Writing Resistance

FRINGE

Series Editors
Alena Ledeneva and Peter Zusi, School of Slavonic and
East European Studies, UCL

The FRINGE series explores the roles that complexity, ambivalence and immeasurability play in social and cultural phenomena. A cross-disciplinary initiative bringing together researchers from the humanities, social sciences and area studies, the series examines how seemingly opposed notions such as centrality and marginality, clarity and ambiguity, can shift and converge when embedded in everyday practices.

Alena Ledeneva is Professor of Politics and Society at the School of Slavonic and East European Studies of UCL.

Peter Zusi is Associate Professor at the School of Slavonic and East European Studies of UCL.

Writing Resistance
Revolutionary memoirs of Shlissel'burg Prison, 1884–1906

Edited and translated by

Sarah J. Young

First published in 2021 by
UCL Press
University College London
Gower Street
London WC1E 6BT

Available to download free: www.uclpress.co.uk

Text © Author, 2021
Images © Copyright holders named in captions, 2021

The author has asserted her rights under the Copyright, Designs and Patents Act 1988 to be identified as the author of this work.

A CIP catalogue record for this book is available from the British Library.

This book is published under a Creative Commons Attribution-ShareAlike 4.0 International licence (CC BY-SA 4.0). This licence allows you to share, copy and redistribute the work; and to adapt the work providing attribution is made to the author. If you remix, transform or build upon the work, you must distribute your contributions under the same licence as the original. Attribution should include the following information:

Young, S. J. 2021. *Writing Resistance: Revolutionary memoirs of Shlissel'burg Prison, 1884–1906*. London: UCL Press. https://doi.org/10.14324/111.9781787359918

Further details about Creative Commons licences are available at http://creativecommons.org/licenses/

Any third-party material in this book is published under the book's Creative Commons licence unless indicated otherwise in the credit line to the material. If you would like to reuse any third-party material not covered by the book's Creative Commons licence, you will need to obtain permission directly from the copyright holder.

ISBN: 978-1-78735-993-2 (Hbk.)
ISBN: 978-1-78735-992-5 (Pbk.)
ISBN: 978-1-78735-991-8 (PDF)
ISBN: 978-1-78735-994-9 (epub)
ISBN: 978-1-78735-995-6 (mobi)
DOI: https://doi.org/10.14324/111.9781787359918

For my parents, Jean Young (1943–2012) and Wilson Young, for their unconditional support and love. They never understood where on earth my interest in Russian carceral literature came from, and never really suspected that it was at least in part inspired by the copy of Solzhenitsyn's *The Gulag Archipelago* sitting incongruously on their bookshelves when I was young.

Contents

List of figures ix
List of tables xi
Series editors' preface xiii
Editor's preface xv
Note on transliteration xix

1 Introduction: surviving Shlissel'burg, writing resistance 1

2 Liudmila Volkenshtein, *Thirteen years in Shlissel'burg Fortress* 36

3 Mikhail Ashenbrenner, *Two decades in Shlissel'burg Prison* 82

4 Vasilii Pankratov, *Life in Shlissel'burg Fortress* 133

   Appendix: Shlissel'burg's inmates, 1884–1906 215

Glossary 239
Bibliography 241
Index 246

List of figures

1.1 Shlisselburg Fortress, by Artem https://commons.wikimedia.org/wiki/File:Shlisselburg.jpg. CC BY-SA 2.0.   3

1.2 Plan of Shlissel'burg Fortress, 7 May 1906. Redrawn from the original in Iuvachev, I. P. *Shlissel'burgskaia krepost'*. Moscow: Izdatel'stvo 'Posrednik', 1907, endleaves.   8

1.3 Plan of the new two-storey prison at Shlissel'burg Fortress, opened in August 1884. Cell assignments of the inmates at the end of 1884. Redrawn from the original in Kolosov, E. E. *Gosudareva tiur'ma - Shlissel'burg. Po ofitsial'nym dannym*. 2nd ed. Moscow: Izdatel'stvo Vsesoiuznogo obshchestva politkatorzhan i ssyl'no-poselentsev, 1930, 85.   11

2.1 Portrait of Liudmila Volkenshtein. From Annenskii, N. F. et al., eds. *Gallereia Shlissel'burgskikh uznikov*. St Petersburg: Tipografiia M. M. Stasiulevicha, 1907, between pp. 222 and 223. Public domain/orphan work. Digitization by LSE Library.   37

3.1 Portrait of Mikhail Ashenbrenner before his arrest. From Annenskii, N. F. et al., eds. *Gallereia Shlissel'burgskikh uznikov*. St Petersburg: Tipografiia M. M. Stasiulevicha, 1907, between pp. 188 and 189. Public domain/orphan work. Digitization by LSE Library.   83

4.1 Portrait of Vasilii Pankratov during his exile in Iakutsk. From Pankratov, V. S. *S tsarem v Tobol'ske: iz vospominanii*. Leningrad: Kooperativnoe izdatel'stvo tovarishchestvo 'Byloe', 1925, frontispiece. Public domain/orphan work. Digitization by LSE Library.   134

List of tables

1.1 The Russian prison 'wall alphabet', invented in Shlissel'burg Fortress in 1826 by the Decembrist M. A. Bestuzhev. From Venediktov-Beziuk, D. G. *Po kazematam Shlissel'burgskoi kreposti.* Moscow: Izdatel'stvo politkatorzhan, 1928, 43.   10

2.1 List of convicts imprisoned in Shlissel'burg Fortress from 1884 to 1896. From Volkenshtein, L. A. *13 let v Shlissel'burgskoi kreposti: Zapiski*. Edited by V. L. Burtsev. Purleigh: Izdanie Svobodnogo slova, 1900, 8–9.   43

Series editors' preface

The UCL Press FRINGE series presents work related to the themes of the UCL FRINGE Centre for the Study of Social and Cultural Complexity.

The FRINGE series is a platform for cross-disciplinary analysis and the development of 'area studies without borders'. 'FRINGE' is an acronym standing for <u>F</u>luidity, <u>R</u>esistance, <u>I</u>nvisibility, <u>N</u>eutrality, <u>G</u>rey zones, and <u>E</u>lusiveness – categories fundamental to the themes that the Centre supports. The oxymoron in the notion of a 'FRINGE CENTRE' expresses our interest in (1) the tensions between 'area studies' and more traditional academic disciplines; and (2) social, political, and cultural trajectories from 'centres to fringes' and inversely from 'fringes to centres'.

The series pursues an innovative understanding of the significance of fringes: rather than taking 'fringe areas' to designate the world's peripheries or non-mainstream subject matters (as in 'fringe politics' or 'fringe theatre'), we are committed to exploring the patterns of social and cultural complexity characteristic of fringes and emerging from the areas we research. We aim to develop forms of analysis of those elements of complexity that are resistant to articulation, visualisation or measurement.

The present volume unites three previously untranslated and largely forgotten memoirs by Russian revolutionaries incarcerated in strict solitary confinement in the notorious Shlissel'burg Fortress outside St Petersburg between 1884 and 1905. Out of this unique experience of banishment, these writers went on to contribute fundamentally to the forging of Russian revolutionary mythology, though that contribution has since become obscure. In addition to salvaging these memoirs from the neglect into which they have fallen, the volume contains an extensive editor's introduction that frames these memoirs as exercises in resistance, explores the practices enabled by constraint, and captures the textual strategies that transform traumatic individual experience into collective memory of injustice.

Alena Ledeneva and Peter Zusi,
School of Slavonic and East European Studies, UCL

Editor's preface

My interest in the Populist prisoners incarcerated in Shlissel'burg Fortress was sparked many years ago when, pursuing references in Evgeniia Ginzburg's Gulag memoir, I read Vera Figner's *Memoirs of a Revolutionist*. Later, working on my ongoing book project on Russian carceral narratives, I began tracking down and reading memoirs by some of Figner's fellow inmates for a section of a chapter on prisoner networks and carceral topographies. The extraordinary situation of these prisoners, and the fact that so many of the survivors wrote about their incarceration and their prison comrades – in memoirs, poetry and letters – immediately struck me with the immense power of the stories they had to tell, the appalling suffering they endured, and their resilience and willpower in overcoming a seemingly hopeless situation.

I realized that these texts would make a fascinating case study on the construction of an exemplary prison community. I could also see their potential for corpus analysis. I have been experimenting with distant reading techniques for the last few years, not least in response to the vast and still proliferating number of Gulag narratives that have been published (not to mention those in the archives of the human rights organization 'Memorial' and elsewhere), which is far beyond the ability of any single individual to read. The Shlissel'burg corpus, comprising 25 texts and less than half a million words, is certainly readable – and I have indeed read all the texts, some several times. But focusing on the type of patterns and congruences that can be revealed by distant reading seemed particularly worthwhile in relation to such a unified and complete corpus. As the representation of a significant episode in both Russian carceral history and revolutionary history, written by such a large proportion of those involved (at least, of those who survived), the corpus provides a rare opportunity to interrogate the way memoirs construct their story. Indeed, as I argue in my Introduction, the very point of the majority of these texts – especially those published before 1917 – was to take control of the narrative of their imprisonment. I use concordance analysis techniques on the corpus to show how their inscription of the process of challenging and transforming the conditions of their incarceration, through the collective they forge, lies at the heart of the story they are advancing.

At the same time, the consistent political aims of the texts notwithstanding, their authors' different perspectives enable us to build a rounded picture of life and death in the prison, the fortress's culture and the changes that took place over the two decades of the Populists' incarceration. This overcomes some of the limitations of using individual memoirs as historical sources, such as the reliance on anecdote and single points of view. As a corpus, the texts allow us insights into the experience of solitary confinement, the techniques of resistance the revolutionaries brought to bear to help them survive their imprisonment, and the reasons for the failure of the fortress's harsh regime.

The II International Congress on the History of Prisons and Punitive Institutions, held at the University of Castilla-La Mancha in Albacete in September 2019, gave me an opportunity to present some of this work for the first time, and I am very grateful to Manuel Maroto Calatayud for inviting me to speak at the conference. By the time I had finished writing the paper for the associated conference proceedings, I had well and truly caught the Shlissel'burg bug, and quickly sought out the few remaining primary texts that I hadn't yet read. I was amazed that only the memoirs of Figner, Ivan Iuvachev and, more recently, Grigorii Gershuni, had previously been translated into English, and that many of the memoirs have not even been reprinted in Russian since the early Soviet period, despite the prominence given to the prisoners as revolutionary martyrs in the late Imperial era, and the notoriety of Shlissel'burg Fortress itself. The decision to translate these three texts, and restore their authors and the collective voice they are part of, to Russian history and penal history, was therefore not a difficult one. I also viewed this book from the start as an opportunity to retrieve the memory of this group of prisoners more broadly, and make their writings more readily accessible. Alongside this book I have set up a website, shlisselburg.net, as a repository for the memoirs and other texts that were not otherwise available in plain text on the internet, and in some cases were not available online in any form. I have also started a Twitter bot, @shlisselbot, to bring the story of the fortress and its prisoners to a wider audience.

*

I am very grateful to UCL SSEES for granting me the research leave during which I began this project, for enabling the reduced teaching load that allowed me to bring it to a timely conclusion, and for their support as I took a slightly off-piste journey and thereby exacerbated the already considerable delays to my main book project. No academic book appears in isolation, and I would like to express my gratitude to a number of people who contributed to the preparation and publication of this volume. The two anonymous readers for UCL Press gave me excellent guidance for widening the appeal of this book beyond Russian area studies as well as for reinforcing its value within Russian studies. Their suggestions for revisions helped strengthen the Introduction in particular. The support of my colleagues Alena Ledeneva and Peter Zusi for publishing this book as part of the FRINGE series was essential. Lydia Buravova clarified some impenetrable phrasing in the original texts. Uilleam Blacker confirmed the meaning of a Ukrainian proverb. Cathy McAteer helped me identify an elusive variety of strawberry (a sentence that will resonate with translators everywhere!). Bryan Karetnyk suggested an initial approach to an especially challenging translation conundrum that ultimately – after a number of further twists and turns – led to a viable solution, and he, Julia Leikin and Stuart Finkel all helped me track down digitized versions of Russian sources where print copies were not readily available. Rachel Morley put me in contact with Hilde Hoogenboom, who kindly sent me a copy of her essay on Vera Figner and the genre of revolutionary autobiography when libraries were closed due to the COVID-19 pandemic. Bilal Siddiqi brought me books from SSEES library and my office that allowed me to finish checks of all my references while I was shielding.

During and after a sabbatical research presentation at SSEES, questions and comments from a number of colleagues, but particularly Pamela Davidson, Agnieszka Kubal, Ben Noble and Anne White, were very useful in clarifying my thinking and confirming my sense of the subject's intrinsic interest. I would also like to thank Pamela Davidson for kindly sharing her photographs of the fortress after my own trip to St Petersburg had to be cancelled because of the pandemic. Chiara Clouzeau checked old- and new-style dates for consistency. Lisa McCormick did a beautiful job of redrawing the plans of Shlissel'burg Fortress from Iuvachev's memoirs, and the cell assignments in the new prison from Kolosov's study, with English captions. Wojciech Janik at SSEES Library and colleagues at UCL digital collections gave up their valuable time in very tricky circumstances to track down the original digitization of the 1740 map of Lake Ladoga and the surrounding area that I wanted to use for the cover of the book. Daniel Payne, Curator for Politics and International Relations at LSE Library, provided digitized copies of portraits of my three authors in timely fashion at a point when academic libraries were coping with the challenges of reopening. Two people deserve special thanks. Maurits Westbroek's careful reading of the draft translations picked up numerous errors and omissions, and provided much-needed clarification on the aforementioned conundrum, as well as various very useful suggestions for stylistic improvements. He also checked the final manuscript with a fine-tooth comb. Lynn Patyk read the entire draft manuscript with exactly the sort of perceptive eye I needed, and raised a number of penetrating questions and comments. Both of them helped this become the book I knew it could be, for which I am extremely grateful. Any remaining errors and infelicities are, of course, my own responsibility.

My thanks also to Dr Alexandra Nanzer-Kelly and specialist asthma nurse Linda Green at Guy's Hospital, and Dr Irem Patel at King's College Hospital, who helped to keep me healthy enough to see this book through to completion. David McCormick encouraged me to take on the project in its early stages. Our neighbours Mark Lewis and Susie Grimshaw have been an enormous source of support while I have been shielding during the pandemic and revising the book. For long periods over the last year, our weekly over-the-garden-wall cocktail hour was the only direct human contact I had apart from my partner, and that, alongside the regular exchange of the cakes we have both been baking, has done wonders for maintaining my mental health (if not my waistline) during this very challenging time. The friendship and support of Alex Harrington and Helen Brennan has done more to sustain me over the last year than they realize. Much-needed entertainment and distractions were provided by our three red cats, Vera (originally named after Zasulich, rather than Figner, though we now think of her as embodying both revolutionary women), and her silly boys Victor and Serge (who really don't resemble their namesake in any way, although Serge's pen-stealing propensities make us wonder if one day he's going to reveal that he has in fact been writing his magnum opus: *Birth of our Purr*). My partner John Levin did everything he possibly could to keep me safe during the pandemic, and provided technical assistance, helpful comments on drafts, and all the love, support, wine and chocolate I could ever need.

London, 14 April 2021.

Note on transliteration

Throughout the text of this book, I have used the Library of Congress romanization system (without diacritics) to transliterate the Cyrillic, except where a standard Europeanized version exists (e.g., for tsars' names; Herzen rather than Gertsen).

1.
Introduction: surviving Shlissel'burg, writing resistance

> Citadel of freedom in misfortune's hour
> Crypt of friends of the people's will,
> In this bulwark of Liberty – slaves…
> Oh, thou irony of fate!
>
> German Lopatin, 'Oreshek' (1887)[1]

I. The revolutionary prisoners of Shlissel'burg Fortress

On 2 (14) August 1884,[2] 11 convicts – Populist revolutionaries and members of the terrorist organization the People's Will (*Narodnaia volia*)[3] – arrived at the notorious Shlissel'burg Fortress near St Petersburg, the first inmates to be housed in its newly-constructed prison. A further 27 prisoners were transferred to the fortress before the end of the year, and from 1885 to 1890, another 18 were sent there. Seven of these convicts were taken to Shlissel'burg for execution, but most of the rest had received long – frequently life – terms of hard labour, in most cases commuted from death sentences. Many of the prisoners expressed the feeling upon arrival that the fortress was intended to be their living tomb, and that they would never see the outside world again. This proved to be true for more than half the inmates. But others did survive, and more than 21 years later, the final prisoners were freed or transferred.

Of the 30 long-term survivors of Shlissel'burg, 18, who served sentences averaging over 15 years, wrote memoirs of their incarceration or about their fellow prisoners, testifying to '[t]he remarkable literary productivity of the populist movement's surviving veterans'.[4] These memoirs played a crucial role in Russian revolutionary mythology. Following the 1905 revolution, a minor industry within the revolutionary movement was devoted to the publication of their works. The prisoners were exalted as 'exemplary models of self-sacrifice, [and] revolutionary heroism',[5] and as martyrs to the injustice and illegitimacy of tsarist rule.[6] Their heroic resistance to the exceptionally harsh regime instituted at the fortress was celebrated, and names that the authorities wanted to obliterate were restored to revolutionary history. The prison itself became their 'place of triumph and suffering', the 'Golgotha of the Russian revolution', their 'holy Jerusalem'.[7] Beyond their role in revolutionary history, in which the experience of incarceration became a central trope and rite of passage in the creation of revolutionary identity, these memoirs also played a major role in the development of the tradition of prison writing and memorialization that has been part of the Russian experience of punishment for political crimes for well over 150 years. The three texts included in this volume, by Liudmila Volkenshtein (1857–1906), Mikhail Ashenbrenner (1842–1926) and Vasilii Pankratov (1864–1925) – none of them republished in the original Russian since the 1920s, or previously translated into English – present very different perspectives on the experience of incarceration in Shlissel'burg. However, they reveal a common cause in framing the understanding of the punitive institution itself, and of the behaviours developed by the inmates to contend with, and ultimately overcome, its predations, that became central to forging their identity as revolutionary martyrs. In doing so, these memoirs not only advance a particular interpretation of their authors' situation, but also illuminate the experience of harsh prison regimes and the detrimental effects of solitary confinement more generally.

II. Shlissel'burg Fortress and its prison

Even before the construction of the new prison at Shlissel'burg, the fortress had a fearsome reputation.[8] Situated on Orekhovets (Nut) Island, at the mouth of the Neva river on Lake Ladoga, 35 km to the east of St Petersburg, the original wooden fortress (known as Orekhov or Oreshek) was built in 1323 by Prince Yuri of Moscow,[9] in his capacity as Prince of Novgorod, following the capture of the island from the Swedes. A location of strategic importance, the fortress changed hands several times over the next four centuries. In the late fifteenth century, under the Novgorod Republic, the wooden fortress was replaced by a stone citadel occupying practically the entire island (see Figure 1.1). Its final capture by Peter the Great took place in 1702 during the Great Northern War.[10]

Figure 1.1 Shlisselburg Fortress, by Artem https://commons.wikimedia.org/wiki/File:Shlisselburg.jpg. CC BY-SA 2.0.

Renamed Shlissel'burg by Peter, the fortress's military function was quickly superseded by the carceral role for which it became infamous. Between 1711 and the February revolution of 1917, Shlissel'burg Prison was used for all but short periods to hold primarily political prisoners, including top-secret state prisoners and some of Russia's most serious criminal offenders.[11]

In the eighteenth century, the prison at Shlissel'burg was a small-scale institution, generally housing fewer than five inmates at any time. Relatively short periods of incarceration were the norm. Only four of the known eighteenth-century prisoners were held at Shlissel'burg for over 15 years, including Ernest Biron (1690–1772), regent to Ioann Antonovich (Emperor Ivan VI), imprisoned 1741–62, and economist and alchemist Filipp Belikov, incarcerated 1746–64.[12] A significant proportion of the prisoners were victims or perpetrators (perceived or actual) of political conspiracies. A small number of writers and publishers of seditious material, as well as independence fighters from Russia's colonial borderlands, and religious sectarians, were sent to the prison. Notable political prisoners included Maria Romanova, half-sister of Peter the Great (imprisoned 1718–21), and Evdokiia Lopukhina, Peter's first wife (1725–7). The most famous prisoner from this era – and the one most frequently referred to by the Populist revolutionaries as their most august and tragic predecessor[13] – was Ioann Antonovich, who as Emperor Ivan VI was deposed at the age of one by Empress Elizabeth of Russia in 1741, and spent his entire life in prison. He was incarcerated in secret in Shlissel'burg from 1756 to 1764, and murdered there on Catherine the Great's orders during an attempt to release him. Following Ioann Antonovich's death, no further prisoners were sent to the fortress until 1775. Shlissel'burg came into increased use in the 1790s as a place to isolate a small number of intellectuals. Previously tolerated by Catherine the Great, their arrest reflected fears of revolutionary ideas spreading from France. However, the most famous of this group of prisoners, the Enlightenment writer and journalist Nikolai Novikov,[14] was incarcerated ostensibly for his activities as a freemason.[15]

Novikov's four-year incarceration, like others' in the eighteenth century, was the subject of Imperial decree. No judicial process or formal sentencing procedures were in place at this stage. In the early nineteenth century, court intrigues among branches of the Imperial family ceased to play a significant role, but Shlissel'burg was still occasionally used to imprison by administrative fiat members of the nobility who intervened in politics. For example, Baron Timotheus von Bock spent 10 years in the fortress for sending a letter to Tsar Alexander I calling for a constitution. Following the 1826 trials of participants in the failed December 1825 uprising, more regular judicial processes were generally employed to send prisoners to Shlissel'burg. Administrative sentences remained in use throughout the nineteenth century, however, as they did elsewhere in the Russian penal system, usually as a speedy means of sending a wide variety of perceived undesirables to Siberian exile, often irrespective of whether they had actually committed any crime.[16] Of the 102 prisoners known to have spent time in Shlissel'burg between 1800 and 1870, 57 were incarcerated for political reasons, including 13 Decembrist revolutionaries and six national liberation fighters, mainly from Poland.[17]

For both political prisoners and others, periods of incarceration in Shlissel'burg in the nineteenth century were typically short. The most common term served was one year or less (41 prisoners). Eighty-one of the 102 prisoners from this period served terms of 10 years or less. Among those who served five years or less, 40 were sentenced for political activities, four for criminal acts, and four for heresy and sectarianism. In 21 cases the reason for imprisonment is unknown. The very short-term political prisoners included all but one of the Decembrists, who spent between three and seven months at the fortress, before being transferred to Eastern Siberia for terms of hard labour. Of those who served over 15 years, six were political prisoners, two were convicted of fraud and two were incarcerated for religious reasons (heresy and conscientious objection). No information is available on one of the long-term prisoners. Of the political prisoners, political and republican deeds were more likely to result in short than long terms of imprisonment (26 served five years or less, 11 served more than this). Seditious words (including unpublished writings) were generally, but not always, punished with shorter terms: in 14 cases, five years or less. Six attracted longer terms, including two sentences of over 10 years.

Conditions in the original prison were harsh. Cells in the main prison building were badly affected by damp and a lack of light, with detrimental effects on the health of the inmates.[18] This was exacerbated by the lack of exercise space,[19] and enforced inactivity: no work was provided. Prisoners were kept in solitary confinement, with a regime of total silence. Inmates were generally not permitted writing materials, and were given access to devotional books only as a reward for good behaviour. Food in many cases was extremely poor. Gernet ascribes differential treatment to class difference, with peasants receiving much worse food than members of the nobility.[20] Von Bock was provided with luxury foods, and even had a grand piano installed in his cell.[21] Yet Mikhail Bakunin – also a member of the nobility, albeit one who had long since eschewed its privileges – was apparently allocated a smaller sum for food than other prisoners in the 1850s – 18, rather than 30, kopeks per day[22] – and famously lost his teeth to scurvy while incarcerated in the fortress.

Before 1849, treatment was dictated by individual instructions. For 'secret prisoners' whose presence in the fortress was hidden from the outside world, instructions not only stated that guards should not know who their charges were, but forbade even official acknowledgement of the inmates' existence. In practice, however, levels of secrecy were inconsistently maintained. The deposed emperor Ioann Antonovich was taught to read by a sympathetic guard, despite orders not to communicate with him.[23] Von Bock's wife did not know his whereabouts for several years, but they were permitted to exchange letters via a German Baptist pastor who was allowed to visit the prisoner.[24] The Polish freedom fighter Walerian Łukasiński spent 38 years in almost total isolation at the fortress until his death in 1868, but was seen during walks by both Bakunin and, later, Bronisław Szwarce, and reports suggest that Bakunin even managed to speak to him briefly on one occasion.[25] The absence of references to Łukasiński in the memoirs of the next generation of prisoners, however, indicates that in his case secrecy was maintained to the extent that outsiders knew nothing about him. Vera Figner, the only memoirist to mention him, notes that, 'The secret about Łukasiński was kept so strictly that in 1850 an administrator from the Third Section [the tsarist secret police department] approached War Minister Chernyshev to ask who the old Pole locked up in Shlissel'burg was.'[26]

In 1849, conditions were regularized with two sets of instructions, for ordinary and secret prisoners. These primarily concerned the tightening of security at the prison and establishing a harsher regime overall, for example, depriving inmates of all communications, both with each other and beyond the fortress.[27] Prisoners 'died for the outside world from the moment they stepped over the threshold of the Secret House'.[28] They were to be kept under constant surveillance, and denied any form of communication, even with their own jailers. At the same time, the nineteenth century saw a gradual decrease in use of the prison, albeit with increased length of incarceration for those who ended up there. From 1812 (when the fortress received its first inmate for over 10 years) to 1829, 45 prisoners were sent to Shlissel'burg, but over half spent less than two years there. From 1830 to 1848, 40 prisoners arrived, including those who served the longest sentences: 11 were still incarcerated in 1849. However, in the 18 years from that point, until the last prisoner of this era arrived, in 1866, there were only 15 new inmates, eight of whom arrived during the final years of Nicholas I's reign. The prison was not used, for example, to incarcerate members of the Petrashevskii Circle, who were arrested for seditious activity in 1849.[29] Instead, it gradually emptied out, and during the 1870s the fortress housed a penal battalion.

III. The new prison

Up to 1870, therefore, Shlissel'burg Fortress functioned both as an ordinary prison and an exceptional space of 'secret' incarceration. Although renowned for its harsh environment, the fortress's fearsome reputation rested primarily upon its role as a secret prison, and on the very long sentences endured by a small minority of prisoners. Despite its frequent use to hold more regular inmates, it remained in the eyes of the authorities – and of revolutionary circles – an exceptional institution.[30] This was undoubtedly one of the reasons for it being brought back into use in the 1880s, following the assassination of Alexander II in March 1881 by members of the People's Will.[31] Five of the revolutionaries directly responsible for the Tsar's death were executed, but as the rest of the organization was gradually rounded up (175 members were tried between 1880 and 1890),[32] the question of secure facilities became pressing. Not only was the Russian penal system as a whole notoriously porous,[33] but the escape of prominent prisoners even from high-security institutions – notably that of Prince Petr Kropotkin from St Petersburg's Peter and Paul Fortress in 1876 – suggested that nowhere within existing provision could be considered sufficiently secure to isolate those deemed the most dangerous state criminals.

The new prison built in Shlissel'burg Fortress in the early 1880s represented an unprecedented development in Russian carceral history. In a perpetually underfunded and chronically corrupt system that lacked even basic oversight in most parts of the Russian Empire,[34] the decision to lavish huge amounts of money on constructing a new high-security prison was remarkable. Meanwhile, the fact that Shlissel'burg Fortress maximized surveillance, and close control by the authorities in St Petersburg, indicates the importance of these prisoners and the perceived extremity of the situation faced by the state.[35] The most expensive of three proposed schemes to increase capacity at the fortress was adopted,[36] leading to the construction of a two-storey, 40-cell prison (see Figure 1.2). The prison cells initially impressed the inmates with their modern facilities (including plumbed toilets), cleanliness and light – at least by comparison with the gloomy, if larger, cells at the Peter and Paul Fortress, where many of the prisoners had previously been held.[37] The existing 14-cell prison, referred to as the 'old prison' or the 'hut' (*sarai*) in memoirs,[38] which itself had been rebuilt in the 1850s, was renovated to serve as the punishment block.

The new prison was administered from the Police Department in the Imperial capital, and was commanded by Viacheslav von Plehve, who had also been responsible for its construction.[39] The decision to guard the inmates at Shlissel'burg using gendarmes, and only experienced non-commissioned officers, indicated that the fortress was considered different from other places of confinement.[40] The basic chain of command went from the superintendent of the gendarmes, to the fortress commandant, to the Chief of the Corps of Gendarmes, who was also the head of the Third Section.[41] In the first, harshest years of the prison's operation, the ineffectual commandant, Kasper Kazimirovich Pokroshinskii was, however, effectively subordinate to Matvei Sokolov, the superintendent of the gendarmes, who to all intents and purposes ran the entire fortress.[42] The first Chief of the Corps of Gendarmes, General Orzhevskii,[43] directed the prison and wrote the instructions that governed its operation until 1897.[44]

The arrangements instituted at Shlissel'burg Fortress in many ways resembled the 'complete and austere institutions' of the Eastern State (Pennsylvania) Penitentiary type, with individual facilities enabling the primary aim of absolute isolation.[45] But in fact the regime at the new prison differed little from that of earlier eras.[46] Discipline at the fortress took the form of a regime of complete silence and total solitary confinement, with no communication among the prisoners or with the outside world. Surveillance was conducted via spy holes in the cell doors,

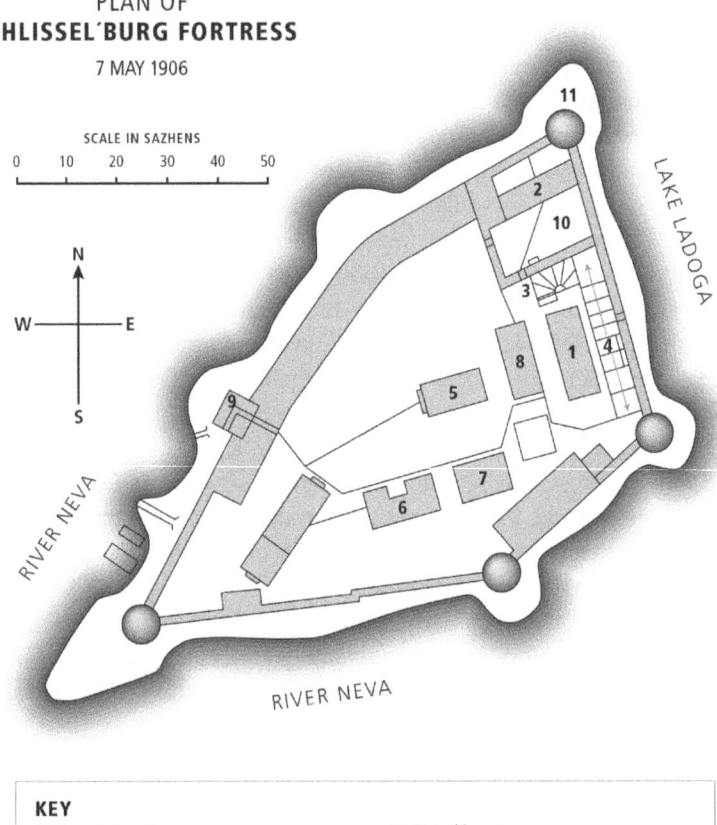

KEY
1 New state prison
2 Old prison and citadel
3 First yards for solitary exercise (partitions later removed)
4 Pens, later prisoners' allotments
5 Church of John the Baptist
6 Commandant's house and chancellery
7 Officers' quarters
8 Guard house
9 Fortress gates and Sovereign's Tower
10 Orchard planted by prisoners
11 Burial site for executed prisoners and other prisoners who died in the fortress

One sazhen' equals 2.1336 metres or 7 feet

Figure 1.2 Plan of Shlissel'burg Fortress, 7 May 1906. Redrawn from the original in Iuvachev, I. P. *Shlissel'burgskaia krepost'*. Moscow: Izdatel'stvo 'Posrednik', 1907, endleaves.

and guards wore soft boots so that they could approach the doors without being heard by the inmates. Although the fortress was officially designated a hard labour (*katorga*) prison, work was neither viewed as transformative, nor imposed as a punishment, as was generally the case both in the tsarist system and in Foucault's definition of 'complete and austere institutions'.⁴⁷ Instead, work was provided as a reward for good behaviour – and only after the regime had been relaxed. Books – consisting, as previously, solely of religious works that could be of little interest to the materialist and atheist mindset of most of these Populist revolutionaries⁴⁸ – also constituted rewards for good behaviour. Short periods of exercise (as little as 30 minutes each per day) were granted, and withdrawn as punishment, but prisoners remained isolated in separate yards, under constant surveillance to prevent not only communication with each other, but also interaction between inmates and guards. The aim was to leave prisoners with nothing to do but focus on the workings of their own conscience.⁴⁹ The strictness of the regime was enforced by an escalating series of punishments for infractions of prison regulations, from withdrawal of privileges, to confinement in the punishment cells, to birching, and ultimately the death penalty for assaulting guards or other members of the administration.⁵⁰

The appalling effects of this exceptionally harsh regime – alongside extremely poor and meagre food, and exceptionally cold cells⁵¹ – on the physical and mental health of the prisoners are all too apparent in the distressing descriptions of the first two years of imprisonment in many of the memoirs, including those in the present volume. The oppressive experience of total isolation and inactivity is depicted as a 'living death' or a 'grave' by almost every memoirist.⁵² It was literally fatal to their less fortunate comrades. Beyond the presence of a prison doctor, whose ability or inclination to help the prisoners was often very limited, there were no medical facilities, and practically no treatment was given to the physically or mentally sick. As a result, of the 38 prisoners who arrived at the fortress in 1884, 16 died, 11 within two years, with tuberculosis and scurvy being the main killers. A further two died by suicide, and two were executed for assaulting the prison doctor and the superintendent of the guards. The psychological state of many of the prisoners was also badly affected, not least because they were surrounded by so many comrades dying agonizing deaths in complete isolation and without medical intervention. This led to various degrees of mental breakdown, and in several cases to permanent insanity.

Ultimately, the harshness of the initial regime was its own undoing, and revealed fundamental contradictions in the prison's operation.⁵³ The very high mortality rate was unsustainable in the longer term. At the levels of attrition of the first two years, the guards would soon have no-one left to guard, which, no matter how much secrecy surrounded the fortress, risked creating a scandal in Russian society. At the same time, transferring new prisoners to the fortress brought its own difficulties, as they undermined the strict isolation of the existing inmates from the outside world. If some easing of the regime was inevitable and necessary to ensure the fortress continued to function, the vicissitudes of Russian politics also played a role in improving conditions after the first period. But the memoirs all contend that it was the actions of the prisoners themselves, and their refusal to accept the conduct of a state they continued to view as illegitimate, that were instrumental in improving their situation. One might observe that the very decision of the authorities to bring this group of extremely combative prisoners together without, apparently, any expectation that they would rebel collectively against such appalling conditions, seems questionable. And indeed, it is in relation to the idea of the collective that the memoirs frame the prisoners' fightback.

Survivors and memoirists, including several who themselves recovered from severe illnesses, depict resisting the regime, and striving for more humane conditions that no longer endangered the lives or sanity of the prisoners, as a constant task. Establishing communications represented the first stage, and is portrayed as a transformative moment. It took the form of tapping on the walls of cells, using the 'prison alphabet' originally developed in Shlissel'burg itself by the Decembrist Mikhail Bestuzhev, during his three-month incarceration at the fortress in 1826 (see Table 1.1), and familiar to readers from many Gulag memoirs.[54] A very laborious method, involving a series of taps to denote each letter's place on the horizontal and vertical axes of a grid, this nevertheless acted as the primary means of communication for several years. With the new prison essentially full from the end of 1884

Table 1.1 The Russian prison 'wall alphabet', invented in Shlissel'burg Fortress in 1826 by the Decembrist M. A. Bestuzhev. From Venediktov-Beziuk, D. G. *Po kazematam Shlissel'burgskoi kreposti*. Moscow: Izdatel'stvo politkatorzhan, 1928, 43.

	I	II	III	IV	V
1	А	Б	В	Г	Д
2	Е	Ж	З	И	К
3	Л	М	Н	О	П
4	Р	С	Т	У	Ф
5	Х	Ц	Ч	Ш	Щ
6	Ы	Ю	Я		

PLAN OF THE NEW PRISON
Distribution of the inmates transferred in 1884

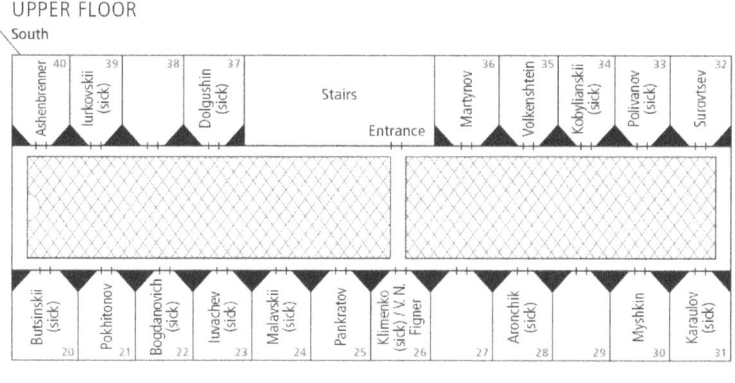

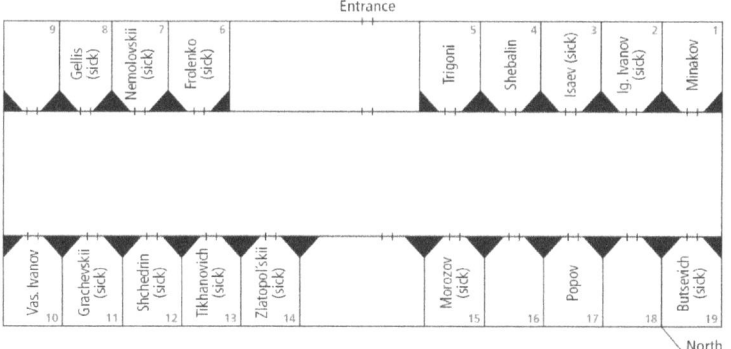

Figure 1.3 Plan of the new two-storey prison at Shlissel'burg Fortress, opened in August 1884. Cell assignments of the inmates at the end of 1884. Redrawn from the original in Kolosov, E. E. *Gosudareva tiur'ma - Shlissel'burg. Po ofitsial'nym dannym.* 2nd ed. Moscow: Izdatel'stvo Vsesoiuznogo obshchestva politkatorzhan i ssyl'no-poselentsev, 1930, 85.

(see Figure 1.3), the initial strategy of separating inmates by leaving empty cells between them, thereby thwarting communication via the cell walls, was no longer viable. The sort of secrecy, isolation and silence that had been possible with small numbers of prisoners in previous periods proved difficult to maintain with a larger – and more unruly – group, many of whom already knew each other. Survivors record that tapping on the walls was punished at first, but soon became the norm, with the guards more or less turning a blind eye to it. Yet the very fact of establishing communication, however limited, breached the prison's strict policy of isolation and silence. One important effect of communication was to enable organization, albeit haltingly, and, as the memoirists acknowledge, with inconsistent results, including outright failures. Even where concessions were won, they were often not applied to all – and certainly not to new prisoners who were brought in.[55] The privileges gained were also frequently reversed. The memoirs record a constant state of tension as the prisoners sought to normalize and extend rights to all their comrades, and the authorities repeatedly pushed back, at times attempting to revert to the harsher early regime. Indeed, the story they advance is one in which to a great extent the prisoners remain powerless, and the administration fundamentally retains the cruel instincts that inmates sought to curb.

Nevertheless, the general trajectory after the first two years was undoubtedly one of improvement. Gradually inmates were assigned partners for exercise periods, in effect bringing to an end the regime of absolute solitary confinement. Allotments were established, enabling the prisoners to grow food and improve their diets. These were followed by workshops, giving most of the prisoners useful activity throughout the day. As a result of these changes, many of the inmates were restored to good physical and mental health. The range of books and journals available to the prisoners improved, although this remained a significant battleground.

When such reading material was provided, it allowed an extraordinary flourishing of intellectual activity to take place. Many of the prisoners undertook serious studies and original research,[56] learned foreign languages, translated books, and so on. Prisoners delivered lectures to each other on specialist subjects, and reports on their reading. This type of activity very much resembles that seen among other groups of intellectuals imprisoned in Russia, from the Decembrists' 'Academy' at Chita, to the lecture series given by victims of the Stalinist purges in the overcrowded cells of the Lubianka and other prisons. Memoirs of both earlier and later periods represent this transformation of the prison space as a unique form of university.[57] The situation of the Shlissel'burg prisoners was particularly remarkable because they achieved this from a starting point not of communal imprisonment and relatively free association, but of strict solitary confinement, and despite the authorities' determination that no form of collective spirit or action should develop.

IV. Unity and resistance

The fortress administration's efforts to maintain the prisoners' separation is exemplified by a reprimand attributed by Volkenshtein to the first superintendent of the guards, the notorious Sokolov: 'Don't you dare talk about others; it's none of your business – there are no "others" here!' (Volkenshtein, Chapter I). Yet the prisoners themselves emphasize the other as their primary concern. As Ashenbrenner states, 'we were tied together by fellowship, a common enemy and a common duty' (Ashenbrenner, Chapter I). Indeed, as members of the same groups, participants in the same actions and defendants in the same trials, they were part of a movement, not lone fighters against injustice, and saw their own roles very much in the context of the revolutionary community.[58] That sense of unity becomes central to the forms of resistance the memoirs depict. Resistance can be defined as 'the process and act of challenging one's subordinated position in a given social system'.[59] The 'subordinated position' of the Shlissel'burg inmates was unusual: oppressed but not exploited, and to a great extent coming from elite sectors of Russian society – certainly on the whole from more powerful and educated backgrounds than their jailers – they retained a strong sense of their own legitimacy and morality, while rejecting those of the state and its representatives.

These were not therefore, even under conditions of imprisonment, the weakest members of society enacting 'reluctant compliance' and 'symbolic conformity' in the context of 'the day-to-day imperative of earning a living'.[60] Far from this type of covert and individual 'everyday resistance', the memoirs depict open and determinedly collective defiance. Emphasis is placed on the absence of hierarchical divisions between the inmates, which allowed them to forge a strong sense of group identity that was no longer predicated solely on their common revolutionary cause, but also on their shared opposition to the prison authorities. Haslam and Reicher's study of prison resistance shows how shared identity and the sense of a common fate can become a source of social power and agency that enables groups of inmates to contest their environment. In this sense, the situation of the Shlissel'burg prisoners resembles two of Haslam and Reicher's case studies, of Irish republicans incarcerated in the Maze Prison near Belfast from 1972 to 1994, and political prisoners of the South African Apartheid regime imprisoned on Robben Island between 1962 and 1991.[61] In all three cases, housing the inmates together enabled them to organize effectively, and underpinned their 'willingness to promote the collective cause to the total exclusion of personal interests', to the extent of conducting hunger strikes at the Maze and Shlissel'burg.[62] Of particular significance in each case is the educational dimension, in the form of political lectures at the Maze, and on Robben Island the institution of 'a self-regulated "university" with its own faculty, courses, and curriculum' which, as with the shared intellectual activities of the Shlissel'burg prisoners, proved essential to their 'creation of alternative communities and cultures'.[63]

The Shlissel'burg collective may ultimately have been limited in its successes because of two crucial differences from the situations discussed by Haslam and Reicher, relating to internal organization and external, third-party support.[64] The latter was never available to the Populist prisoners, as they were completely cut off from the outside world. But internal organization proved difficult as well, with memoirs highlighting the obstacles to collective decision-making in the context of severely restricted communication. Moreover, the ideological rejection of leadership and the hierarchical organization that implied, and the reluctance in practice of some of the prisoners to take on any form of supervisory role that entailed interaction with the fortress authorities, may further have hampered their efforts. Yet despite these limitations, the memoirs consistently place the sense of a shared identity and the prisoners' collective at the centre of their story of resistance, and in many situations their intransigence and refusal to negotiate on key issues is in fact depicted as the reason for the victories they managed to achieve.

The importance of shared identity is evident in every description of actions that unite the inmates against the administration, but is also reflected in the memoirs' emphasis on establishing communications between the prisoners, and the story they advance of their development as writers and lecturers within the fortress. It also impacts on the memoirs' language, not least in the pronouns adopted in many of the texts that draw attention to the collective. Both Ashenbrenner and Volkenshtein strongly favour 'we'/'us' forms over 'I'/'me'. In the 13,400 words of Volkenshtein's original text, she uses 'I'-forms only 15 times, but 'we' 163 times; Ashenbrenner's slightly longer memoir has 39 occurrences of 'I'-forms compared to 293 of 'we.' Pankratov's usage is more evenly balanced, although still favouring 'we,' with 180 occurrences, compared to 162 for 'I'. His use of possessives strongly tends towards 'our' rather than 'my', however, with 103 uses of the former, but only 14 of the latter. Similar patterns, foregrounding the group over the individual writer, are apparent, especially in the memoirs of Mikhail Frolenko and Grigorii Gershuni.[65]

Other forms of self-effacement and de-personalization promote the collective in different ways. Volkenshtein, her regular evocation of the common 'we' notwithstanding, avoids using the form altogether when dealing with herself and Figner, the only long-term female prisoners. From describing their arrival onwards, she refers to them collectively in the third person only: 'In October 1884, nine people from the Trial of the 14 were brought in. Two of them were women, and four were from the military' (Volkenshtein, [Introduction]). In this way she rejects any separation or possible alternative source of solidarity, even when addressing differential treatment, such as the humiliating personal searches of the women, or the fact that they were forbidden any direct contact with the male prisoners. Pankratov takes a different approach, obscuring his own personality at times by using his initial, as he does with other prisoners. He thus places himself on the same level as those around him, without privileging his own actions or experience within his narrative.

De-personalization further manifests itself in Pankratov's and Ashenbrenner's tendency to switch to the second person singular, to express the impact of the prison on the individual inmate.[66] This is particularly prominent in Pankratov's memoir: 'You start feeling completely bound, but bound now by invisible shackles; an oppressive feeling begins to agitate and mortify you, a consciousness that you do not belong to yourself, but solely to these warders, who can do whatever they want to you' (Pankratov, Chapter I). Ashenbrenner employs the same technique: 'And when you are forced in this way to spend many years under the regime of the "unsleeping eye", which gnaws at you like an indestructible worm, you ask yourself why they needed to employ such subtle torture on people who are either working or sick?..' (Ashenbrenner, Chapter II). Volkenshtein uses the same technique when she turns to general reflections on the prison experience (Volkenshtein, Chapter III). The use of the second person removes the observation from the purview of the individual writer, to encompass its commonality as an experience for all of the inmates – and one which, moreover, the reader can share, as the addressee moves outside the text and, implicitly, outside the prison.[67] This type of deflection away from the self may also reflect the traumatic nature of the experience, and the author's need to a create a sense of separation in order to be able to represent it adequately.[68] By introducing the second person, Ashenbrenner and Pankratov suggest theirs is an alienated subjectivity, dictated to from the outside,[69] and deprived of the normal contact with the other that characterizes the reciprocal and interchangeable nature of the 'I–you' relationship. Pankratov's emphatic use of the familiar 'you' in this way closely coincides with the administration's announcement that this is how the prisoners will be addressed – something that practically all the memoirs mention:

> 'As you are deprived of all rights', says the superintendent, enunciating every word distinctly, 'I will use the familiar form of "you." If you behave yourself, you will get everything: books, work, conversation with a priest (!). Here are the instructions, you can read them.' A manner like this immediately makes you hostile to this person. From the very first words he offends you, from the very first words he mocks you, pointing out your impotence and his own omnipotence.
> (Pankratov, Chapter I)

The change to second person singular forms thus acts as a reminder throughout these texts of the inmates' subordinate position, of the sense of humiliation associated with its use by the administration, and of the authorities' refusal to acknowledge the existence of the collective that would be indicated by the plural 'vy'. But the voluntary turn to the second person singular in these texts also alludes to the existence of a different 'you', one that acknowledges interdependence and community, and brings the prisoners' collective back into focus in the form of 'you–us', rather than 'I–we'.[70]

The use of familiar, informal forms of 'you' by the administration indicates the way that language exercises power to become a punishment in itself, but the reactions to this also show its capacity to become a form of defence. Pankratov, like others, records that some prisoners responded in kind, addressing the superintendent with the familiar form, even though this led to punishments. Such regulations ultimately create trouble for the authorities themselves, as they lead to further distortions of language. Pankratov observes the unnatural form of address the fortress commandant uses to avoid the familiar 'you' (by contrast with the gleeful adoption of this rule by the superintendent): 'how is the convict's health? Have meals been taken? Walks? Does the convict have any complaints, requests?' (Pankratov, Chapter I). Although such forms are aimed at denying the inmate's identity, the accompanying description nevertheless renders the scene comic, as the elderly commandant is pictured, '[b]owing exquisitely, stroking his grey beard and swaying from side to side, like a polar bear on a hot day'. In this way, a regulation intended to underline the convicts' powerlessness, loss of status and personality within the fortress, in the memoirs instead become a means of undermining the perceived authority of the jailers.

The subversion of authority through language is also apparent in the memoirs' repeated recourse to quasi-passive forms. The impersonal active voice in the Russian, using plural verbs without a subject, appears repeatedly, particularly in Ashenbrenner's and Volkenshtein's texts. It is frequently used in relation to the administration's actions, as when Volkenshtein comments, 'all hope had probably been lost of absolutely isolating the inmates, which was apparent from the fact that meetings began to be granted' (Volkenshtein, Chapter I). On the one hand, this implies the extent to which the authorities were effectively at the mercy of the prisoners' behaviour, and on the other, it removes any sense of the human from the authorities' decision-making process. Although certain individuals from the administration, notably the much-hated 'Herod', are vividly depicted, and the differences in the prison regime enacted by more or less humane commandants and superintendents are acknowledged, overall the memoirs frame the problem as an institutional one, rather than being caused by its specific personalities. Thus the penal system acts as a synecdoche for tsarism as a whole. Allusions to the passive indicate that even high-level representatives of the system are mere proxies, with relatively little agency of their own.

Elsewhere, however, similar constructions are used to underline the prisoners' even greater powerlessness and loss of agency, as in Volkenshtein's description of the treatment meted out to Nikolai Shchedrin, one of the most acutely mentally ill inmates: 'The most terrible thing of all was that he was punished for contravening discipline as if he were healthy, because his illness wasn't believed. And so his cell was invaded day and night, and he was often taken away to the old prison' (Volkenshtein, Chapter I). Here, removing direct reference to the guards and administration shifts the focus solely to what is being done to the unfortunate prisoner. The precise source of the ill-treatment is ultimately unimportant; the effect is not. Of course, the same construction may erase the pronoun 'we' as much as 'they', and there is also evidence of a more playful usage, when it is employed to refer to the prisoners' own actions, especially those that break the fortress regulations. Such instances function ironically as a means of obscuring agency, and therefore deflect the blame for supposed wrongdoing. Thus, discussing the boiled sweets the inmates made for their sick colleagues, Volkenshtein states, 'They were often buried in the beds, during work in the allotments' (Volkenshtein, Chapter II), as if the inmates had nothing to do with this. Similarly, when Ashenbrenner recalls efforts to remove barriers to conversation between prisoners in neighbouring allotments, he refers to the most significant actions around the fence as though they had been performed by anonymous or uninvolved bystanders:

> These boards were pulled off with the help of shovels and stakes. [...] The boards were fastened back in place in our absence; but they were torn down again, [...] very quickly a window of approximately six inches in both directions was cut in the fence to the neighbouring allotment, and the neighbouring pairs shook hands.
> (Ashenbrenner, Chapter III)

By conjoining verbs that omit reference to both the administration ('were fastened back in place') and the prisoners ('were torn down again'), Ashenbrenner implies an equivalence to their actions that questions the authority of the institution and its actors. When he reveals the administration's solution at the end of the episode – to ask the prisoners to make shutters for the fence, and keep them closed during inspections – it becomes clear that the power dynamic has shifted, and that the administration is now, in certain areas at least, colluding with the prisoners, rather than imposing its will on them. Indeed, the depiction of such moments suggests that, far from the inmates performing acts of 'symbolic compliance' as a form of everyday resistance in Scott's terms, it is instead the local administration that is staging 'the *impression* of compliance without its substance', revealing its own subordination to the higher authorities.[71]

The battle over the fences is represented as a key moment in establishing direct contact between the inmates and changing the dynamics of their environment. Not for nothing does Ashenbrenner describe their victory as 'an earthquake that shook the foundations of the prison' (Ashenbrenner, Chapter III). The significance of the physical separation of the prisoners, and their need to break down the barriers the prison places between them, is apparent in all the survivors' memoirs. And for all that these texts unfailingly highlight the isolation of life in the prison, particularly in the first years, and the hopelessness it inspires, the emphasis ultimately is placed more on overcoming those barriers than on their simple existence. Across the corpus of Shlissel'burg memoirs,[72] references to doors are collocated with 'open' and its synonyms (*otkryt, otper, otvorit'*) almost three times more frequently than they are with 'shut', 'locked', and so on (notably *zakryt, zaper, zatvor, khlopnut'*); for example, 'Now the door opened and I was admonished for reading aloud.'[73] Similarly, references to the small ventilation pane in the windows (*fortochka*) are collocated with synonyms for 'open', or the preposition 'through' (*cherez*), almost eight times more frequently than references to them as closed, as in Frolenko's description of one social gathering: 'Through the open window vent, conversation, tea-drinking and snacks began'.[74] As jailers are depicted opening doors and windows more frequently than closing them, the memoirists emphasize that the obstacles separating the prisoners are permeable, and surmountable.

As the memoirs make clear, the door and window to the workshop set aside for Figner and Volkenshtein become especially popular spaces for congregation. That becomes possible because of their location on the old prison corridor, and Pankratov in particular emphasizes the significance of the latter as a conduit to communication and interaction, and, at times, confrontation with the administration. From the early stages of solitary confinement, when listening to movement in the corridor could provide inmates with important information about the number of comrades in the institution, and what was happening to them, to the later days of relatively free movement, corridors serve to connect the prisoners to each other and mitigate isolation.

Within the prison infrastructure, doors, windows and corridors all have a necessarily communicative function, hence the administration's periodic attempts to limit or prevent their use by the prisoners, and the determination of the prisoners to defend the rights they have gained to use them or keep them open. However, the primary structures devoted to separation of the inmates – the walls – also prove to be surprisingly porous. The collocations one would expect here ('high', 'stone') are present, and the walls are described, for example by Frolenko, as 'gloomy',[75] while in Morozov's poem 'A Meeting', 'Damp, cheerless, stupefying,/ The walls from the gloom look out'.[76] Yet marginally the most frequent single word collocated with 'wall(s)' is in fact, again, 'through', as in Figner's description of Volkenshtein's actions:

> Thus, S. A. Ivanov, at one time almost doomed to die as a result of throat haemorrhages, ascribes his resurrection to nothing more than the sympathy and moral support L. A. provided to him during his illness, purposely moving into the cell next to his, so as to render him friendly help through the wall.[77]

'Tapping' also features significantly, as when Iuvachev describes evading the attention of the guards: 'it was necessary to tap like thieves, sneakily, i.e. to wait for the moment when the guard leaves the door, and with a bent finger to tap on the wall until his return.'⁷⁸ The wall alphabet provides a means of communication that uses the very barriers intended to prevent contact; if they cannot be physically torn down, as in the case of the fences between allotments, the writings of this determined group of prisoners show how barriers can be breached in other ways to overcome their separation.

Just as the communicative potential of the prison's infrastructure is foregrounded in the memoirs, so are the actions and senses associated with communication. Given the fortress's silent regime, the three Russian words for silence (*molchanie, tishina* and the less common *bezmolvie*), unsurprisingly, appear regularly (with 145, 87 and 35 occurrences respectively), while *tikho* (quietly) appears 112 times. Yet they are significantly outstripped by references to noise and human cries: *shum, krik/krichat', zvuk, zvon* (109, 182, 120 and 47 occurrences). Volkenshtein depicts clearly the role of noise in the prisoners' resistance:

> In the event of a tap, several guards would usually burst into the cell [...]. If a prisoner answered back, at the superintendent's command the guards would attack him, push him to the floor, beat him on the pretext of resistance, and, putting him in a straitjacket, tether him to the iron bed for several hours, often inserting a wooden gag into his mouth to stop him screaming. His neighbours, hearing the brawl, would start to protest, shouting, 'what are you doing to him?' Then they would be pounced on and tied up. The commotion became unspeakable, with screams, clattering, brawls and the croaks of those lying there with wooden gags in their mouths.
>
> (Volkenshtein, Chapter I)

The emphasis on sound indicates that any rupture to the habitual silence in itself becomes an event, and in the context of writing about the experience of solitary confinement, the uneventfulness of daily life in the early years, once it has been described, inevitably assumes lesser importance than anything that disrupts the monotony and is therefore narratable. At the same time, it is notable that while silence within the prison denotes stasis, the breaking of that silence is indicative of human action, of the real people who remain alive within the 'deathly silence' of this 'living crypt' (Pankratov, Chapters III; II).⁷⁹ Moreover, the use of noise as a form of protest, either by shouting or banging on the cell doors, in addition to the more normal practice of tapping to communicate, is depicted as leading the guards to break the silent regime, as they respond to noise by making it themselves in order to drown out the sounds the prisoners were making.[80] Thus sound becomes a further way in which the harshness of the regime results in the administration becoming party to its own undoing.

The corollary of sound is hearing, and even when cut off from the rest of the world physically, the ability to hear what is going on in the prison – aided by the echoing acoustics of the building – is emphasized as an important connection that reduced the inmates' sense of isolation. Immediately following the above quotation, Volkenshtein notes that 'In all corners of the prison what was going on in any individual cell could be heard quite clearly' (Volkenshtein, Chapter I). Interpreting the noises from the corridor and other cells and spaces of the prison became a significant activity: as Janavičius states, 'All these sounds were comprehensible to the experienced ear of an inmate'.[81] Communication via tapping on the walls also required careful listening. There are no references to deafness among the prisoners, but such an inmate would have been truly alone, in the way that a blind inmate would not. Indeed, the eyesight of most of the prisoners deteriorated acutely because of the poor light in the cells; Ashenbrenner notes that the choice was 'either to save one's eyes, not read and go out of one's mind from depression, or go blind and save oneself from madness' (Ashenbrenner, Chapter II). Those who were able chose the latter option, with the result that their hearing became more acute.

The patterns of usage of hearing and listening across the corpus reflect some of the preoccupations identified above. In terms of sounds heard in the prison and recorded in the memoirs, only 15 per cent have an agent; beyond these, as doors slam and steps resound in the corridor, the decision not to mention the guards frames the institution as animated by itself, not by its personnel, as with the use of third-person forms identified above: 'The door slammed, and exhausted, I sank down onto the bed';[82] '[b]ehind the door you hear a slight rustle, quiet steps' (Pankratov, Chapter II). However, allusions to general sounds account for only 14 per cent of all occurrences of hearing verbs (*slyshat'*). Notably, the majority of references to hearing (over 60 per cent) focus on the prisoners hearing each other, in both positive and negative contexts, as when Volkenshtein records Mikhail Grachevskii's terrible fate:

> Over the course of two weeks his neighbours heard him talking to the gendarmes and demanding execution, but he spoke calmly, and perhaps for that reason the authorities did not especially fear

his threat to end his life. Having noticed that Grachevskii's conversations could be heard by his neighbours, he was transferred to the adjoining cell.

(Volkenshtein, Chapter I)

By contrast, only four per cent refer to the inmates hearing the guards, and two per cent to the guards hearing the inmates. In relation to listening (*slushat'*), 20 per cent of references are associated with members of the administration listening to the prisoners, of which almost two thirds refer to the guards' surveillance of the inmates. The remainder have more positive connotations of doctors listening to their hearts, and inspectors listening to their complaints. In any case, this is greater that the 15 per cent of references to the prisoners listening to the guards, half of which, moreover, are negated, as in Figner's description of the boycott of Shebeko, Deputy Minister of Internal Affairs: 'do not make statements, do not answer questions, do not listen to any messages, and in one form or another ask him to get out.'[83] Significantly, the fact that in the Russian, 'obedience' (*po<u>slush</u>anie*) is derived from, and predicated on, listening, suggests that directing their listening *away* from the administration in itself represents an act of resistance. Instead, the act of listening, like hearing, is focused primarily on the prisoners themselves, relating to one third of all references. In particular, the lectures they deliver to each other in the allotments alone account for 18 per cent of all listening verbs, with the remainder referring to conversations and other sounds from the prisoners.

Similarly, and remarkably, given the authorities' ultimately hapless attempts to maintain the principle of solitary confinement, references to conversation (*beseda* and *razgovor*) overwhelmingly relate to the prisoners talking to each other, with 88 per cent and 81 per cent of occurrences respectively (in the latter case 18 per cent refer to the prisoners' interactions with the administration), including references to conversations held through the walls: 'Loud taps could be heard two cells away, and above and below, and therefore we had general conversations in various corners' (Ashenbrenner, Chapter II). Meanwhile, every reference to argument (*spor*) relates to intellectual disputes between the inmates, which, as Figner notes, became ubiquitous: 'The same arguments with our Social Democrats that Liudmila Aleksandrovna and I waged in the fifth or sixth pens, also occurred in other places where S. Ivanov would explode, and M. Popov sound off and shout, along with the like-minded Trigoni'.[84] This indicates the degree of debate and disagreement that existed among the prisoners. They were far from a homogenous group, despite their common cause, as Pankratov's memoir in particular makes clear. But it also emphasizes the connections between them, and the community they created. As conversation brings the inmates together (even if to disagree), it destroys the silence of the prison, and restores their voices. Vera Figner states that, 'when there is no voice, no words, there is nothing'.[85] In the memoirs, 81 per cent of uses of the word 'voice' (*golos*) are attributed to the prisoners themselves, including a small number of references to voting (*golosovanie*) that confirm the democratic, collective perspective of this group of revolutionaries. By contrast, less than 14 per cent of such references relate to the fortress commandant and other members of the administration. The silence of the gendarmes who guard the prisoners is highlighted, moreover, as they are described in several memoirs as 'dumb' (*nemoi*): 'in our presence the conscripted soldiers were required to be as dumb as fish'.[86] Thus after the initial period of deadly silence, it is the voices of the surviving prisoners that are represented as emerging from Shlissel'burg, while the administration becomes voiceless.

This portrayal of the revolutionaries' voices re-awakening within the fortress is crucial, because it challenges the authorities' fundamental objective for the prison: 'They wanted to isolate us, so that young Russia would forget our names; they wanted our silent removal from the scene' (Ashenbrenner, Chapter IV). As these prisoners were prepared to remain neither separated nor silent, their resistance through communication undermines this aim. It also points to the role of their memoirs in continuing this struggle. The community developed by the prisoners is depicted in several memoirs specifically as a writerly community, their endeavours replicating the structures of literary production in the outside world, from producing 'fat journals' to the appointment of a censor.[87] The foregrounding of literary activity in this way draws attention to the role of the memoirs themselves, as the survivors widened the scope of that literary community, and its communicative strategies, to a reading public already well versed in the tropes of Russian carceral writing, from Dostoevskii's *Notes from the House of the Dead*, to more recent, prominent publications such as Anton Chekhov's *Sakhalin Island* (1893–4) and Vlas Doroshevich's *Sakhalin (Hard Labour)* (1903). In doing so they endowed the genre with a distinctive revolutionary dimension that proved transformative.[88] In the nineteenth century, Dostoevskii's influential meditation on the so-called 'executioner within' identified the carceral chronotope primarily with the human capacity for evil.[89] The Shlissel'burg survivors, however, shifted emphasis to the state's violence and oppression, an argument that remains prominent in Gulag narratives throughout the Soviet period. Moreover, the primary setting of earlier carceral texts, likewise taking their cue from Dostoevskii, was the labour camp, with the focus on Siberian imprisonment and exile. The *prisons* of Siberia tend to be depicted from without, in the travelogues and campaigning texts of visitors such as George Kennan.[90] By contrast, the memoirs of Shlissel'burg survivors brought concentrated attention to the prison settings and penal institutions of European Russia – close to the Empire's centre of power – for the first time. Again, this had a lasting effect on the genre. Many narratives of the Stalinist Gulag, such as Evgeniia Ginzburg's seminal memoir *Into the Whirlwind*, place a disproportionate emphasis on the (generally relatively short) initiatory experience of the prison, usually in European Russia or the USSR's European republics. In such texts, as in the case of Ginzburg, Shlissel'burg Prison and its revolutionary inmates frequently become a key point of reference.[91] The very much longer periods of survivors' sentences in labour camps in Siberia and the Soviet Union's peripheries, by contrast, tend to be given much more minimal treatment.

V. Politicizing prison writing

The vision of the prisoners' collective regaining its voice in the fortress not only becomes a central theme of the texts, but extends beyond the fortress as a motivation for the memoirs. As Ashenbrenner contemplates the effect of multiple memoirs of incarceration being published, he emphasizes the collaborative voice they produce: 'if each of those who is freed writes their own notes about the prison, then our collective work will, perhaps, provide something significant' – which sentiment the editors endorse in a footnote in the original journal publication (Ashenbrenner, Chapter III). Indeed, many of these memoirs refer to works by their fellow survivors, pointing to the place of their own work within that collective text.[92] Determined that neither the living nor the dead will be forgotten, several memoirs seek to document as completely as possible the names and fates of prisoners, as we see in the data Volkenshtein presents in the first pages of her text.[93] Frolenko notes the difficulty of maintaining records of the dead because of the limited communication in the early, most fatal period: 'as many unknown people were brought in, and their cells were a long way from mine, I didn't know about other deaths.'[94] In this context, the collaborative effort to memorialize the prisoners becomes particularly important as a means of assuring no-one is forgotten.[95] The memoirs also reinforce the identity of the group of prisoners as a 'mnemonic communit[y]' that, 'through introducing and familiarizing new arrivals to their collective past, ensure[s] that new members, by identifying with the groups' past, attain a required social identity.'[96] Gershuni's first chapter on Shlissel'burg, in which he records the harsh regime of the 1880s and the deaths of many inmates, long before his own transfer there in 1904, performs this function, bringing the experience of two different revolutionary generations together.[97] But even Pankratov – among the last of the prisoners to arrive in 1884 – employs a similar device to denote the connection between his own experience and that of the first prisoners to be transferred. He uses the words of two comrades who did not survive, Nikolai Pokhitonov and Dmitrii Butsinskii, to describe the prisoners' impressions of the fortress upon arrival (Pankratov, Chapter I). Framed as the collective memory of a group of prisoners the tsarist state wanted to expunge, these memoirs transcend their status as personal documents.

As their memoirs restore the prisoners' communication with the outside world, and perform this memorializing function, their political dimension becomes clear. They take on a significant role in advancing revolutionary aims in a number of ways. By highlighting the brutality of the prison regime and positioning the inmates as its martyrs, they endow the survivors – and the revolutionary movement of which they are a part – with moral authority, and question the legitimacy of the tsarist autocracy.[98] At the same time, stories of the prisoners' resilience, their determination to fight back and the numerous victories they managed to achieve to ameliorate their situation, held out hope for the revived revolutionary movement in the early 1900s. And the story they tell of challenging authority and reorganizing the social order within the prison represents a template for the revolutionary future. Therefore, although a significant number of the Shlissel'burg prisoners had been convicted for their involvement, direct or otherwise, in political assassinations,[99] their promotion as ethical models following their release, as well as the emphasis placed on their martyrdom at the hands of the tsarist autocracy, make these texts notable in terms of clarifying the emotional and moral appeal of the revolution. They suggest that whatever moral high ground the Russian authorities might have expected to occupy as victims of a campaign of political terror, was relinquished as a result of the treatment meted out to the prisoners.

The dictates of the former inmates' continued political objectives prior to 1917 shaped the genre conventions of their memoirs, which comprised the four major factors introduced in the analysis above, through which their experience is refracted. First, the scope of the memoirs was confined to what occurred within the walls of the fortress and the terms of incarceration the prisoners endured, excluding all references to life before imprisonment and after release. Second, they set up the fundamental opposition of the prisoners and the administration, creating a clear 'us' vs 'them' dynamic through which the state's violence is filtered. Third, even if not narrated chronologically, they depict the transition from solitary confinement to communal life that reflects the gradual ascendency of 'us' over 'them'. Finally, they provide a guide to correct conduct for revolutionaries, which includes the suppression of personal feelings for the sake of the collective, and which ultimately enables that ascendancy.

The first set of memoirs by former Shlissel'burg inmates conforms to these conventions to a remarkable degree. Of all the texts published before the 1917 revolutions, only Janavičius's gives any sort of wider perspective on the revolutionary life such as that we see in Figner's, Frolenko's and Morozov's later memoirs, which, as Hilde Hoogenboom has shown, focus instead on the question of 'How I became a revolutionary'.[100] Janavičius aside, none of the earlier writers makes any reference to the activities that led to their arrest. Nor do other memoirs provide the sort of justification for revolutionary action that Figner advances so eloquently.[101] Undoubtedly, the censorship and the need to protect both comrades and the secrets of the revolutionary underground played a significant role in these omissions. But this determinedly narrow scope also reflects the uncompromising self-sacrifice necessary for revolutionary life. Gershuni, whose memoirs cover his imprisonment in the Peter and Paul Fortress as well as Shlissel'burg, strongly equates carceral experience with revolutionary activity, his translator noting that he perceived this text as 'a sort of survival guide for newcomers to the revolutionary life'.[102] He explicitly rejects the preoccupations of bourgeois life-writing:

> Does it really matter where, when, to whom and why I was born, how I grew up, how my childhood was spent, and so on, all the things that autobiographies are filled with? All that satisfies only the idle curiosity of idle people, and is not for revolutionaries like us to indulge in.[103]

Devotion to the cause endowed these revolutionaries with a single-mindedness that displaced the personal in the service of the whole. These memoirs – particularly those written during the revolutionary upheavals of the last years of the tsarist autocracy – are fundamentally *not* portrayals of individuals who experienced imprisonment. They are, instead, the story of the collective that emerged in the fortress. This in many ways accounts for the differences between the Shlissel'burg memoirs and other carceral writing, in Russia and beyond. As I have argued elsewhere, memoirs of incarceration in the Gulag, particularly relating to the Stalinist era, tend to incorporate the experience of imprisonment into a wider perspective on the survivor's life, so that they are not defined by their incarceration alone.[104] By contrast, the survivors of Shlissel'burg, particularly while their comrades remained imprisoned there and elsewhere, define themselves precisely by their carceral experience. At the same time, their political aims mean that these works are not framed primarily as therapeutic narratives of survival, despite their common emphasis on overcoming the predations of the prison regime. They are, however, narratives of non-survival, as they seek to create witnesses to what was intended to remain hidden from the world – the deaths of their comrades, and the authorities' attempts to eliminate this revolutionary generation. That aim suggests a traumatic core to the texts – perhaps most strongly in evidence in the final words of Volkenshtein's and Ashenbrenner's memoirs – but it remains one that looks principally beyond the self. Moreover, the impersonal, collective approach they adopt to a great extent precludes the sort of introspection normally associated with prison writing from Boethius onwards. To be sure, they retain a similar sense of 'defend[ing] their ideas and cultural values against a dominant persecuting power', and 'creat[ing] order from chaos to focus willpower and resistance'.[105] But the revolutionary cause, rather than God, is the faith that sustains these prisoners, their adoption of Christian imagery to draw attention to the martyrdom of their comrades and the morality of their cause notwithstanding.[106] The collective order they create as the source of resistance co-opts the genre of prison memoir in the service of the revolution, but in fulfilling this aim, the authors contribute new features to the Russian tradition of carceral writing.

*

To the extent that Shlissel'burg Prison retains today any of the notoriety it had a hundred years ago is due to Vera Figner's memoir, which is indisputably a classic, and required reading for anyone interested either in the history of the Russian revolutionary movement or in Russian penal history. It is, however, representative of only one side of the body of memoirs of imprisonment in Shlissel'burg Fortress, because of its wider perspective on the revolutionary life, while in its greater focus on the development of the individual than the collective it deviates significantly from the genre conventions the prison's memoirists established. It is therefore particularly ironic that – largely owing to the vicissitudes of ideology in the Stalinist period, and contrary to the author's wishes – it became the text that represented this episode in revolutionary and penal history, with Figner standing in for the entire group of prisoners, indeed almost for an entire revolutionary generation, to the exclusion of the other memoirs that foreground the collective.[107]

The present volume aims to restore the collective voice of the Shlissel'burg prisoners. The texts, translated here for the first time, have been selected in part at least because of their typicality, the fact that they contribute to a greater whole and gain from being read together. They complement each other, and between them tell the story of the trauma of the early period of imprisonment and the resilience of those who survived, the battles they fought and the establishment of a more relaxed regime. They offer a wide range of detail about the techniques of imprisonment, their effect on daily life and the activities the prisoners engaged in. They reflect the monotony of everyday life in the fortress, and depict the dramatic incidents that punctuated it. The pen portraits they include bring to life different facets of both the prisoners' and administration's personalities, providing us with a more rounded view than a single text might achieve. And by building a cumulative picture across a body of texts, they overcome some of the limitations associated with using memoirs as historical sources. While we should always remain aware that the choices the survivors made about what to include and exclude from their memoirs were dictated by their political aims, nevertheless they have a great deal to tell the careful reader about the operation of harsh carceral regimes and the extent to which they are the product of mismanagement. They also grant important insights into prisoner behaviour and the effects of solitary confinement, and the limitations of severe mechanisms of punishment and control in the face of determined opposition.

For all that they cover the same ground and reflect similar aims, the three authors take different approaches to portraying the prisoners' life in Shlissel'burg fortress. Liudmila Volkenshtein's focus on the human tragedy of the prison, and on the dreadful emotional and psychological impact of living surrounded by so much death and insanity, while completely unable to render assistance to others or improve one's own situation, is particularly painful. Her memoir is never hopeless, however, and the constant striving she depicts of all the prisoners – as indicated above, she almost never refers to her own thoughts, feelings or actions in isolation – on behalf of their comrades, means that it ultimately becomes an account of collective recovery and compassion, even as it mourns the dead. At the same time, that impersonal approach – which leads to silence about all intimate and family matters, including her feelings about her separation from her child, and an implicit denial of any gender-based difference in her experience – means that when she does reflect on her inner life, the result is an abstract, almost existential feeling.[108] Volkenshtein's own untimely death during a demonstration in Vladivostok in 1906 was undoubtedly a factor in her disappearance from public memory, despite the various articles devoted to her in the revolutionary journal *The Past* (*Byloe*) in that year. Yet it is evident from other survivors' memoirs that they held her in as high esteem as they did Vera Figner. For many years she has appeared, if at all, as a footnote to revolutionary and carceral history, a mere sidekick to Figner.[109] But her memoir represents an early example of Russian women's writing about imprisonment, in addition to being the first by a Populist incarcerated in Shlissel'burg, and established many of the conventions that both traditions subsequently followed. For that reason, as well as the power of her own depiction of life in the fortress, her voice deserves to be heard in its own right once more.

Mikhail Ashenbrenner, the oldest of the prisoners sent to the fortress in 1884, was one of several military officers incarcerated in Shlissel'burg. His is the most cerebral and technical of the three memoirs, and his narrative is full of fascinating detail that tells us a great deal about both everyday and intellectual life in the fortress, although in places he too turns to existential reflections. Focusing more on the later period, once solitary confinement had been scaled back through meetings with comrades during exercise, Ashenbrenner reveals the exceptional range of activity and accomplishment among the prisoners, although he always remains modest about the latter. He represents incarceration as a space for education and development, but at the same time views it as a form of sociological experiment, as he explores group behaviours in close confinement – another way in which the collective is emphasized in the face of the authorities' attempts to maintain the prisoners' isolation from each other as well as from the outside world. Ashenbrenner's preoccupations reflect the erudition others identified in him, yet his writing is curiously unstructured, with some abrupt changes of subject – at times within a single paragraph – making the direction of his thought processes unclear, particularly in the opening pages of his memoir. But his insights into prisoner behaviour as well as the rigour of his descriptions of daily life in the fortress, make persistence more than worthwhile.

Vasilii Pankratov was both the youngest of the early arrivals at the fortress, and the only prisoner of proletarian origin to leave behind a memoir – in itself testimony to the education he gained in Shlissel'burg. His text in many ways complements the others translated here, in that his approach is, like Volkenshtein's, primarily psychological, yet his focus, like Ashenbrenner's, is on the communal life established by the prisoners after the initial period of solitary confinement. Pankratov avoids simplistic appeals to the idea of unity. Although there is evidently great solidarity among the inmates in relation to their opposition to the prison administration, he also confronts the tensions between the members of the group that are often glossed over elsewhere. A very lively narrator, Pankratov regularly slips between present and past tense, giving his descriptions a striking immediacy. This is augmented by a significant amount of dialogue, bringing many of the personalities in the fortress vividly to life, and reinforcing the many absurdities of the situation they faced. Perhaps as a result of his working-class background, his language is in places somewhat earthier than the other memoirs, which the translation does not try to obscure.

The three memoirs share the anger and urgency of political writing that has an immediate objective, as implied by the rather breathless tone of the publisher's preface to the first edition of Volkenshtein's memoir.[110] That immediacy is also undoubtedly one of the reasons why all three texts show signs of being hurriedly written and published. They are in places unrevised and untidy, with numerous spelling, grammatical and typographical errors. While occasionally it proved necessary to smooth out some phrasing in order to clarify the precise meaning, and some sentences in all three memoirs have been split to aid readability, the aim of the translations overall has been not to polish the texts unduly, but rather to preserve that sense of urgency. Differences in the authors' terminologies have been retained, but the translations try to reflect as much as possible the common modes of inscribing resistance, overcoming separation and forging the collective outlined above.

The intersection of Russian literature and the country's carceral history has a long pedigree, to which these memoirs make a significant contribution. From the time of their writing to the present day they have made the very name of Shlissel'burg synonymous with unjust incarceration and despotism – as well as the possibility of resistance.[111] The three works translated here – and those by other survivors such as Vera Figner – introduce us to a remarkable group of people, most of whom have been forgotten.[112] The appalling conditions they endured, the resilience and resourcefulness with which they overcame their situation, and their overwhelming concern for others, are intensely moving. The carceral practices of late nineteenth-century Russia may seem very distant from today's world. Yet the operation of a harsh (if largely communally-based) penal culture rooted in the Gulag and resistant to reform in post-Soviet Russia;[113] the imprisonment by the Russian government of political opponents such as Oleg Sentsov and, most recently, Aleksei Navalnyi, amid credible allegations of the withholding of medical treatment and other abuses; the use of solitary confinement in HM Prison Service in the UK and in the US Federal Prison System;[114] the poor conditions of prison facilities and long sentences meted out by criminal justice systems in all three countries and many others; the legacy of Guantanamo Bay, rendition, and the long-term imprisonment of terrorist suspects without judicial process; and the mass incarceration of asylum seekers in many parts of the first world, all indicate that punishment, confinement and their institutionalization remain burning questions across the world. It is in this context that reintroducing these memoirs to a new audience makes sense. They still have a great deal to say to us today.

Notes

1 Shilov (ed.) *German Aleksandrovich Lopatin*, 187.
2 In the Introduction and editorial material, dates from pre-revolutionary Russia refer to the Julian (old-style) calendar, with new-style (Gregorian) dates given in brackets. In the translations, old-style dates have been retained, with inaccuracies highlighted in endnotes.
3 Not to be confused with political populism as it is more commonly understood, the Russian Populists (*Narodniki*) were socialist revolutionaries who championed the rights of the peasantry (*narod*) and espoused social reorganization based on the model of the peasants' traditional commune.
4 Goodwin, 'The afterlife of terrorists', 230.
5 Goodwin, 'The afterlife of terrorists', 230.
6 Chatterjee, 'Imperial incarcerations', 2015, 850–72. http://www.jstor.org/stable/10.5612/slavicreview.74.4.850, albeit using different sources, identifies the remarkable success of the Russian Populists in publicizing their prison experiences as means of challenging the legitimacy of the tsarist regime.
7 Gershuni, *Iz nedavnego proshlogo*, 122–3.
8 The following historical sketch is adapted from Young, 'Isolation, control and resistance', 635–48. http://doi.org/10.18239/jornadas_2020.25.44.
9 Yuri Danilovich (1281–1325), was Prince of Moscow from 1303, and Grand Prince of Vladimir from 1318.
10 The Great Northern War (1700–21), for supremacy over Northern, Central and Eastern Europe, was fought between an alliance led by Peter the Great, and the Swedish Empire.
11 Venediktov-Beziuk, *Po kazematam Shlissel'burgskoi kreposti*, 13; Gernet, *Istoriia tsarskoi tiur'my*, 1:222.
12 Gernet, *Istoriia tsarskoi tiur'my*, 1:233–5.
13 See, for example, Iuvachev, *Shlissel'burgskaia krepost'*, 173–85; or Frolenko, *Zapiski semidesiatnika*, 232, 245.
14 Nikolai Ivanovich Novikov (1744–1818), writer, publisher, philanthropist and prominent freemason, was involved in the 1767 Legislative Assembly to produce a new code of laws, and

produced satirical journals that were entertained by Catherine the Great until the French revolution.
15 Anti-masonic measures were introduced by Catherine the Great, who suspected the freemasons of turning her son Paul against her.
16 Sentence to exile by administrative process (that is, without recourse to the justice system) was enshrined in the legal code in 1669, and became a means of colonizing Siberia; it remained in use throughout the tsarist era and continued in other forms during the Soviet period. See Wood, 'Administrative exile and the criminals' communes in Siberia', 397; Beer, *The House of the Dead*, 23–5.
17 Data on prisoners is derived from Gernet, *Istoriia tsarskoi tiur'my*, 1:222–65; 2:397–403; and Koniaev, *Shlissel'burgskie psalmy*, 529–603.
18 See Szwarce, *Siedm lat w Szlyselburgu*, 78; 118–9.
19 Gernet, *Istoriia tsarskoi tiur'my*, 2:224.
20 Gernet, *Istoriia tsarskoi tiur'my*, 2:388.
21 O'Meara, 'Timotheus von Bock', 2012, 114–5. https://www.jstor.org/stable/10.5699/slaveasteurorev2.90.1.0098.
22 Bakunin, *Sobranie sochinenii i pisem 1828–1876*, 4:567.
23 Prugavin, 'Shlissel'burgskaia krepost'', 1:ix.
24 O'Meara, 'Timotheus von Bock', 114.
25 Szwarce, *Siedm lat w Szlyselburgu*, 102; Gernet, *Istoriia tsarskoi tiur'my*, 2:439; Koniaev, *Shlissel'burgskie psalmy*, 235.
26 Figner, *Zapechatlennyi trud*, 2:40. Aleksandr Ivanovich Chernyshev (1786–1857), officer, diplomat and statesman, was Minister of War from 1827 to 1852, and chair of the State Council of Ministers from 1848 to 1856.
27 Gernet, *Istoriia tsarskoi tiur'my*, 2:382–6.
28 Gernet, *Istoriia tsarskoi tiur'my*, 2:382.
29 The Petrashevskii Circle, named for utopian theorist Mikhail Vasil'evich Butashevich-Petrashevskii (1821–66), at whose home meetings were held, was a radical philosophical discussion group whose members arrested in 1849 included Fedor Dostoevskii (1821–81).
30 As Doreen Massey argues, '[t]he identity of places is very much bound up with the *histories* which are told of them, *how* those histories are told, and which history turns out to be dominant'. 'Places and their pasts', 186. https://www.jstor.org/stable/4289361. In the case of Shlissel'burg, the 'secret' history and its telling as a tale of terror has always dominated, and the writings of the Populist prisoners only served to reinforce that reputation.
31 The classic account of the development of the revolutionary movement is Venturi, *Roots of Revolution*. On the practical and organizational dimensions of the Populist revolutionaries, see Ely, *Underground Petersburg*.
32 Daly, *Crime and Punishment in Russia*, 67.
33 On the high number of escapees, see Daly, 'Criminal punishment and Europeanization in late Imperial Russia', 2000, 353; 359. http://www.jstor.org/stable/41050588.
34 See Adams, *The Politics of Punishment*, 58.
35 The location of the prison so close to the centre of Imperial power is contrary to the usual practice of 'exile imprisonment' in Russia, which 'encapsulates the idea that a custodial sentence necessarily involves being sent to a distant location.' Badcock and Pallot, 'Russia and the Soviet Union from the nineteenth to the twenty-first century', 272.
36 Gernet, *Istoriia tsarskoi tiur'my*, 3:217–8.
37 Frolenko, *Zapiski semidesiatnika*, 214; Polivanov, 'Otryvki iz pisem byvshego shlissel'burzhtsa', 1906, 273.
38 Novorusskii, *Zapiski shlissel'burzhtsa: 1887–1905 gg.*, 26–7.
39 Viacheslav Konstantinovich von Plehve (1846–1904), Director of the Imperial Police and later Minister of Internal Affairs (1902–4), when he was assassinated by a member of the Socialist Revolutionary Party, Egor Sozonov, who was imprisoned in Shlissel'burg (1905–6) before being transferred to hard labour at Nerchinsk.
40 See Kolosov, *Gosudareva tiur'ma - Shlissel'burg*, 36–7. The gendarmes were uniformed security police, first established as an army regiment in 1826 following the Decembrist uprising.
41 Kolosov, *Gosudareva tiur'ma*, 65.
42 Kolosov, *Gosudareva tiur'ma*, 69–71. See also Ianovich, *Shlissel'burzhets L. F. Ianovich*, 51.
43 Petr Vasil'evich Orzhevskii (1839–97), Deputy Minister of Internal Affairs.

44 As Ashenbrenner indicates (Chapter II), the turnover of fortress commandants and superintendents was relatively high, reflecting a similar situation in the upper echelons of the Imperial bureaucracy and the Police Department in particular. See Daly, *Autocracy Under Siege*, 29.
45 Foucault, *Discipline and Punish*, 231–9.
46 In the 1845 penal reforms, Shlissel'burg Prison, despite already functioning as a local example of single-cell incarceration, was overlooked as a potential model in favour of Pentonville Prison in an ultimately unsuccessful attempt to modernize the tsarist penal system. See Adams, *The Politics of Punishment*, 39. The fact that Adams's study makes no reference at all to Shlissel'burg beyond his critique of Gernet's *Istoriia tsarskoi tiur'my* is an indication of the extent to which the fortress remained outside the normal workings of the Imperial carceral system.
47 Foucault, *Discipline and Punish*, 239–42.
48 Nikolai Morozov, however, notes that he at least found material of interest in these religious works. Morozov, *Povesti moei zhizni*, 3:10.
49 Foucault, *Discipline and Punish*, 238.
50 The instructions are set out in Novorusskii, *Zapiski shlissel'burzhtsa*, 32–3.
51 Almost all the memoirs mention both the dreadful food and the cold in the cells. Kolosov, *Gosudareva tiur'ma*, 98, notes that most cells had average temperatures of 8–10° Réaumur (10–12.5° Celsius), with the warmest only reaching 11–12° (13.75–15° Celsius).
52 See, for example, Novorusskii, *Zapiski shlissel'burzhtsa*, 208.
53 See Young, 'Isolation, control and resistance', 639–42.
54 See, for example, Ginzburg, *Into the Whirlwind*, 59–61.
55 Polivanov, 'Otryvki iz pisem', 276.
56 Nikolai Morozov's work, in particular his controversial *Revelation in Storm and Thunder (Otkrovenie v groze i bure)*, is the best known product of the prisoners' intellectual activities.
57 On the Decembrists, see, e.g., Lorer, 'Zapiski moego vremeni', 415–6. On intellectual activities in Soviet prisons, see, e.g., Polak, *Bylo tak*, 71, or Shumovskii, *Svet s vostoka*, 78.
58 The fortress effectively gave these revolutionaries the opportunity to construct the sort of commune beloved of Populist theoreticians. In the early post-revolutionary years as well, the imprisonment of members of the Socialist Revolutionary Party and others was seized upon as a chance to organize communes, as on the Solovetskii islands in 1923. See Gullotta, *Intellectual Life and Literature at Solovki 1923–1930*, 61.
59 Haslam and Reicher, 'When prisoners take over the prison', 2012, 155. https://doi.org/10.1177/1088868311419864.
60 Scott, *Weapons of the Weak*, 26; 33; 246.
61 Haslam and Reicher, 'When prisoners take over the prison': 161–5. Haslam and Reicher's third case study, of the uprising at Sobibor Extermination Camp in 1943, seems less relevant here.
62 Haslam and Reicher, 'When prisoners take over the prison': 162. By the time Shlissel'burg's new prison opened, hunger striking was already a relatively common tactic of the Populist revolutionaries. See Grant, 'British suffragettes and the Russian method of hunger strike', 2011, 113–24. http://www.jstor.com/stable/41241735.
63 Haslam and Reicher, 'When prisoners take over the prison', 164; 160.
64 Haslam and Reicher, 'When prisoners take over the prison': 170–1.
65 By contrast, in Figner's memoirs, the use of 'I'-forms dominates, appearing twice as frequently as 'we', and reflecting her greater emphasis on the repression of the individual personality by the prison and consequent development of the 'I' as an ethical subject.
66 Gershuni, by contrast, uses the second person plural to broaden out his observations from the self to all the prisoners. *Iz nedavnego proshlogo*, 125–7.
67 On the implications of second person narration for the relationship between author and reader, see Mildorf, 'Reconsidering second-person narration and involvement', 2016, 146. https://www.jstor.org/stable/10.5250/storyworlds.4.2012.0075.
68 This might be compared to Dostoevskii's decision to distance himself from the experience of incarceration through the use of a fictional narrator, Gorianchikov, in his *Notes from the House of the Dead*. Robert Louis Jackson has argued that overtly separating the observational, engaged Gorianchikov of the main text, from the reclusive figure depicted in the Introduction of *House of the Dead*, enabled Dostoevskii to compartmentalize the trauma of his own experience and thereby concentrate on the objective portrayal of the other convicts. See Jackson, *The Art of Dostoevsky*, 54–7. On the use of the second person to enable the present self

to address the past self, see Fludernik, 'Introduction: Second-person narrative and related issues', 1994, 288. https://www.jstor.org/stable/42946253.
69 DelConte, 'Why you can't speak', 2003, 205. https://www.jstor.org/stable/10.5325/style.37.2.204.
70 On the interdependence implied by the second person, see Code, 'Second persons', 1987, 377–8. https://doi.org/10.1080/00455091.1987.10715942. On the second person as rejecting the individualism of the Cartesian 'I', see Bal, 'First person, second person, same person', 1993, 300–1. https://www.jstor.org/stable/469408.
71 Scott, *Weapons of the Weak*, 26. Emphasis in the original.
72 25 texts by 15 authors, containing 442,024 words, and 58,681 unique words. Texts used for the corpus are indicated in the bibliography. Analysis was conducted using *AntConc* (version 3.5.7), a free desktop concordance application, available at: http://www.laurenceanthony.net/software/antconc/.
73 Iuvachev, *Shlissel'burgskaia krepost'*, 54.
74 Frolenko, *Zapiski semidesiatnika*, 247.
75 Frolenko, *Zapiski semidesiatnika*, 247.
76 Morozov, *Iz sten nevoli*, 42.
77 Figner, 'Shlissel'burgskaia uznitsa Liudmila Aleksandrovna Volkenshtein', 1906, 274.
78 Iuvachev, *Shlissel'burgskaia krepost'*, 35.
79 Many of the Shlissel'burg texts, including those translated here, refer to the prison in poetic terms as a crypt (погреб) or a sepulchre (усыпальница) to convey its deathly atmosphere.
80 See *Shlissel'burzhets L. F. Ianovich*, 62.
81 *Shlissel'burzhets L. F. Ianovich*, 47.
82 Figner, *Zapechatlennyi trud*, 2:10.
83 Figner, 'Shlissel'burgskaia uznitsa': 257.
84 Figner, *Zapechatlennyi trud*, 2:170.
85 Figner, *Zapechatlennyi trud*, 2:215.
86 Popov, 'Mechti o svobode', 1917, 263.
87 My thanks to Lynn Patyk for pointing out this resemblance.
88 On the interplay between the revolutionary movement and Russian literature in the nineteenth century, see Patyk, *Written in Blood*.
89 Dostoevsky, *Notes from the House of the Dead*, trans. Boris Jakim, 204–6. Dostoevskii himself does not in fact use the term 'executioner within'.
90 On the externalized perspective of Kennan's *Siberia and the Exile System* (1891), see Young, 'Knowing Russia's convicts', 2013, 1702–5. https://doi.org/10.1080/09668136.2013.844509.
91 Ginzburg, *Into the Whirlwind*, 199, 202–3. Notably, even in the *Kolyma Stories* of Varlam Shalamov, which focus almost entirely on depictions of the hard labour camps of the most notorious part of the Gulag, the few tales set in Moscow's Butyrka Prison in 1937 are closely related to the imprisonment of revolutionaries in the late Imperial era through the recurring character Aleksandr Georgievich Andreev, a member of the SR Party and general secretary of the Society for Former Political Prisoners, with references to Shlissel'burg prisoners including not only Figner and Morozov, but also Gershuni, Sozonov and Ivan Kaliaev. 'Luchshaia pokhvala' ('The Highest Praise'), in Shalamov, *Sobranie sochinenii*, 1:284.
92 See, for example, Iuvachev's use of other prisoners' memoirs and poetry (notably by Figner and Morozov, but also including the words of Ashenbrenner, Polivanov and Volkenshtein) as epigraphs to chapters of his *Shlissel'burgskaia krepost'*; Popov's citation of an incident described in detail in Novorusskii's memoir, 'Mechti o svobode', 265; or Morozov's reference to reading Frolenko's and Novorusskii's memoirs, *Povesti moei zhizni*, 3:6.
93 In the first edition of Volkenshtein's memoir, the revolutionary and publicist Vladimir Burtsev appended expanded notes on the Shlissel'burg inmates: Volkenshtein, *13 let v Shlissel'burgskoi kreposti: Zapiski*, ed. V. L. Burtsev, 41–53. Tabularized data is also provided in Novorusskii, *Zapiski shlissel'burzhtsa*, 214–5, while Iuvachev, *Shlissel'burgskaia krepost'*, 150–61, includes plans of the cells in the new prison and details of their occupants.
94 Frolenko, *Zapiski semidesiatnika*, 208.
95 On the privileging of written forms of memorialization in Russia, see Etkind, 'Hard and soft in cultural memory', 2004, 36–59. http://www.jstor.org/stable/20442652.
96 Misztal, *Theories of Social Remembering*, 15.
97 Gershuni, *Iz nedavnego proshlogo*, 113–20.

98 It is notable that different aspects of this story were emphasized for different audiences. In the international press, feeding into wider campaigns about Russian prison conditions by the Society of Friends of Russian Freedom, among others, the extremity of the fortress's regime and length of the sentences were the sole focus, with almost no reference to any of the concessions gained through the prisoners' actions. See, for example, Wallace, 'Horrors of Schlusselburg Fortress', 1910, 16 (based on an interview with Figner), or Kropotkin, 'The revolution in Russia', 1905, 877. In the Russian domestic press, the resistance of the inmates and their ability to challenge the prison regime is highlighted, as in Noskov, 'V russkoi bastilii', 1905, 339–43 (based on Volkenshtein's memoirs).
99 Others had participated solely in peaceful propaganda, and at least one prisoner, Vladimir Malavskii, had only the most tenuous connection to the revolutionary movement. On the latter, see Kolosov, *Gosudareva tiur'ma*, 78–80.
100 Hoogenboom, 'Vera Figner and revolutionary autobiographies', 78–82. Janavičius's memoir, published in Russian under the title *Shlissel'burzhets L. F. Ianovich*, may be something of an outlier due to his rather different revolutionary aims, rooted in the Polish independence movement, as well as the context in which he was writing. His text breaks off abruptly, and he did not complete it before his suicide.
101 Figner, *Zapechatlennyi trud*, 1:280–8.
102 Katya Vladimirov, 'Introduction', in Gershuni, *From My Recent Past*, xii.
103 Gershuni, *Iz nedavnego proshlogo*, 6–7.
104 Young, 'Framing Gulag memoirs'.
105 Zim, *The Consolations of Writing*, 16, 18. https://www.jstor.org/stable/10.2307/j.ctt6wq0m7.
106 See, for example, quotations by Gershuni (Introduction, I) and Figner (Introduction, III) above. We might associate the appearance of Christian imagery with Anatolii Lunacharskii's later attempt to place socialism in a religious context with the concept of 'God-building' (*Bogostroitel'stvo*). See Boer, 'Religion and socialism', 2014, 188–209. https://doi.org/10.1179/1462317X13Z.00000000074.
107 Attempts to restore the memory of some of the Shlissel'burg inmates to revolutionary history were made in the 1970s and 80s in contributions to the 'Fiery Revolutionaries' (*Plamennye revoliutsionery*) series of biographical novels: Trifonov, *Neterpenie: Povest' ob A. Zheliabove*, 1973, in which, among others, Aronchik, Bogdanovich, Butsinskii, Dolgushin, Frolenko, Grachevskii, Isaev, Myshkin and Trigoni feature; Voinovich, *Stepen' doveriia: Povest' o Vere Figner*, 1973; Gladilin, *Sny Shlissel'burgskoi kreposti: Povest' ob Ippolite Myshkine*, 1974; Popovskii, *Pobezhdennoe vremia: Povest' o Nikolae Morozove*, 1975; Davydov, *Dve sviazki pisem: Povest' o Germane Lopatine*, 1983. On the 'Fiery Revolutionaries' series, see Jones, *Revolution Rekindled*. https://dx.doi.org/10.1093/oso/9780198804345.001.0001.
108 My thanks to Lynn Patyk for this observation.
109 See, in particular, Hartnett, *The Defiant Life of Vera Figner*, 160–171.
110 The publisher's preface to the second edition takes on a more Gothic slant. My thanks to Lynn Patyk for this observation.
111 On Ginzburg's and Shalamov's references to the Shlissel'burg prisoners, see note 91 above. Nadya Tolokonnikova of Pussy Riot has described Figner, whose memoirs she read in the high security prison in Omsk, as a sartorial inspiration. See Tolokonnikova, *Read and Riot*, 166.
112 Beyond the limited memory of Volkenshtein mentioned above, of the other survivors translated here, Ashenbrenner is seldom mentioned beyond the fact that he was arrested alongside Figner, while Pankratov is remembered more for the role he played in the fate of the Imperial family following the October Revolution, as detailed in Koniaev, *Shlissel'burgskie psalmy*, 408–33. Of all the prisoners who entered Shlissel'burg Fortress between 1884 and 1906, only Figner, Morozov (albeit for his scientific work, rather than his imprisonment), and perhaps Lenin's brother Aleksandr Ul'ianov remain well-known names.
113 On Russia's harsh penal culture, see Pallot, 'The Gulag as the crucible of Russia's 21st-century system of punishment', 2015, 681–710. https://muse.jhu.edu/journals/kritika/v016/16.3.pallot.html. On conditions in the post-Soviet Russian penal system, see Piacentini, *Surviving Russian Prisons*.
114 See Shalev, *A Sourcebook on Solitary Confinement*. www.solitaryconfinement.org/sourcebook, and Shalev, *Supermax: Controlling risk through solitary confinement*.

2.
Liudmila Volkenshtein, *Thirteen years in Shlissel'burg Fortress*

I. Liudmila Volkenshtein (née Aleksandrova), 1857–1906

Liudmila Aleksandrovna Volkenshtein (see Figure 2.1) was born in Kiev on 18 (30) September 1857 to a family of minor gentry. Her father, Aleksandr Petrovich Aleksandrov, the son of a small landowner, was the chief forestry officer of the Kiev state forest. Her mother, Evdokiia Karpovna (née Kryzhanovskaia), was from a wealthier background, and owned several houses in Kiev.

Educated at the local gymnasium until 1875, in the following year Liudmila married Aleksandr Aleksandrovich Volkenshtein, a young *zemstvo* doctor.[1] In the summer of 1877, her husband was arrested for propaganda activities associated with the 'Going to the People' movement, and was one of the defendants in the 'Trial of the 193', which took place in St Petersburg between 18 (30) October 1877 and 23 January (4 February) 1878.[2] Although he was acquitted, the trial proved a turning point for Liudmila Aleksandrovna. She left her husband and family life, and, with her newborn son, joined the revolutionary movement. She assisted in the assassination by Grigorii Gol'denberg of Prince D. N. Kropotkin in February 1879, running the safe house where plans for the attack were made.[3] She escaped Russia in November 1879, leaving her two-year-old son

Figure 2.1 Portrait of Liudmila Volkenshtein. From Annenskii, N. F. et al., eds. *Gallereia Shlissel'burgskikh uznikov*. St Petersburg: Tipografiia M. M. Stasiulevicha, 1907, between pp. 222 and 223. Public domain/ orphan work. Digitization by LSE Library.

Sergei in the care of his father and maternal grandmother, and spent almost four years living in Europe under the name Anna Andreevna Pavlova.

In August 1883, travelling on a fake passport, Volkenshtein returned to Petersburg, where she was arrested the following month. She was one of the defendants in the 'Trial of the 14', of members of the Executive Committee of the People's Will, alongside Mikhail Ashenbrenner and Vera Figner, six others who were subsequently incarcerated in Shlissel'burg Prison, and two who were sent there for execution.[4] Volkenshtein received the death sentence, commuted to 15 years' hard labour. She was transferred to the Shlissel'burg Fortress on 13 (25) October 1884.

In 1896 an amnesty declared to mark the coronation of Nicholas II[5] ordered Volkenshtein's transfer to exile on Sakhalin Island.[6] She left the fortress on 23 September (5 October) 1896, and was incarcerated in the Peter and Paul Fortress in St Petersburg until March 1897, when she was transferred to Odessa. There she was reunited with her husband, who travelled with her to Sakhalin. They arrived at Korsakov port on Sakhalin on 2 (14) November 1897 after 52 days at sea. Volkenshtein worked as a medical assistant and pharmacist at the Korsakov hospital, but the couple had to move to Aleksandrovsk in 1900 because their closeness to many of the hard labour convicts in the hospital brought them into conflict with the prison authorities. In 1902 they settled in Vladivostok, where Aleksandr set up the town's first public health unit, and Liudmila at first engaged in social work, and later, during the Russo-Japanese War, worked as a medical assistant.

During unrest in Vladivostok following the Russo-Japanese War and the October Manifesto of 1905, Liudmila Volkenshtein participated in a number of demonstrations. On 10 (23) January 1906, soldiers fired on a demonstration demanding the release of prisoners from the town's fortress. Volkenshtein was among those killed. She was buried in Vladivostok's Pokrovskii cemetery three days later.

Disliked by the gendarmes who guarded the prisoners because of her 'remonstrative character',[7] Liudmila Volkenshtein was described by fellow Shlissel'burg inmate Nikolai Morozov as 'an angel of light'.[8] For Vera Figner, she was 'my comfort, my joy and happiness. ... the personification of tenderness, kindness, and humaneness. All the treasures of her loving spirit she gave me with a generous hand'.[9] While Figner's role as a moral centre and guiding light for the prisoners has become legendary, all the memoirs by survivors of Shlissel'burg make it clear that Volkenshtein was an equally powerful and influential figure during her 12 years at the fortress.

Volkenshtein's memoir was the first to be published by this group of prisoners, and in many ways set out a framework for subsequent publications by her fellow survivors. Written in transit to exile on Sakhalin Island, her husband's Tolstoian connections led to the first edition being published in Great Britain by the Free Word Press, edited by Vladimir Chertkov,[10] and with notes by the revolutionary and publicist Vladimir Burtsev.[11] A second edition appeared in Berlin two years later, with slightly updated footnotes. The present translation includes the editors' forewords for both editions, and footnotes indicate where the second edition expanded or altered information from Burtsev's original notes.

Thirteen years in Shlissel'burg Fortress: the notes of Liudmila Aleksandrovna Volkenshtein

Publisher's Foreword to the first edition[12]

These *Notes* we are publishing by Liudmila Aleksandrovna Volkenshtein about Shlissel'burg Fortress were written by her in the winter of 1896 on the way to Sakhalin, immediately after her departure from the fortress following 13 years of imprisonment. This is what she wrote to us about this in a letter of 10 (23) April 1900:

> Sitting in Odessa prison I hurried to set down the most important things, wanting to respond as quickly as possible to inquiries about what is happening in Shlissel'burg Fortress. The intention is to quickly produce copies of these *Notes* in Russia, and for that reason we decided that this would be best done in impersonal form, and in that way avoid the most terrible thing for us *at that time* – being deprived of meetings.

These *Notes* were delivered to our Editors in April 1900.

Wishing to supply readers with a possibility of constructing for themselves a certain understanding of the people mentioned in these *Notes* and more generally to gain a more detailed acquaintance with what happened in Shlissel'burg, we have included here, in the form of an appendix and footnotes, first, brief biographical sketches of all those incarcerated there in the period 1884–1896 and, second, bibliographical references to articles relating to Shlissel'burg Fortress and imprisonment there in the same period, that have appeared up to the present day in the Russian and foreign press.[13]

Both, on our request, were kindly prepared for us by Vladimir L'vovich Burtsev, using – as a consequence of his tireless study and collection of materials concerning the revolutionary movement in

Russia over many years – the most accurate and complete information on this question.

V. Chertkov.

Publisher's Foreword to the second edition[14]

From Shlissel'burg Fortress, where Russia's best people are buried alive, nothing reaches the world of the living. Only the few who have been freed from this living grave can tell the world about all its horrors, and the hopeless life of the revolutionary martyrs imprisoned there. Liudmila Aleksandrovna Volkenshtein, who spent 13 years in Shlissel'burg Fortress, in her notes gives an introduction to the fortress and life of the prisoners. L. A. Volkenshtein belonged to the 'People's Will' Party, and was in the fortress from 1883 to 1896.[15] Because she was covered by the terms of an amnesty, her sentence was reduced by a third, and she was sent to Sakhalin in the winter of 1896. During her journey to Sakhalin she wrote the notes published herewith.

Notes on Shlissel'burg Fortress

L. A. Volkenshtein

[Introduction]

These sketches of 13 years of life in Shlissel'burg Fortress have been constructed in the most general outlines simply so as to give the reader an understanding of the main events in that time span. Describing life in detail over such a long period – a life in which so much was lived internally, and so little externally – is very difficult. It could only be done in exactly the right frame of mind. The description of the details themselves, deprived of their inner meaning, would probably end up being one-sided and insipid, all the more so as I do not consider it appropriate to touch upon many aspects of life in prison, for both internal and external reasons.

It has turned out, I think, free of exaggeration, as although I have only selected the most vivid facts, the minor facts brought to bear daily were ultimately no less terrible, if not more so, because they haunted the prisoners every day, every minute, and there was no hope whatsoever of escaping them. But these have been omitted. There is probably some muddle in the chronological order, but little has been forgotten all the same. The factual side itself is accurate throughout, except where caveats are made. In any case, these sketches may give a certain understanding of Shlissel'burg Prison and serve as material for its future historian.

I will first tell the story of the old and new prisons, where the inmates lived and died. The new prison in Shlissel'burg was opened in August 1884. Before the construction of the new building there was an old, single-storey prison for ten people, which still exists today. This is not the historic prison; it was built thirty years ago in place of the old prison, of which remained only one cell in the tower adjoining the present-day prison.

Who was incarcerated in the old prison before our arrival, I don't know. In our time, during the first seven years, it served as a punishment block and generally as a place for dumping the most troublesome and sick prisoners. Those brought for the execution of death sentences were also kept there. Finally, every new arrival was locked up in there for three or four months so that they initially endured the most severe conditions possible. In the last six years workshops for the prisoners were opened there, but when somebody needed to be isolated, work ceased on the pretext of renovating the building. Executions initially took place in the yard of this prison; in later years they constructed allotments, planted trees, and so on. Besides this large yard, situated in front of the old prison, there is a small yard behind the building, between the back wall of the prison and the centuries-old wall surrounding it. Onto here look windows both from the prison and the cell in the tower in which, apparently, Ioann Antonovich was kept.[16] In this little yard the segregated prisoners were taken for exercise. There is only one entrance to the old prison via the yard of the new prison, and from the windows we could sometimes see the segregated prisoners and new arrivals being led out there. The old prison was surrounded on all four sides by ancient walls. The new prison was a two-storey brick building, red in colour, narrow, long. The windows were low, one *arshin* long, 14 *vershoks* high, with opaque glass.[17] In the yard of the new prison were allotments and a place for exercise.

In the 12 years described, 48 people were in Shlissel'burg Fortress,[18] of whom 21 died in the first six years and three more in the second six. The new prison replaced the defunct Alekseevskii Ravelin at the Peter and Paul Fortress in Petersburg, from where in August 1884 all the inmates and the entire administration and inventory were brought. The new arrivals (nine people)[19] were very weak, emaciated and suffering from scurvy.

The Alekseevskii Ravelin, as a matter of fact, had held the majority of those convicted in the trial of Aleksandr Mikhailov, which took place in 1882.[20] Six of them died in a year: Kolotkevich [sic], Barannikov, Langans, A. Mikhailov, Kletochnikov, Teterka,[21] while one, Aronchik, went insane. The others were rotting to death when suddenly the conditions they were in were 'noticed'.[22] This was on Orzhevskii's second or third visit to the Alekseevskii Ravelin.[23] Earlier nothing was 'noticed' and the doctor,[24] poking a finger into the swollen legs of the sick prisoners, said, 'it's still small potatoes', and gave them a tablespoon of milk and, to improve the putrid food, *shchi* and *kasha*.[25] Everyone treated the prisoners cynically, indifferently, and crudely.

In the Alekseevskii Ravelin, apart from other prisoners, there were 14 people from the Mikhailov trial. Among them were three women: Lebedeva, Iakimova, with her child, and Terent'eva. In summer 1883, also rotting to death, they were taken to Kara,[26] except for Terent'eva, who disappeared God knows where: she wasn't delivered to the House of Preliminary Detention before the transfer.[27] The prisoners in the Ravelin later said that the rats in the curtain wall had almost eaten Iakimova's baby, and testified to the terrible bread they were fed. However, all this was put down in black and white in the pamphlets 'From the Dead to the Living' and 'Torture and Penal Servitude in the Peter and Paul Fortress', published in 1878,[28] so I'm not going to talk about it in any more detail. I will add only to the history of the 'Ravelinites' that of the 14 inmates of the Ravelin from this trial, only three remained alive: Frolenko, Morozov and Trigoni; they are all now at Shlissel'burg.[29]

In August 1884, prisoners from both the Alekseevskii Ravelin and the Trubetskoi [Bastion] were transferred to our fortress. These convicts – there were 10 of them in number – were transferred from Kara, where they had been sentenced to penal servitude; they were sent here as the 'most restive'. Many of them had already spent several years in prison in pre-trial detention and at hard labour. The conditions of their life in Kara were a little better than in the fortresses, but nevertheless so terrible that they had decided to escape, and if they failed, to burn themselves alive in the prison. A tunnel was dug, a fire prepared, but their plans were discovered. For their transport to Petersburg via the Kama river and the Volga a special barge without windows was constructed, with single berths and a guard at every door. They were all shackled with fetters.

In October 1884, nine people from the Trial of the 14 were brought in. Two of them were women, and four were from the military. [See Table 2.1.]

After 1891 no-one else was brought to us.

Table 2.1 List of convicts imprisoned in Shlissel'burg Fortress from 1884 to 1896. From Volkenshtein, L. A. *13 let v Shlissel'burgskoi kreposti: Zapiski*. Edited by V. L. Burtsev. Purleigh: Izdanie Svobodnogo slova, 1900, 8–9.

When arrived?	From where?	Surnames	Total
August 1884	Alekseevskii Ravelin	Frolenko (arrested 1881), Morozov (arr. '81), Trigoni (arr. '81), Grachevskii (arr. '82), Aronchik (arr. '81), Isaev (arr. '81), Iurii Bogdanovich (arr. '82), Polivanov (arr. '82), S. Zlatopol'skii (arr. '81)	9
August 1884	Kara	Myshkin (arr. '75) and Popov (arr. '79), initially held in the Alekseevskii Ravelin. Malavskii (arr. '77), Shchedrin (arr. '81), Butsinskii (arr. '79), Iurkovskii (arr. '80), Kobylianskii (arr. 79), Minakov (arr. '79), Gellis (arr. '79), Dolgushin (arr. '73), initially held at the Trubetskoi Ravelin (Peter and Paul Fortress)	10

(Continued table 2.1)

(Continued table 2.1)

When arrived?	From where?	Surnames	Total
August 1884	Peter and Paul Fortress	Klimenko (arr. '82), Butsevich (arr. '82)	2
August 1884	Kazan' lunatic asylum	Ignatii Ivanov (arr. '79)	1
October 1884	Peter and Paul Fortress, Trial of the 14	Vera Figner (arr. '83), Liudmila Volkenshtein (arr. '83), Ashenbrener [sic] (arr. '83), Pokhitonov (arr. '83), Iuvachev (arr. '83), Tikhanovich (arr. 83), Nemolovskii (arr. '83), Vasilii Ivanov (arr. '83), Surovtsev (arr. '82)	9
December 1884	Kiev Trial	Shebalin (arr. '84), Pankratov (arr. '84), Martynov (Borisevich) (arr. '84), Karaulov (arr. '84)	4
1885	Odessa	Manucharov (arr. '84), tried alone	1
1885	Peter and Paul Fortress	Administratively sentenced to 5 years, former solider Logovskoi [sic] (arr. '84)	1
1886	Warsaw Trial	Waryński (arr. '83) and Janavičius (arr. '84)	2
1887	Petersburg Trial of 1 March	Lukaszewicz (arr. '87) and Novorusskii (arr. '87)	2
1887	Petersburg Trial	German Lopatin (arr. '84), Starodvorskii (arr. '84), Sergei Ivanov (arr. '86), Konoshevich [sic] (arr. '84), Antonov (arr. '85)	5
1888	Petersburg Trial	Orzhikh (arr. '86)	1
1891	Petersburg Trial	Sof'ia Ginsburg (arr. '89)	1
		Total:	48

List of the dead at Shlissel'burg 1884–96, the remaining prisoners and those taken away.

The first six years, to 1891.
Executed: Minakov (6 September 1884), Myshkin (at the beginning of January 1885).[30]
Suicides: Klimenko (hanged himself in September 1884), Grachevskii (in 1888 burned himself alive, by dousing himself with kerosene).[31]
Insane: Shchedrin, Iuvachev, Konoshevich [sic].
Died from illness: Malavskii, Butsevich, Tikhanovich, S. Zlatopol'skii, Kobylianskii, Isaev, Ignatii Ivanov, Dolgushin, Gellis, Iurii Bogdanovich, Nemolovskii, Aronchik, Waryński. – Tihkanovich, Aronchik and Ignatii Ivanov died insane.

In the last six years.
Became mentally incapacitated: Pokhitonov.
Died from illness: Butsinskii, Iurkovskii.
Suicide:[32] Sof'ia Ginsburg.
In total 24 people died.
Transferred: in 1888 Karaulov (to Siberia); in 1895 Logovskii [sic] (to Siberia); in 1895 Manucharov (to Sakhalin); in 1896 Shebalin, Martynov, Janavičius, Surovtsev (to Siberia); Liudmila Volkenshtein (to Sakhalin).
Transferred insane: in 1887 Iuvachev,[33] in 1896 Pokhitonov, to the Petersburg Nikolaevskii hospital, Shchedrin and Konoshevich [sic], to Kazan'.
Remained in Shlissel'burg Fortress:
Vera Figner, Petr Antonov, Iulii Ashenbrener [sic], Sergei Ivanov, Vasilii Ivanov, Jyzef Lukaszewicz, German Lopatin, Nikolai Morozov, Mikhail Novorusskii, Boris Orzhikh, Petr Polivanov, Mikhail Popov, Vasilii Pankratov, Nikolai Starodvorskii, Mikhail Trigoni, Mikhail Frolenko.[34]

Chapter I.

I have already mentioned that everyone brought to Shlissel'burg in 1884 was kept first at the Peter and Paul Fortress. We already sensed there what was in store for us. The tone, although not always crude, was petty and spiteful. Why, for instance, in the case of people who were there only temporarily after trials – for all of a few days – was it necessary to read the instructions for hard labour convicts, that threatened birching and suchlike? The mood here was extremely despondent: every one of us felt all the horror of the long period of solitary confinement that awaited us without books, distanced from everything human. Sitting all day in one's cell without anything to read or any work seemed tantamount to death – and that's exactly what it was. Our thoughts were so gloomy that at first it seemed they really wanted to kill us, and when they were leading each prisoner in chains by the arm to the steam boat at the landing stage on the quay, many of us wondered whether they intended to drown us. They also led us by the arm to the prison – practically carrying us, although each of us was able to walk freely in our fetters. All this was done despite it being a convoy of only around ten people. On the steam boat, of course, we guessed where we were being taken. One's imagination painted the most terrible pictures, envisioning an underground cell with no light or air, eternal torpor in fetters.

We were mistaken: the time of dungeons, like physical tortures, was obsolete. In their place something more subtle and less conspicuous prevailed. Our first impression of Shlissel'burg Fortress was even pleasant: clean, dry cells – true, with opaque glass, but quite bright all the same. Fine, clean bed linen; a sink for washing and plumbed water closets.[35] The cell was small – seven paces long and five wide – and of the type common to Houses of Preliminary Detention and therefore, perhaps even more pleasant on account of the memory of the last days of 'freedom' – of course, relative freedom… The bunks were locked shut, and apart from a bench, there was nothing in the cell.

At the entrance to the cell the superintendent informed us that according to the obligations of his service he had to address those deprived of their rights with the familiar form of 'you',[36] but would try to address us in the third person. Soon tea was brought – with a lump of sugar, but not fresh boiling water, as was the case in Petersburg. Later it turned out that not everyone was treated like that. This was also a sort of system: it was done in part to separate our interests, in part to cajole us – in the hope that not everybody would tap, and that was how the authorities hoped to achieve full solitary confinement, if the majority didn't tap.[37]

With that aim we were at first accommodated in every other cell; but when that became impossible because of the arrival of many new convicts, tapping increased. We tapped very quietly and tried to choose the most opportune moments for this, for example while food was being doled out, when the guards were busy with their own duties. But of course, despite our precautions we were caught red-handed, and in such situations the most outrageous scenes would ensue: they'd begin to address us in the familiar form and put a gendarme at the spyhole in the door, who would clatter on the door as soon as he heard a tap. Reprimands would start: 'This is childish', they'd say, 'it's shameful'. They'd deprive us of books – it's true, the books were mainly ecclesiastical tomes or some sort of rubbish, but all the same they were precious to those who didn't want to go out of their minds without a fight. Finally, they even put us in straitjackets.

I'll tell everything in the right order.

At first we also tried to act with conviction. We said that everyone here is condemned, so there was no point banning tapping. We reasoned that a system where you're physically able to speak, but forced under duress to be silent, is tantamount to torture, so they shouldn't be surprised if this wasn't met with obedience on our part. However, these naive suppositions were only granted to us initially. Those who had arrived earlier had not reckoned on any conversations. In the event of a tap, several guards[38] would usually burst into the cell, and abuse would be dispensed and rain down, using that familiar 'you'.[39] If a prisoner answered back, at the superintendent's[40] command the guards would attack him, push him to the floor, beat him on the pretext of resistance and, putting him in a straitjacket, tether him to the iron bed for several hours, often inserting a wooden gag into his mouth to stop him screaming. His neighbours, hearing the brawl, would start to protest, shouting, 'what are you doing to him?' Then they would be pounced on and tied up. The commotion became unspeakable, with screams, clattering, brawls and the croaks of those lying there with wooden gags in their mouths. In all corners of the prison what was going on in any individual cell could be heard quite clearly. To avoid such turmoil the guilty parties soon began to be removed to the old prison, put in punishment cells[41] and dealt with there.

One of our comrades said that the superintendent came into his cell and uttered with a hiss, 'ban-dit, scum – I'll get you!' To which he replied: 'Savage'. Then the gendarmes hurled themselves on him, pinned him down and beat him like that until he was covered in blood. But when he demanded a medical examination, the doctor pronounced, 'bruised while resisting!'[42]

Once during an inspection we started talking about the beatings, but Orzhevskii replied: 'this cannot be so, because the entire guard denies it.'

Fighting the administration was very difficult for us. The majority of the prisoners had already been worn out by a dreadful life of hard labour or in the Ravelin, and lived with the sole hope that things were about to get better. Newcomers thought that this hell would continue for no more than one or two years and decided, as far as their strength allowed, to endure these torments. But the experienced people knew that they wouldn't have brought us here from the Ravelin for a short time. They also knew that there were no laws demanding such inhuman savagery, that a great deal depended on the whims of the authorities, and that we had to fight these whims…

And so as a result, after three months of life in Shlissel'burg, in September 1884, Minakov decided to go on hunger strike to demand books and meetings with his comrades.

When his strength had weakened, and he was going to be fed artificially, he spat in the doctor's face, demanding the death penalty 'for violent assault',[43] as it said in the instructions hanging on the wall. A few days later he was taken for trial and read the death sentence. It was suggested he petition for clemency, but he refused. On the day of his execution he asked for permission to write to his family, but wasn't allowed to do so. And so in the morning the measured steps of the escort[44] were heard. The whole prison began to listen keenly, and was paralysed in anticipation. Several men went into Minakov's cell; the superintendent said, 'you don't need a smock, but you can take a hood.' Thereafter Minakov's shouts resounded: 'goodbye, dear friends – I'm being taken to be shot!' and about ten minutes later a volley reached us from the large yard… He'd been shot almost in front of our very eyes!

A few days after that all the ventilation units from the cells and latches from the windows began to be removed: later it emerged that Klimenko had hanged himself.

After another two months, on the first day of Christmas, amid general silence suddenly there was the sound of a metal plate being dropped, then feet stamping, a scuffle and a scream from Myshkin: 'execute me… don't beat me, execute me!' Everyone was paralysed in horror, afraid to believe their ears and not understanding what was going on, as no-one apart from Myshkin's neighbour knew of his intention to commit a violent assault and demand execution in the hope of drawing attention to what was going on at Shlissel'burg.[45]

Three weeks later Myshkin was tried, and we only found out about his execution from an inscription discovered later: 'Myshkin is sentenced to death.'

The battle continued to escalate; the inmates had already begun to tap via the corridor with the hope of agreeing a more general course of action. The most disobedient, as far as the authorities were concerned, were taken away to the old prison, but those who remained began to tap even louder, demanding to be taken there as well and hoping, in this way, to make isolating comrades in punishment cells meaningless, as there were only ten cells in the old prison. In the old prison it reached the point where the gendarmes had to wear themselves out creating a commotion of their own just to prevent the prisoners tapping. However, they continued to separate the inmates as much as possible.

Around this time,[46] we began to fall ill. There proved to be no treatment whatsoever for the sick. Those suffering from scurvy and pulmonary haemoptysis[47] were given the same food as the healthy, that is, meatless *shchi* and *kasha* twice a week, and on the other days the same with a minute piece of beef from the soup. Many were positively starving, especially those who had been in prison a long time, who had already acquired terrible catarrhal gastritis. Some started having hallucinations, others lay motionless on the stone floor, being in no condition to sit on a bench all day. There were bunks, but they were raised and locked to the wall from six in the morning to eight in the evening. The women also lay on the floor, in very poor, thin dresses for good measure, as aside from a smock with a diamond-shaped patch,[48] and underwear, they were not given woollen underclothes, unlike the men. The men had motley coats, made half from black felt and half grey, with stencilled yellow diamonds – these have now been abolished.

There was no hospital, and there still isn't one now. The doctor came on call or when the superintendent deemed it necessary. The doctor was a young man who had only just finished his course, with the surname Zvonkevich. He wasn't an evil man, but he had no will, and subordinated himself almost unquestioningly to the 'established procedure',[49] obviously considering it something preordained: and so it was, since it was instituted 'from above'. Some drugs or other were dispensed, but no-one got an invalid diet. There was no care whatsoever for the sick. Tikhanovich was one of the first to die. When he was dying, he suffered enormously. He never tapped, probably because of his illness. Even at his trial he was very mournful and dejected. Judging from the few words that reached his closest neighbours, it appears he was mad. He died, I think, from pneumonia. Apparently, during his final agony he was taken to die in the old prison so as to avoid unrest among the prisoners. Aronchik didn't tap either, and certain signs made us fear very much for his life…[50]

The prison was getting more and more agitated; many had individual clashes with the authorities. Shebalin went on hunger strike and demanded meetings with his family. After a 31-day strike he fell into semi-consciousness and began to eat. Ignatii Ivanov, who had been brought from Kazan' as a convalescent, began to suffer from insomnia and then melancholy, and his footsteps echoed loudly in his neighbours' cells day and night. The nights began to reverberate with screams: it emerged that Shchedrin had gone insane. The most terrible thing of all was that he was punished for contravening discipline as if he were healthy, because his illness wasn't believed. And so his cell was invaded day and night, and he was often taken away to the old prison. Shchedrin had already twice been sentenced to death, the second time in transit to Siberia for 'violent assault', when Koval'skaia had been tied up for some reason.[51] In Kara he was chained to a wheelbarrow.[52] Ending up in Shlissel'burg, he began to talk gibberish from the very start. He thought that the gendarmes had set out to 'deprive him of his mental faculties', so started incessantly peeping through the spy hole in his door. He suddenly imagined that half his head had already disappeared, but that he still had half left, and one eye, and he had to save them come what may, by not letting anyone see them. The trouble was that these were not simple gendarmes, but 'special ones who knew everything about contemporary science'. Throughout his entire delirium he tapped to his neighbours. He had fits of rage, he tried to stop the guards looking through the spy hole… But as they looked all the more frequently, of course, he couldn't sleep and raved day and night. Obviously, his obduracy perplexed even Herod (as we called the superintendent).[53] The poor madman was nevertheless tied up and, when he took a particularly long time to calm down, dragged off to a punishment cell. His illness wasn't acknowledged until 1891, when he finally fell into insanity and insensibility.

Finally, people began to die, and die in front of everybody's eyes without any treatment. Only a few days before death were the dying given a meat patty. Malavskii died, Butsevich and Nemolovskii were dying – all of tuberculosis. Several people could barely move because of emaciation, scurvy and haemoptysis. Probably in view of such a terrible state of affairs and for fear of new executions being repeated after Minakov and Myshkin, it was decided to give six people meetings,[54] no more. The meetings lasted half an hour, just twice a week. Everyone in fact generally exercised alone every day, also for half an hour, but under various pretexts we often weren't allowed out for exercise. Among the ones who received this benefit were, fortunately, those who had tapped less, that is, effectively, those whose minds were only half disordered. The dying Butsevich was also granted meetings, but after two or three times he had to refuse because he could no longer get up from his bed. As he was dying, he very much regretted that he could no longer take his exercise partner two or three lumps of sugar. That's the strength of the need for love in the soul of someone living in solitary confinement. Merely the sight of a living person who understands you brings a sort of childish delight and tenderness!

Butsevich died quietly. We heard them going into his cell two days before his death, and then everything went silent. Maybe he had been taken to the old prison to die.

Soon after two more died: Nemolovskii and Dolgushin – the first of tuberculosis, the second of emaciation. They suffered terribly, and were taken to the old prison in agony two or three days before their deaths.

This time it was quite clear that they were being taken away to die. The old prison was very damp and cold, and besides, these poor half-dead creatures, regaining consciousness, would have guessed why they were being taken away, so that when they were dying they wouldn't even be able to tap to their comrades. Several tapped goodbye to their neighbours a few hours before they died.

In view of all this many began to demand that the dying 'were not taken to the morgue'.[55] This demand was respected, and Gellis and S. Zlatopol'skii, who also soon died, were returned to the new prison.[56] When they were dying, they suffered dreadfully.

It's terrible to remember that entire time, especially the first two years of our Shlissel'burg life. The smell of death was in the air, and what death – in total isolation, with the dying not hearing the single sound of a friendly voice! The situation for the dying was dreadful. No-one even went to them to change the bed linen or help them to the toilet. Later, in better times, we knew this for a fact.

Many were very often convinced they were dying. The consumptives frequently had haemorrhages, after which they couldn't even tap with a finger on the bed, and if they did tap, it was so inaccurate that it was difficult to understand them. More than once in such a state they said goodbye to their comrades, thinking they were about to die.

In these two years the mortality rate was horrific. There was always somebody dying, so the impression was of daily agony. Tuberculosis was killing more and more people. But not even all the dying were forgiven for 'tapping' and 'being disrespectful'.[57] Thus, for example, the consumptive Kobylianskii, who tapped and used familiar forms when speaking to the superintendent, was not given meetings, although he was promised them if he tapped less. He really did start to tap less, but by that time he was so weak that he couldn't get out of bed. He died like that, with the unrequited dream of hugging his comrades, which he talked about movingly before his own death, when he knew it was close...

In truth, tapping at that time was persecuted less: all hope had probably been lost of absolutely isolating the inmates, which was apparent from the fact that meetings began to be granted. But the gendarmes still tried to discipline the prisoners and for that reason horribly persecuted any 'arrogance',[58] that is, feeling of one's own worth, and protested when the prisoners started to 'defend' the weak and sick, especially if this was done collectively. Screeching and foaming at the mouth, Herod would bawl: 'Don't you dare talk about others; it's none of your business – there are no "others" here!'

The higher powers also tried to drive us all to despair. Inspections took place about four times a year. Once the Deputy Minister of Internal Affairs visited, with the head of the Corps of Gendarmes, once the director of the department,[59] twice the head of the gendarmes' staff, sometime the public prosecutor as well. They asked us questions about our health, exercise, and so on. We answered just to have done with it, knowing how utterly pointless the conversation was. Sometimes Deputy Minister Orzhevskii put in a *mot juste* about the impossibility of leaving here or made an indirect allusion: 'a great deal, they say, depends on you'. However, he did the latter rarely.

Just how futile these inspections were was apparent, incidentally, from the continuing hopeless situation of the severely ill, dying and mad. At this point Iuvachev went insane. He began experiencing religious ecstasies: he'd kneel down and pray to the cross on the fortress chapel that was visible [from his cell]. On the whole it was a mild insanity. Orzhevskii, perhaps thinking he was a hypocrite, suggested he become a monk. Iuvachev replied: 'I'm not worthy.' His neighbours heard this conversation. Soon afterwards Iuvachev was taken away somewhere unknown.[60]

Aronchik was apparently offered meetings, but never went out for exercise. Suffering from permanently being watched through the spy hole in his door, he began to hide in the corner so as not to be seen, but that ended with the corners being sealed off with triangular brick columns.

The women withstood an unremitting battle with Herod. Every Saturday he brought a woman to their cells for a search. These searches were a horrible thing: pointless, crude to the point of cynicism and excruciating. During the search Herod spied with no inhibitions through the door at what was going on in the cell. When the women noticed this and raised a hue and cry, Herod answered, 'what, you think we've never seen naked women before? You're talking nonsense!'

On the whole the women were treated better than the men. They weren't tied up or beaten. Sometimes in the event of a clash with the authorities they were just 'inadvertently' pushed and sent to the punishment cells. They were treated less crudely – in truth, they were seldom treated crudely. Obviously the plan was to keep them among the living. When one of them was ill, she was given medicine and fed assiduously, although there was still no nursing whatsoever. Meanwhile she had a fever, and for three weeks couldn't get up without the help of another person. Nobody ever came into her cell, except for when food was being distributed, or for a search.

The women's bunks had been kept unlocked for a year. However, by that time many of the inmates already enjoyed that privilege, as a consequence of the terrible death rate among the prisoners.

Most of all the question of meetings angered us at this point. Many were absolutely forbidden to see anyone, even the dying, as said above. The situation was dreadful: there were practically no books apart from ones with spiritual or moral content, or like Gillies' history of Greece[61] in an old typeface – and that was one of the best books; there were some about pilgrimages to holy places, and so on, all of the same sort. There was no work whatsoever, and of course, writing wasn't permitted. Many composed poetry and immediately scratched it onto the walls, but the gendarmes erased it with crude reprimands. The only thing that saved us from madness was tapping, but what was it worth? For many, it was life – or then again, madness.

You have to experience solitary confinement yourself to understand the whole of its horror for a living person. It is the most barbaric punishment, equivalent to torture. Alas! How little the mass of even enlightened nations understands this! If a person ends up confined in a punishment cell or spends some time in semi-free solitude in hospital – with what aversion he talks about it afterwards! Why is solitary confinement in prison forgotten, when you're forced to live in a tomb for many years? However, perhaps this is beginning to be recognized. At least, in criminal prisons solitary confinement is limited to one and a half years, and two days are counted as three.[62] If I'm not mistaken, this law is spreading to life in the fortresses as well. Besides, I think that here too there exist limits to sentences of solitary confinement (nearly a third of the sentence, after which one has to be moved to better conditions). Some of our comrade lawyers somehow asked one of the bureaucrats from the public prosecutor's office about this, as they were already insisting too much on the legality of our confinement. In reply to their question he said that Shlissel'burg had its own laws. And so it turned out in reality.

But I'll continue.

I recall this now and am surprised at the passion with which we sought meetings – and for all of half an hour twice a week! Could these meetings be called an alleviation of solitary confinement? Yes, without question. You need to know what it means not to hear the sound of a friendly voice, not to see a person who understands you, not to have the possibility of exchanging your feelings and ideas in the way people do. Tapping is really only a lifeline you seize in despair, and for a long period that consolation would not be enough.

Our administration tried to allow meetings on the basis of the prisoners' behaviour, but this system met with energetic protests. All those exercising in pairs refused such meetings, saying that 'it is immoral to be well-fed among the starving'. The authorities, of course, were incensed, but our solidarity scared them, and the main thing was that they were taken aback by the huge number of people dying – which was more than enough evidence of the conditions in which convicts were being kept in Shlissel'burg Fortress.

At this point Isaev died of a pulmonary illness; he suffered terribly and coughed in agony and, I think, died in a coma. Soon after, in the cell next to his, Ignatii Ivanov died. It was difficult to find out what was wrong with him, but the night before he died he tapped to bid his neighbours farewell.

Thanks to meetings it became possible to make connections between separated parts of the prison. Now when meetings ceased, tapping increased; conversations began via the corridor. Herod did not crack down on those tapping as savagely as before, but on the other hand he tried to divide the tappers through the question of meetings with greater energy than previously, because this sort of collective decision by the prisoners fundamentally undermined the system of complete isolation. Several people were put in the old prison and were kept in the old, damp building for six months, some of the sick among them. The ones who were being taken away kept being prodded and 'crushed',[63] even though they were going voluntarily. Several convicts insisted on being taken to the old prison so as to not leave their comrades totally alone, and besides, they judged that the administration would in fact be afraid of a larger number of detainees.

At this point Grachevskii, who was incarcerated in the old prison, declared to his neighbours[64] that he could no longer endure living in these conditions and had decided to strike the doctor in order to land a death sentence. As a matter of fact, the doctor got more of his share than Herod, because it was easier to gain access to him, while Herod always stood behind the backs of two gendarmes.[65] It was impossible even to throw anything at him, because after the incident with Myshkin crockery was no longer left in the cells.

Grachevskii carried out his intention and demanded execution. This was already in '88.[66] The authorities took fright, but decided not to give the affair any publicity. The commandant appeared and said that the mentally ill wouldn't be tried. Then Grachevskii declared that if they wouldn't execute him, he'd kill himself anyway. He was moved within the old prison to the most isolated cell (no. 10) and his surveillance was enhanced. Over the course of two weeks his neighbours heard him talking to the gendarmes and demanding execution, but he spoke calmly, and perhaps for that reason the administration did not especially fear his threat to end his life. Having noticed that Grachevskii's conversations could be heard by his neighbours, he was transferred to the adjoining cell (no. 9), which faced onto a remote little corridor that separated cell no. 9 from no. 10.

Suddenly one evening a cry rang out – terrible, inhuman, but short. This was followed by commotion, an indistinct dragging noise, and the vibration of wire ringing the bell in the corridor to alert the sergeant-major.[67] The bewildered voices of the duty non-commissioned officers[68] could be heard and, finally, the smell of burning and smoke filtered into the cells. A slight groaning could be heard, then a door hastily being opened, the voice of the doctor and the superintendent. It was difficult to figure out immediately what was going on, but there was no doubt something terrible had happened to Grachevskii. The next day he wasn't taken any food. It was clear he had set himself on fire. Later it emerged that he'd poured kerosene over himself. He obviously died within a few minutes, as his weak groaning only continued for about two or three minutes. The superintendent and doctor quickly left, and the prison settled into its usual silence; only the reek of burnt clothes and something organic remained the following day. On the second and third day after this event Chief of Staff Petrov[69] went round the cells, and after that Herod disappeared and another superintendent was appointed in his place.

Finally, I will give a few more details on Herod, although what I've already said is enough to characterize him. We found out his biography after he left the prison. He was a converted Jew and advanced up the ranks from soldier to officer. Up to 1884 he was at the Alekseevskii Ravelin; both there, and at the Shlissel'burg Fortress, he was notable most of all for his astonishing zeal in performing his duties. How vigilantly, how feverishly, he attended to every little detail carried out by the non-commissioned officers under his command! Distributing underwear to the prisoners, he would make a remarkably meticulous examination of every item and move it to another place. Dealing with the convicts' leftover food, he would watch with unusual attention how and where it was put. Day and night he would be in the corridor, even on holidays. Once on Easter morning, at dawn, around five o'clock, we began tapping, still lying in our beds, hoping that on such a day it wouldn't lead to banging on the doors, reprimands and so on. When suddenly – even now I can't remember this calmly – Herod burst in with a crowd of non-commissioned officers and uttered a frenzied shriek: 'Even on holidays they behave disgracefully! Will you never stop?'

He was a great fan of tormenting the prisoners, and how much pleasure this gave him! So, for instance, he would deliberately choose Christmas to distribute new, unwashed underwear to the prisoners – very rough and scratchy – and then ask, with a radiant look, 'what, does it sting?' And he could have waited a little while, because the old underwear wasn't thrown away, but redistributed later. On the whole he was an extremely undeveloped person, both intellectually and morally.

After Grachevskii's death he caught it so much from Petrov right here in the prison that he had a stroke. He later recovered, but by that time was no longer working and lived on a pension. From time to time, meeting Shlissel'burg non-commissioned officers who had served under him, he very much liked to reminisce with them about the past; they felt the same respect and fear of him as before. It emerged that he kept them in very strict subordination. They lived on Shlissel'burg island like exiles. They were not allowed into the town more than twice a week for a very short time. Their food was brought to the gates of the fortress, no-one was allowed inside. Note that these were all experienced old hands, and the majority of them had already served at the Ravelin. They put up with such a life thanks to the double salary, which was also drawn by all the rest serving at Shlissel'burg; it wasn't for nothing that they boasted the fortress cost tens of thousands a year. The entire guard was no less than 40 strong. But why such precautions against people sitting in solitary confinement, under several locks, without the least communication with anyone except Herod? The warders[70] let no-one near the fortress, that is, the island, either. Besides, the director of the fortress had at his disposal a whole company of soldiers in the barracks and guardhouse.

Chapter II.

With Herod's departure life at the fortress improved.

It's likely that Grachevskii's horrific death, the extraordinary mortality rate, the large numbers of the sick and weakened, and finally several madmen, made a certain impression in higher circles, and it was decided there to change the policy with regard to Shlissel'burg. On his final visit Petrov, going round all the convicts, emphatically asked them not to keep silent 'as always', and to say what was particularly onerous for them. One way or another, from that time our jailers were more careful; the new superintendent treated the convicts politely and tried not to aggravate them.

The first act on the part of the administration was to put to rest the question of the protest we had undertaken with the aim of securing the return of our comrades from the old prison (they had been locked up there for six months), or at least to get information about them. Everyone guessed that something had happened there, because after Grachevskii's death immediately in all the cells the lamps were adapted and started being kept locked.[71] These sorts of changes usually took place always after some sort of catastrophe; for example, after Klimenko's death by hanging himself they broke off the latches from the windows in all the cells.

The prisoners' agitation grew; everyone in concert began to shout, tap and demand to be taken to the old prison or for the return to us of those locked up there. The superintendent immediately hastened to 'appease' us, declaring that the transfer had already been decided. It's true that it was very convenient for them to make this retreat, as several new prisoners had been brought in, and the old prison was needed to isolate these new arrivals. But they weren't kept there for long either.

Then we were promised history books, true, nothing later than the eighteenth century, but nevertheless these books were, of course, better than the old ones. Until that point we'd been given books only relating to the ancient world and the Middle Ages; we'd also previously been allowed whatever textbooks we wanted. Until these books were sent (official permission was needed in order to obtain them), it was suggested that we take books that some of us had brought in with us, without any particular restraint in the choice.

The cancellation of Saturday searches, which were so insulting and distressing in their pointlessness and crudeness, also dated to this time.

An invalid diet was made more accessible, and exercise was increased. Soon everyone was exercising in pairs. Certain improvements had been made earlier, but after such haggling that they inspired only revulsion. Thus, a year ago, still during Herod's reign, activities on allotments were arranged, but it was all done in such a way as to make the work not entirely pleasant. The women were given embroidery hoops, but this soon bored them.

Soon after Petrov's visit one of the convicts made an unexpected discovery which brought everyone a lot of joy: he showed how it was possible to hold conversations via the water closet plumbing, which connected several cells above and below. Restraining oneself from such a 'club' would have been beyond human strength, so a 'telephone', as we called it, appeared on the scene for us. The gendarmes were afraid of entering into battle with us; as it then seemed to us (alas, mistakenly!), they silently decided to tolerate our clubs.

We sat in session at the club for several hours and came to life in our conversations with each other. We even began group readings: sometimes something from the new life at liberty, from notes compiled by recent arrivals,[72] sometimes something from our life in this place. It was already a year since we'd been given notebooks, which were taken off us every evening for inspection. Many wrote poetry and in it often laughed through tears, recalling facts from the Herod era. Views were expressed on our recent activities in freedom, the future of the parties, chances of a constitution, and so on. All this had to be shouted, as otherwise it was impossible to speak or hear.

Meanwhile at this point Waryński and Bogdanovich were in the final stages of tuberculosis. Waryński begged not to be banished from the 'telephone', because it was better to die ten times sooner, but feeling the proximity of comrades, than to die in total isolation. Bogdanovich, on the other hand, soon didn't have the strength to scoop out the water in order to say even a single word. Normally the pipes were filled with water, and then it was impossible to speak via them.

For four months we lived harmoniously as a single family. How great was our surprise when suddenly Shebeko appeared and burst into insults and abuse.[73] We hadn't had to face such behaviour from a high-ranking figure. The notes in the penalty journals served as an official excuse for his ire (perhaps this was in fact half the reason). It emerged that a diary was being kept about the conversations in our clubs. Shebeko burst into each cell in turn and spat out: 'Regicides, and sleeping in soft beds. They should all be hanged, and they're debating, inciting rebellion!' 'Colonel – whip them – whip them!... you hear?' Quickly slamming the door and moving from one convict to another, he would let rip at times with words such as: 'What an impertinent face! Who is this?' – 'Ah, you were in the punishment cells not long ago; your behaviour is disgusting. There's the rod for this as well!' – and on he rushed again. At last, the yelling grew fainter, and by the final cells he was already speaking in the tones of an offended man. The prison was stupefied, and almost no-one managed to answer Shebeko in any substantive way.

After his visit all the books the prisoners had brought with them were taken away from us. Meeting that evening at the club and informing each other of all the details of that day, we didn't know what to talk about. For the first time since the opening of the clubs everyone felt on the edge of the abyss, and nothing gladdened us. We avoided speaking of the insults and threats, and many probably kept their gloomy thoughts to themselves. We conferred more about the future his visit promised, and about the books that had been removed. Everyone was very afraid that the clubs would be closed down.

At this point Bogdanovich was in his death throes. We agitated for permission for someone to be let into his cell to alleviate his suffering and say goodbye to him, but were refused. Everybody's mood was so grave that the decision was taken by everyone to go on hunger strike and demand books. This was at the end of 1888 or the beginning of 1889.[74] In the first days of the hunger strike we still talked via the plumbing, but by the fourth or fifth day decided to stop our conversations so as not to waste energy; moreover when tormented by hunger it would be difficult not to speak of one's own suffering. For me, the most agonizing days were the third, fourth and fifth. Later it became easier to endure the hunger, but I felt so weak that it was impossible to stand up. Towards the end of the hunger strike we were communicating with each other only via taps. On the ninth day some started to cough, and their weakness increased even more. The administration remained aloof, silent, and behaved as if indifferently. Petrov visited, but didn't go to see anyone.

Before the start of the hunger strike there had been no agreement about how to end it. Some proposed resorting to violent measures, but the majority were against this. Owing to the irreproachable behaviour of the administration, it seemed to us that Shebeko's stunt was explained by his own motivations, and we decided that it wasn't worth venting our outrage at the local authorities, at least until they themselves gave occasion for it, and therefore on the tenth day we decided to give up and started eating. I think that at another time the action would have ended with something serious, but on this occasion everyone was saved by the tactical behaviour of the administration, who did not cast a single spark in those overwrought days. Besides, such behaviour forced everyone to think even more that we had to deal with Shebeko himself.

To finish with the Shebeko incident, I will say now that he never went into anyone's cell during his visits in the next year (he was with us twice), and after that he never came again. Just once, accompanying the Minister of Internal Affairs, Durnovo,[75] he followed him into one cell with the words: 'your mother…'; but he was not allowed to finish; no-one even wanted to hear about their mother from him. He was confused and left in silence.[76]

After the hunger strike – about two weeks later – we were all read out a memo from the Police Department, saying money, books and items on the 'inventories' of the prisoners in Shlissel'burg Fortress would be sent to their families. This was the answer to the hunger strike. Soon a heavy, almost unexpected blow struck us: the 'telephones' suddenly stopped working – it was impossible to talk any longer because the water in the pipes didn't go down, however much you scooped out… It turned out they had been sealed somehow from the cellar. Our club existed for around six months, and now we were submerged again in the gloom of solitary confinement. The very walls once more seemed alien to us, unbearable…

There was no longer the strength to endure loneliness. Five or six years after being locked up together, many had never once spoken to each other, as meetings were assigned by the superintendent and seldom changed. The women never saw anyone at all – and no-one saw them. Nerves were in such a state that it could no longer be endured in silence. After the hunger strike many fell ill although, perhaps, the reason for their illness was not the hunger strike alone, but the fact that influenza filtered through to us. During the existence of the club the general uplift to our spirits was so powerful that we either didn't notice ill health, or didn't feel it very much. Now everything had changed, the gloom was significantly intensified – and a daily war had again begun. First of all we began to clamber up the windows to see our comrades walking in the yard. A punishment would follow, of course, but not in such a brutal form as previously: in the majority of cases exercise was curtailed. There was one incident that almost went to trial, but the administration decided to hush it up.

The administration often tried to conduct peaceable conversations with us along the following lines: 'Why', they'd say, 'do you want to achieve everything by force? You went on hunger strike – and as a result many are sick. Now you want to get meetings by force. You'd be better off making the case and asking.' But no-one agreed with this: no-one wanted to ask.

There were bitter clashes over the sick; we demanded that everyone, not just a few, should be given invalid diets. Thus, for example, Butsinskii, who died after two years with stomach cancer and suffered from terrible pain during that time, ate exactly the same food as the healthy, that is, borscht, porridge and black bread. Many refused to accept better food if it wasn't given to those who needed it most. Aronchik soon died from progressive paralysis; he died as quietly as he had lived for six whole years, never once leaving his cell…[77] Waryński was in a very bad way: after the hunger strike he began bleeding from his throat. Sergei Ivanov almost died from a monumental haemorrhage. We demanded the doctor see him, even tapping on our doors at night and insisting on this. The doctor came. He was called Naryshkin. He was a lazy, careless, fat slob, indifferent to everything, but it was possible to rattle him, and then he would do something. Morozov also had serious haemorrhages. Scurvy had never remotely been eradicated among the prisoners, to say nothing of catarrhal gastritis.

At the same time one occurrence seriously agitated everyone. Logovskoi [sic] had been incarcerated in Shlissel'burg Fortress by administrative sentence.[78] He had already finished his term: when he was brought to Shlissel'burg Fortress, the commandant had read him a memo assigning him a five-year term, and in fact, on the day his sentence ended they came to see Logovskoi with a document, but… read out a new five-year sentence… He had been kept all this time in the conditions of a hard-labour convict, with the only difference that he was allowed to wear his own clothes. But as he wasn't granted meetings with his family, he wasn't able to make use of this privilege.

Meanwhile Waryński got even worse. He had long been on an invalid diet and medicine, but it was clear that he didn't have long to live. His terrible cough echoed round the whole prison. The only concession we won was permission for one of his friends to go into the cell next to his,[79] which we had striven for in vain for Iurii Bogdanovich. He could no longer go out, but he was allowed the joy, at least, of tapping to someone close to him. This was very easy, as even a tap of the finger on the wall could be heard in the next room. Waryński died at ten in the morning, but at eight he said good morning as usual to all his neighbours above and below…

Deprived of the club, we now began to seek some other means of associating with each other. We had already long since noticed gaps in the fences and began to use them to deliver various homemade sweets to the sick. Sugar was difficult to pass on, so we made sugar ice out of it, dropping it onto slips of paper. Others did their best – of course, mainly the women – to make toffee out of milk and sugar. You had to stand still for three or four hours, holding your hand above the lamp, to boil the milk until it went thick. One of the 'confectioners' contrived to make sweets out of turnips. All these treats were intended for the sick, to give them pleasure.

They were often buried in the beds, during work in the allotments. But soon the gendarmes noticed our ruse and two or three times searched the allotment, and tiny bundles of these meagre treats were triumphantly pulled out… However, they couldn't find it in themselves to call us properly to account for this crime, and only told us that we mustn't do it. On the platform[80] from where everyone exercising and working in the allotments was observed, they began watching much more attentively, never moving even a pace to the side, which had never happened before. They didn't notice the gaps in the fences for some time, and anyway they were much more important to us, because through them you could see your neighbours exercising. I remember how lively and rosy-cheeked Waryński looked to me two months before his death. This was his last flush of life.

However, soon the gaps were noticed as well, despite our very careful use of them, and they started to be blocked up. This upset us terribly. A struggle began. We tore off splinters and not only that, but started to talk to each other louder still. We were taken to our cells, but that only exasperated everyone. We began to shout through the fences, and some even clambered up them. The administration tried to persuade us, but as that didn't work they decided to make concessions themselves. They promised us meetings in the evenings, books and workshops. It was difficult to believe this, of course, but all the same it was clear there must be a grain of truth in it all, and that they had probably decided in essence to improve our situation somewhat. All the more so as there were still people dying and many sick, while behind us lay a whole crowd of fatalities – 20 people in six years! At this point the gendarmes already probably knew about Konoshevich's [sic] madness, which we still doubted.

But in any case, the women knew that they wouldn't be allowed meetings, except with each other. They had been exercising like that for five years, and their desire to see new people was particularly strong.

Our hopes in fact came true. The authorities agreed to cut gaps in the fences. True, we couldn't get along without a fight – about the size of the gaps. At first the holes were made one and a half inches high, so that we had to squint terribly to see each other. A few months later they were changed into little apertures, but of such dimensions that you could in no way get your head through them. Finally, ten months after the hunger strike, we were still waiting for books. We were brought quite a lot of works on history – Schlosser, Solov'ev, Kostomarov,[81] but all these works related to events only up to the eighteenth century. We were brought many textbooks on natural sciences (although completely unsystematically), and also for studying languages, all the volumes of Reclus,[82] Livingstone and Stanley's travelogues,[83] and so on. Literary works were considered harmful and not given to us. We couldn't receive journals, even old ones.

This sort of flexibility by the administration extended to the sick: we were allowed to start looking after them. At this point everyone knew about Konoshevich's insanity. It was an unassuming insanity, although at times he became angry at not being addressed Konoshevich-Sagaidachnyi, whose descendent he began to consider himself.[84] When he bothered the administration too much with his miscellaneous trivial demands he was taken to the old prison, but this was stopped when we reproached the doctor. Konoshevich was constantly making some sort of flying projectiles and doing research into hypnotism. Even in the Peter and Paul Fortress before his trial he was suffering from hallucinations, thinking that they were trying to hypnotize him and find out everything, but then he recovered, and until 1889 he was healthy. Afterwards he began to write some sort of essay about making the whole world happy. Almost at the same time another person became mentally ill as well, but subsequently made a full recovery.

Chapter III.

From around 1890 a new period of life began in Shlissel'burg Fortress. One might think the authorities were sick of the endless battle with the prisoners. They were persuaded of the stupidity of a prison system where conditions of incarceration of the convicts depended on their 'requests and petitions',[85] and felt the need to introduce mandatory rules for all.

At this point a new commandant was appointed to our fortress, Gangart. For several months before his appointment he had been with us as acting commandant, and during that time had tried to acquaint himself with our needs and the reasons for our discontent and disquiet. Several times he proposed applying a system in which there would be nothing to argue about, at least in questions of everyday life. Thus, for example, although at that time our food had improved, this had happened individually after appeals, which meant it wasn't as the result of a general rule, but the wishes of the administration. Moreover, each one of us was at risk of the sum provided for invalids not being sufficient for all. The commandant endeavoured to improve the allowance for food – if I'm not mistaken from 12 to 22 kopeks per day, deeming such food necessary for us all. He did the same in other instances. It seems probable that Gangart was under the impression that the Police Department had supplied him with instructions for a new regime for the convicts, and what's more, that these were based on his observations during his tenure as acting commandant.

Consequently we gradually gained the following reforms:

1) meetings (in pairs) in cells were introduced, and this resolved a truly burning question – the possibility of the sick having a comrade at the most difficult moment for a human being. But how dreadfully late to be given this permission! By this point, besides suicides and executions, 14 people had died – and they were all completely alone and totally helpless. But there were still sick people who could not always go out for exercise and therefore especially needed visits from their comrades.

2) Workshops were organized, where two people could work together for three hours per day. Here they had also wanted to arrange work on the former privileges system, that is, not giving it to all, but at the discretion of the authorities, but the commandant objected, saying that this would sabotage his entire system. Everyone was so sick of these 'rewards' and 'punishments' that they shunned anything that looked like them with disgust, preferring either to refuse them outright or accept them only after a fight; and if we started refusing work and so on, again we'd end up in a hostile relationship with the administration.

3) As we had expressed discontent at the books being too old, we were promised permission to petition to be allowed to present[86] a list of desirable books ourselves.[87] We wrote two or three times, requesting well-known books, but they rarely sent us what we wanted. However, the books we were permitted were not so much strict as absurd. For example, we were twice sent 18 volumes of Solov'ev, and 8 volumes of Schlosser, and so on. Almost half the books were duplicates – obviously the people we were reliant on to send books never bothered to glance at the list of what had already been sent, or the catalogue of books we already had. We were allowed literary works, but weren't given even old runs of journals. Fortunately it turned out that we received things that we weren't officially permitted. Local Shlissel'burg officers were allowed to give us

books for binding. The bookbinding workshop for that reason flourished; this work soon became essential for everyone who was fit. The only trouble was that we were given piles of rubbish to bind, completely useless for reading, like the Bible and other spiritual books, fortune-telling books, the most stupid novels. Sometimes we came across several copies of journals from the same year, but they were the most uninteresting things – military journals, illustrated ones, *The Russian Herald*.[88] The best were *The Herald of Europe* and *The Northern Herald*.[89] All the journals were, of course, old issues. Of new journals we received only foreign ones – French and English – of course, the emptiest kind. Sometimes we came upon *The Grainfield*,[90] and some specialist journals: *The Proprietor*, *The Doctor*, and *The Paramedic*.[91]

4) Our food began to improve. Every day a meals menu was posted up. Soon they suggested we manage our own domestic affairs, that is, order food according to our own taste. We were allowed to draw up our own schedule for exercise, that is, who wanted to exercise with whom, and where; and we also chose our own comrades for activities in the workshops. This sort of autonomy is often practised in prisons: it relieves the administration of very tiresome work, but most importantly, it saves them from many clashes and complaints.[92]

Gradually they decided to transfer the money we earned to our management – for the entire time that never amounted to more than 200 rubles. We were paid for wood-turning as well; all the turned fencing in Shlissel'burg Fortress was made by us. We made cabinets and a few other things for the barracks, and for the school, voluntarily – and without payment – desks, blackboards, easels and so on. The sum of 50 rubles per month was also handed over to us for materials for our work. Thanks to this our seamstresses could knit jerseys and so on for our comrades. Finally, we were allowed to take control of the money for tea – one ruble 25 kopeks per month, so that those who didn't drink tea could buy coffee or milk. Instead of sugar, some bought acid drops. If someone couldn't eat bread at all (bread was credited at five kopeks each per day), then from the gradual savings they could buy themselves milk, cheese, herrings, and so on. Our allotments and greenhouses were a major support to us. Beside the fact that working in the vegetable gardens and greenhouses was in itself absorbing, thanks to them we could improve our own food.

5) At this point we began to receive extracts from family enquiries[93] that had been sent to the Police Department. These enquiries had

probably been sent by our families frequently, for years, but had lain untouched all this time. The news was very brief, transmitted to us in the administration's paraphrasing, and consisted of a few words: alive, healthy, living in such-and-such a place, and requesting a reply. Of course, we began to reply; we were allowed to do so once or twice a year.

Many received very painful news. In these six or seven years, not only had the old died, but the young as well: someone's wife, another's child… But soon the banality of all this news began to irritate us; we even doubted whether it was real. In our letters we asked our parents about their old illnesses, but never received any reply to this. Postcards from our families reached us, informing us of their important news, but we only managed to receive these rarely: in all likelihood, our families didn't know or didn't believe their letters would reach us.

6) Finally, we were allowed to congregate sometimes, and we called these meetings 'clubs'. In the pens where we exercised, where windows had already been knocked in the walls so that we could see each other, the upper part – a third of the whole wall – was turned into a grille. Consequently from one pen all those exercising in the other pens were visible. Adjacent to the little windows, benches had at some point been fixed at half the height of the wall. Grilles were put in the walls on the pretext of increasing the light in the allotments and pens, where at that time flowers were being grown and bushes planted. That sort of circumvention of the rules was necessary, because solitary confinement for the Shlissel'burg prisoners had not been eliminated in principle. But these changes could not go entirely unnoticed, and the inspectors visiting the prison saw all this, of course, however much they tried to shut their eyes to it. Here, in these clubs, at first we converged and chatted, but later began to arrange group readings and activities. As there were very few books on social questions, we mainly studied natural sciences, which was very convenient at that time, as we had just, by chance, acquired a decent microscope with 300x magnification. We were absorbed by studies of physiology and histology (human and plant), mineralogy, zoology, anatomy, botany and so on. Often we shivered for several hours in the frost in this original auditorium. There were natural scientists among us who knew their subject well and shared their knowledge with love and enthusiasm, and they prepared magnificent templates for these activities.

Later we began to receive annual statistics from abroad, and the Police Department sent us *The Financial Herald*.[94] Thanks to that, statistical work became possible. Some studied historical-philosophical questions. Reports were delivered on all these subjects, ideas exchanged, speculation about the fate of the near future… Here as well from time to time domestic celebrations took place. In the fifth pen we placed a table and organized tea with homemade treats cooked on the lamps, to the surprise and laughter of the gendarmes, who at first, I think, doubted how edible such preparations would be. Sometimes there was even singing. The authorities at first thought of protesting, but then gave it up as a bad job. The 'platforms' from where we were supervised were not idle, however; the guards constantly watched over us, and they didn't stop conducting the prisoners between two gendarmes either.

Often, when we congregated at the club, we reminisced about the years we had just lived through, and our dead comrades in Shlissel'burg Fortress. It's said they were buried near the walls of the fortress:[95] four soldiers carried the coffin with a sergeant-major in front, and they were buried without any rites. Granted, the rites were not recognized by any of us, and the dying had themselves refused to see a priest. But from the point of view of the authorities, it was so bad that later they boasted of improvements and related expenditure: they began to invite a cleric to perform funeral rites and seal the coffin.

During our meetings for the first time we learned for sure what we'd previously only heard fragments of. It emerged that in 1887 five men had been executed in the large yard: Ul'ianov, Generalov, Andreiushkin, Osipanov and Shevyrev. They were convicted in the 1 March '87 case. The trial ended two months after the first arrests, and probably for that reason, little is known publicly about the case. Of the main defendants, almost all were students from Petersburg University, arrested with a bomb in their hands *en route* to Kazan' cathedral,[96] and at the cathedral doors, where they were awaiting Alexander III for the 1 March requiem service.[97] When they were arrested all four [sic] were seized at once by the arm. They had of course been betrayed.

Two months later the case ended; five were sentenced to death, two to incarceration in Shlissel'burg Fortress. All of them were brought to Shlissel'burg.

Only now did we learn where the five people we'd seen from windows in '87 had disappeared to. When they were brought here, we were surprised, because soon after only two were transferred to us from the old prison instead of seven.[98] Comrades said they had conducted themselves very bravely during the trial; rumours said they died bravely as well. They were all young – from 21 to 27 years old. They left the old prison at five in the morning and did not return...

Apropos of that I will report on other executions at Shlissel'burg.

In '84 two soldiers from the trial of the 14,[99] Rogachev and Shtromberg, were brought here for death sentences to be carried out. Somebody managed to exchange taps with Shtromberg, but the next day both he and Rogachev disappeared. According to rumours, they were hanged. It's said that Rogachev broke the gallows and they had to string him up a second time... It appears that no-one else was brought to Shlissel'burg for execution.[100]

In '91, as we later learned, Sof'ia Ginsburg was brought to us from Petersburg, although what for isn't known.[101] She was locked up in the old prison (in cell no. 1). A week later she somehow slit her wrists (with scissors, it seems), so nobody ever saw her. We learned about all this from certain prison sources about five years later. She probably found it too terrifying as there wasn't then a single living creature like her nearby. She must have thought that's how it would be forever. I will allude here to just one more rumour: it's said that she had attempted suicide in the House of Preliminary Detention, but only badly wounded herself, and after that she was immediately transferred to Shlissel'burg Fortress. Whatever the case, there's no doubt that she died in the old prison in December '90 or January '91.[102]

The sources of all this information were either 'new' comrades brought in from outside, who told us this news, for the most part confirming our own observations, or we ourselves saw new arrivals from the windows, and later a comrade who remained among the living gave us news about the executions. We were always inclined to see signs of new arrivals in everything, and we were often mistaken, although it was scarcely possible to hide it from us if someone had indeed been brought in. We found out from work in the workshops in the old prison being curtailed (this is how we guessed that Ginsburg had been transferred), the late distribution of food, or there being too much haste and commotion in the prison. Then we would open the ventilation panes in the windows that faced on to the south west, and listen out for the clanging of chains – the sound of chains could be heard from half the yard. Climbing up to the windows without a moveable bench was so hard that there was a risk of falling down if you couldn't maintain a foothold; sometimes we made a ladder from sheets and towels, and hung it from the window latch. The difficulty was increased by the fact that at such times the gendarmes were particularly vigilant and might notice us scaling the windows, and drag us down. But all the same someone would always manage to see who had arrived, and would tell those who hadn't. The new arrivals were usually brought in 'under the arms', almost carried.

The impatience with which we awaited 'newcomers' will probably seem strange. Yes, that must be acknowledged! But it's more understandable because not only in the first days, but even right to the final days, the majority – both those with fixed terms and life sentences – didn't expect ever to leave the walls of the prison.[103] It's difficult to imagine how much a person's soul needs to think eternally about liberty, be inseparably linked with this idea, desire to see someone from liberty and, what's more, know what new things have happened, and even more so, know this from one's own comrade. At times you feel a spiritual and intellectual hunger – not longing, not apathy, but sometimes approaching an instinctive fear before the dead emptiness not only of your own life but also the life of your comrades in prison; no, that feeling you carry with you to your life outside, forever and in everything. Such feelings are probably familiar to everyone who has experienced a long period of imprisonment. Everything surrounding you – the sun, the sky, people, sounds – seems totally other, not connected to your usual ideas, and for that reason appears somehow strange, alien, like it's all incomprehensible and hostile. Probably for some this mood leads to the question: why live? For others it leads to insanity; semi-insanity didn't pass any of us by. The most frequent dreams for everyone without exception were of escape – the most unbelievable, always ending in capture. And these dreams don't end for those in prison even after ten years in captivity… Yes, you very often experience this longing and feel this pent-up desire for new comrades to arrive. And that's all the more natural because, despite improvements in conditions you remain constantly aware of the terrible oppression of an aimless, pointless life!

Now, when I am far away from Shlissel'burg I often imagine everyone living there as nothing less than half alive. Everything there is divided into minutes, so poor are the contents and events of one's inner life; tomorrow will be exactly the same as yesterday. Often, when getting up in the morning, you think: 'just let there be something new, even if it's worse', and once more you walk with aversion down the same path that you've gone down for 12–13 years, with the same two gendarmes, not allowing you a step out of line. No-one ever went outside the prison walls, and sometimes it seemed that you'd give half your life just to be able to glimpse liberty, there in the distance, from the tower. During the day, when you're busy reading books or with some domestic task, it's at least somewhat bearable. But how much torture you experience at night! You often experience that torture in the daytime as well, sometimes for days in a row. Now I understand that only people with a strong will have the ability within themselves to live in prison. Precisely that dead stillness, hopelessness, inactivity, becomes unbearable. Judging from external appearances, people may appear healthy, and sometimes even have a tendency to be overweight, but the state of their soul can best be gleaned from the subsequent description of events, and the attempt to take away the privileges granted to us.

The issue was that all our liberties remained 'semi-acknowledged', not confirmed 'from above'. The system of solitary confinement had not been eradicated, and as a result the local administration could always return to the old system without any obstruction. On the other hand, privileges themselves were often inhibited as a consequence of the very strict implementation of all the rules. Thus, permission to see someone at set hours and in a set place[104] was very arduous: you go to meetings when you want to be alone, and vice versa. Not to mention that many of our rights were achieved with great difficulty. Thus when Iurkovskii was dying in '96, we were allowed to look after him at night, but very begrudgingly. During exercise it was only possible to be in pairs. However hard we strove for permission to exercise in threes, they would not concede this for anything. As a result we could all be together only in the 'club', but even then we were all separated by fences in twos, and could only see each other through the grilles in the fences. In order to see one's comrades, one had to shiver through exercise for the entire long Petersburg winter, get soaked by the rain practically the whole year round, although some sort of wooden awning was constructed. The sick nevertheless often had to return from exercise to their cells owing to the cold and rain, and so on. This was why we began to talk about opening the ventilation panes in the doors, at least in the workshops while we were working, on the pretext that this was essential when several people were making the same thing, while later we began to insist on permission to go into the corridor for materials for our work. This was essential, because the workshops could not accommodate large pieces of wood, and it was only in the corridor that one could assemble large items. The commandant agreed to our request, albeit reluctantly.

In 1895 we were again allowed into the large yard, and also to the greenhouses in pairs after lunch. In the old prison there was a kitchen with a window looking out onto that yard. For the last two years we had been allowed to cook up something there on festive days or on some other pretext. So we started to organize tea and conversation by this window. Another little 'club' came into existence in this way, and our meetings there went on from one hour to three or four. We also began studying and reading by the workshop windows. The authorities didn't like all these meetings, and constantly asked us to gather together in groups less frequently. This begged the question of why constraint was necessary? It was later explained to us that they feared us clashing with the sentries.[105] But there were no conflicts at all, as long as the sentries weren't called upon to 'chase us away' or 'banish'[106] us by force from the windows. This prohibition began to seriously annoy us, and we constantly experienced it as a form of coercion, as if we were some sort of beasts without any reason, any thoughts… Why were we being watched so carefully? Weren't there enough locks already: 1) on the cell, 2) on the prison door, 3) on the doors to the prison yard, 4) on the fortress gates? The guards walked day and night on and along the walls of the prison. There were crowds of non-commissioned officers inside the prison, a guard house packed full of guards, and whole barracks of soldiers. These locks and guardians[107] were often completely unbearable just to contemplate; a single sound from a jailer would agitate us. And all this was performed in relation to people who had been torn away from liberty 14 years ago, who were living as if in the next world, and had lost any clear idea of real life! Relations with the town across the canal at that time were, as always, severely limited, so it was impossible to explain to oneself why such security was called for.

Recently, in the period of improvements, it was as if we'd been forgotten – inspections took place very rarely. With the commencement of the new Tsar's reign (Nicholas II) again something sinister blew in. Attention was paid to us once more, and a decision was taken to bring us back to the situation we were in previously, that is, to subject us to strict discipline and subordination. It was found that we'd been left to our own devices and had become masters of our own situation. That this was not the only threat was soon proved by the visiting inspector – some colonel of the gendarmes, who was not ashamed to conduct searches everywhere, even under the beds in our absence. It was said that the Police Department thought that we were practically making bombs and that we were communicating with the outside world. The inspector conducted himself like a superior, entering without a bow, looking round and silently leaving. As a result of his visit the receipt of books was tightened up, there were attempts to close the workshop windows and destroy the 'clubs'. At one point the windows were closed, but comrades who hadn't yet gone into their cells refused to leave the corridor, created a disturbance and began to discuss with those already locked up about how to win back open windows. The newly appointed superintendent Dubrovin, who had very tactlessly boasted that in the Cadet Corps he had even brought troublemakers to heel, ordered them to be opened, saying that this had been done by mistake. But following this attempt to return to the old ways there were new attempts, and with that a despairing, stubborn struggle began. No-one wanted to give way, no-one wanted to hear about the old order. Once things even reached the stage of the guards being called out – for the first time in 12 years.[108] However, on this occasion the duty non-commissioned officer probably overdid it – on the whole, many of the older servicemen, remembering the old days, were very willing to overdo it in their zeal. The guards did not let the sentries themselves into the prison building, because a major confrontation might have awaited them. The guards were obliged to seize those not obeying orders (and there were many), restrain them, and even bring cold steel into play, on the command of the guards' officer. There was a serious commotion among the prisoners. One threatened with a raised axe, if any of the guards said 'just one more offensive word'[109]...

Clashes with the administration began to happen very frequently, but the authorities didn't punish any of us, alleging that all the prisoners were 'mentally ill'. It was obvious that no-one could stand a regime like this any longer. We were afraid even to talk about the destruction of our clubs, although it was hinted that the grilles might be closed up if we didn't become more subdued. 'So it's worth you doing that if only for form's sake', we were told. However, we were deprived all the same of the right to go out into the corridor more than two at a time, and the 'little club' by the kitchen window was broken up, so that in the summer of 1896 there was more unpleasantness from conflicts with the authorities about the right to see comrades than there was pleasure from being together. We even wondered whether a backlash against all of us was being intentionally provoked by these means. The fact was that all this began right after the coronation amnesty, and we thought the government wanted to find some justification to itself to not apply the amnesty to us. However, that was only a guess, and as it later turned out, it was mistaken.

There were no longer people dying. The last to die (in 1891 or 1892) was Butsinskii.[110] He died alone in his cell, because the comrades who were nursing him were only allowed in his cell at specified hours. He was also buried God knows how. Butsinskii until the last day was (if I'm not mistaken) occupied with statistical work, although he'd already long been confined to his bed by illness, so that he could no longer go out to exercise himself, and comrades would carry him out to the yard to breathe fresh air. He suffered from stomach cancer and died – very quickly, it seems – from a cardiac rupture. The others with chronic pulmonary illnesses recovered and on the whole were physically more or less healthy. In the last two years we could exercise for six hours in summer (in the morning from 8 to 12 and in the afternoon from 4 to 6). The sick could go into the yard after lunch as well – the healthy always gave them their shifts.

Now nervous and mental illnesses began to take over. Right before his comrades' eyes, Pokhitonov went insane. He was an officer, charged in 1884 with belonging to the military organization.[111] He had been in Shlissel'burg for ten years, and everybody loved him. Suddenly he began to argue over every little thing and, in the main, over political and social questions, he proposed organizing a commune of a rather strange character, and so on. He grasped at everything, convinced it would be a great success, gave lectures on the preparation of good tobacco from the basic kind we propagated,[112] planted flowers by some sort of unusual method, invented an outlandish machine. Everything he did turned out absurdly, but he was convinced it was excellent. It was clear to everyone, of course, what was happening to him. Then he began to spend whole days and nights writing: he fabricated theories of how to make people happy – at this point he was completely delusional. Finally, he became violent, began to attack the gendarmes and his comrades, and attempted suicide. The gendarmes and doctor played along as much as they could, and endured all the sick man's caprices and moods, as did we, and they attended him continually during his violent period. The doctor himself began to petition for him to be taken away, as Pokhitonov was capable of killing himself or others. Once he almost crushed his cervical vertebrae, by inserting the sharp leg of a heavy iron bunk into his mouth and falling from this hook with great force. Fortunately he was taken to Nikolaevskii military hospital in Petersburg after 6–7 months of illness. Pokhitonov was a hopeless case: he had progressive paralysis.

Meanwhile Shchedrin had sunk into complete insanity. For six whole years he didn't appear out of his cell, but in the last two years he began to come out to see us at meetings. He put on airs, puffed himself up, treated everyone high-handedly, and in a more turbulent period castigated both us and the gendarmes, calling them lackeys and blaming us for being insufficiently revolutionary.

Konoshevich almost never left his cell. He made himself a daily schedule – at times, like Pokhitonov, writing a work about how to make the world happy, then singing, then whistling, then dancing… And that continued every day over the course of a year and a half or two years. His wild howling and whistling echoed round the prison day and night, and upset everyone terribly. However, only after Pokhitonov had been removed did we decide to petition about Konoshevich. We had been afraid of him being isolated in the old prison, where the non-commissioned officers would insult him: because of him they would have had to increase their hours on duty. But we decided to petition, because it was impossible to support the mentally ill without suitable supervision and nursing, and, what's more, right before the eyes of healthy people who are stuck in the same place. At the same time we made arrangements to defend him if they tried to take him away to the old prison. In summer 1896, Minister of Internal Affairs Goremykin came to visit us,[113] and heard Konoshevich's howling and raving for himself. We once more repeated our petition to him. The minister listened to us with displeasure and after two or three phrases became impatient at the very first words about 'mental illness'. Whenever they tried to stop him, he'd continue to speak and, raising his voice, answer, 'I know, I know already'. Two months later both of them – Shchedrin and Konoshevich – were taken to Kazan'. Shchedrin had been sick for 11 years, Konoshevich for eight.

On 5 September 1896 Iurkovskii died of kidney disease and oedema.[114] He had been sick for many years and was always irritable, but as he didn't like to talk about his illness, the administration and doctor ascribed his irritation to a bad temper, and ruthlessly recorded him in the penalties book; however, they avoided directly punishing him. In the end, two months before Iurkovskii's death, on the earnest request of his comrades, the doctor came to see him – and two days later we discovered that he had an oedema. The administration and doctor apparently felt some qualms of conscience, and for two months took as much care of him as they could. When he was completely helpless, they tried to organize a transfer to a hospital in Petersburg for a visit from his mother – an eighty-year-old woman who in vain had pleaded for a meeting and, finally, in the summer of 1896, in a letter full of despair, sent him her last blessings, a crucifix and the prayer book from which she had prayed during the whole time of Iurkovskii's imprisonment, that is, 16 years, with the inscription that she no longer had the strength to get to Petersburg. Iurkovskii desperately wanted not to die in his hated cell, but at least on the road, or a steamship, which he loved so much from family and personal memories. But he died in his cell. He met his death bravely. One night he was offered the services of a priest, but refused and asked the comrades keeping watch over him to send a request to the commandant to allow him to say goodbye to both women. This request was fulfilled, and he bade them farewell in full consciousness, although he was already struggling to breathe at all. Two hours later he died. His body, prepared by his comrades, lay in an open cell. It took some time to get permission for this, and the cell was locked for about three hours. When the coffin was brought, everyone bade him farewell for the last time, and his mother's blessing was placed on his chest. The next day at six in the morning when tea was being handed out, the prison gates creaked, and our comrades on watch let everyone know that the coffin had been taken out. Four soldiers carried out the pine box, with an officer in front of them, beyond the fortress gates. Ultimately he was the only one of the sick who benefitted from this degree of care and attention from his comrades and the administration. Earlier it had been impossible to give anyone any kind of help.

The request to transfer Iurkovskii to Petersburg turned out to be possible due to the deliberations going on at that time – or even somewhat earlier – or the decision that had already been made to apply the amnesty to those locked up in Shlissel'burg, which we had no idea about before then. Iurkovskii would certainly have been removed from Shlissel'burg according to the terms of this amnesty, because he had served his 15-year term and had remained locked up for his escape from Kara. Nobody even thought about the amnesty being put into practice. We were all convinced that Shlissel'burg was exempt from all normal prison rules – and moreover in the last year an unceasing struggle had taken place as a consequence of the new crackdown. Then suddenly (this was seven months after the coronation), when we were working as usual in the workshops, ten convicts were called to the commandant. This had never happened before. Everyone's imagination was so stressed that we were expecting something ominous, if not for everybody, then for those who had been called. The others waited in terrible agitation for an hour and a half, until their comrades, returning, informed them of a memo from the Ministry of Internal Affairs that had been read to them. The document said that the Minister of Internal Affairs in counsel with the Minister of Justice, found it possible, in view of the good behaviour of so-and-so, to submit to the discretion of the sovereign a reduction of the sentence of hard labour by one third, and for those who had finished two thirds of their sentence, to commute imprisonment in the fortress to exile to settlement – 'which the sovereign graciously deigned to permit'.

Only six people received serious mitigation (at this time 21 people were incarcerated): three had their life sentences commuted to twenty years; three had their terms reduced by six years. Five would be sent on 23 November 1896 to Siberia: Shebalin, Martynov, Surovtsev, and Janavičius to Iakutsk district; and I – to Sakhalin.

For two weeks, during preparations for the dispatch of the five there were many conversations with the administration. There was speculation that they wanted to bring Shlissel'burg Fortress into line with the general prison situation. I don't know whether that's true. I only know that even with a reduced sentence, you need a terrible intensity of will to survive in that place, and when conditions worsen, no-one can endure it for even two or three years. I can say that with full confidence – the administration had long been convinced of it. Convicts in Shlissel'burg Fortress can survive to the end of their sentence only in reformed conditions, that is, if they are given new books and journals, permitted correspondence and meetings with family and full association with each other, without any threats from the administration.

Thinking about how little hope for the best there is for those remaining in Shlissel'burg, I remember our stay there and am astonished that I am still able to speak, study, read, work, sing, laugh… It's strange, as if it's not me doing these things.

Earlier it was mentioned that many were mentally ill – indeed, at least one third (some of them died, others were transferred from Shlissel'burg, and others still recovered). Two or three people are still at Shlissel'burg from among those who recovered. Looking at them, you see how close the danger of going out of their minds again remains – they are aware of this themselves, and often talk about it with the usual anxiety of the sick.

Now, from a distance, life in that place appears to me to be the life of half-dead people… A common idea exists about the possibility of getting used to prison to the extent of not wanting to leave it. Not only can I not confirm this, but I don't even understand it: I suppose something of that kind might happen either with very undeveloped people, for whom a very unsophisticated mental life is possible, or as an abnormal manifestation of illness. Thus, Shchedrin, for example, having not left his cell for six years, screamed when they decided to open his ventilation window: fresh air had become unbearable to him. Yet after six years he again experienced the pleasure of leaving his cell and enjoying the summer sun and warmth…

It's difficult to block up the soul and mind of a living and developed person, and no matter how much the thought of the benefits of suffering for an idea supports them, their mind and soul will thirst for life and development: indeed, 'whoever does not go forwards, goes backwards…' Locked in the prison, you find a certain satisfaction only in the constant struggle for the feeling of human dignity, as a consequence of the incessant attempts to stifle it. But you also get used to danger, and over time it loses its sustaining meaning. And everything that is left then, in the end, is devoid of life.

Notes

1. After the emancipation of the serfs in 1861, medical care in the Russian provinces was provided by the local *zemstvo*. Many of the doctors who took up such posts were motivated by a commitment to social justice and service to society.
2. The 'Going to the People' movement began in 1874, when thousands of students and other young people went out into the Russian countryside to educate the peasantry and help spread revolutionary ideas. The subsequent arrest of many participants on charges of spreading propaganda and unrest led to two famous trials in 1877. Many of the defendants in the 'Trial of the 50' were sentenced to hard labour or Siberian exile. Almost half the defendants in the 'Trial of the 193' were acquitted, but many still received long sentences, including Ippolit Myshkin, who was sentenced to 10 years' hard labour, and delivered a famous speech at the trial on the revolutionary movement and the illegitimacy of the court. Other future Shlissel'burg prisoners tried in the 'Trial of the 193' were Grachevskii, Lopatin and Morozov (sentenced to time served), Sergei Ivanov and Lukaszewicz (exile), Rogachev (10 years' hard labour) and Shevyrev (acquitted).
3. Prince Dmitrii Nikolaevich Kropotkin (1836–79), first cousin of the anarchist Prince Petr Alekseevich Kropotkin (1842–1921), was governor of Kharkiv province. Grigorii Davydovich Gol'denberg (1855–80), a member of the Executive Committee of the People's Will, in addition to the successful assassination of Kropotkin, was involved in 1879 in an attempt on the life of Alexander II, leading to his arrest. He died by suicide in his cell in the Peter and Paul Fortress in St Petersburg.
4. Ivan Iuvachev, Vasilii Ivanov, Appolon Nemolovskii, Nikolai Pokhitonov, Dmitrii Surovtsev and Aleksandr Tikhanovich also served their sentences in Shlissel'burg Fortress. Nikolai Rogachev and Aleksandr Shtromberg were executed there on 10 (22) October 1884. Three further defendants, L. V. Chemodanova (1848–1931), V. I. Chuiko (1857–after 1934) and A. A. Spadoni-Basmandzhi (1853–1906), were sentenced to Siberian hard labour.
5. Nicholas II reigned from 1894, but his coronation was held on 14 (26) May 1896.
6. From 1857 to 1905 the penal colony on Sakhalin Island, in the North Pacific, was one of the major destinations for both hard labour convicts and exile settlers who had completed their sentences.
7. Kolosov, *Gosudareva tiur'ma*, 64.
8. Morozov, *Iz sten nevoli*, 23.
9. Figner, *Memoirs of a Revolutionist*, 196.
10. The pacifist, ascetic Tolstoian movement, inspired by the religious and philosophical teachings of the novelist Lev Tolstoi, established numerous colonies in Europe, many with the help of Tolstoi's editor, Vladimir Grigor'evich Chertkov (1854–1936). The short-lived English colony founded in Purleigh, Essex, was associated with the Free Word Press.
11. Vladimir L'vovich Burtsev (1862–1942), activist and publisher of numerous revolutionary journals, was most famous for his exposure of the tsarist double agent Evno Azef (1869–1918) in 1908.
12. L. A. Volkenshtein, *13 let v Shlissel'burgskoi kreposti: Zapiski*, ed. V. L. Burtsev. Purleigh: Izdanie Svobodnogo slova, 1900.
13. Information from the prisoner biographies from the first edition has been incorporated into the appendix of the present volume. Vladimir Burtsev's and later editors' notes, as well as the author's notes, are indicated, and the translator's additions to original notes are marked by square brackets. Most of the bibliographic sources listed in Burtsev's notes relate to the trials of the Shlissel'burg prisoners, and those that refer to the prison itself are exclusively from the émigré revolutionary press.
14. L. A. Volkenshtein, *13 let v Shlissel'burgskoi kreposti: Zapiski*. Berlin: Izdanie Gugo Shteinitsa, 1902.
15. Volkenshtein actually arrived at the fortress in October 1884.
16. On Ioann Antonovich, see the Introduction, part II, above.
17. Definitions of Russian terms included in the text are given in the glossary.
18. Besides seven people brought to Shlissel'burg fortress for execution – Rogachev, Shtromberg, Ul'ianov, Generalov, Osipanov, Andreiushkin and Shevyrev. *Burtsev's note*. [Aleksandr Ul'ianov was Lenin's elder brother. *Translator's note*.]
19. In fact, 11 prisoners were transferred on the first day of the new prison's operation. See the Introduction, part I above.

20   The so-called 'Trial of the Twenty'. Aleksandr Dmitrievich Mikhailov (1855–84) was the *de facto* leader of the People's Will. See Ely, *Underground Petersburg*, 172–6.
21   Nikolai Nikolaevich Kolodkevich (1849–84), Aleksandr Ivanovich Barannikov (1858–83), Vil'gel'm-Martyn Rudol'fovich Langans (1852–83), Nikolai Vasil'evich Kletochnikov (1846–83), all members of the Executive Committee of the People's Will; Makar Vasil'evich Teterka (1853–83), worker and member of the People's Will.
22   Russian: 'заметили' ... ничего 'не замечали'. Volkenshtein's use of quotation marks often indicates her interpolation of official discourse.
23   On Orzhevskii, see note 43 above, Introduction, part III.
24   An old man – his surname was Williams, first name William. *Author's note.*
25   Traditional cabbage soup and grain porridge, usually made with buckwheat. Volkenshtein's formulation – 'щи и каша' – ironically echoes the Russian saying 'щи и каша – пища наша' ('cabbage soup and porridge are what we eat', figuratively meaning 'whatever happens in Russia, we live the same way').
26   A network of high-security hard labour prisons along the Kara River to the east of Lake Baikal, part of the Nerchinsk hard labour system.
27   Terent'eva [Liudmila Dement'evna, 1862–83] was a defendant in the trial of Aleksandr Mikhailov. Soon after the trial, in the Peter and Paul Fortress, the doctor accidentally gave her atropine instead of medicine, and she died. Lebedeva, Tat'iana Ivanovna [1850–87], a defendant in the Trial of the 193, was acquitted, but by evading arrest ended up living outside the law. With Frolenko she took part in an attempt on the life of Alexander II near Odessa in 1879, and participated in arranging secret safehouses during preparations for the 1881 attempt. She was arrested in autumn 1881, tried in the Trial of the 20, and sentenced to hard labour. She died in 1887 or 1888 in Kara. Iakimova, Anna Vasil'evna [1856–1942], participated in the Trial of the 193, was acquitted, but nevertheless sent to Viatka Governorate, from where she escaped in 1878. In 1879 she joined the Executive Committee of the People's Will, participated in the attempt on the life of Alexander II near Aleksandrovsk, with Isaev organized a dynamite workshop and, finally, participated in two underground tunnelling plots, in Odessa and Petersburg (by Malaia Sadovaia). Arrested in spring 1881 in Kiev. *Burtsev's note.*
28   Figner dates these pamphlets, published by a press organized by Mikhail Shebalin and Petr Filippovich Iakubovich (1860–1911) for the People's Will, to 1882 and 1883 respectively. Figner, *Zapechatlennyi trud*, 2:117.
29   As far as is known, Iakimova is also still alive. *Burtsev's note.* [Trigoni was transferred to Sakhalin in 1902. Morozov and Frolenko remained in Shlissel'burg until 1905. *Translator's note.*]
30   Minakov's execution actually took place on 21 September (3 October) 1884, and Myshkin's on 26 January (7 February) 1885.
31   Grachevskii's suicide actually took place on 26 October (7 November) 1887.
32   See below. *Author's note.*
33   Ivan Iuvachev subsequently recovered and wrote, among other things, his own memoir and history of the fortress, *Shlissel'burgskaia krepost'* (1907), available in English as: Youvatshev, *The Russian Bastille, or the Schluesselburg Fortress*.
34   At the present time from these 16, two are no longer at Shlissel'burg fortress: Orzhikh (he is now in Vladivostok), and Pankratov (in Iakutsk region). *Burtsev's note. Note to the 1902 edition continues:* ... and Trigoni (on Sakhalin). In 1901 Karpovich was imprisoned in the fortress for the murder of the Minister of Public Education, [Nikolai Pavlovich] Bogolepov [1846–1901].
35   In relation to the purges of the 1930s, Evgeniia Ginzburg observed a basic rule: 'the dirtier the prison ... the less danger there was to life. The cleaner the jail ... the closer we were to death'. *Into the Whirlwind*, 83. See Peterson, 'Dirty women', 179–82.
36   That is, using 'ты' as opposed to the polite 'вы'.
37   Russian: стук, стучать. A reference to the 'wall alphabet' used by the inmates to communicate. See Introduction, part III above.
38   Russian: страж.
39   Russian: 'ты' так и сыпалось, раздавались ругательства.
40   Russian: смотритель.
41   Russian: карцер.
42   Russian: 'помяли во время сопротивления!'

43 Russian: 'за оскорбление действием'.
44 Russian: караул.
45 His neighbour was Mikhail Popov, who wrote about the incident: Popov, 'K biografii Ippolita Nikiticha Myshkina', 1906, 250–68.
46 About six months later. *Author's note.*
47 Coughing up blood, usually as the result of tuberculosis.
48 Convict uniforms had a diamond-shaped patch, usually in black or yellow, sewn on to the back of their uniform.
49 Russian: 'установленный режим'.
50 On Aronchik's presence and death in the fortress, see note 77 below.
51 Elizaveta Nikolaevna Koval'skaia (1851–1943), member of the Chaikovskii Circle (named for its founder Nikolai Vasil'evich Chaikovskii, 1850–1926), Land and Liberty (*Zemlia i volia*), and Black Partition (*Chernyi peredel*) revolutionary groups. She organized the Southern Russian Workers' Union with Shchedrin in 1880, but was arrested in October 1880.
52 Recidivist convicts in the hard labour system were frequently chained to wheelbarrows for as long as 10 years, as 'a punishment that was both a moral torment and an obstacle to escape'. Beer, *The House of the Dead*, 287.
53 His surname was Sokolov. *Author's note.*
54 Meeting each other in pairs during exercise. *Author's note.*
55 Russian: 'не уносили в мертвецкую'.
56 Actually this wasn't difficult to achieve. The administration was very afraid of any incident; and as soon as the convicts themselves protested against the dying being taken away, it wasn't worth continuing. *Author's note.*
57 Russian: 'трубость'.
58 Russian: 'заносчивость'.
59 The Police Department; along with the *Okhrana*, successor from 1880 to the Third Section of His Imperial Majesty's Own Chancellery, the tsarist secret police force.
60 Iuvachev is now at liberty. *Publisher's note.*
61 John Gillies (1747–1836), Scottish historian and writer. His *History of Ancient Greece, its Colonies and Conquests* was published in 1786.
62 This method of calculating reductions in sentences was used in both the Imperial and Soviet eras.
63 Russian: Уводимых продолжали толкать и 'мять'.
64 We learned about this later. *Author's note.*
65 This arrangement was also used to separate prisoners from doctors and other officials.
66 On the date of Grachevskii's suicide, see note 31 above.
67 Russian: вахмистр.
68 Russian: дежурный унтер-офицер.
69 Nikolai Ivanovich Petrov (1841–1905), Chief of Staff of the Corps of Gendarmes from 1884 to 1893, and Director of the Police Department 1893–5.
70 Russian: часовые.
71 That is, so that the prisoners could not remove the lamps from the walls to repeat Grachevskii's method of suicide. Electric lights were installed around 1895, as Pankratov (Chapter IV) states.
72 Lagovskii arrived in 1885; Janavičius, Manucharov and Waryński in 1886; Antonov, Sergei Ivanov, Konashevich, Lopatin, Lukaszewicz, Novorusskii and Starodvorskii in 1887; and Orzhikh in 1890.
73 [Nikolai Ignat'evich Shebeko (1834–1904)] Deputy Minister of Internal Affairs and head of the Corps of Gendarmes. *Author's note.*
74 Bogdanovich died in July 1888.
75 Petr Nikolaevich Durnovo (1845–1915).
76 This episode happened to the author of the memoir published by us, L. A. Volkenshtein. Another author of memoirs about Shlissel'burg Fortress writes the following about the clash between Volkenshtein and Shebeko: Shebeko started to say to Liudmila Volkenshtein: 'Your mother came to see me, I can say…' but she interrupted him: 'are you General Shebeko?' 'I am.' 'I don't want to know anything from you, even about my mother.' *Burtsev's note.*
77 Morozov notes that Aronchik's mental breakdown was manifested by a silence so absolute that his presence in the fortress was unknown to the other prisoners until long after his death,

which they learned about from an officer: 'He never uttered a single word to anyone during his imprisonment in Shlissel'burg, and in the last two or three years he never even got out of bed. His entire body was covered in gangrenous ulcers.' Morozov, *Povesti moei zhizni*, 3:296. See also Lopatin's poem 'On the Death of Aronchik', *German Aleksandrovich Lopatin, 1845–1918*, 188–9.

78 On the use of administrative sentences, see the Introduction, note 16. An administrative sentence to imprisonment with hard labour was unusual (Shlissel'burg was legally defined as a hard labour prison, even if no labour took place there).

79 This was probably Janavičius, whose own memoir emphasizes his closeness to Waryński: *Shlissel'burzhets L. F. Ianovich*, 55–60.

80 Russian: вышки.

81 Friedrich Christoph Schlosser (1776–1861), German historian, whose multi-volume *World History* began appearing in 1815; Sergei Mikhailovich Solov'ev (1820–79), one of Russia's most distinguished and influential historians, notable particularly for his 29-volume *History of Russia from the Earliest Times* (1851–79); Nikolai Ivanovich Kostomarov (1817–85), Professor of History at the St Vladimir University of Kiev and St Petersburg University, most famous for his three-volume *Russian History in the Biographies of its Main Figures*.

82 The anarchist and geographer Jacques Élisée-Reclus (1830–1905) was best known for his 19-volume *Universal Geography*.

83 David Livingstone (1813–73), Scottish physician, explorer and missionary, author of *Missionary Travels and Researches in South Africa* (1857). Henry Morton Stanley (1841–1904), Welsh journalist and explorer, most famous for finding Livingstone in present-day Tanzania in 1871; author of *How I Found Livingstone* (1872) and *In Darkest Africa* (1890).

84 Hetman Petro Konashevich-Sagaidachnyi (c.1586–1622) was leader of the Ukrainian Cossacks in the first half of the seventeenth century.

85 Russian: 'просьбы и заявления'.

86 Russian: нам обещали хлопотать о том, чтобы нам самим разрешали представлять список желательных книг. The convoluted phrasing here creates an ample reflection of the sort of hoops the prisoners were forced to jump through to achieve concessions.

87 The department now assigns 130–140 rubles per year to replenish the prison library. *Author's note*.

88 *The Russian Herald* (*Russkii vestnik*) was one of the most famous 'fat' literary journals of the nineteenth century, notable for publishing the major novels of Dostoevskii and Tolstoi as well as works by other prominent writers including Ivan Turgenev, Nikolai Leskov and Afanasii Fet. It became renowned for its increasingly reactionary stance under the editorship of the conservative publicist Mikhail Katkov (1818–87).

89 *The Herald of Europe* (*Vestnik Evropy*) was a major liberal monthly journal, published in St Petersburg from 1866 to 1918, until 1909 under the editorship of its founder, historian and scholar Mikhail Matveevich Stasiulevich (1826–1911). *The Northern Herald* (*Severnyi vestnik*), founded in 1885 by Russian feminist writer and lawyer Anna Mikhailovna Evreinova (1844–1919), was associated with the Populists in its early years. In the 1890s it was edited by writer Mikhail Nilovich Al'bov (1851–1911). Later, under author, translator and critic Liubov' Iakovlevna Gurevich (1866–1940), it was associated with the Decadent movement.

90 *The Grainfield* (*Niva*) was a popular 'thin' journal, focusing on literature, politics and modern life, published in St Petersburg from 1870 to 1918.

91 Although many journals devoted to agriculture and related subjects were published in Imperial Russia, none named *The Proprietor* (*Khoziain*) is listed in *Gazety dorevoliutsionnoi Rossii, 1703–1917*; *The Doctor* (*Vrach*) was a monthly medical journal, published from 1880, edited by Sergei Vasil'evich Vladislavlev (1859–1916), a staff physician at the Obukhov hospital in St Petersburg; *The Paramedic* (*Fel'dsher*) was a medical newspaper published from 1891–1917, edited by medic and public health official Boris Abramovich Oks (1851–1926).

92 This type of self-governing is a common practice in Russian prisons that continues to this day.

93 Russian: запросы.

94 *Vestnik finansov*, not listed in *Gazety dorevoliutsionnoi Rossii*.

95 The burial ground was outside the northern tip of the fortress, by the Royal Tower (Korolevskaia bashnia). See point 11 on the plan of the fortress, Figure 1.2.

96 Kazan' cathedral, dedicated to the icon of Our Lady of Kazan', is on Nevskii Prospekt in St Petersburg.

97 That is, the requiem service for Tsar Alexander II on the anniversary of his assassination.

98 Jyzef Lukaszewicz and Mikhail Novorusskii were brought to the fortress on the same day as the five executed men.
99 On the defendants in the 'Trial of the 14', see note 4 above.
100 Executions resumed at Shlissel'burg in 1902 with the hanging of Stepan Balmashev. Three people were executed in 1905 (Ivan Kaliaev, Girsh Gershkovich and Aleksandr Vasil'ev), and two in 1906 (Zinaida Konopliannikova and Iakov Vasil'ev-Finkel'shtein), after the departure of the remaining group of prisoners.
101 Ginsburg was an active member of the 'Allied Terrorist Circle', formed in Switzerland in 1888 by remaining members of the People's Will still at liberty in emigration. She returned to Russia to test the political mood, establish connections and prepare terrorist acts. Gernet, *Istoriia tsarskoi tiur'my*, 3:127.
102 Ginsburg's suicide took place on 7 (19) January 1891. She had in fact been in the old prison since 1 (13) December 1890.
103 28 of the longer-term inmates (excluding those sent to the fortress for execution) were originally sentenced to death. In 24 cases this was commuted to perpetual hard labour, with specified sentences of between 10 and 20 years in the other four. Nine others were sentenced to lifelong hard labour. Ten received sentences of 20 years or more (the result of increases to the original term). Six had sentences of between 10 and 19 years.
104 Now the convicts can see each other from 9 in the morning until 9 at night, and an exception exists only for the women: they are allowed to see each other only during morning exercise from 8 to 12. At the present time the inmates of Shlissel'burg Prison often tap to each other during long winter nights – they also tap like that from 6 to 8 in the morning. *Author's note.*
105 Russian: дежурные.
106 Russian: 'разгонять' и 'отгонять'.
107 Russian: аргусы.
108 This incident is described in detail in Chapter IV of Vasilii Pankratov's memoir.
109 Russian: 'еще одно грубое слово'.
110 Butsinskii's death was on 16 July 1891.
111 The People's Will's military centre, to which Ashenbrenner, Butsevich and others also belonged.
112 We weren't given any other tobacco, and the smokers, having tried smoking nettles, moss, grass, and so on, somehow managed to get hold of seeds for flowering varieties of tobacco. Now they are allowed to buy real tobacco with the money they earn. *Author's note.*
113 Ivan Logginovich Goremykin (1839–1917).
114 Iurkovskii's death was actually on 30 August (11 September) 1896.

3.
Mikhail Ashenbrenner, *Two decades in Shlissel'burg Prison*

I. Mikhail Ashenbrenner, 1842-1926

Mikhail Iul'evich Ashenbrenner (Figure 3.1) was born in Moscow on 9 (21) September 1842 to a gentry family. His father, Iulii Iul'evich, was a Russified German who served as a military engineer. His mother was one of the daughters of General Mikhail Fedorovich Naumov, military commandant of Smolensk and veteran of the Patriotic War of 1812.[1] After a childhood spent in the Caucasus, St Petersburg and Moscow, Ashenbrenner was enrolled in the Moscow Cadet Academy in 1853. An initially harsh regime at the school gave way to reforms, and he was able to take university courses, including history lectures by S. M. Solov'ev and literature lectures by N. S. Tikhonravov.[2] Through the latter, Ashenbrenner was introduced to radical literature, including journalistic writings by Belinskii, Dobroliubov, and Chernyshevskii,[3] as well as illegally obtained copies of *The Bell* (*Kolokol*) and *The Polar Star* (*Poliarnaia Zvezda*), edited in emigration by Alexander Herzen,[4] and philosophical works by Hegel, Feuerbach, Fourier, and Robert Owen.[5]

In 1863 Ashenbrenner was assigned to a guards' regiment as a commissioned officer, but in 1864 he refused to participate in the suppression of the Polish Uprising[6] and was sent to serve in Russian Turkestan,[7] returning to European Russia five years later. In the mid-1870s he met various future members of the

Михаилъ Юльевичъ
АШЕНБРЕНЕРЪ.

Figure 3.1 Portrait of Mikhail Ashenbrenner before his arrest. From Annenskii, N. F. et al., eds. *Gallereia Shlissel'burgskikh uznikov*. St Petersburg: Tipografiia M. M. Stasiulevicha, 1907, between pp. 188 and 189. Public domain/orphan work. Digitization by LSE Library.

People's Will, including Mikhail Frolenko. Based in Odessa and Nikolaev in present-day Ukraine, he participated in officers' reading and educational circles, where socialist theories were studied and a political programme for reforming the army was planned. In 1881 he met Vera Figner, and Aleksandr Butsevich, a lieutenant in the Russian navy and leader of the military centre of the People's Will. Ashenbrenner's group joined the military centre, adopting a more radical programme and increasing propaganda efforts among conscripted soldiers and sailors. In 1883, Ashenbrenner, Figner and others were betrayed and arrested.[8]

Ashenbrenner was transferred to the Peter and Paul Fortress in St Petersburg, and convicted in the 'Trial of the 14'. He was sentenced to death, commuted to lifelong hard labour, and transferred to Shlissel'burg Fortress on 14 October 1884. He spent almost 20 years in the prison, finally leaving for exile in Smolensk on 28 September 1904. Remaining under police surveillance, he nevertheless returned to revolutionary activity, assisting the Socialist Revolutionaries, but never joined the party due to differences over the use of terrorist tactics.[9] His civil rights were restored in 1917, and he spent his final years in the Il'ich rest home for revolutionary veterans in Moscow. He died on 11 November 1926, and is buried in the city's Novodevich'e Cemetery.

Ivan Iuvachev, who met Ashenbrenner as an officer before his arrest, noted, 'It seemed to me that [other officers'] love for him almost turned into hero worship. Military campaigns in Central Asia turned him into a good, sincere comrade, prepared even to give up his life for a friend'.[10] Figner described Ashenbrenner as 'an educated and erudite man', who appeared to be 'the natural leader of [his] fraternity'. He was 'a very affectionate man, flexible and gentle in his relations with others', who 'had a high opinion of his friends and colleagues'.[11]

Mikhail Ashenbrenner, *Two decades in Shlissel'burg Prison, 1884–1904*[12]

(A memoir)[13]

Chapter I.

These are the key aspects of prison life. Our life was full of contrasts. There was no influx of living, external impressions, and no material from outside was forthcoming for normal mental life. Years went by without bringing anything new from outside, because we lived in a communal grave, separated from the world of the living by an unbridgeable chasm. Neither books, nor meetings, nor news about our families, nor about what was happening in the world. The Bible, the works of Saint Dmitrii of Rostov,[14] two or three old years of ecclesiastical journals, and about three dozen ancient books on poor quality paper, written in language that pre-dated Pushkin[15] – that was the entirety of our library. Communicating by tapping on the walls was annoying rather than satisfying, because it was impossible not only to exchange arguments, but even to express oneself. To all appearances our life was colourless, empty, meaningless, but the absence of external impressions was replaced in abundance by the ordeals and experiences of the material that the prison gave. We lived intensely, in a state close to boiling over, interrupted only by exhaustion. The tragedy of our position consisted precisely in this. In moments of rest one could live by one's memories, a purely contemplative life, and become stupefied by dreams. Or in order to save one's soul from madness, one could take on serious work and bury oneself in it, forming a special, perfect, theoretically constructed world for oneself – detaching oneself with a protective shell – and surviving through speculation, theories, hypotheses, as the only content of life. But it was impossible to withdraw into this world. Every day, dreadful reality destroyed this illusion. Constant conflict, unpleasant petty quarrels, everyone's inevitable participation in battles, wherever they arose, because we were tied together by fellowship, a common enemy and a common duty, perpetual anxiety, unbearable constraints and the impossibility of being reconciled to the regime – that was the material for life the prison gave us. A state of stress was followed by fatigue, the need to rest and forget. But an agitated soul only comes back into balance slowly. An involuntary desire arose to avoid wasting one's strength on trivial matters, to endure in silence and respond with contempt. This was possible sometimes, 10 or 15 times, but resentment grew and flashpoints became all the more inevitable, to the point that such-and-such a plan seldom turned out for the best. Clashes and disturbances happened rarely, but became much more toxic, and actions in response were, moreover, not always proportionate. But peace returned more slowly, and insomnia became more tormenting. Many began to entertain the idea that in such a petty and cruel struggle one becomes petty oneself, and that it's not worth dragging out such an existence. Perhaps that sort of feeling acted as one of the reasons for suicide. But the daily struggle, suppressed resentment, the consciousness of one's powerlessness and the hopelessness of the situation, the impossibility of pacifying a frustrated, exhausted person, the tense situation even when you're avoiding conflict, and especially the alternation between agitation and prostration – all that led to madness. The desperate struggle for life, for moderation, for a more reasonable existence, dragged on for a long time, and we achieved concessions at the price of great sacrifices. Ten years passed. In the first years almost 50 per cent died, including two who were shot for violent assault. Then almost an epidemic of madness began.[16] Myshkin and Minakov tapped to their neighbours that they no longer wished to live, but wanted to die in a way that wasn't useless for their comrades, so they would demand books, journals, meetings with comrades, correspondence with family, workshops. By some unknown route certain news about Shlissel'burg reached the foreign press, for example about the terrible death of Grachevskii, who burned himself alive with kerosene. The calculations of the authorities did not include the transformation of a political prison into a lunatic asylum, but that was exactly where it was heading. And the insane were too dangerous for them personally as well, tremendously increasing the work of supervision and restraint.

The very rapid depopulation was a blatant scandal: without a doubt, a protest in this form would ruin their plans. That is why the authorities little by little agreed to concessions, and all these concessions and privileges were purchased at the price of blood. The main privileges that had a salutary value were books and journals, fellowship and exercise. All these privileges began to be felt to a minimal degree at the end of Alexander III's reign, and, finally, in '95–7, our 'golden age' began, which lasted for several years (until autumn 1901). Things started to tighten up again and return to the former rules under Sipiagin,[17] and under Plehve.[18] When there were only 13 of us left out of 51, when we had lost our youth, strength, health and endurance, we were returned to the old regime. Such was our state of mind from the beginning to the very end of our stay in the prison, with minor fluctuations for the better in the best periods.

Chapter II.

Soon after the deaths of Myshkin and Minakov[19] we were each given small boards (made of card) and notebooks of three quartos, with numbered pages and countersigned by the superintendent. We were each given a pencil and asked what textbooks each of us would like for studying. Giving me a pencil, Sokolov-Herod said, 'If the pencil breaks, tell us: we will sharpen it; when the notebook is full, hand it in, we will give you a new one.' Some wanted to do mathematics, others to study languages, natural sciences, applied sciences, for which books, textbooks and dictionaries were ordered. When the books that had been bought were distributed, we were disillusioned: those who wanted to study advanced mathematics received arithmetic and concise geometry books for primary schools. For studying foreign languages instruction books for the youngest age group were given out, with 40–50 pages and the most stupid questions and answers. This probably happened out of ignorance or for economic reasons. When we complained about the unsuitability of such textbooks, and after multiple statements to the local administration and inspectors, we finally received the textbooks we wanted, as well as the dictionaries we had been deprived of upon our arrest. On his visit to the prison I asked Minister Durnovo to sell my medals,[20] among other items confiscated from me, and buy three dictionaries with the proceeds. The minister replied, 'There will be dictionaries'. The next day the commandant told me that the minister had been offended by my statement, considering it a demonstrable expression of disrespect for decorations for distinguished service. Be that as it may, I was given three dictionaries and it was announced that my medals would be returned to my family. However, on returning home, it emerged that my family had never received these medals. Several years later General Petrov sent us,[21] on our request, the complete collected works of Spencer in Russian,[22] and the collected works of Macaulay in English, and then Solov'ev's *History of Russia* and the collected works of Kostomarov.[23] And soon, on our request, we were given books confiscated on our arrests, with some exceptions, however (I wasn't returned a collection of articles by Prof. Ziber on Marx's economic theory,[24] or Lopatin, apparently, the first volume of *Capital*).[25] But soon these books were taken away because an inspector saw Mignet's or Quinet's *History of the Revolution* on someone's table.[26]

The confiscation of books was followed first by a suspension of walks, and then by a hunger strike. For conversation then we 'for the first time ever'[27] used the toilet and its pipes, for which the bowl had to be cleaned carefully and then the water scooped out, and in that way the toilet was turned into a 'telephone'. Via these telephone clubs we exchanged opinions about the most reliable methods of suicide. The hunger strike was quite sustained, and shattered the health of many. The administration could consider itself the victor, but the commune did not sustain total defeat, as most of the books were returned.[28]

*

At the same time, by the right hand corner adjoining the old, miniature pens for exercise, eight more spacious pens were constructed. Earth was brought out, and in this way our future flower beds and allotments began to take shape, and we started to be taken out in pairs for walks. I was designated M. P. Shebalin,[29] whom I saw every other day at first, and then every day. After a year and a half the authorities for their own reasons gave me F. N. Iurkovskii,[30] instead of Shebalin, with whom my meetings also continued for more than a year. M. F. Frolenko was the third to be assigned.[31] Then we were entitled to choose our comrades for exercise ourselves, and change them after short intervals, and, finally, there was the following order for assigning exercise: we chose a comrade as 'promenade-master',[32] who scheduled us in daily pairs according to our nominations and gave the timetable to the sergeant-major in the morning. In the end, when exercise was extended until lunch, that is, from eight to twelve o'clock, changing partners for exercise was accomplished via our personal requests to the duty non-commissioned officer on the watchtower, so that it was possible to see everybody in turn. Moreover the gendarmes only watched to make sure there were no more than two people in one pen. At that point the duty of the promenade-master was discontinued as superfluous.

*

I think it was in 1890 that we were told that workshops were already being planned, but in the meantime those who wanted it were offered fretwork. Many declared their desire to do this. Then in the old prison, which was located in the citadel, that is, in the nearest adjoining yard, in the cells that had previously served as punishment cells, joinery, turning, bookbinding and shoemaking workshops were established. Alongside this we were allocated, I think, 180 rubles a year for the gardens, tools for the allotments, seeds, fertilizer and materials for the workshops. Everyone wanted to get busy in the workshops, but very few had any skills, and the administration didn't want to allow us in the workshops in pairs and suggested that the beginners have gendarme non-coms[33] as tutors. We refused that sort of mentor. It was such an absurdity: the workshops were permitted, organized – and empty, amid our general desire to learn and to work. Little by little the administration acquiesced, and started taking us there in pairs. Thus many of us taught ourselves skills, but not many turned into good craftsmen. We produced elegant, artistic things, but worked on them for so long that at normal market rate we couldn't have earned more than 20 kopeks per day. On the whole in the workshops and our bookish activities we didn't achieve great success: it's difficult to work productively in captivity, and we had no means of selling our wares either. It is true that many of us achieved significant success, but at the cost of so much time and labour that our success would have been many times greater in other circumstances. When the allotment fences had been constructed and a watchtower installed for the duty officers, we were distributed among the allotments. The available personnel were divided up into pairs for the small gardens, and threes and fours to work in the large ones. Vegetable seeds were distributed, water was brought out for each of the eight allotments, garden tools were given out. Everyone had to plant their own seedbed. The cells where we lived were very small: you could go from the door to the window in five or six paces – the corners were filled in and it was impossible to walk diagonally. We suffered from lack of movement and static gymnastics did not compensate for this lack, and it led, at least in the first years, to acrimony, making the duty officers in the corridor bewildered and uneasy. Therefore in each allotment we made a wide path for the movement of two together, paving it with old, broken flagstones. Along these paths we sauntered, holding conversations, and if we happened to be in an allotment alone, then we'd walk with a book: reading and walking at the same time, combining motion with interesting reading. We went out for exercise a great deal: this was necessary and saved our health. One comrade calculated that in 20 years in prison he walked the distance round the earth's equator 12 times. Leaving space for walking meant having to narrow the beds. Every inch of earth was precious, so it was necessary to save space between the beds, and we decided to lay boards at the sides of the beds. In the yard by the old prison there was a pile of wood, and we saw some long, thick logs. We asked to be given these logs and, using an axe, wedges and a rough plane, made boards from them. This was our first major work. We sowed red and black radishes, and swede, turnips, carrots, onions, fennel, parsley, peas, garlic, cabbage and cauliflower – all in small quantities. The swede turned out best of all, the turnips and cauliflower the worst: it was too overcrowded. The fortress walls, the prison and the high fences round the allotments shut out the sun for most of the day. In well-lit places we planted flowers, and along the fences raspberry canes, black and red currants and gooseberries. Subsequently we planted some apple trees. In the eighth allotment there is now a small apple tree grown from a pip and grafted by M. F. Frolenko, and a cherry tree grown from a stone.

When the workshops opened and practical conversations with the superintendent, commandant and officer in charge of the workshops entered into the picture, the need emerged for a delegate to speak on behalf of everyone. This delegate was known as the elder[34] and served, I think, a year at first, and later six months. The local administration willingly agreed to this, because it was more convenient for them to negotiate with a representative of the entire commune, particularly as some comrades simply could not speak to their jailers[35] dispassionately. The elder was obliged to monitor the condition of the tools, the issue and use of materials, and settle accounts on the expenditure of the sum allocated for the workshops and allotments. This sum was divided into two parts: one for common needs, the other split into equal shares in cash and spent by each person on buying materials at their own discretion. It should not be supposed that any money was handed out. All the accounts were done on paper.

*

In the first six years 11 kopeks per day were allocated for our rations, including black bread. We were given 2½ pounds of bread each. The bread was always poor quality, undercooked and separated from the crust. For lunch we got two dishes: soup, *shchi*, borscht or thin pea gruel; for the second buckwheat or millet porridge, or slop. For dinner we got the reheated liquid dish left over from lunch. On fast days and on Wednesdays and Fridays we were given a Lenten diet. This wasn't done out of piety, of course, but to subdue us, because we were given Lenten food on Wednesdays and Fridays even in Holy Week and at Christmas.

The food was inferior: hot dishes without any fat, with only traces of meat; porridge with hardly any oil, Lenten stew from rotten smelt, mushroom *shchi* with a minimal quantity of cabbage and mushrooms, thin pea soup floating with worms. On Sundays we were given as a second dish a few small, chopped up pieces of roast beef with potatoes and beans, and for dessert a tart with lingonberry jam. At Easter a small loaf was given out by way of Easter sweet bread, and a small – three mouthfuls – Passover cake made with sweetened curds, and some decorated eggs. In 1889 our invalid ration turned into the ordinary one: 23 kopeks per day plus bread were given as our allowance, with permission to swap the black bread for white, made with sifted flour, at half the quantity, that is, instead of 2½ pounds of black, 1¼ of white. From this point on the food was reasonable, and more varied than previously. In addition we were allowed to put the menus together ourselves, on condition of not going above 23 kopeks. For compiling the menus we began to elect a 'menu-master',[36] who had the difficult and thankless role of trying to please everyone without going over budget. For such a hopeless job our menu-masters needed a lot of wit and zeal, and from time to time they began to make creative referendums: each dish was repeated for two, three or four weeks proportional to the number of votes cast. Two or of three times a week we received milky soup, meatballs, rice porridge, macaroni, cheese pancakes, filled dumplings, the same festive tarts with lingonberries, or pies with cabbage and meat; for dinner on Saturdays we received herring with potatoes, and for Sunday dinners around ¼ pound of cheese. This food would have been good, except that for the hot dish we always received boiled meat, because with our means it was impossible to make a roast of good, tender meat. Fats were given out very rarely, yet at the latitude where we were living, the need for fats and carbohydrates was more urgent than anywhere else. Dr Nikolai Sergeevich Bezrodnov,[37] who did us a lot of good, came to our aid. He began to distribute sunflower oil to the whole of our fraternity to the tune of 10 pounds a month from the hospital budget. At first we stirred this oil into our porridge, potatoes and so on with displeasure, but then got used to it, and it even became pleasant. At first we were each given a mug of tea and piece of lump sugar twice a day. Many years later, under commandant Gangart, each person got two teapots: one for boiling water, the other for brewing tea, and they began to allocate us ½ pound of tea and 3 pounds of sugar a month. The tea was of reasonable quality, at 90 kopeks for two pounds, but the sugar was very expensive, at 18 kopeks a pound. Purchasing wholesale, and with a regular customer discount, ½ a pound of tea came out at 77 kopeks, so the tea allowance per person came out at one ruble 31 kopeks per month. Subsequently we were allowed to order not only tea with this money, but coffee, cocoa, lemons, acid drops and cranberries. Many took only ¼ pound of tea, and with the rest of the money bought something else. Some didn't take tea at all, but drank malted coffee.

*

At first we tapped very unskilfully, and barely understood each other, so that conversations by tapping didn't satisfy us, but rather exasperated us because it was impossible to express ourselves. Then, gradually we began to tap very quickly and distinctly, and understood each other so well that we didn't need to tap words to the end. Frequently used words we exchanged for a single letter, or an agreed signal. At first we exchanged taps only with our neighbours and needlessly tapped too loudly, but when we got used to the prison acoustics we began to tap very quietly so as to not disturb other comrades or introduce an unwanted witness into the conversation: the duty gendarme. Loud taps could be heard two cells away, and above and below, and therefore we had general conversations in various corners. The administration persecuted us for tapping, punished us, interrupted our taps in every way, including by leaving water to stream from a tap in an unoccupied cell: the gurgle of water drowned out our taps, and horribly aggravated our nerves to boot. But the need for communication with others was so great that the administration had to yield. Then for communication with the other side [of the corridor] we tapped on the iron heaters (steam heating), or on the door. Such taps could be heard by everybody and involuntarily attracted general attention, so we only tapped on the door and the heater in extreme cases, when we needed to exchange thoughts or news with everybody, trying not to disturb for no reason comrades who were busy or resting. When we began to see each other frequently, tapping gradually fell out of use, but the administration sometimes invited the elder to tap on the door to advertise to the whole house, for example, thus: 'Please can you tap that today exercise will begin at 9 o'clock, as works are being carried out in the yard.' General, furious tapping on the doors and stoves, and moreover tapping with anything that came to hand, developed as a form of protest.

*

Aside from the usual punishments, such as being deprived of tea, books, walks and work in the workshops, or a dark punishment cell without a bed on rations of bread and water, the following was also employed: prolonged incarceration in a punishment cell in fetters and a straitjacket. Incarceration in fetters was only employed once, on K. F. Martynov,[38] for spitting in the face of Superintendent Fedorov. Removal to the punishment cells was sometimes accompanied by a beating. The brutal upstart Sokolov, alias Herod, a.k.a. Cerberus, responded to protests against violence with apparent distress: 'ah! But if we were really to follow the instructions', indicating the point in the instructions that mentioned 50 lashes with the birch. General protests, which took the form of minor mayhem, remained unpunished: the authorities were too anxious of an incident ending in a major scandal, and resorted to exhortations and promises to pacify us. In the second decade punishments were applied more rarely, although there were just as many reasons for them, as we became very cantankerous: each of us was like a bomb filled with pyroxylin, and we often went from defence onto the offensive. In the mornings when hot water was being distributed, we had to raise our heavy iron bedsteads, together with the bedding, up against the wall and lock them up, and in the evening at 7 o'clock put them down again. That arrangement existed for a long time, but then we no longer raised the beds.

The first superintendent, Sokolov, initially tried to address us in the familiar form, and when we replied to him in the same fashion, he was extremely offended: 'Why, you've been deprived of all your rights. According to the instructions, when you address me, you're ordered to say, Your Excellency, and then I'll speak!' Later on we were addressed in the third person, for example, the first commandant Pokroshinskii, in the fourth year of imprisonment, asked me: 'Is the convict healthy?'—Well, I replied—'And in all this time the convict hasn't once been sick?'—Not once.—'And the convict's health is not declining in any way?'—No decline.—'Remarkable!' he concluded.

The high position of the windows in the cells, the thick iron bars and double frames in summer and winter took away a lot of light, and the opaque glass created eternal twilight in the cells. This continued for a long time, long enough to ruin the eyesight of everyone who managed to stay among the living. Our insistent requests remained unanswered, or we were offered striated glass instead of opaque, which would be no less detrimental. After about 10 or 12 years, when we were all suffering from acute eye pain, we had clear glass installed, and we could finally see the moon and star-filled sky. When we were allowed to have homemade stools in the cells, some would read while standing on the stool by the window. The administration, unable to put itself in our shoes, viewed this as a violation of order, when in fact this means of reading was the only possibility for people whose vision had been wrecked. We read a great deal, without pitying our painful eyes. To do otherwise would have been impossible, because the choice we faced was either to save one's eyes, not read and go out of one's mind from depression, or go blind and save oneself from madness. For this reason we read a lot during exercise as well. To restore our eyes it was necessary, every day, all year round, to bathe them morning and night with boric lotion.

*

For 20 years we lived as if under a bell-jar. When being taken out for exercise, to the workshops and back to the cells, two non-commissioned officers accompanied the convict, while the superintendent or sergeant-major also observed from the side-lines. Moreover the gendarme in front turned his head first to the right, then to the left. Along the pens and allotments a gallery with an awning was constructed, from where those exercising were constantly watched by the duty non-com, who listened to our conversations. The first superintendent, who himself shut and opened the cell doors, kept constant vigil from this watch platform. In the cells and workshops we were spied upon via the little windows in the doors, which were closed from the outside by iron shutters. Along the cells lay matting, and the sentries walked along it in soft shoes in summer and felt boots in the winter. They sneaked up on the little windows every five or ten minutes. The sentries' manoeuvres, approaching silently and raising the shutter unexpectedly, were absurd, because they spied at regular intervals and it was clear that their precautions were in vain. A rustle, when a gendarme sneaks along the wall and brushes his back against it, interrupts one's activities and forces one to follow these antics and lie in wait for them. These antics outraged us as something pointless that we were involuntarily forced to attend to; pointless because the innumerable attempts to catch the convicts in the act of committing an imaginary crime didn't come to anything. Making each of us the object of multiple daily observations, they knew perfectly well in advance who, and at what time, would be doing what, because over the years we developed our habits and unchanging domestic customs. And meanwhile, in full knowledge of the uselessness, absurdity and impropriety of the sentry's observations, the convict, instead of calmly continuing his activities, stiffens in tense expectation, sometimes fearing to change the position of his body under these suspicious eyes. And when you are forced in this way to spend many years under the regime of the 'unsleeping eye', which gnaws at you like an indestructible worm, you ask yourself why they needed to employ such subtle torture on people who are either working or sick?.. In any case it would have been difficult to catch us red-handed committing a crime: we were always on guard when we needed to be and were able to draw our own conclusions from their countless observations, while our hearing had been so sharpened by the prison that from the habits of the sentry, via a multitude of small signs, we knew exactly who was on duty and what they were doing outside the door in the corridor. On the whole we acted and spoke straightforwardly and openly, resorting to conspiracy only rarely, and this confused them all the more. And not only did we speak openly, but to keep the curious at bay, for example, we deliberately raised conversations that the gendarmes were uncomfortable listening to, and that helped. It's entirely understandable that the damned bit of glass outraged many, and that the non-coms were driven from the door with fierce abuse. This helped for a while, but then the same story would begin again, as if we were dealing with an implacable element against which curses were useless. However, this incessant surveillance was completely ineffectual from the point of view of prevention and interruption: for instance, it did not prevent suicide, but was very subtle as a means of torture (Tikhonovich hanged himself,[39] Grachevskii burned himself alive, Sof'ia Ginsburg slit a vein, Pokhitonov was stopped in time and saved, not by the gendarmes, but by L. A. Volkenshtein).

For a long time we did not succeed in our attempts to get better ventilation in the cells, which were poisoned by the smell from the toilet bowls. The window ventilation panes tilted downwards and gave too little fresh air, because they were connected by iron bands to another pane in the external frame and could only be opened a small crack; and these ventilation panes at first were opened only twice a day, for a quarter of an hour. After about 10–12 years the windows were altered so that the upper part of the frame tilted down. Now we could ourselves open the panes at our own discretion, having fitted two cords for the purpose.

*

Applying the instructions – which mentioned fetters, straitjackets and firing squads – broadly, the administration hung these instructions in our cells, evidently because there was a reference to ignominious punishments in order to achieve submission and humility. It was too dangerous to apply this instruction because it would have led to attempts on the lives of the foot soldiers[40] and to wholesale suicide, but they nevertheless wanted to humiliate and insult us. One way or another the convicts removed these written or printed instructions. New copies were hung up, which were again removed, and in the end they disappeared. Besides these instructions the commandant undoubtedly also received secret guidelines to be employed with extensive powers in extreme cases, and such extremes were to be determined at his discretion. The best of the commandants said to us: 'Believe me, if I applied the instructions in all their severity, not a single one of you would be alive after six months!' The prison administration consisted of experienced, committed, decisive people, I even think incorruptible, and very likely serving as a vocation. How, one wonders, did this eternal, petty but cruel war with the prisoners affect their souls? The story of our commandants and superintendents during those 20 years answers the question: the first commandant, Pokroshinskii, went mad and died, the first superintendent, the infamous Herod Sokolov, was knocked out by a stroke after Grachevskii's death, the second commandant, Dobrodeev, went mad, the second superintendent, Fedorov, drank heavily, composed denunciations about everybody, and in the end wrote a denunciation against himself by accident and was dismissed, but with a large pension. The third commandant, Korenev, kind, and completely unsuitable for this place, was with us about four months, or something like that, and then transferred to Arkhangel'sk. The third superintendent, Dubrovin – not unintelligent, strict, but tactful and independent – and the fourth superintendent, the cultured officer Provorotov, arrived at the best time, but didn't stay long: the first left because he didn't want to serve in this place, and the second because, in his words, he feared going mad. The best commandant, Gangart – a reformer, a clever man, considerate and with great tact – rubbed along with us quite successfully. The most substantial reforms were introduced under him. Sipiagin found him weak, and he was transferred, and soon retired. The fifth superintendent, Guz', and the fifth commandant, Obukhov, were accommodating in Sipiagin's reign and, although under them the return to the old regime was already starting to make itself felt, they tried to alleviate it. But with the appointment of Plehve, they made an abrupt turn, opening a campaign against us with senseless, cruel and unprovoked violence against a sick comrade, for which the younger of them received a violent assault, and the older avoided the same retaliation only because he hid. Obukhov was pensioned off for letting the prison get out of hand; Guz' as well, but he later obtained some sort of job in the Caucasus. Is it not clear that this barbaric system of persecution was ruinous, or at least not harmless, to the jailers themselves? Not only was lifelong retribution carried out there for acts that were, in the view of the authorities, criminal, but they looked upon the convicts as hostages, on whom impotent rage was wreaked for their every misfortune.

*

Conversations with the authorities were very unpleasant, and for some simply unbearable, and even when we behaved peacefully their usual harsh way of dealing with us turned into a satirical or ironical one. But others, to the contrary, were, so to speak, in a constant state of single combat with the local administration and did not allow any incident to pass by without testing them with complaints and protests, or by seeking clarifications. But meanwhile we needed designated people who could get practical solutions from the prison administration on a daily basis. Establishing duty positions was in part motivated by the calculation that the elder's or librarian's voice in the name of the entire commune would have greater weight, and at the same time would save comrades from unpleasant and distressing conversations with their jailers. So much higher was the merit of those who always readily agreed to serve the community. One comrade, S. A. Ivanov, was elder almost perpetually (resting for six months a year). M. P. Popov willingly alternated with him, although the administration didn't like these representatives we chose.[41] The more complex duties of the elder were particularly arduous because our personal communications were so constrained, which made for a lot of extra work. Orders that under normal circumstances could have been made very quickly and easily in oral form, had to be tapped on a door, or passed via a note through the sergeant-major with inevitable allusions, omissions and circumlocutions, but paper communications created misunderstandings. So the police bureaucracy, through our contact with it, contaminated us with bureaucratism. It's understandable that these duties were accepted reluctantly, and we repeatedly raised the question of their abolition. However, these duties nevertheless facilitated the commune's practical relations and the administration treated our representative with great attention, knowing that the commune unanimously and vigorously supported him. Therefore these posts survived, only service ceased to be obligatory, and was subject to the consent of those elected.

Chapter III.

The gloomy clouds pressing on the prison did not even allow refreshing rain before the appearance of the god of thunder: quite the opposite.

A visit from the authorities brought us new anxiety. Wishing to show the visitor the prison in the full glare of its perfection, the local administration acted as if they were ashamed to appear too liberal in the eyes of the distinguished guest, or were afraid to offend his gaze with those little deviations from the instructions that among us were known as 'privileges'. Books were hidden: only one was left, with the most innocent title. Cutlery, penknives (this had all become available to us very slowly indeed), tools for working in the cells – it was all removed. Notably, the patched, torn, worn-out rags we wore (jackets, pants, underwear) were left, as if for show.

The dignitaries were very polite, with the exception of General Shebeko, who screamed – in the corridor, it's true, so that not many understood him – that we 'should be whipped'…, while General Orzhevskii behaved politely, but strangely. One of our comrades informed him that the opaque glass was ruining our eyesight and if it was not replaced with clear glass, we would go blind. To this Orzhevskii replied that replacing the glass depended entirely on his will, and the opaque glass was not replaced; true, he'd never promised to do so. At that point Staff Captain M. F. Lagovskii was in the prison, incarcerated administratively without trial, a situation that differed from ours in a way that was not in his favour, although we had been sentenced to hard labour, while he still remained an officer.[42] He was sent here for five years, and five years had already passed. Lagovskii asked Orzhevskii: 'why aren't I being released?' Orzhevskii replied: 'No-one's released from here, they're carried out!' Then after a few days Lagovskii was read a document from the Police Department about the continuation of his punishment for another five years. Of the high-ranking visitors, only the head of the Corps of Gendarmes visited us promptly and annually. The directors of the Police Department, Durnovo and Zvolianskii, visited twice each; Ministers Durnovo and Goremykin once;[43] then inspectors or investigators from the Police Department also came on various occasions for inquiries. We would unfailingly and almost without success request books, journals, newspapers, meetings with comrades, workshops, correspondence with families, and these privileges were prescribed to us after a year on a teaspoon.[44] What's more, we were always warned that privileges were granted for the time being, and could be taken away on discretion without any cause on our part.

Visitations to a convict from the higher authorities took place in the following manner: the superintendent opened the door; two gendarme non-commissioned officers entered and stood to the sides and back of the convict. They didn't take their eyes off him and were in a state of perfect readiness to seize him by the throat at the least suspicious movement. Then the superintendent and commandant came in and stood between the visitor and the prisoner. The local authorities met us with the same precautions in the first years. Later, when the era of 'trust' began, they would come into the cell either with the sergeant-major or with one sentry. For trivial declarations they just opened the window in the door. The doctor was never allowed to see either the sick or the healthy without the superintendent. Only Dr Bezrodnov insistently demanded that no gendarmes accompany him. The fortress chaplain visited us at first likewise with the superintendent, but the preacher soon stopped these visits because we didn't like each other. On his first visit to Iurkovskii, seeing several secular books on the table, he started flinging them aside in disdain: 'Why are you reading this? Read the Bible: there are too many books, you can't read them all!' To which followed the reply: 'There's a lot of bread as well: you can't eat all the bread, but without bread you'll die!'

*

The burning question of authorizing communication between us had to be resolved come what may. Walking in pairs didn't satisfy us even when we assembled not by assignment but according to our own choice; it was more like a marriage of convenience, a compulsory bond, and not an alliance made by inclination. Monologues and dialogues were pleasant for the time being; but the prison inhabitant's thirst for wider association is such a natural need that no persecution can eradicate it. Long and in vain did we ask for exercise in threes. The administration recognized all the strength of our arguments, but flatly refused to raise this impractical question, considering our desire utopian, and all further negotiations and attempts have shown that on this point, on the basis of unknown considerations, the Police Department wouldn't make any concessions. Long did we yearn for this, and in the end found a solution by a roundabout means. The fences separating the pens and allotments abutted onto the fortress walls, and the place where the fence met the wall was blocked by a vertical board. One comrade realized that the position of the board left a gap at this point. Research confirmed the hunch. These boards were pulled off with the help of shovels and stakes. Of course, there was a hue and cry. The boards were fastened back in place in our absence; but they were torn down again, and so we managed through a gap an inch wide to kind of see and talk to our neighbouring pairs. But such a game wasn't worth the candle: too little was visible, and it wasn't particularly convenient to speak. However, we had fallen on the right path, and our brains continued to work in this particular direction. Our prison social life at every step confirmed the sociological view of Tarde on the exceptional significance of the factors of invention and imitation.[45] The complicating factor in our society was always this: an innovator would appear who was not, however, always a leader: our innovators were often the more impetuous and impulsive people, and the imitators turned out to be the gifted ones, and that, perhaps, hinged on the fact that our innovators had purely practical characters. Efficient application was the job of the more gifted, who picked up and developed the innovator's raw idea.

And this wasn't 'unconscious and accidental imitation' (N. K. Mikhailovskii).[46] Then wholesale imitation began, in this case taking the form of joint action. In other situations, which will be mentioned below, imitation took on the character of 'psychic contagion' (Mikhailovskii) and could be explained, perhaps, by our psychic dislocation. But in this instance it was like this: the same thought preoccupied everyone. One day, God knows on what inspiration, one comrade rushed from the allotment to the workshop and returned with a drill bit and a hacksaw (a little hand saw). In a few words he explained to his partner what needed to be done. One turned the bit through the holes in the fence, while the other sawed the board between the holes with the hacksaw. He chose a moment when the sentry gendarme was beginning his walk round, and very quickly a window of approximately six inches in both directions was cut in the fence to the neighbouring allotment, and the neighbouring pairs shook hands. Only then did the gendarmes come running with the superintendent in front. At the same time the news that so-and-so had 'cut a window'[47] between two allotments spread everywhere, and at that moment, while an investigation and war of words were getting underway, others were running to the workshops and all down the line work was in full swing. By the time we had been separated in our cells, several such windows had already appeared. The next day these windows had been nailed shut, but removing the boards covering them was not remotely difficult. However, this *pro* and *contra* did not continue for long, and the windows were vanquished. In every prison, order is inevitably disrupted, but it also inevitably recovers. But what happened next could be called an earthquake that shook the foundations of the prison: the achievement of a new right. How can such flexibility by the authorities be explained? The commandant couldn't legitimize such a revolution through his own power. Evidently, he persistently interceded for us because he was faced with reasons that were all too valid. In the prison the epidemic of mortality had only just come to a halt; but no prophet could have predicted what would happen next. Tuberculosis and scurvy had stopped mowing us down, but now death assumed an even more terrible form – the form of madness. The mentally ill lived among us, turning our abode into hell. Looking at the insane, the healthy saw their own terrible fate at first hand, and fully appreciated how treacherous a gift was a life term in prison instead of a death sentence. In this situation voluntary death is the best way out. What measures could the authorities take to restore order? Remove our tools? Close the workshops? But we might, in the image and likeness of cavemen, act in primitive ways, without drill bits and hacksaws. We might, in the end, start jumping over the fence to see each other. Consequently it would have been necessary to lock us all in our cells and deprive us of exercise forever, in other words, to exterminate us. But this the authorities did not dare to do, so they offered us a compromise: we were asked to make moveable shutters from the boards, so that these square holes did not gape open in our absence, and asked not to use the windows during high-ranking visits.

The other side of our activity, that is, our occupations, recreation and crazes, also developed in a peculiar way. It couldn't be otherwise, because our life proceeded under such unusual circumstances. These particular cases more obviously speak of 'unconscious imitation', which is explained partly by the poverty and dullness of our existence, partly by our shattered nerves. Perhaps a chance circumstance or a particular mood led an innovator to their enterprise, but he only had to take the first step or show an example for a wholesale craze to begin, and such crazes sometimes continued for a very long time, and then would be unexpectedly swapped for a new craze, to which we would abandon ourselves with no less passion.

An outside observer wouldn't have predicted what form our new craze would take. But it would be all the more apparent to them from the sidelines that the fervour with which people abandoned themselves to the latest occupation or craze was a contrived fervour, artificial, that these people were deceiving themselves in order to forget, or to supplement their existence somehow. Sooner or later our beloved occupation would cool off. But that being said, an interesting choice arose. Some deserted it definitively, while others remained with these occupations to the end, because they had responded to their real, rather than fictitious, inclinations, that is, they had discovered their favourite occupation.

The chess epidemic overcame us at the deadest time, when there were no decent books, the workshops and allotments were just being contemplated, and walks were short. Before then no-one except Butsinskii[48] and Shebalin knew this game or was at all interested in it. Then Butsinskii and Shebalin explained the rules of the game to their neighbours through the walls, and suddenly everywhere chess tournaments were starting up. The difficulty of learning through the wall was serious, of course, but this shouldn't come as a surprise; even the very smallest problems in prison are not easily resolved. And perhaps the persistent energy needed to achieve any aim whatsoever revived us and saved us from death. M. P. Shebalin, a mathematician and an excellent teacher, gave his neighbour, the worker K. F. Martynov, a course on geometry via the ventilation pane in the window, and he clung to the wall by the window like a swift, holding onto the sharply angled windowsill, and drawing diagrams with his fingers. We sculpted chess pieces out of bread, drew boards on the tables or on paper, and round the prison echoed taps such as e2-e4, b1-c3, and so on. When the workshops were opened, everyone had finely turned figures and chessboards, and when we began to get the 'Literary Appendix' to *The Grainfield* for bookbinding,[49] we started solving chess problems, following the games of famous players, and wrote out a guide to playing chess. Then, gradually this game lost its fascination for the majority. But two comrades became inveterate players and probably competed until their release. When I left, they had played more than 10,000 games with each other.

However, our chess obsession left enough scope for other crazes, for example the poetry-writing craze. If I'm not mistaken, the first poems were published by Iurii Bogdanovich, and then every day brought a new poem and a new poet, until the whole prison turned into a Parnassus, which also, under sufferance, overcame the author of these notes, who not only had not the slightest capacity for poetic creation, but even for versification. One day, quite to my surprise, a poem appeared with my signature. It emerged that my neighbour G. A. Lopatin wrote counterfeit poetry, like Chatterton.[50] Lyric poetry flourished among us most of all, and of this kind, by common consent, we encountered several true poetic works by V. N. Figner, N. A. Morozov and P. S. Polivanov.[51] We wrote elegies, meditations, songs, epistles, epigrams, long poems and even long novels in verse. In the 1900s, when the clampdown began again, I seized some papers from M. F. Frolenko that he was intending to destroy, and found among them beautiful poetry, in both its musical form and the power of its simple and movingly expressed feelings. Frolenko, with his phenomenal modesty, had decided not to show these to his comrades. He remained true to himself in this case as well, doing silently more than others. That's how he always was: silent and working for ten. Poetry fever, however, did not last long. The audience moved on from poetry to prosaic creations, and there remained only one songbird, who could have been called our laureate, although he wrote in a special way. G. A. Lopatin responded to almost every event in our world, large and small, with an epigram or satire, so that through his poetic chronicle it was possible to reconstruct our entire life. Always brilliant and witty, his poetry reminded us somewhat of Heine's verses.[52] They were often very wicked, and the scourge of his satire lashed both friend and foe mercilessly. Our prosaic writings were very varied. In this we found a rational and popular activity that met an urgent need for meaningful work, the exchange of ideas and the free expression of our convictions. Each of the prisoners resolved to keep a journal, but unfortunately this was impossible, because we were carefully searched until around '96, and even after that they'd poke around in our papers, and we didn't want to pour out our souls before the eyes of our persecutors. Journals would have shown a vivid picture of our tragic life, in which so many characters perished, or at least would have given us photographic snapshots of this life. The present notes are only a pale outline, devoid of brightness, vividness and pathos. But if each of those who is freed writes their own notes about the prison, then our collective work will, perhaps, provide something significant.[53]

From the very beginning we worked on translations, both for practice and so that comrades who didn't read foreign languages could become acquainted with interesting books or articles. By the end almost all of us could read fluently in two or three foreign languages, and beyond that some studied others; for example, Vera Figner studied Italian; Polivanov – Italian, Spanish and Polish; and Lopatin – Latin and Greek. Vera Nikolaevna did very good translations into beautiful Russian from German and English. She produced an excellent translation of the most difficult East-India stories by Kipling.[54] Her final work in prison was a translation of Kipling's novel *Kim*. Maudsley's *Body and Will* was translated twice, by Pokhitonov and Shebalin, and besides that the book was translated into an abridged version. Then three volumes of Macaulay's *History of England* were translated, the first volume of Thackeray's *Vanity Fair*,[55] and three of Shakespeare's dramatic chronicles: *Henry IV [Parts I and II]* and *Henry V*. We translated nothing more by these authors, as we received their complete collected works in Russian. Pankratov translated Taine's *Origins of Contemporary France* from French. Polivanov translated several verses by his favourite poet, Ackermann.[56] Subsequently interesting articles were translated from the journals *Review of Reviews* and *Times Weekly*.[57] Our original prosaic literature was quite wide-ranging: several novels were written. In an unfinished novel

Iurkovskii depicted vivid, fascinating scenes of the lives of revolutionaries;[58] his story of escape from Kara hard labour prison was very interesting. Novels from the world of factories by another very observant author authentically portrayed the types and features of working life. Undoubtedly talented, although not very prolific, in my opinion, were V. N. Figner, Polivanov (the story 'It Seems to be Over') and S. A. Ivanov. V. N. Figner wrote charming folktales and poetic reminiscences of her early life. S. A. Ivanov depicted in a very gifted way the life of political exiles in Western Siberia and northern Russia, and the escape and ordeals of an exile – before he found solace and refuge in an illegal circle – were described with considerable humour. I won't write about other authors' literary works, because I'm speaking of what I think is outstanding and most characteristic. I will mention only N. A. Morozov's witty fantasies, written to promote certain concepts from the natural sciences. In their wit and clarity they resembled those pages from Dühring,[59] where he speaks of the absolute difference between the infinitely large and the infinite.[60] Besides this we wrote provocative, boisterous pamphlets about representative government, minority and majority rights, and proportional representation. Abstracts, monographs and treatises were written on the commune, capitalism, Populism and Marxism. Here the major dispute was between N. P. Starodovrskii on one side and J. D. Lukaszewicz on the other. Almost everyone made copies, extracts and compilations from books, while Morozov and Lukaszewicz wrote extensive research, the former on the 'structure of matter', while the latter created a whole philosophical system. By philosophy he understood not a theory of science itself, not a theory of cognitive knowledge, but a general body of individual scientific deductions, that is, an encyclopaedia of knowledge. The study of absolute elements served as an introduction to his system. This was followed by an exposition of data and deductions in physics, chemistry, mineralogy, geology, biology, psychology – as a division of biology – sociology, and his concluding observations. The sociology and concluding observations remained unfinished. His psychological ideas were interesting. Strongly rejecting psychological parallelism, he spoke, however, of the functional relations between the phenomena of consciousness and what lay outside them. He called the phenomena of consciousness 'psychic energy', which appears in organized bodies as a new form of transformed physical energy. Moreover the transformation of one form into another, of course, occurs on the basis of equivalence. He did not recognize the explanation and objections to such theories by Paulsen and Wundt, and considered them metaphysicians.[61] I listened to Lukaszewicz's lectures: he was a brilliant speaker with huge knowledge and a gift for beautiful, clear and precise presentation. His lectures (that is, only on psychology, the theory of cognitive knowledge, and sociology) inspired great controversy. Morozov's multi-volume study *On the Structure of Matter* was not entirely accessible to non-specialists: there was too much mathematics in it. Knowing his ability to popularize the most complex questions, we ignoramuses asked him to present his books in a more accessible form for us, and he skilfully coped with that difficult task. The fate of his work was as follows: he asked one of the high ranking visitors to pass on his work to Professor Mendeleev for scrutiny.[62] Permission for a long time was not granted, but finally, after repeated requests, he was allowed to send his work for review not to Mendeleev, but to Professor Konovalov.[63] Konovalov returned the manuscript with an extremely flattering review. He acknowledged the author's great erudition and wit, but found that Morozov's hypotheses did not always allow for experimental verification, given the present state of knowledge. After this Morozov asked for his book to be sent to his mother for printing, but this was flatly refused.

Journals, or rather, periodically produced collections of various articles, did not take root among us. The majority participated in the first collection, *Vinaigrette*, with illustrations and caricatures provided by Lukaszewicz. Lopatin composed a monthly chronicle. Another, smaller group turned out the journal *The Dawn*, under Lagovskii's editorship. *Vinaigrette* and *The Dawn* soon entered into a bitter polemic. A seasoned and poisonous polemicist for *Vinaigrette* plagued his opponents too much with his sarcasm, as did another contributor with his wicked caricatures. Combative people on the opposing side responded sharply. Some contributors to *Vinaigrette*, who considered the situation undesirable, left the editorial board and started to put out a third journal, *The Cobweb* – a collection free of polemics. Soon all three ceased to exist.

*

Alongside our poetry and writing activity, many developed a passion for taming birds, at first pigeons and sparrows, then swallows and even blue tits. This passion really emerged from the wind, or from the yard. Polivanov first fed a bird in the yard; he then decided to lure them through the window into his cell, and succeeded, although pigeons were more trusting than sparrows. In the cells above the doors there were two airholes, for some reason called ventilators. Pigeons began to breed in them. The ancestor of this vast flock was the popular favourite 'Heat', who died at a great age soon after Polivanov's departure. Watching

Polivanov, others began to copy him, but soon it became overwhelming. Uninvited pigeons flew in through all the open ventilation panes, treating the cells like home. Nets had to be placed in front of the windows. Thus ended this diversion. Only Polivanov bred pigeons until his departure, and one other comrade used to pick up young swallows ejected from the nests during storms and feed them insects until their departure in the autumn.

*

Our love of flowers was somehow uneven, spasmodic: first it would vanish, then return. The eyes, jaded by the gloomy background of our life, with grey overcoats and blue uniforms passing by, found repose in our bright and fragrant flower beds. Everyone had flower beds. There were roses, sweet peas, lily of the valley, lilac, diaphanous jasmine, forget-me-nots and many annual and perennial plants. We liked night phlox, and because it smelled so sweet at night, we planted it in pots and took it to our cells with us in the evenings. Our real florists were S. A. Ivanov and especially J. D. Lukaszewicz. S. A. Ivanov's flower beds were always beautiful: when some flowers faded, others came into bloom – violets, superlative gillyflowers, fragrant verbena, beautiful zinnia and lush, fragrant peonies, and then perennial phlox, luxurious asters, delphiniums, gladioli and Maltese Cross campions. Lukaszewicz turned his entire allotment into a flower garden. He planted bulbs and greenhouse plants, for which he built two hothouses. In addition to hyacinths, wallflowers, narcissus, lilies, tulips and irises, he had begonias, azaleas, Chinese roses, gloxinia, pelargoniums and many rare flowers. We had so many flowers that on our festive days the entire pen where V. N. Figner and L. A. Volkenshtein exercised was filled with wreathes, garlands and bouquets. Polivanov had an original, colourful flowerbed: he sowed it thickly with only double-petalled poppies. Each allotment and pen had arbours, up which grew hops, or morning glory or Ipomoea.

*

The allotment enterprise was not only established, but constantly improved, in part because we had two experienced leaders: the former Peter and Paul men M. F. Frolenko and M. P. Popov,[64] who tended the gardens with great passion; in part because horticulture, when taken seriously, demands communal work; and also because it brought us visible benefits, improving our diet and introducing the sort of greens needed by those suffering from scurvy. When cold frames were set up for us, preparatory work in the workshops even began in winter: casing and sub-casing, and screens for covering the cold frames, were made anew or repaired, strawboards were woven. In the autumn we planted young berry bushes and dug up the old ones, and planted fruit trees, for which we dug deep holes. Earth from the beds was dumped in a single heap and sifted, for which we made several filtering pans. On the site of former seed beds we dug deep pits, sometimes to a depth of 1½ yards, down to the subsoil, and carried away rocks and flagstones on a stretcher; then we brought humus from the greenhouses and mixed it in with the allotment soil. In early spring we dragged manure on stretchers to the greenhouses and pits for our future flower beds. Such work made you sweat, and it was necessary to change your shirt on returning to your cell. Some had a second shirt, but others didn't, so instead of damp shirts had to put on their canvas summer jackets. When lots of cold frames appeared, we had to help the gardeners take down the casing and cover the frames, and water the plants as well. The allotments gave us sufficient quantities of all kinds of vegetables. We baked swede and kohlrabi, or boiled and ate them with vegetable oil. Radishes, onions and lettuce we ate all summer. There were enough onions, garlic and cucumbers to last us to the new year in the years we harvested them. We salted cucumbers. In winter we ate radishes grated with vegetable oil. Leeks were stuffed for our harvest festival. Everyone got cauliflower about four times in the summer. We pickled beetroot. We dried green dill in the sun and stored it as a powder. In successful years the cold frames gave us many tomatoes, so that two or three times a week comrades would take turns in the workshop kitchen to cook a sauce of tomatoes, vegetable oil and paprika. This sauce was added to cabbage soup and porridge. We also grew a few potatoes and heads of cabbage. S. A. Ivanov and M. P. Popov also grew two or three melons and two or three pumpkins. S. A. Ivanov tried to grow Japanese cucumbers, physalis, Aldan (Iakutsk) grapes,[65] mushrooms and corn. He and Frolenko fed the entire fraternity with excellent strawberries (Laxton, Koch).[66] Raspberries and currants were abundant, but there were few gooseberries. The apple trees for a long time gave us nothing. Later, even in the best years the wind would damage the blossom and bring down the fruit; sometimes the Borovinka apples would ripen enough to eat; the Antonovka and Aport apples and others didn't ripen, and we ate them baked or in tarts.[67]

After Grachevskii's death,[68] the kerosene lamps illuminating the cells were inserted into a ring, and something like a muzzle was placed on top of them, which the sergeant-major locked; the lamps were shackled. On the glass of the lamps we placed a light trivet made of tin, on which it was possible to place an enamelled plate or even small enamelled teapot. That's how we made cranberry jam and sweets from milk and sugar. Under Colonel Gangart three small kerosene stoves were purchased for the shoemaking, carpentry and bookbinding workshops, for making glue, preparing flour paste and so on. We were not forbidden to take these kerosene stoves to our cells when necessary. We made ourselves tin griddles, moulds and ovens. Our oven was the size and shape of a *garnets*. The oven was positioned on the kerosene lamp, and in it was placed a mould filled with a paste of whisked egg whites and yolks with sugar. All this was covered with a lid, and in 15 minutes a small cake was ready. Several of these cakes, one placed on top of the other, and interlaid with cranberry jam, were sent to name day celebrants.[69] Having received such offerings from all sides, they would divide them up and share them out, so that everyone participated equally in the feast. That's how pastry and confectionary art was born, but it gained much wider development later, when a kitchen with a stove and real oven was opened for us in the workshops in the old prison. Jam from our berries was cooked on the stove in an enamel pot. In the oven were baked various large cakes, pastries, gingerbread, pies, sweet buns and simple rolls, soft and hard rolls, and sweet Easter bread. At Shrovetide we made pancakes. S. A. Ivanov and P. L. Antonov were the real pastry chefs and bakers. We gathered together the necessary ingredients for baking thus: flour was often replaced with crushed white breadcrumbs; milk was left over from lunch; we were given oil for porridge and herrings and it could be saved up, while a couple of raw eggs were given out, if desired, in exchange for dinner. Cinnamon, cloves, almonds, cocoa and vanilla could all be obtained instead of tea.

Chapter IV.

Essentially we didn't need flowers, birds, chess, cakes or allotments. We needed freedom. We were fighting for human dignity that had been trampled underfoot, for a legitimate life, for natural rights. Of course the allotments were useful to us, but they were no less useful to our administration. The authorities turned them into eye-catching stages to exhibit us for inspection. The grandees who visited the prison were shown our flowers, cold frames, carpentry, museum, when it was organized. Visitors were delighted and thanked the commandant. They wanted to isolate us, so that young Russia would forget our names; they wanted our silent removal from the scene. But we had been removed from life, and removed with scandalous speed and publicity. These people, who believed themselves to be mind-readers, didn't know prisoner psychology at all. At first they wanted to break us: but we could only be killed, not conquered. Then they thought of bringing us to obedience and submission through kindness, that is, they thought they could buy our souls with a 20 kopek piece. The devil himself valued the human soul incomparably higher; he paid for it with omnipotence. When the decision had already been made to reform the prison regime, the best and most reasonable commandant said that, 'alleviating our situation had to be done with great care, because if a finger was stretched out to us, we'd walk all over them!' This effectively revealed the general tendency of our internal politics: one hand promotes, while the other abolishes. And in fact, every new commander considered it his duty to invent some new constraint. Even in the liberal period we were deprived of half a cubic fathom of air in our cells: the corners of the cells nearest the door were filled in so that the small, four-cornered cells became six-cornered. From the commandant's explanations, it turned out that this had been done for our benefit: 'Don't you see what's going on? When you're in those corners the sentries lose sight of you, and they worry, get nervous and aggravate you!' In that case, so the sentries don't get nervous, the toilets should be moved to the centre of the cells, so that wherever you go, the toilet's right there. As they were unable or unwilling to make any major mitigation to our situation, a truly hellish system was adopted: we would be given a privilege, then restrictions would begin, the privilege would be removed, and then bestowed upon us again after some religious fast or other, as if it were a new privilege. In this way a single privilege multiplied like a magic ruble,[70] while we had to suffer the torments of a Tantalus and aggravation that drove us to fury. 'Don't you see', said one superintendent, 'we want to bring our system to ultimate perfection!' Therefore, they were acting not accidentally, but by calculation. For that reason, when they gave privileges, the authorities didn't foresee the consequences that necessarily followed them. These consequences were closely linked with the privileges themselves, but for the authorities they were, apparently, an unexpected surprise which had to be acknowledged or ignored.

Non-recognition deprived privileges of any meaning or significance, turning them into empty noise. As a result, recognition of all the consequences of privileges was inevitable. But the authorities dragged it out tediously, as if to tease us, which led to the idea that they were deceiving us, mocking us, that they wanted to drive us mad with trivial things. And at the same time they assured us that these privileges horribly complicated the work of surveillance and the whole service of the supervisors,[71] that they were run off their feet, that they had to plead for an increase in the team of supervisors – all of this was unjustified because the team of supervisors remained exactly the same, while our number had been cut by 50 per cent, so the gendarmes' work had become easier. Shortly I will show how many guards there were for each of us, but first I'll give some explanations of what I wrote above. We were allowed to use the three kerosene stoves for making glue and paste in our cells because some things were made and glued together in our cells. The kerosene stoves were also allowed in the bookbinding and other workshops in the living-quarters prison, where there wasn't a kitchen. This led to the confectionery and cake production, a complication the authorities hadn't counted on. In the old prison there were ten cells and a kitchen with a stove. Glue was heated up in the kitchen. One cell was occupied by the non-commissioned officer in charge of the workshops, another was too damp, and we made it into a pantry for our vegetables for the winter, and our pickles, conserves and so on. Of eight workshops, two cells, nos. 1 and 10, looked out onto the yard with the hothouses and flowerbeds, and the sun often peeped in there, so we allocated these workshops to V. N. Figner and L. A. Volkenshtein. In the remaining six workshops, which faced the other direction, where the sun never fell (the windows opened onto the yard where Ioann Antonovich's prison was located), there were five carpentry workshops and one for turning. As there were more carpenters than there were workshops, each carpentry workshop in the old prison had to have two occupants. Each of them made his own workbench. The cells were very small and it was difficult to turn around. That meant that many items necessary for the work had to be kept outside the cell, not to mention that the wood for our work could only be piled up in the corridor outside the workshops. That was where the grindstone for sharpening axes, cutting tools and chisels was also located. The round timbers for turning were also impossible to keep in the work cell, while the trestles for the large jig-saws also stood outside the prison in the yard. As soon as work began (from ten to three o'clock), the duty officer constantly had to open up the cells: one person needed to choose a board and saw off a piece of it; another to pick a round log and saw it into pieces on the trestle; a third needed glue or a vice for gluing boards together (the vice was near the kitchen); a fourth to sharpen an axe or another tool, and so on. And this merry-go-round was performed incessantly for five hours. Such a regime was really inconvenient for the gendarmes, and it ended with us no longer being locked in the workshops, leaving everyone to go where they needed for their work. And the following regime was established: the officer and sentries watched only so that no more than two people were in the corridor at the same time, two in the kitchen, and two in the yard, and also that our ladies did not meet anyone in the corridor, yard or kitchen. But then the windows to the ladies' workshop were always open and next to them, on the invitation of V. N. Figner and L. A. Volkenshtein, two men would stand, chatting, drinking tea or reading. In 1895, the prison itself where the workshops were located stopped being locked up, and much wider communication was established: in the corridor, kitchen and workshops we gathered endlessly, and only when the commandant visited were we asked to disperse to our cells. With this it became much easier for the sentries; they ceased tormenting themselves with unnecessary supervision.

How untenable the avowals of the administration were about privileges increasing the work of the supervisors, can be seen from the following calculation, not to mention the logical absurdity of such an assertion, because privileges meant freedom from supervision. We were supervised by the commandant, his two senior assistants (one of whom was the superintendent), a junior assistant or manager of the workshops and kitchens, the head of the combat attachment and his assistants – in total, two staff officers, four company officers, 30 non-commissioned officers with a sergeant-major and a kitchen supervisor, a combat attachment of 75 enlisted soldiers with several non-commissioned officers and 30 non-combat troops. This made 105 enlisted soldiers – that is, each of us required five enlisted soldiers and half a non-commissioned officer, with one officer for every three prisoners. This level of supervision cost the state 80,000 rubles per year. In 1904, when only 12 people remained, the upkeep for each of them was 6,666 rubles a year. Of this, very little was spent on the prisoners themselves, of course. When there were 20 of us, our subsistence cost 1,656 rubles; tea 212 rubles; around 200 rubles for the workshops; then they began to give us 140 rubles for books, and 10 rubles for Christmas and Easter for the whole prison. In total, 2,228 rubles for the entire fraternity. Very little of our portion was accounted for by heating: it was always cold. Illumination accounted for too much, because they never allowed the lamps to be extinguished at night.[72] Our clothes, underwear and shoes were very inexpensive.

What has been said about the privileges granted by the administration, and their expansion through our personal efforts, should not lead to conclusions about the stability of these improvements. In my opinion, in the final analysis everything depended on the trends that existed in the highest spheres of the Russian state. And it seemed to us that in the local administration's relations to us and our affairs, we could gain an idea, rather vague of course, of the present mood of the government. Depending on these moods and trends, the success of the development of our community in prison was like a devout Muslim's pilgrimage to Mecca: in happier times we took two steps forward and one step back, in less happy times two steps back and one step forward.

*

After the publication of the coronation amnesty, Minister Goremykin visited us. In terms of its consequences this was an important event for us. Until then Shlissel'burg prisoners had not only been exempt from all amnesties, but general administrative reductions in sentences for criminal and political hard labour convicts did not apply to them either. A year of our hard labour confinement consisted of the entire 12 months; there was no division into categories of unreformed and reformed convicts;[73] everyone was unreformed; transfer to unrestricted work teams was not allowed. We were repeatedly informed that Shlissel'burg Prison was a special prison, that it was outside the law, that those with indefinite sentences would remain incarcerated until their deaths, and that those with fixed terms would, at the end of their sentences – to the day – be sent to settlement in the most remote places. We asked the minister about permission to receive Russian and foreign journals and newspapers; about correspondence with our families and permission to receive books and money from our families; and about meetings with our comrades in the cells; about exercising in threes; about replacing the three top boards in the fences surrounding our allotments with wooden grilles, so that gardening and allotment work would actually be possible, and in order at least to be able to see our neighbours through the grilles; and about taking the mentally ill to psychiatric hospitals. Our requests were respected in part: we were permitted to exchange letters with our families (mother, father, brother sister, husband, wife, son, daughter) twice a year, but with correspondence subjected to the prison and departmental censorship, and an obligation to write nothing about the prison or its regime. Money, books, and other parcels from families were not permitted, but for books and journals we were given, I think, 140 or 130 rubles a year. We were not allowed to subscribe to Russian newspapers, but foreign newspapers even for the current year were allowed. We could receive Russian journals only for the previous year, foreign ones for the current year. Meetings in threes were forbidden. The grilles for the allotments were made, and, finally, they began to take the sick to psychiatric hospitals. Even before this, old copies of *The Grainfield* for '83, 84, '85 and, I think, '86 had been sent from the department. Our desire to know what was going on in Russia, what our motherland was going through now, was so great that we treasured every printed sheet of paper. We treasured every dirty scrap of newspaper blown into the yard by the wind. The gendarmes gave us their own books to bind, and we subjected them to careful scrutiny in the hope of finding, if not any direct indication of events, then at least some foundation for our inferences about events. But all our searches were in vain: they weren't those sorts of books, but we kept up this hopeless task with the obstinacy of maniacs. The word 'news' had very great significance for us. It was the first word we exchanged when we met each other in the morning.

In the absence of anything better, we eagerly seized and passed on our domestic news. This shows what an event for our personal and communal lives was the receipt of journals even for the previous year. Money was assigned, and we subscribed to *Russian Wealth, God's World*, [74] *Review of Reviews, Times Weekly, Revue des Revues*.[75] With what painful and joyful feeling did we experience those final days, those final hours of waiting! For reading Russian journals, we divided into two equal groups. Issues were given out for four days, and an order was set out for them to go from one to another within the group. After the last person had read issue no. 12, there would be an exchange of journals between the groups. Later, to give everyone the opportunity to quickly become acquainted with particularly interesting sections of the journal, this system was reformed, and books were given out not for four days, but sometimes for one or two days, and then each book was issued in the same sequence for a second time for another two days. Later we subscribed to *The Scientific Review*[76] and *The Proprietor*. Foreign journals were read without a time-limit, but we didn't linger. We liked Stead's illustrated journal *Review of Reviews*,[77] because for seven shillings it gave us a lot of interesting material, in abbreviated form of course, from English, American, Australian, French, German and Italian journals. Besides leading articles reviewing the events for the month, every issue included a biography of some prominent figure, for example, Gladstone, Havelock [sic] (a friend and student of Robert Owen, interviewed about the 100th anniversary of his life [sic]), Burns, Ruskin, Victoria, McKinley and so on,[78] and, at the end of the issue, a novel by some famous author in an abridged edition.

The *Times Weekly* included all the editorial and most important articles on the week's parliamentary hearings from the daily *Times*, and so on. One year, by mistake, we received *The Idler*, an illustrated monthly publication, in which the adventures of Conan Doyle's detective Sherlock

Holmes proved to be the most interesting thing, and the French nationalist newspaper *The Echo of Paris* – we were punished for being tempted by its cheapness. Morozov subscribed for himself to the Crookes' journal *The Chemical News*.[79]

Finally, with friendly pressure on commandant Obukhov we gained permission to receive Sheller's *Son of the Fatherland* for the current year and Molchanov's cheap newspaper *Petersburg*.[80] We received *Son of the Fatherland* for less than a year, but *Petersburg*, I think, for two years. But this victory brought us much grief. *Son of the Fatherland* was delivered to us in a very slipshod way: some issues were delayed, others arrived with bits cut out. In that very year *Son of the Fatherland* ceased publication.[81] The administration hastened to make use of this, and didn't allow us to subscribe to another newspaper. People repent of bad deeds, but our guardians repented of good ones: newspapers were forbidden, and forbidden 'for our own good': 'Newspapers excite you too much!' The Department irrevocably banned newspapers. And with the same beneficial aim they soon confiscated *The Proprietor* and Wol'f's *Book News*.[82] I think the publishers of *Book News* would be astonished to discover there are people who are excited by their catalogues.

Colonel Gangart gave us *Russian Thought*, and the *Historical Herald* for the previous year,[83] and *The Grainfield* with the supplement for the current year. The next commandant gave us only the *Herald of Foreign Literature*.[84] We returned all the journals that were bought from the prison administration fully bound or stitched and, although we were offered pay for this work, we refused it because we had a great deal of bookbinding work, and it would have turned it into an obligation. Each had to be bound as a year for 12 medium-sized books or stitched for 24 books. A large book, for example *The Grainfield*, was counted as two. After subscriptions for journals and newspapers, around 50 rubles a year was left for books; on top of that M. N. Trigoni[85] handed over for books 100 rubles that had been confiscated at the time of his arrest, and had been preserved by some miracle and sent to him by the department. Our doctor N. S. Bezrodnov who, unfortunately, wasn't with us long, did us a great service: he began to bring us new books and journals from the Salt Town museum collection:[86] *Russian Wealth*, *God's World*, the *Herald of Europe*, *Life*, *New Word*, *Revue de deux Mondes*.[87] As payment for examining the collections, we bound the museum's books and journals, and sent our own collections to the museum: very elegant organography work on glass plates (V. N. Figner, M. B. Novorusskii, J. D. Lukaszewicz, V. G. Ivanov) and herbariums, and we fulfilled other work for schools on request; for example, we traced and illuminated tables and diagrams in large scale from foreign statistical chronicles. Second copies of all of this were kept for our own museum. Apart from this we received two big orders from our administrators: making a fence of turned columns for a monument to the soldiers who fell in the storming of Shlissel'burg,[88] and making desks and blackboards for the school opened on the island for the children of the gendarmes. Money for this went towards the purchase of books. Thus by 1904 we had built up a sizeable library of 2,000-odd volumes. If we exclude the completely useless and unnecessary books from the original library, then the extensive section of belles-lettres, there still remained several hundred good books.

We greedily devoured books, especially journals, reading day and night. Some people absorbed 300 pages a day, and one cannot say that such reading was useless. We lagged a long way behind current life. In journalism we encountered new names, 'new words', new ideas, new framings of questions, new formulas, and at first we had to get to know these unfamiliar phenomena personally, without trusting our comrades' retelling. Therefore it was necessary to read everything right to the end, firstly as a 'rough draft,' in order to grasp the entire picture at once, and later dwell on the details that merited particular attention – that is, reading everything remarkable 'cleanly' a second time. We were all industrious. At first, when there were no decent books and when we were possessed by philological and allotment fever, one convict copied out Aleksandrov's dictionary for himself, and another a *Guide to Botany*.[89] Such industriousness, perhaps, can be explained by the emptiness and dullness of prison life. But the capacity for work of other comrades was more surprising because with it the beneficial, healing power of labour was manifested. S. A. Ivanov and N. A. Morozov were apparently fading and dying before our eyes, but never wallowed in their beds and, enduring their suffering on their feet and working, they recovered. For example S. A. Ivanov had haemorrhages, could barely breathe, but would run out early to the allotment, and there he would dig, drag barrows, do hard work, but work he was used to. From there he'd rush to the carpentry workshop, chop and plane wood; then he'd hurry to the kitchen and cook, pickle, or make pastries, which he'd send to his comrades for lunch. After lunch he'd already be in the cobbler's workshop making slippers for V. N. Figner or L. A. Volkenshtein. On evening walks he'd listen to lectures or take an active part in debates. And if in the midst of this maelstrom of activities that interested him one of his comrades called for his help, he'd abandon his own tasks and help them with the same enthusiasm. On top of all that he'd carry out community service as the elder or librarian, and find time to read and make wide-ranging abstracts and compilations, and write beautiful and original stories. Thus in his work he forgot all about himself and his ailments, and his ailments forgot all about him too. Exactly the same could be said of M. F. Frolenko, who arrived from the Alekseevskii Ravelin barely alive: only a miracle could save him, and that miracle was tireless work. Frolenko belonged to that most appealing type of eternal seekers of the truth, who even forget about themselves when they're being burned at the stake. The speeches of this man, who sought a pure and bright truth, but always had in front of him one injustice, were very touching. N. A. Morozov, likewise, was so absorbed in his ideas and scientific work that he had no time to think about his illness, and this saved him. And yet in prison hypochondria and the tendency to give too much space to introspection can easily develop.

*

The grilles were made, and the allotments began to get more light. But we needed meetings. The first, most extensive allotment had common fences on one side with pens nos. 5 and 6, and here three pairs could see each other; but as the fences were very high, to see each other through the grille a platform with steps was needed. Harmonious work was in full swing, and the administration hadn't managed to get a grip before covered meeting places sprung up everywhere and meetings began. The administration was apparently looking for a decent excuse to concede, and a decent excuse was at hand: we needed somewhere to shelter from the incessant summer rain. In the first allotment, where three pairs converged – and moreover, the fifth pen was where the ladies usually were – an auditorium and club were opened, and we gathered for meetings. It was there that Lukaszewicz gave his lectures for several years, our own and others' collections were displayed, reports were read, group readings of certain journals and books took place, debates were held on certain burning questions that were exercising Russia. This was where communal feasts were held on our festive days: some would leave, others would come to take their place, so that everyone was able to participate in the general merriment, or express their opinion at a meeting. Debates were held there with books in hand. These debates proceeded in a purely Russian way: we barely gave each other a fair hearing, all spoke at once, failed to clarify the matter in substance, resorted to refined, scholastic interpretations of trivial things, and brought too much heat and intolerance to our objections. However, objections and comments at lectures and reports were submitted with parliamentary correctness. The heat of our debates must be attributed to our painful irritability, rather than theoretical disagreement, while in practical matters we were always unanimous. Remember how our great forefathers disagreed for many weeks about Hegel's phenomenology (see *My Past and Thoughts*),[90] or because of different understandings of the mysterious process of the 'transformation and manifestation of the spirit'![91] And then it will become clear that a different understanding even of inconsequential questions can serve as a reason for quarrels among inhabitants behind bars. Our practical work pacified and united us; our quarrels, most likely, served as an indicator that the pressure exerted on us from outside was favourable. We argued and were able to make our peace, but as our circle was depopulated, we drew closer and more harmoniously together, and when only 13 of us remained, any quarrel was removed to the realm of legend. It is notable that at the first meetings through the grille we did not adjust the strength of our voices according to the distance separating the pairs: we all shouted as though we were talking across a river, and meanwhile the prison had sharpened our hearing. Later this gradually stopped.

With the assistance of N. S. Bezrodnov, we acquired an inexpensive microscope, and under the direction of Lukaszewicz made simple observations, while Morozov constructed a small chemistry laboratory, where he also gave lectures on chemistry.

*

All our privileges, in essence, consisted of allowing us to skim the cream from already skimmed and watered-down milk; thus, for example, we were allowed to eat just one part of our bread ration, and with the other, buy confectionery, milk, oil, flour, raisins, coffee, cocoa and so on. I took half a pound of black bread a day, and in that way I made monthly savings of one ruble 50 to one ruble 55 kopeks. I cannot say who gave the signal for our new, almost universal pastime: we took up distilling. Our workers and skilled craftsmen made several beakers with coiled condensers out of tin. Sugar syrup with raisins in a soup cup was placed next to the heater. When the fermentation reached a certain strength, the fermented liquid flowed into a beaker; the beaker was sealed and placed on a kerosene stove; and the coiled condenser was placed under the tap in a sink so that the water cooled the alcohol vapours. In winter we cooled it with snow, which we dragged in from the yard in a pillowcase. Then we distilled it a second time through powdered carbon, and obtained strong and pure vodka, but it was terribly expensive. From the vodka we made liqueurs by adding berry juice. It was remarkable that the sentries saw all this and kept quiet. Such connivance was incomprehensible. During the fermentation and distilling, the heavy smell of a tavern hung around the cells, but they didn't even bother taking a look. Besides, the finished vodka was stored in a cell, and they saw it in our absence. The commandant knew nothing about the still; Superintendent Fedorov was keeping quiet about it until the time was right, in order to undermine the commandant. Then, with the aim of unseating the commandant, he wrote a denunciation, not realizing that he was also denouncing himself. An inspector came. We managed to anticipate this, and everything was hidden: the inspector found only a lid for a beaker. The superintendent was dismissed, while we were asked to liquidate the still, and so there wouldn't be any temptation we were banned from buying raisins.

*

One comrade smoked cabbage leaves, but in the flowerbeds between other flowers we came across nicotiana. This was apparently the beginnings of our tobacco plantation. Someone had the idea of ordering tobacco seeds and a guide to cultivating and preparing tobacco. According to our written codex the list of books we wanted to buy was subject to strict, multi-level censorship. Ordering seeds for the flowerbeds and allotments was free of censorship. Thus we obtained and sowed Havana, Ohio, Gundi Virgin, a hardy variety, and Amersfoort, that is, Dutch shag. The first time round the harvest was good, especially the Virgin and shag. Havana didn't work, but the Virgin also had to be mixed with the shag to be smoked. In the second year the summer was dry and sunny. The harvest was big, and the preparation of tobacco more successful. The tobacco beds very much beautified the allotments and the administration admired them, not suspecting a thing. The sentries were perplexed when we lay out and folded the tobacco sheets into bundles in the cells, swathing piles of it in bedsheets and smocks, took apart and sorted the bundles, then, having strung the sheets on twine, hung them up in the workshops and allotments to dry. The elder obtained flints, craftsmen made steel strikers, and each person made tinder from old footcloths. Our mysterious manoeuvres became clear when we started smoking our own cigarettes and small cigars. The non-coms were overcome with delight at our fiery shag, and the higher administration wondered at our ingenuity. I think it was in the third year that Dr Bezrodnov persuaded us to stop smoking home-grown tobacco, declaring it harmful and poisonous to air quality, especially during the stage of fermenting in bundles, and he promised to make efforts to supply us with real tobacco, in view of the fact that scurvy had never been eradicated in the prison. Permission did indeed follow, and a small sum was assigned, and each smoker could receive one pound of tobacco for one ruble, cigarette papers and several boxes of matches. Then we liquidated tobacco cultivation.

*

In November 1896 the commandant read out a document to those concerned about the implementation of the coronation amnesty. Those with fixed-term sentences had them reduced by a third, and were to be transferred to settlements: L. A. Volkenshtein and Manucharov to Sakhalin, Shebalin and Martynov to Viliuisk, Surovtsev and Janavičius to Srednekolymsk.[92] Pankratov had his sentence reduced, but had to remain in the prison until 1898. Three prisoners with indefinite sentences – Polivanov, Starodvorskii and I – were transferred to the 20-year category. The amnesty did not affect the rest.

Chapter V.

Dear comrades were leaving. Our life became even poorer, and we sank deeper into our books. A time of specialization in various scientific fields began. In this period lectures flourished. Besides Lukaszewicz's regular courses and Morozov's readings there were also occasional lectures. One comrade, at the request of V. N. Figner, whose word was law for him, as it was for many others – otherwise he would never have dared take the floor as a lecturer – read, or, to be more precise, delivered in his own words Riehl's excellent work *The Theory of Science and Metaphysics*,[93] which we had in an impossible translation, overflowing with wild terminology.[94] Everyone was interested in sociology. The most popular authors were Giddings, Arnoldi and Stemler;[95] Engels and Kautsky had their proponents among us.[96] Alongside Russian society, we were interested in philosophy, or specifically epistemology. Popular authors were: Riehl, Avenarius, Høffding, Mach and Ostwald.[97] We read with great attention the books and articles of Mikhailovskii, Chernov, Struve, Bel'tov, Il'in, Tugan-Baranovskii, S. Bulgakov and Berdiaev.[98] Literary writers Korolenko, Chekhov, Gor'kii and Veresaev had particular significance for us.[99] Someone said that a writer is a prophet of a new age. We needed a prophet-accuser, to show us the way out of this barren, waterless, silent desert. A stream of fresh poetry, if it didn't quite intoxicate us, at least revived our hopes and refreshed our faith in the imminent future. The same could be said, in my opinion, about recent journalism. The books we subscribed to were exposed to inexplicable censorship, as if whimsy were guiding the censor's hand. The commandant explained to us: 'I know that no book will spoil you (read: 'a leopard can't change its spots'); but the department is guided by its own considerations…' The department allowed the second and third volumes of *Capital* to be read, but Ianzhul's *Free Trade* was forbidden,[100] Dostoevskii's works were deemed dangerous to the shattered nerves of the prisoners, but the insane, whose continued presence among us was incomparably more dangerous, were ignored, until they began to smash in the heads of the gendarmes.

*

At this point we began to breed rabbits. They multiplied too quickly and spoiled the allotments and shrubs, so we decided to sell them, but there were no buyers, and we didn't want to eat creatures we had reared ourselves, so we had to give them to the gendarmes.

Whenever a similar enthusiasm passed, we asked ourselves what new passion would appear in its place. Someone on this occasion offered a prize for the correct prediction, and no predictor was found, but a few days later a rooster and hen appeared in one pen, and poultry farming began. The hobby was so serious that in two pens we built little huts for the chickens. Our poultry farming brought us substantial benefits: we ate chickens and fresh eggs. Poultry farming was banned during the pogrom, of which more later.

In 1898 V. S. Pankratov was taken to Viliuisk; in 1901 M. N. Trigoni, having served his entire 20 years, was sent to Sakhalin; and in 1902 Polivanov was sent to Stepnoi Krai.[101] There remained 12 old prisoners and one newly arrived: P. V. Karpovich. Between 1887 and 1901 we did not gain any new comrades. We suspected nothing of the arrival and tragic death of Sof'ia Ginsburg. Much later a gendarme told us that she had spent several days in the old prison, and that on her request she was given sewing work, needles and scissors. That night she opened up an artery, and in the morning the sentries found her dead. Karpovich arrived in June, when our roses were in bloom, and we welcomed him with flowers and gifts, that is, we sent him everything he couldn't get from the gendarmes, but had to acquire gradually: a towel, handkerchiefs, a comb, a mirror, a chair, a coffee pot, jam, coffee, oil, eggs, cakes, paper, a pencil, a penknife. We made his acquaintance on that very day. It was impossible to tap with him: he didn't know our system, and indeed he wouldn't learn it later, but we went straight to the door of his cell and chatted with him for a minute or two. He brought us good news about the awakening of Russia. His first words were: 'In 3–4 years there will be a revolution in Russia and the Russian Bastille will fall!' For exercise he was assigned the furthest away, no. 1 pen, which was separated from the neighbouring no. 2 pen with a fence with no grille. We talked to him via the door leading to his pen.

It could be said that over the course of three months a free political newspaper appeared among us, which gave an exhaustive account of recent events. Karpovich, gifted with an extraordinary memory, communicated party programmes, resolutions of congresses, recapitulated the content of illegal publications and acquainted us with interesting literary works, such as Stepniak's novel *Andrei Kozhukhov*,[102] in abridged form. We, in turn, introduced him to our life and routines, and our past activities.

The administration began to limit our relations with him, whereupon one comrade jumped over the fence to see Karpovich. The next day, when we were gathered in the yard by the hothouses, Karpovich came to visit us by the same method. The commandant entered into negotiations. We demanded Karpovich be given meetings. The commandant swore it was outside his powers. Conversations by the doors continued. After three months Karpovich demanded to be given work in the carpentry workshop under the guidance of a comrade. We supported his demand. The administration tried to convince us that it was impossible to bank on this before a year was out. Karpovich started a hunger strike, while we stopped going out for exercise and to work. Karpovich struck for nine days. In the prison, impassioned representations to the administration became a daily occurrence, and in our impatience these could have turned at any moment into fisticuffs. A doctor was sent from Petersburg for diplomatic negotiations. Karpovich was informed that he would be allowed to work in the workshops shortly, if he gave up his hunger strike. He would make no compromises whatsoever, and declared that while he had been drinking water up till that point, from now, to accelerate the outcome, he wouldn't drink either. This went on for two more days. On the 11th day he was informed that his wish would be fulfilled immediately. In a short time they began to bring him out to us for exercise. The first meetings with him face to face in our club were a remarkable moment in prison life. He seemed to rejuvenate us, infected us with his enthusiasm, energy, inexhaustible liveliness and his firm convictions. One comrade rotated with another around him, and loud conversations, animated speeches and general exclamations never subsided.

Each of us had some sort of nickname. Discussions began about what to christen Karpovich. Someone suggested calling him 'The luck of a roaring camp!' (see Bret Harte's story of the same name).[103] That was very apposite, but it was a long name, so he was called 'Benjamin'. Karpovich was a very talented man: his hands were truly golden. In less than a year he became an excellent carpenter, a good bookbinder, sewed shoes for comrades, became a metalworker and a blacksmith, a kitchen gardener, a florist and a beautiful draughtsman. He sketched 25 or more large-scale botanical tables from small drawings taken from the *Universal Encyclopaedia*,[104] and from textbooks, elegantly decorating them in paint. For my departure he took two or three lessons from V. N. Figner and knitted me a thick woollen sweater. He just never learned to tap.

One thinker has said that everything that happens unexpectedly or comes from some unknown quarter, is dangerous. The essence of our imprisonment consisted in us being rendered deaf, blind and isolated, in order to paralyse the self-defence mechanism that united us. It is clear that unforeseen danger is the main element of prison life, and the inhabitant of a prison is as if at every moment dwelling on a volcano.

We imagined that our liberties had taken root at exactly the time when a thunderstorm was approaching that would carry them away. First they took away the old prison with the kitchen, which was so necessary to us. This was equivalent to the abolition of all eight workshops. They proposed transferring the workshops to the general prison, but this was unfeasible, even if there had been enough space, because noisy work in the residential prison would have agitated the sick and prevented the healthy prisoners resting and studying. Before our eyes the old prison was converted to house new convicts. Two cells, nos. 2 and 6, were hastily completed and heated daily. From this we correctly concluded that within days new prisoners would be brought in. At the same time we were also deprived of the large yard next to the old prison. Thus our cold frame facilities and flowerbeds were eliminated. Berry bushes, and 15 or 20 apple and pear trees that were only just coming into fruit, disappeared for us. We were deprived of the ice cellar we had set up in the yard, and lost the opportunity to use the circular saw, as there was nowhere to move the long shed needed for this saw. The forge had to be moved to one of the allotments. Then our correspondence with our families began to be limited. It was forbidden to write about our activities or our health, so there only remained the weather to write about. And finally, we were told that receiving Russian and foreign journals was forbidden, we would no longer be given the gendarmes' copies of *The Grainfield* for binding, or the only Russian newspaper we received,

The Proprietor. Even Wol'f's *Book News* and Gatstuk's *Calendar* were banned.[105] All this pointed to some important event in Russia. At that moment a fragment of newspaper was blown into our allotment by the wind, from which we learned about the death of Sipiagin. We were put on the alert. From the end cell on the upper floor, no. 4, part of the fortress yard was visible where the officers' annexe, administrative office, commandant's house, and fortress gates were located. From the gendarmes' yard, the route to our's and the old prison went through the guard house, which stood about 15 paces away, opposite the general prison. Only our dead were taken through the gates by the guard house, while firewood, sand, manure and bulky items were brought in. One day at dusk the tenant of no. 4 noticed unusual movement in the fortress yard. A mattress and pillow were being carried into the office. Then the commandant, officers and an armed company went through the fortress gates to the quay. The crowd soon returned, stopped for a minute near the office, and then dispersed to the different buildings. P. L. Antonov said that he saw a tall blonde man in the crowd – nothing else was visible, as it was getting dark. Later that evening the iron gates next to the guard house creaked, and soldiers carried several logs through to the old prison, behind which was located the courtyard (next to Ioann Antonovich's tower) where executions were carried out. At the dead of night a large crowd proceeded via the door of the guard house to the old prison. At dawn they went back in groups: the commandant with the officers, the priest, behind him a soldier with a folded robe under his arms, the doctor, the company. Then later in the day they carried back the logs, tools, and an empty bucket, which had obviously contained lime. The observations indicated that an execution had been carried out that morning. Later I learned that Balmashev had been executed. But how and when they had brought Sazonov (no. 2?) and Kachura (no. 6) to the prison, we didn't notice. We just realized there were newcomers when they began to take in covered dishes at lunch and dinner time.

Finally, in order to complete the return to the old order, Commandant Obukhov and Superintendent Guz', without any provocation on our part, committed violence against a sick comrade. It happened like this: in the auxiliary team that cleaned the corridors, swept wood shavings from the workshops, brought in lunch and boiling water and so on, there was one very helpful, good natured and talkative soldier. He couldn't tell us anything interesting, because he wasn't interested in what was important to us. M. R. Popov, outraged by the latest constraints to our correspondence, persuaded this soldier to drop a letter written by Popov to his mother into a post box in the town. In this way Popov hoped to avoid the cruel censorship. The soldier took up the case. The addresses of our families and our handwriting were known to the authorities, and Popov asked the soldier to write the address in his own hand. The soldier didn't know how to write, so he asked a colleague for help, and then dropped the letter in the post box fastened to the commandant's door. Popov never suspected of the existence of a post box in the fortress, and the solider out of naivety didn't guess that all fortress correspondence, even that coming from the officers, was examined by the commandant. The next day, Obukhov, assessing the letters to be sent to the Shlissel'burg post office, noticed a letter addressed to Popov's mother. The soldier who had written the address on the envelope was brought in for interrogation and implicated his colleague, who admitted everything. Obukhov announced to Popov that he was going to report his action. That same evening, Obukhov, Guz' and a crowd of guards suddenly burst into S. A. Ivanov's cell, knocked him to the ground, put a straitjacket on him, and gagged him. He had a hysterical fit, and muffled sounds and commotion were heard. A hellish uproar was raised in the prison: expletives rang out, and demands for explanation. We protested against Obukhov's and Guz''s pacifying statements with offensive words and demands for them to open the cells and show us S. A. Ivanov. One comrade was taken to see Ivanov, who was no longer wearing the straitjacket. This violence against a sick person was, in Obukhov's explanation, a perfectly plausible punishment for tapping with a neighbour. Such a severe measure had never been taken before for tapping, and even according to the instructions, the punishment for minor instances of tapping should have been applied somewhat gradually. But the commandant needed the first excuse that turned up in order to inaugurate the new era. The next day V. N. Figner demanded to see the commandant. He didn't come, but sent Guz'. With the words, 'we'll answer violence with violence', Vera Nikolaevna tore off his epaulets and shouted to us about this. A quarter of an hour later the sergeant-major came to her and politely asked, 'Excuse me, please, perhaps I'm disturbing you? But the superintendent asks whether you have any black thread for sewing on epaulets. We only have white!..' V. N. asked us, out of respect and love for her, not to avenge the punishment that awaited her, approach her door or question her and, if she was taken away to be isolated, to treat this with all possible restraint. The best, most beloved, most selfless comrade, whose moral influence was so salutary for those who were suffering, had fallen into the claws of an evil enemy – this was a defeat. And meanwhile, having such a hostage in their hands and not expecting any resistance from our side, the authorities continued to strip away our liberties: we were told that the grilles on the fence would be covered with boards, and ordered to hand over all our books, allegedly for inspection. The moment was well chosen: at this point, when they had taken such a valuable hostage, we didn't care about the grilles. We fulfilled V. N.'s wishes and didn't disturb her, but each of us decided, without any agreement with the others, to answer violence against Vera Nikolaevna with violence to the bitter end. And this was expressed by one comrade to the commandant. After such a statement, a doctor sent from Petersburg to replace N. E. Bezrodnov pending the appointment of a resident doctor, appealed to us with soothing reassurances that 'Everything would end well!' A few days later an official from the Police Department came to investigate, and a resolution quickly emerged: Popov, for his illicit correspondence, was deprived of exercise for two weeks, I think, while V. N., I think, was deprived of correspondence with her family and left, if I'm not mistaken, without exercise for a month.

From this business it was clear who was in charge: thus Plehve returned us to our primordial condition. Soon von Wahl[106] appeared to complete our pogrom, removing the kerosene stoves on which we brewed our coffee. Now, like Sisyphus, we had to start hauling the stone that had rolled back once more. Of all our privileges, we managed to retain our books, while the grille between the 5th and 6th allotments was left there temporarily (V. N. was the 6th allotment-keeper), so that we could continue meetings with V. N. there, and our lectures. We were allowed to receive just one English monthly natural science journal, *The Knowledge*. Approximately six months after the events described, V. N. received notification about her transfer to the category of 20-year prisoners.

In this lonely period we absorbed a tremendous quantity of novels. We bought, I think, 12 volumes of Dicks' editions in folio;[107] for 10 rubles that gave us 60 complete novels: Thackeray, Dickens, Smollett, Fielding, Cooper, Sterne, Thomas Hood, Eugene Sue, Dumas father and son and, finally, Paul de Kock.[108] Interestingly, we had to read French authors in English, and Walter Scott, for example, in French.[109]

In 1904, from various elusive signals in relation to our requests, the readiness to listen to us and relative consideration we were shown, we became convinced that a new trend had begun. Then we requested subscriptions to Russian and foreign journals for the previous year. The new commandant, Colonel Iakovlev, replied: 'well, times are changing; perhaps I'll give you Russian journals; but I'll just tell you in advance: "I'll crop them!"' And we really were given *Russian Wealth* and *God's World* for 1903, without the chronicle, politics and science sections, and with no bibliography; not even the literary sections were spared: the middle of Veresaev's story 'At the Turning Point' was ripped out, we weren't given

Gor'kii at all, upon which the commandant explained: 'well, you see, Mr Gor'kii isn't liked in the department!'

*

Finally, the day of our departure arrived. We said goodbye: our comrades rejoiced at our release. For those leaving, it felt difficult and shameful to abandon them… V. G. Ivanov and I were transferred to a house of preliminary detention, and V. N. Figner to Petropavlovka.[110] We spent the first nights without sleep. We were tormented by hallucinations: we would barely close our eyes when the animated faces of our abandoned comrades would start to move into our field of vision, we'd hear their voices merge into a single noise, and the noise would grow into a roar, like a swell of surf. Sodium bromide calmed our agitated nerves and drove away the hallucinations.

The first news we received in liberation was very sad: we learned about the death of many comrades who had left the fortress earlier: Janavičius, Martynov, Polivanov had all died by suicide. Trigoni had gone blind! And I soon myself realized how difficult it is to endure such a beneficent change as liberty, after long captivity. At first I was stunned, I feared wide expanses, open spaces, street traffic and noise. I avoided people because I felt like a barbarian, I avoided large gatherings because I had not yet lost 'the taste for solitude', as V. N. Figner said. Then I realized that I was not reacting correctly to things I perceived. Major events and facts did not surprise me, but trivial things took on a value disproportional to their importance. This indicated a breakdown in my ability to rationalize. Such a mass of living, fresh, clear impressions swept over me so quickly that my brain, overwhelmed by all of this, could not make the correct connections, and this abnormality passed only very slowly. I don't know how my highly gifted comrades, endowed with incredible strength, coped with this abrupt change from painful captivity to free life. Their more perfect organisms and nerves differed also in their greater resilience, but sublime development and talents do not save a person from scurvy or other illnesses acquired in prison. Besides, exceptional people also occupy exceptional positions in life, with all the ensuing consequences. For example, G. A. Lopatin, a brilliantly passionate man, sociable to the highest degree, always felt himself alone – and that is indeed the sad privilege of high development. Or V. N. Figner, whose soul, the soul of an apostle chained to a rock, suffered cruelly. A wide arena was not open to her but, suppressing her own suffering, she forgot herself and took on the pain of others, generously taking a share of others' heavy burden and carrying it herself. Energetic, courageous, selfless, she was always out in front; and it is not surprising that in large and small matters all eyes turned to her, in anticipation of a word, a sign or example from her. I think that such an intensive and generous life will never be impoverished due to its wealth, its depth and its fullness.

The last words in the diary of the communard Mayer (I think), when escaping from Cayenne, were: 'in any case I leave for liberty more of a person and less of a mollusc.'[111] I can repeat that only with the proviso: yes! After 22 years of captivity we remained people, but we came out of captivity damaged people.

M. Ashenbrenner.

Notes

1 The invasion of Russia by Napoleon's *Grande armée*.
2 Sergei Mikhailovich Solov'ev: see Volkenshtein, note 81; Nikolai Savvich Tikhonravov (1832–93), philologist and historian of Russian literature.
3 Vissarion Grigor'evich Belinskii (1811–48), prominent literary critic and essayist, and a central figure in the early radical 'Westernizer' movement in the 1830s and 1840s; Nikolai Aleksandrovich Dobroliubov (1836–61), radical critic and journalist, most famous for his essay 'What is Oblomovitis?', a critical diagnosis of the Russian gentry through the eponymous hero of *Oblomov*, the 1859 novel by writer Ivan Aleksandrovich Goncharov (1812–91); Nikolai Gavrilovich Chernyshevskii (1828–89), radical critic and writer, founder of Russian Populism, and author of the novel *What Is To Be Done?*, which inspired many young Russians to join the revolutionary movement.
4 Alexander Ivanovich Herzen (1812–70), Russian writer and publicist, renowned as the 'father of Russian socialism'. A Westernizer in his early years, he was later particularly influential through his émigré publishing ventures, *The Bell* and *The Polar Star*, which were smuggled into Russia in large quantities and were required reading in the late 1850s and early 1860s.
5 Georg Wilhelm Friedrich Hegel (1770–1831), German idealist philosopher, ultimately the most important figure in the assimilation of the German philosophical tradition by the Russian intelligentsia in the 1830s–1840s; Ludwig Andreas von Feuerbach (1804–72), prominent German philosopher associated with Left Hegelianism and best known for his critique of Christianity, *The Essence of Christianity* (1841); François Marie Charles Fourier (1772–1837), founder of utopian socialism, whose concept of the phalanstery as an ideal community was highly influential among Russian radicals; Robert Owen (1771–1858), manufacturer, social reformer and philanthropist.
6 The Polish Uprising, also known as the January Uprising, an insurgency against Russian rule aimed at restoring the Polish-Lithuanian Commonwealth, began in January 1863 and continued until June 1864.
7 Following the conquest of 1865, Russian Turkestan, comprising the Emirate of Bukhara, the Khanate of Khiva and the oasis to the south of the Kazakh Steppe, became a Governor-Generalship in 1867.
8 Sergei Petrovich Degaev (1857–1921), terrorist and secret service agent, betrayed several members of the People's Will, including Ashenbrenner, but subsequently conspired with members of the People's Will to assassinate Georgii Porfir'evich Sudeikin (1850–83), St Petersburg Gendarme Colonel and from 1882 Inspector of the Secret Police. Degaev escaped to America, changed his name to Alexander Pell, and became a prominent mathematician.
9 The use of terrorist tactics was a major debate among Socialist Revolutionaries, who viewed themselves as the heirs of the People's Will, but accepted the necessity of acknowledging

orthodox Marxist doctrine on the limited capacity of individuals to affect the course of history. See Anna Geifman, 'Aspects of early twentieth-century Russian terrorism', 1992, 23–46, https://doi.org/10.1080/09546559208427147. My thanks to Maurits Westbroek for reminding me of the significance of this debate.

10 Iuvachev, *Shlissel'burgskaia krepost'*, 133.
11 Figner, *Zapechatlennyi trud*, 1:295–6.
12 This article is attributed to Mikhail Iul'evich Ashenbrenner, who was sentenced to death by hanging at the trial of Vera Figner in 1884, then 'commuted' to a sentence of 20 years to be spent in the torture chambers of Shlissel'burg. *Editors' note*.
13 M. Iu. Ashenbrenner, 'Shlissel'burgskaia tiur'ma za 20 let, ot 1884 po 1904 gg: vospominaniia', *Byloe*, 1, no.1 (1906): 54–93. Ashenbrenner's memoir was republished in Berlin in 1906 by Steinits (who also republished Volkenshtein's memoir), and an expanded version covering the author's earlier revolutionary career appeared as M. Iu. Ashenbrenner, *Voennaia organizatsiia 'Narodnoi voli' i drugie vospominaniia, 1860–1904 gg*, ed. N. S. Tiutchev (Moscow: Izdatel'stvo politkatorzhan, 1924).
14 A seventeenth-century Kievan monk, famous for his lives of the saints.
15 Aleksandr Sergeevich Pushkin (1799–1837) is often credited as being the creator of the modern Russian literary language.
16 Ignatii Ivanov and Pokhitonov died. Shebalin and Iuvachev recovered. Suicides: Tikhanovich, Grachevskii, Sof'ia Ginsburg, and several other attempts. Myshkin and Minakov were shot. *Author's note*.
17 Dmitrii Sergeevich Sipiagin (1853–1902), Minister of Internal Affairs from 1899 to his assassination in April 1902 by the Socialist Revolutionary Stepan Balmashev, who was executed for the crime at Shlissel'burg the following month.
18 On Viacheslav von Plehve, see Introduction, note 39.
19 According to L. A. Volkenshtein, Minakov was shot on 6 September 1884, and Myshkin at the beginning of January 1885 (*Thirteen Years in Shlissel'burg Fortress*, St Petersburg, 1905, 3). *Author's note*.
20 M. Iu. Ashenbrenner was a lieutenant-colonel at the time of his conviction. *Editors' note*. [On Durnovo, see Volkenshtein, note 75. *Translator's note*.]
21 On Petrov, see Volkenshtein, note 69.
22 Probably a reference to the philosopher and anthropologist Herbert Spencer (1820–1903), who was popular among radicals. Figner records books by Spencer being taken away from them in 1889; Figner, *Zapechatlennyi trud*, 2:68, but Frolenko, *Zapiski semidesiatnika*, 257, states that until the arrival of Gershuni, who persuaded the administration to give them works on sociology, no such books were permitted.
23 Thomas Babington Macaulay (1800–59), British politician and historian. On Solov'ev and Kostomarov, see Volkenshtein, note 81.
24 Nikolai Ivanovich Ziber (1844–88), economist and one of the first advocates of Marxist theory in Russia.
25 German Lopatin began a translation of the first volume of Marx's *Capital* in 1870. It was later completed by the economist Nikolai Frantsevich Daniel'son (1844–1918).
26 François Auguste Marie Mignet (1796–1884), journalist and historian, author of *History of the French Revolution* (1824); Edgar Quinet (1803–75), historian, philosopher and republican, author, among other works, of *The Revolution* (1865).
27 Russian: 'впервые', given in quotation marks in the original, perhaps to suggest this became a legendary moment among the prisoners.
28 Returned: Schlosser's *Universal History*; Ribot's *Heredity, Diseases of the Will*, and *Diseases of the Mind*; Carpenter's *Mental Physiology*; Taine's *On Intelligence*; Mill's *Logic*; Maudsley's *Body and Will*; Wallace's *Island Life*. *Author's note*. [On Schlosser, see Volkenshtein, note 81. Théodule-Armand Ribot (1839–1916), French psychologist; William Benjamin Carpenter (1813–85), English physician and physiologist; Hippolyte Adolphe Taine (1828–93), French historian and critic; John Stuart Mill (1806–73), British philosopher; Henry Maudsley (1835–1918), British psychiatrist; his book is given in English in Ashenbrenner's original as *The Will and Body*; Alfred Russel Wallace, British geographer, explorer and naturalist. *Translator's note*.]
29 Now in Iakutsk region. *Author's note*.
30 Died in Shlissel'burg. *Editors' note*.
31 Amnestied in 1905. *Editors' note*.

32 Russian: 'променадмейстер'.
33 Russian: унтеры.
34 Russian: староста.
35 Russian: тюремщики.
36 Russian: 'менюмейстер'.
37 Bezrodnov (1857–1923) was from 1892 physician to the St Petersburg Division of Gendarmes, and from 1895 physician to the Shlissel'burg Directorate of Gendarmes.
38 After leaving Shlissel'burg, he shot himself dead while in exile in Iakutsk region. *Author's note*.
39 Tikhonovich's death is generally not recorded as suicide, though he apparently died days after a suicide attempt.
40 Russian: исполнители.
41 S. A. Ivanov and M. P. Popov were both amnestied in 1905. *Editors' note*.
42 Prisoners with judicial sentences were deprived of their ranks, while those under administrative sentences were not.
43 Sergei Erastovich Zvolianskii (1855–1912), Director of the Police Department, 1897–1902. On Durnovo and Goremykin, see Volkenshtein, notes 75 and 113 respectively.
44 Russian: 'через год по чайной ложке', that is, slowly and in tiny amounts.
45 Gabriel Tarde (1843–1904), French sociologist and criminologist.
46 Nikolai Konstantinovich Mikhailovskii (1842–1904), Populist theoretician and sociologist. On debates surrounding imitation and contagion in late nineteenth-century Russian discourse, including Mikhailovskii's contribution, see Beer, '"Microbes of the mind"', 2007, 554. http://www.journals.uchicago.edu/doi/abs/10.1086/517981.
47 Russian: 'прорубил окно', an allusion to Pushkin's poem 'The Bronze Horseman', which describes Peter the Great 'cutting a window' to Europe by founding the city of St Petersburg.
48 Died in Shlissel'burg. *Editors' note*.
49 On *The Grainfield*, see Volkenshtein, note 90.
50 Thomas Chatterton (1752–70), English poet and literary forger.
51 Bogdanovich died in Shlissel'burg; G. A. Lopatin and N. A. Morozov were amnestied in 1905, V. N. Figner left Shlissel'burg in autumn 1904, Polivanov was sent to settlement in Siberia, from where he escaped in 1905 and shot himself dead while abroad. *Editors' note*. [In fact, Polivanov's escape and suicide took place in 1903. *Translator's note*.]
52 Christian Johann Heinrich Heine (1797–1856), German poet and essayist, whose later work is renowned for its satirical wit.
53 The editors of *Byloe* heartily endorse these words of the highly esteemed Mikhail Iul'evich. *Editors' note*.
54 Joseph Rudyard Kipling (1865–1936), British colonial writer.
55 William Makepeace Thackeray (1811–63), British novelist.
56 Louise-Victorine Ackermann (1813–90), French poet.
57 *Review of Reviews* and *Times Weekly* were popular British digests of international news.
58 The novel *Bulgakov*, which is dedicated to Liudmila Volkenshtein. Iurkovskii died before he was able to complete it.
59 Eugen Dühring (1833–1921), German philosopher and socialist.
60 A leap into the abyss in the transition from the concept of quantity to quality. *Author's note*.
61 Friedrich Paulsen (1846–1908), German neo-Kantian philosopher; Wilhelm Maximilian Wundt (1832–1920), German physician and one of the founders of modern psychology.
62 Dmitrii Ivanovich Mendeleev (1834–1907), Russian chemist and formulator of the Periodic Table of Elements.
63 Dmitrii Petrovich Konovalov (1856–1929), Russian chemist and student of Mendeleev.
64 Frolenko's memoir, *Zapiski semidesiatnika*, 214–40, records his horticultural activities at the fortress in great detail.
65 Aldan grapes are a large, black variety that grow in Iakutsk and are used for making wine.
66 Laxton, named after the British plant breeder Thomas Laxton (1830–93). Koch, named after Dr Karl Heinrich Emil Koch (1809–79), German botanist.
67 Borovinka is an early fruiting apple variety originating in Russia in the eighteenth century and named Duchess of Oldenburg in Britain and the USA. Antonovka is a popular acidic late autumn/early winter variety, the scent of which was the inspiration of the short story 'Antonovskie iabloki' (Antonov Apples, 1900) by Nobel laureate Ivan Bunin. Aport is a large cooking and eating apple found mainly in Kazakhstan, but brought there by settlers from Voronezh in the mid-nineteenth century.

68 Grachevskii burned himself to death in Shlissel'burg, having poured kerosene over himself. *Editors' note.*
69 In pre-revolutionary Russia, name days – the saint's day after whom people were named – were celebrated as much as, if not more than, birthdays.
70 A silver ruble in Russian and East European folklore that returns to its owner intact no matter how many times it is spent. The writer Nikolai Leskov (1831–95) wrote a short parable for children, 'Nerazmennyi ruble', based on the myth.
71 Russian: надзиратели.
72 Later we had electric lighting, and you could switch off the lamps. *Author's note.*
73 Russian: испытуемых и исправляющихся. While 'испытуемых' might more normally be translated as 'probationary', the association in English of 'probation' with early release from prison makes it inappropriate in the Russian context.
74 *Russian Wealth* (*Russkoe bogatstvo*), published monthly in Petersburg from 1876–1918, was associated with liberal Populists in the 1890s. *God's World* (*Mir bozhii*), a monthly literary and popular science magazine, was published in Petersburg from 1892 to 1906, then as the *Contemporary World* to 1918.
75 *Revue des Revues* was a popular French digest of international news.
76 *Nauchnoe obozrenie*, not listed in *Gazety dorevoliutsionnoi Rossii, 1703–1917*.
77 William Thomas Stead (1849–1912), known as W. T. Stead, influential journalist and newspaper editor, editor of the *Pall Mall Gazette* in the 1880s, then founder of the *Review of Reviews* in 1890.
78 William Ewart Gladstone (1809–98) British statesman who served four terms as Prime Minister of the United Kingdom; Robert Burns (1759–96), Scottish poet; John Ruskin (1819–1900), art critic and social thinker; Queen Victoria ruled the United Kingdom of Great Britain and Ireland from 1837 to 1901; William McKinley, Jr. (1843–1901), 25th US President. Ashenbrenner's memory, however, appears to fail him with regard to Robert Owen: no anniversary coincides with this period, there is no such interview in the *Review of Reviews*, nor is it clear to whom 'Havelock' refers. Unless the piece was actually in another publication, it seems likely that he is in fact referring to a short section in the character sketch on secularist and reformer George Jacob Holyoake (1817–1906), devoted to the subject's encounter with Owen and 'conversion' to cooperativism. *Review of Reviews*, September 1901, 259–60.
79 William Crookes (1832–1919), British chemist and physicist, published the *Chemical News* from 1859.
80 *Son of the Fatherland* (*Syn otechestva*) was a liberal newspaper that took over the name of an earlier journal, edited from 1893 by the writer Aleksandr Konstantinovich Sheller (A. Mikhailov) (1838–1900). *St Petersburg* was edited by journalist and writer Aleksandr Nikolaevich Molchanov (1847–1915).
81 The newspaper ceased publication in 1901.
82 *The Bulletin of Bookstores of M. O. Wol'f Associates*, a monthly illustrated bibliography journal.
83 *Russian Thought* (*Russkaia mysl'*), a popular magazine founded in Moscow in 1880 by the journalist Vukol Mikhailovich Lavrov (1852–1912); *Historical Herald* (*Istoricheskii vestnik*), a popular historical and literary journal published in Petersburg from 1880 to 1917.
84 *Vestnik inostrannoi literatury*, a monthly literary-historical journal published in Petersburg from 1891 to 1916.
85 Sent to Sakhalin after 20 years of imprisonment. *Author's note.*
86 Salt Town is a small area of central St Petersburg, on the River Fontanka opposite the Summer Gardens, where the Agriculture Museum was located after 1859. In 1917, former Shlissel'burg inmate Mikhail Novorusskii became its director.
87 None of the listings in *Gazety dorevoliutsionnoi Rossii* for journals named *Life* [*Zhizn'*] or *New Word* (*Novoe slovo*) fit with the dates of imprisonment. *Revue de deux Mondes* is a monthly French language journal, published since 1829.
88 The final capture of the fortress from the Swedes in 1702, part of the Great Northern War. The Russian forces sustained about 1,500 casualties.
89 A. Aleksandrov was the pseudonym of a group of English and Russian compilers of a renowned English-Russian dictionary published in 1879, and Russian-English dictionary published in 1885. The *Guide to Botany* is possibly *Rukovodstvo k botanike*, compiled by V. V. Grigor'ev. Moscow: Tipografiia V. Got'e, 1861.
90 The memoirs of Alexander Herzen, referring to the early debates of the Westernizers.

91 Russian: 'преобразования и проступления [sic] духа', presumably also a reference to Hegel.
92 Viliuisk is a town in the present-day Sakha Republic, about 600 km (370 miles) from Iakutsk. Srednekolymsk, also in the Sakha Republic, is 1,485 km (920 miles) north-east of Iakutsk, on the left bank of the Kolyma river.
93 Alois Adolf Riehl (1844–1924), Austrian neo-Kantian philosopher. The Russian version is: *Teoriia nauki i metafizika s tochki zreniia filosofskogo krititsizma*, 1887.
94 The scepticism Ashenbrenner expresses here about the translation of Riehl's book, *Der Philosophische Kritizismus Und Seine Bedeutung Für Die Positive Wissenschaft. Zweiter Band. Zweiter Theil (Schluss). Zur Wissenschafttheorie Und Metaphysik* (1887) is somewhat perplexing, as not all the terms he cites from the Russian – 'затреба', 'помета', 'видозвод', 'винословные отношения', and 'мань' – appear as impenetrable as he suggests (at least after typographic errors, of which there are many in the original journal publication of Ashenbrenner's memoir, have been corrected), even if their usage is occasionally odd. His confusion may stem from the fact that the Russian translator, journalist and publisher Evgenii Fedorovich Korsh (1809–97), in places translates a single German term in two different ways, using Slavic and Western roots, and is inconsistent in his usage of these. Conversely (in the case of the first term), he also translates two German words with somewhat different meanings into a single Russian term. 'Затреба' (not a normal Russian term, though obviously derived from the same root as 'требование' and other words relating to 'demand') is used as the translation of the German '*Forderung*' ('demand'), and in this context seems reasonably clear. However, Ashenbrenner's confusion here may have been caused by the same Russian word also being used to render '*Postulat*', despite the German terms not being obvious synonyms. 'Помета' does not appear in the Russian translation of Riehl's book, but we may assume Ashenbrenner means 'подмета', which is used consistently to translate the German '*Wahrnehmung*' ('perception'); indeed the translator at one point offers 'восприятие' as an alternative. This is however somewhat distant from the meaning of related Russian forms. 'Видозвод' (in fact 'видоизвод') is odd and unnecessary in the Russian; it translates the German '*Modus*', which could just as easily, and much more clearly, be rendered in Russian as 'модус'. 'Винословные отношения', in the Russian text in the form 'винословное или причинное отношение' ('causative or causal relation'), appears to be an acceptable translation of the German '*Causalitätsverhältnis*'. Finally, 'мань' (albeit not a normal Russian term in this sense), is used to translate '*Schein*', 'illusion/(false) appearance'.
95 Franklin Henry Giddings (1855–1931), American economist and sociologist; Arnoldi possibly refers to Karl Wilhelm Arnoldi (1809–76), German physician and naturalist; or Johannes von Arnoldi (1751–1827), German archivist, historian and statesman; Stemler possibly refers to Johann Gottlieb Stemler (1788–1856), German physician and politician.
96 Friedrich Engels (1820–95), philosopher, social theorist and industrialist, developer, with Karl Marx (1818–83) of Marxist theory; Karl Johann Kautsky (1854–1938), Czech-Austrian philosopher and Marxist theoretician.
97 Richard Ludwig Heinrich Avenarius (1843–96), German-Swiss positivist philosopher; Harald Høffding (1843–1931), Danish philosopher and theologian; Ernst Waldfried Josef Wenzel Mach (1838–1916), Austrian physicist and philosopher; Friedrich Wilhelm Ostwald (1853–1932), German chemist.
98 Viktor Mikhailovich Chernov (1873–1952), founder and theoretician of the Socialist Revolutionary Party; Petr Berngardovich Struve (1870–1944), political economist and philosopher; Bel'tov was a pseudonym of Georgii Valentinovich Plekhanov (1856–1918), Marxist theoretician and revolutionary; Ivan Mikhailovich Il'in (1873–1954), far right political and religious philosopher; Mikhail Ivanovich Tugan-Baranovskii (1865–1919), Ukrainian politician and economist; Sergei Nikolaevich Bulgakov (1871–1944), Orthodox Christian philosopher and theologian; Nikolai Aleksandrovich Berdiaev (1874–1948), Russian religious and political philosopher. Berdiaev, Bulgakov, Struve and Tugan-Baranovskii all participated in the Legal Marxism movement from the mid-1890s to the early 1900s, and it would be works from this period that the prisoners were reading.
99 Vladimir Galaktionovich Korolenko (1853–1921), activist and writer, famous for his short stories based on his experience of Siberian exile; Anton Pavlovich Chekhov (1860–1904), short story writer and playwright; Maksim Gor'kii (Aleksei Maksimovich Peshkov) (1868–1936), proletarian writer and revolutionary; Vikentii Vikent'evich Veresaev (Smidovich) (1867–1945), doctor and campaigning writer.

100 Ivan Ivanovich Ianzhul (1846–1914), Professor of Financial Law at Moscow University, who established the Russian system of factory inspections. His book *English Free Trade* was published in 1876.
101 Stepnoi Krai was the unofficial name used between 1882 and 1917 to refer to the area around present day north-eastern Kazakhstan.
102 The revolutionary Sergei Mikhailovich Kravchinskii (1851–95), known by the pseudonym Stepniak, assassinated General Nikolai Mezentsov (1827–78), Chief of the Corps of Gendarmes and head of the Russian secret police. Kravchinskii escaped abroad and settled in London from 1880, turning to writing and propaganda, and helping establish the Society of Friends of Russian Freedom. He died after being struck by a train near Chiswick in West London, in what was possibly a suicide. His 1888 novel known in English as *The Career of a Nihilist* was published in Russian after his death under the title *Andrei Kozhukhov*.
103 Francis Bret Harte (1836–1902), American short story writer, known for his fiction about the California gold rush.
104 We hadn't had enough money to buy the Encyclopaedia. N. V. handed over 60 rubles that had been returned to him, and then the Encyclopaedia was ordered. *Author's note.* [It is unclear who 'N. V.' refers to, as it does not correspond to the initials of any of the prisoners. *Translator's note.*]
105 Aleksei Alekseevich Gatstuk (1832–91), archaeologist and writer. Starting from 1865, he published an annual calendar, listing saints' days and religious festivals in the Orthodox church, as well as other practical information, for example on trade and travel.
106 Viktor Vil'gel'movich von Wahl (1840–1915), Deputy Minister of Internal Affairs and Commander of the Special Corps of Gendarmes.
107 John Dicks (1818–81), a London-based publisher specializing in popular, affordable editions.
108 Charles Dickens (1812–70) was one of the most popular British authors in Russia; Tobias Smollett (1721–77), Scottish picaresque novelist and poet, author of *The Adventures of Roderick Random*; Henry Fielding (1707–54), English satirical novelist and dramatist, author of *Tom Jones*; James Fenimore Cooper (1789–1851), writer of historical romances on American frontier life; Laurence Sterne (1713–68), Irish novelist, whose *Sentimental Journey* in particular was highly influential to the development of Russian literature; Thomas Hood (1799–1845), English author and poet; Marie-Joseph 'Eugène' Sue (1804–57), popular French novelist, best known for *The Mysteries of Paris* and the genre of the urban gothic; Alexandre Dumas *père*, born Dumas Davy de la Pailleterie (1802–70), French popular author of novels including *The Three Musketeers* and *The Count of Monte Cristo*; Alexandre Dumas *fils* (1824–95), French novelist and playwright, best known for *The Lady of the Camellias*; Charles Paul de Kock (1793–1871), French novelist with a risqué reputation.
109 Sir Walter Scott (1771–1832), Scottish author and historical novelist of works including *Ivanhoe*, *Rob Roy* and *The Heart of Midlothian*.
110 In the Arkhangel'sk region.
111 Simon Charles Mayer (1820–87), Commandant of the Place Vendôme during the Paris Commune, and author of *Souvenirs d'un déporté: étapes d'un forçat politique*, 1880. Mayer is also mentioned by Figner as a moral example to follow in a moment of weakness (*Zapechatlennyi trud*, 2:17), but the quotation Ashenbrenner gives here does not appear to be from Mayer's book.

4.
Vasilii Pankratov, *Life in Shlissel'burg Fortress*

I. Vasilii Pankratov, 1864-1925

Vasilii Semenovich Pankratov (Figure 4.1) was born on 26 December 1864 (7 January 1865) in the village of Alekseevskoe in Tver' Governate. He was from a large peasant family and lived in great poverty, especially after the death of his father, but nevertheless received a technical education. He worked as a turner and machinist in St Petersburg and other cities, and from 1880 became involved in revolutionary circles and propaganda work.[1] In 1883 he joined the People's Will, and became a member of the armed workers' detachment with his future fellow Shlissel'burg inmates Kalinnik Martynov and Petr Antonov. Resisting arrest in Kiev in 1884, Pankratov wounded, or according to some reports, killed, a gendarme. He was a defendant in the Kiev trial in the same year, alongside Martynov, Vasilii Karaulov and Mikhail Shebalin. The death sentence Pankratov received was commuted to 20 years' hard labour, and with the other defendants he was sent to Shlissel'burg Fortress, where he was the youngest of the long-term prisoners. According to the terms of the 1896 coronation amnesty his sentence was reduced by one third, and on 9 (21) March 1898 he was transferred from the prison to exile in Viliuisk, near Iakutsk.

In 1903 Pankratov joined the Socialist Revolutionary Party, and in 1905 escaped from exile to return to Moscow. He

Василий Семенович Панкратов
в Якутской обл.

Figure 4.1 Portrait of Vasilii Pankratov during his exile in Iakutsk. From Pankratov, V. S. *S tsarem v Tobol'ske: iz vospominanii*. Leningrad: Kooperativnoe izdatel'stvo tovarishchestvo 'Byloe', 1925, frontispiece. Public domain/orphan work. Digitization by LSE Library.

participated in the December Uprising of 1905, and in 1907 was sent back to Iakutsk for five years. He became a member of the SR Party's Central Committee in 1909, and returned to Petersburg in 1912.

In 1917, as a member of the All-Russian Peasant Union, Pankratov participated in the State Conference.[2] He was elected to the All-Union Constituent Assembly from the Iakutsk electoral district on the Socialist Revolutionary list, and was also nominated for the Tobol'sk district. During the July Days,[3] he published a denunciation of Lenin as a German spy. From 1 September 1917 to 26 January 1918 he served as Commissioner for the Provisional Government, with a special operations detachment assigned to guard former Tsar Nicholas II and the Romanov family in Tobol'sk.[4]

In September 1918 Pankratov participated in the Ufa State Conference,[5] where plans to oppose Soviet power were discussed by anti-Bolshevik parties. After the SRs agreed to end opposition to the Bolsheviks in January 1919, Pankratov joined the faction that went over to support Admiral Kolchak, in order to continue the fight against the Bolsheviks. As a result he was ejected from the party in November of that year. After the Civil War, Pankratov returned to Petrograd, where he became a member of the Society for Former Political Prisoners. He died in Leningrad on 5 March 1925.

In Shlissel'burg Prison, Pankratov and Antonov taught their carpentry and turning skills to other prisoners, when the workshops were opened. In addition to Antonov, Pankratov was particularly close to Ashenbrenner, while Figner describes having 'tender, almost maternal feelings' towards him.[6] An autodidact, he took his studies in the prison very seriously, supported by Figner and others, and after his release he participated in scientific and geological explorations in Siberia, making discoveries in the latter field. Figner notes that he could be quick-tempered, although never with her, and that he hated the guards with a passion, as a result of which they were afraid to provoke him.[7] According to a later acquaintance, despite Pankratov's years of imprisonment, 'he was a thoroughly humane man, having not the slightest animosity toward the Czar or toward the old regime.'[8]

Vasilii Pankratov, *Life in Shlissel'burg Fortress*[9]

Chapter I.

The construction of Shlissel'burg Prison was completed in 1883, but it was populated only from August 1884. The first party of Ravelinites[10] was brought to Shlissel'burg Prison on 15 August by a barge on which single cells had been constructed for each person, so that even this short river journey was turned into a floating prison with the full Ravelin regime: the same solitary confinement, only with more cramped, lower, and stuffier cells, with miniature windows and 'eyes' in the doors leading to the corridor, the loyal 'blues' incessantly and silently walking the corridors, glancing repeatedly through the 'eyes'. Those locked in the cells were in chains. Some, for whom fantasy had not yet been smothered under the weight of life in the Ravelin, who still lived in the hope of escaping to better conditions, thought that they weren't being taken to Shlissel'burg, but to Kara,[11] that their solitary life was over, that they would soon find themselves among comrades, that they would not be torn away from free people and their kin. What cruel disappointment! But there were also those who regarded their departure from the Ravelin more gloomily.

The late Pokhitonov and Butsinskii described their first impressions, when they were brought out, or rather carried under the arms, from the Ravelin's walls.[12]

It was night, and quite a dark night; the entire sky was completely covered in unbroken clouds. Suddenly the blues open the cell door and invite them out. Where, why – they won't say and don't answer. 'Why do they need me?' Butsinskii asked himself. 'Maybe they're moving me to a different cell?' But they don't take him to another cell, but to the guard house, where a lot of blues are gathered with a few officers, under the leadership of the commandant. Here he's dressed, inspected, and put in shackles. 'Well, that means I'm being taken away… It must be to Kara', flashed through his head. He was already delighted, and his fantasy worked out how he'd end up there again, see his old friends, be able to write to his family, start reading journals and making statistical abstracts.

'You know', he said to me later, 'I love statistics terribly. In the Ravelin, where we weren't given anything, I would bring figures to mind and, can you imagine, I had memorized a great deal.'

But while his imagination was working in this direction, the blues were whispering about something, running about, bustling – and suddenly, seizing him under the arms as if he were some sort of object there was no reasoning with, he was dragged across the yard. Then he was forced through the gates towards the river, where gangplanks to a barge were laid out. One of the blues lit up the path. What was this? Were they going to drown him? 'Are they really going to throw me into this dark, cold water now?' thought Butsinskii. 'If it weren't for the chains, I'd probably be able to escape. I can swim well, after all, and could survive in the water for a long time. But what about the chains? How can I get rid of them?' he asked himself.

'Did you really seriously think that at that moment, Butsinskii?' we asked him. 'How could you allow such a thought? After all, they had more convenient ways of getting rid of all of us, with no noise, no hassle, no unnecessary eyes watching. And after all, a body might float to the surface. Surely you know how carefully they hide our bodies?'

'That's exactly how seriously I thought about it', he replied: 'I brought to mind everything at that moment: where, how I'd swum, and how often… The mysterious arrangements, the silence, the night, the gendarmes' secretive whispering, their vacant faces – everything led me to those thoughts. Now, of course, it seems funny even to me, but then, oh, then I was ready to make the most terrible assumptions.'

Pokhitonov said almost the same, except that he didn't plan to escape. And they didn't escape after all: they drowned not in the water, but in the stuffy cells of Shlissel'burg Prison. Many, however, guessed where they were being taken, and although they didn't paint a bright picture for themselves of life in a new charnel house, they were still glad of the move, on the basis of the proverb, 'let it be worse, as long as it's different'.[13] That's how repulsive and tedious the entire situation at the Ravelin had become to them.

For the whole of the journey they were forbidden not only to see each other, but also to tap. On arrival at the island, they were taken off the barge one by one. The administration was already waiting for them on the shore in front of the fortress gates: the fortress commandant and his acolytes: officers, the doctor, a platoon of soldiers with gleaming weapons and in full dress, and finally, the blues – the future prison guards. As you can see, the reception was rather formal, but its formality was hollow, dead, ominous.

To a man they are as silent as fish, just surveying each captive from head to toe. With the same silence, but a sort of demonic speed and disrespect, the blues seize each victim, as if afraid they will somehow slip away, and drag them once more inside the walls. They are brought through more iron gates separating the prison yard from the courtyard where the administration, soldiers and blues live, and finally brought to the prison and unchained. Being freed from the fetters makes a strong impression: some sort of hope is reborn, vague and unclear. Thoughts suppressed by the harsh atmosphere and uncertainty of one's subsequent fate come back to life.

Even now I cannot forget what I went through when my chains were removed. I was brought in alone, on a covered wagon, and also led under the stone arches of the gate. There were several gendarmes waiting for me, one with a hammer and chisel. 'You need to put your leg like this!' the superintendent said to me complacently. 'No-one's locked up in chains here.'

I put my leg up. A heavy hammer blow rang out, and one of my legs was free. Another blow – and the chain fell. 'How simple', I thought – and my eyes even grew dim. 'I'm free, free of chains! My legs are now free to move, and I can walk like a man: the chains won't clank, clatter or carve into my soul with their noise. Are they going to remove the chains from my hands as well?' I looked at the fetters on my hands. I wanted to get rid of them as quickly as possible. 'How good, how at ease I'll feel.'

This desire was quickly fulfilled in the prison itself, in the gendarmes' duty office, where another detailed search was carried out, and clothes[14] and underwear changed. All this was done in the presence of the commandant, superintendent and doctor. The latter does an examination, listens to the chest, and asks questions about health. This entire procedure already completely dispels the joyful mood instilled by the removal of the chains. You start feeling completely bound, but bound now by invisible shackles; an oppressive feeling begins to agitate and mortify you, a consciousness that you do not belong to yourself, but solely to these warders, who can do whatever they want to you. Again they lead you somewhere; again dead silence, secrecy, the feline steps of the gendarmes in the corridor, their glances through the 'eyes' in the doors. How slyly, how cautiously, they approach these eyes, like beasts lying in wait and preparing to seize their prey! It's repugnant and tormenting to look at all of this!...

But now the door to the empty cell opens. It appears clean, with a high ceiling, opaque glass window, an iron bedstead fastened to the wall, and a wooden table and seat, also fastened to the floor and wall. The impression it makes is heavy, oppressive: as if you're entering some sort of crypt or metal coffin. The presence of four gendarmes, dumb, resigned, with eyes riveted to you, and the superintendent, whose face says to you: I will do to you everything I'm ordered to, aggravates the unpleasant impression even more.

'As you are deprived of all rights', says the superintendent, enunciating every word distinctly, 'I will use the familiar form of "you." If you behave yourself, you will get everything: books, work, conversation with a priest (!). Here are the instructions, you can read them.' A manner like this immediately makes you hostile to this person. From the very first words he offends you, from the very first words he mocks you, pointing out your impotence and his own omnipotence.

Not everyone, of course, reacted to such statements in the same way. Some hoped to give him a wide berth or if possible avoid conversations with him. But some from the first group declared that they would respond to him in the same form, which, of course, led not only to unpleasantness, but also to the pettiest nit-picking and harassment. A man such as our first superintendent could not forgive such things, and not because he was personally offended by them – no, he was too ill-mannered for that, and a complete stranger to the idea of human dignity – but because he was just unable to understand how it was possible to contradict the administration, dissent, and not fulfil his demands. After all, he did not invent this familiar 'you' himself; he was ordered to use this form of address, and come what may, he had to use it. He was ordered to keep the prisoners subordinated and obedient, and he had to do this, no matter what it led to. And he really didn't back down.

When the first group was brought in (15 people),[15] he separated them in such a way that it was impossible to tap, which was easy to do as he had 40 cells at his disposal. But later, when seven more people were brought, it became impossible to do that. Tapping began, and with it incessant reprimands, incessant threats of incarceration in the punishment cells, not being given books. The late Malevskii [sic], in the final stages of tuberculosis, was not given books until December because of tapping. For such an executor of the higher will as our superintendent, no extenuating circumstances existed whatsoever.

The superintendent Sokolov or, as we called him, 'Herod', a.k.a. 'Cerberus',[16] was elderly, of medium height, thickset, with a round face, and a head covered with thick grey hair, trimmed round, obviously so as not to change the shape of his face, with dark grey eyes that always glittered with a sort of soulless coldness, detachment and sense of duty. His eyes always told you on his behalf: 'It's nothing to do with me, I only carry out the administration's orders; what I am ordered to do is what I will do. If they order me to feed you hazel-grouse and kow-tow to you, I'll feed you hazel-grouse and kow-tow to you; if they order me to torment, torture and shoot you like partridges, I'll shoot you all, tear you all to pieces. I have no personal involvement. I was raised to carry out orders unquestioningly, without reasoning.' And that's exactly how he had been raised. By birth he was Jewish, then converted to Orthodoxy, was handed over as a cantonist, where he probably had a taste of everything, including the lash and punishment cells, and the most important thing is that there he was taught the strictest discipline, obedience, and was taught how himself to demand and achieve obedience and submission from others. From the cantonists he became a soldier, then an orderly to General Potapov,[17] the very same general whom Nechaev had struck on the cheek for the repugnant offer of gaining his freedom by giving up his comrades.[18] Sokolov also served as a gendarme under Sudeikin's leadership,[19] and captured a printing press in Sapernyi Lane in an 'assault'.[20] But how he was made an officer, and how he got the Cross of St George,[21] nobody knew. He was a completely illiterate man, but with a proud consciousness that he was a captain, the superintendent of an important prison, that he had the keys to this prison, to these cells, in his hands. He would rattle the keys with pleasure, and wouldn't hand them over to anyone else, wouldn't trust them. Oh, how he loved to jangle those keys, how self-satisfied he was as he unlocked and locked the cells. You should have seen his beaming face. With what skill he flicked the key, apparently enjoying his own dexterity. And no wonder. He had been the superintendent at the Ravelin, after all, and had locked and unlocked the cells there as well.

Strictly fulfilling the orders of the higher authorities, he was mercilessly demanding towards his own subordinates. No matter that many of them had three stripes on their sleeves and a big medal, he treated them like raw recruits, demanded unconditional obedience from them, and schooled them so that in his presence they behaved more like automatons, like soulless machines, than living people.

Not one of them dared to say a word to him. Once one new gendarme, an old man, replied 'very well' to one of the prisoners who posed him a question. Herod jumped into the cell like a madman, grabbed the gendarme by the collar, pulled him out and, slamming the door, began to berate the poor man with the choicest Russian abuse, and what's more, threw him in a punishment cell for four days. Even at home, in their flats, he forbade the gendarmes to speak much. Complete dummies were found who carried out his orders to the letter; one even went totally dumb, and forgot how to speak. When the workshops were opened for us, and the gendarmes were allowed to answer our questions, that poor man couldn't say a word. Later one of the blues himself said how bad it was under Sokolov, and how glad they were when he was removed. 'He tormented you, but us as well, and no less. Our share was likely even bigger', he would say.

'Who forced you to serve here? You could have left', we'd argue.

'Where would I go? Where can you find this sort of service, this salary? I've got a family, children.'

Herod knew this very well and chose just such subordinates for himself. Apparently he knew how to pick people out: not a single one of his subordinates ever broke their oath. That was Herod. He dressed neatly and loved his overcoat with its wide, very deep collar. He wore that overcoat even in summer. Both of the first two groups brought in comprised his old acquaintances from the Ravelin, whom he'd managed to study well over the previous two or three years, so he was able to distribute them around the cells so that they would tap as little as possible. He placed the sick and those who didn't want to tap between the 'inveterate tappers', in the hope, he said, that if they won't listen to me, they might feel sorry for their friends, and not want to upset or disturb them with their tapping. But his reasoning was wrong. The desire to share ideas, feelings, to know who was in which cell, how someone's health was, whether they had any news – all that was so strong that they tapped through the cells, not always even considering the condition of a silent neighbour. They were even angry at them.

The Ravelin regime was transferred in full to Shlissel'burg: the same severity; the same food, poor quality and stingy; the same short, daily exercise of 20–30 minutes; the same categorical refusal to allow any kind of correspondence with family, or to make use of one's own things or money; finally, the same constant surveillance of every move, both in the cell and during exercise. All this, of course, created an oppressive, hopeless impression. And then some had the idea of seeking changes to these conditions one way or another. This was the beginning of the first protest, which couldn't be across the board. Indeed, where could such a thing have come from? Communications between comrades were very constrained; many were suffering from tuberculosis, nerves, and even refused to tap. Reluctance to have it out with Herod, to listen to his reprimands and threats, also kept some from tapping. And indeed, how repellent, how unbearable was this familiar 'you', was Herod's presumptuous face when he started threatening you with something, hiding behind the backs of two gendarmes who were ready at his very first signal to do all sorts of nasty things to you. You needed nerves of steel to endure all this. But our nerves were shattered, shattered to the utmost degree. Shchedrin was already on the edge of madness. Butsevich likewise. Ignatii Ivanov, although he'd recovered in Kazan' hospital, once he ended up in Shlissel'burg Prison again fell ill both physically and mentally. Grachevskii was so overwrought that a tap on his door or window during mealtimes would upset him. Gellis and Malavskii were suffering from tuberculosis, Isaev as well, Frolenko was permanently ailing, Klimenko was, I think, already completely insane. Morozov was spitting blood, Iurkovskii was in some sort of strange mental state: he remembered nothing, was conscious of nothing going on around him, only he screamed terribly at night. Aronchik fell into insanity and didn't tap with anyone or leave his cell. Dolgushin had only just recovered from smallpox. Of the more or less healthy there remained only Popov, Myshkin, Trigoni, Kobylianskii, Bogdanovich, Polivanov and Butsinskii. But the last two could in no way be considered healthy: the first suffered from nerves and even hallucinations, while the second had already been hallucinating for an entire year. And Zlatopol'skii started with tuberculosis as well.

It's clear that no general protest could come about. It had to be done individually. Minakov, Myshkin and Popov began to demand correspondence with their families, meetings with comrades, smoking tobacco and so on. Of course, these were refused. Then Minakov began to starve himself. The doctor was ordered to feed him artificially. You can imagine Minakov's anger and resentment. In the broad sense he couldn't feel any malice towards the doctor, not least because the doctor – everyone knew this, everyone saw it – was not himself an evil man, but completely spineless, timid and lacking in character. Herod and the commandant treated him like a child. Herod's unceremonious treatment of him frequently overstepped the boundaries of simple politeness. When he spent a long time talking to one of the sick, Herod would begin shouting: 'Well, stop this, get out, I've not time for this!' And sometimes he even grabbed him by the sleeve when he said these words. Even vicariously one felt insulted for the doctor. After all, he was a free man, with an education and even a diploma, in a military uniform, and suddenly he's treated so disrespectfully and rudely. As he allowed himself to be treated this way, of course he wasn't going to refuse to force feed Minakov. What prompted him to take on such a role is difficult to say. But he got a slap to the face from Minakov. Both the forced feeding and the hunger strike – it all ended with this smack. A few days later Minakov was sentenced to death, although how he was tried, and where, is unknown.

After the smack, they say, he almost stopped tapping. All this created the most painful impression on the other comrades, all the more so as it was a mystery to all of them what had happened and why exactly it was the doctor who had suffered, not Herod, who deserved a punch every day, every hour.

On the day of his execution Herod appeared before Minakov with some document and said loudly, 'sign, and nothing will happen'! [sic] 'I don't want to!' rang out the emphatic reply, which Minakov's neighbour heard. 'Then let's go!' screamed Herod. Leaving his cell, Minakov cried out: 'Farewell, comrades! They're taking me for execution!' In reply there was not a single sound. And what answer could there be, except a silent 'forgive me', unaccountable grief, pain and crushing thoughts?.. That was in September, almost a month after the first group had arrived.

Shortly after that, Klimenko attempted suicide, which was revealed only when the cords and hooks for opening the ventilators were removed.

These incidents apparently worried the authorities. General Orzhevskii, deputy Minister of Internal Affairs, began to come every month from Petersburg. The commandant also visited everyone each week. These visits were like having a living statue periodically appear in one's cell.

An attentive, grey-haired, tall old man with a polite demeanour, inevitably appeared every Saturday at the doors of the cell. Bowing exquisitely, stroking his grey beard and swaying from side to side, like a polar bear on a hot day, he always asked everyone exactly the same questions: 'how is the convict's health? Have meals[22] been taken? exercise? Does the convict have any complaints, requests?' He avoided using the familiar 'you', but didn't want to use the formal form, so used the third person.

At first the most varied requests were made: about books, the food, correspondence with families and establishing special facilities for the sick. But no benefit came from any of this.

'This must be declared to the inspector on his first visit, the request may be taken into account', the commandant would reply, tottering and smoothing his beard, 'I can't do this "myself" – it all depends on the higher authorities.'

'Then why am I asked about requests?' the dissatisfied prisoner objects.

'Perhaps the prisoner has inadequate food?' the commandant unsuccessfully avoids answering.

But the prisoner is already sick of this comedy.

'It's not that the food's inadequate, but it's bad; there are many sick people here for whom it's not suitable.'

'That's a matter for the doctor', the commandant interposes: 'complaints about that must go to him.'

But the doctor is standing right there as silent as a corpse. But what could he say? He knows that by referring to him, the commandant is dodging; he knows that he, the doctor, can do nothing, that everything depends on the higher authorities.

The same conversations are repeated in other cells as well. Beyond the formalities they mean nothing, give nothing, but nevertheless these tiresome, fruitless visits gave subjects for tapping amid this desolate life divorced from everything. Comrades start asking each other: what did the commandant say? what was requested, and so on, and so forth. These visits constituted another interest: many comrades used them to count how many altogether were in the prison, for which they stood at their doors and listened for how many doors were unlocked. Some became so accustomed to such observations that they made them completely unconsciously, listening with keen attention to every tap, every rustle. One comrade maintained this habit until the very last days, despite the fact that communications had become free.

Before any visit to the cells a detailed search took place – not in the presence of the convict, of course, but during exercise. Moreover everyone was searched, stripped naked and had their underwear changed. Everything found that had not been issued by Herod – scraps, threads, little stones – was all taken away somewhere.

'What do you need all this for?' Herod would sometimes ask meaningfully, pointing to a chip of wood or a tiny stick – the stalk of a bay leaf found in soup and sharpened.

'Sewing on a button', his addressee replies unwillingly.

'None of that is necessary here', Herod declares firmly and aggressively. 'Say what's needed, and it will be sewn. I am always here, whatever is needed must be asked for immediately. Don't do it yourself.'

Having finished his little speech he calls in an imperious tone for the blues, of whom at this time there were never fewer than four, and sometimes up to six were sent for, depending on the state the inmate was in.

Despite his boorishness, Herod kept a close eye on everyone, demanded the same of the gendarmes and, besides, made them give the most detailed reports. On leaving each cell, he usually issued them with instructions, in a whisper, of course. Oh, how that whisper aggravated and tormented us! Like a snake hissing behind the door. This whisper was also heard every time before the cell door was going to be opened: the gendarmes told Herod everything they had seen and noticed.

The indefatigable Herod fulfilled his duties so precisely and scrupulously, believed so completely in his own loyalty and integrity, and so little relied on his subordinates that he never for a minute left them alone with the convicts. Not to mention the fact that there existed among the gendarmes a Jesuitical system of spying on each other, not to mention that they were the chosen of the chosen, Herod always himself accompanied them when they were taking one of the victims somewhere: one of Herod's eyes would be trained on the victim, the other on those accompanying him.

For example, the exercise hour would arrive: Herod unlocks the door, two gendarmes fly into the cell, two remain by the door and stand silently on both sides, like a pair of idols. 'To exercise!' Herod says. And a solemn procession begins: a gendarme marches in front, the 'captive'[23] behind him, behind the latter another gendarme, and, finally, Herod himself. Having locked one in a pen for exercise, he sets off for another, and so on, until all the pens are full. Then he climbs up to the watchtower, where there are already three blues walking, and observes who is exercising in what way, standing all the while in a general's pose and repeatedly checking the clock to see whether it's time to take one shift back and replace it with another.

Thus, day in, day out, did he perform his sacred routine. And apparently it never bored him; he always remained impassively calm, and the complacency on his face was easy to see. But it was a servile complacency. And bath days! He'd spend two days in a row sitting in the bath room, where it was unbearably hot from the boiler and the stove.

In the first years we were taken to the baths only once a month. At the same time everyone without fail had to be shaved bald. But how they shaved us! Like sheep, without a comb, and simply thus: someone from the gendarmes – whomever Herod orders, of course – takes the scissors and starts hacking any old how, as long as there's less hair left. One's head ends up looking like badly mown tussocks. Herod doesn't let anyone out of his sight. When one head is ready, the shearling doesn't utter a word, but just glances silently at Herod, who pronounces: 'ready! You can wash!' He himself observes how the blues do the search, inspect the underwear, clothes, shoes. Without fail he obliges clean underwear, which is brought from a closet, to be unfolded, shaken out, in order to make sure nothing forbidden has ended up in there.

These baths sometimes dragged out for the whole day. For the whole day Herod would stew and sweat in his blue uniform with the medal round his neck. But it didn't bother him at all. I don't really know whether he was executing orders from above or simply being zealous of his own accord; but I think if he'd been ordered to wash everyone personally, he would have fulfilled that order as well, without any hesitation.

Chapter II.

In October 1884 those convicted in V. Figner's trial were sent to Shlissel'burg Prison, of whom two had ceased to be by the next day…[24]

In December of the same year those convicted in the Kiev trial were brought in,[25] not all at once, but one by one. For journeys during winter on the whole they were taken one by one in covered wagons, accompanied by blues, and several gendarmes were assigned to each station, who had to meet, guard the station and bid farewell to the 'condemned man passing through'. Excessive precautions were taken with cuffs on the wrists and ankles.

I've already had reason to speak of the oppressive impression made by the Shlissel'burg crypt, despite its very clean, high-ceilinged cells. In those first minutes the consciousness of being buried alive so takes over that it's impossible to drive away the thought that 'it's all over'… But then, recovering a little, you rush round to look at the bare walls – to see whether there are any inscriptions there – but instead you find the instructions, which advise you to behave quietly, obediently, to obey all the ranks and all the requirements of the ranks, for which you will be rewarded with conversations with a priest and work in the workshops, which at that time did not exist. If you fail to obey – that is, if you violate the silence and 'discipline', the instructions promise punishment cells, deprivation of books, deprivation of a bed and hot food; for more serious misdemeanours they promise up to 50 lashes, and for assaulting officials – the death penalty. In helpless indignation you turn away from this half sheet of paper covered in writing, and again look around the walls. Behind the door you hear a slight rustle, quiet steps: your diligent watchman is looking through the eye in the door, watching your every move. You begin to strain your ears. Measured, monotonous steps echo – a feeling of the greatest joy suffuses everything: it's probably a comrade walking… I'm not alone here… Gloomy thoughts become lighter, as if the crypt is becoming warmer and friendlier – so strong is the desire to have someone close to you nearby, even if through a thick, solid wall. This feeling is followed by another – to ask who's there as soon as possible, exchange at least a few words, find out if there's any link with the living world.

Dead silence all around, only from time to time terrible coughs ring out here and there. One's imagination rushes ahead and draws the pale, exhausted faces of comrades. We try to tap. The ventilation pane opens, and the disgruntled physiognomy of Herod appears, on which you can read at first glance: aha, got you! 'There must be no tapping here, I'll send you to the punishment cells.' And the window swings shut again. With what incredible speed and dexterity he did all this! 'Is it really worth living in such conditions?' you ask yourself: 'some executioner with neither god nor man in his heart is going to follow your every step, insult you and judge your behaviour to boot! No, it's more than you can stand'…

You begin to think of different methods,[26] running back and forth. But then your disgust weakens, you reproach yourself for your cowardice. Again you try to tap. Finally you manage to understand your neighbours. Your heart becomes lighter.

Despite all the inconvenience of communicating with each other, news of the arrival of 'newcomers' quickly spreads. Amid the sepulchral silence you only have to listen out for the taps of distant neighbours to know what they're tapping about. 'A newcomer's been brought in!.. Who is it? From which trial? Where from? Find out whether so-and-so's still alive, whether so-and-so's still in one piece, what's going on outside?'

The novice is swamped with endless questions, although he himself wants to find out as much as possible, as quickly as possible, about his comrades' daily life in prison. We had brought sad news with us. We didn't even want to impart a lot of it, so as to avoid causing pain and despair, but concealing the situation would have simply been dishonest… Pogroms, treachery on the widest scale, the indiscretion of certain people, courtesy of which so many were crushed – this was the most important news we brought with us.

'So it's all over?' one comrade asks somehow nervously.

'Well, we're not going to bring you any joy with the news here. Almost half are sick: Malavskii has TB, Isaev as well, Nemolovskii has a stomach ulcer; Shchedrin is mentally ill, Gellis has TB', and so on, they catalogue all the details for us. Meanwhile a blue creeps up to the door… The little window opens and the unhappy conversation ceases. The topics of conversation were most diverse, exclusively related to prison life, and most of all there were enquiries about the condition of sick comrades. The fact was that thanks to the constant silence, every groan, every cough from one of the sick could be heard clearly. During the visits of the doctor, who came every day and saw everyone, you couldn't help standing by the door, listening to what the doctor was saying and what the sick person replied. 'I'll send powders', the doctor would say softly. 'Unlock the bed', he adds, as the door swings shut. 'Unlock the bed?' you ask yourself. 'That means it's a serious illness, death is just round the corner;

a few days and all the suffering and captivity will end.' A gloomy feeling, malice boils over in the soul. 'But really that's the end that awaits us all', somehow calms you, and drives away oppressive thoughts.

In the first years beds were only unlocked during the daytime on the doctor's orders, and for the weakest of the sick... Two hours after the doctor's round medicine is brought. Don't imagine it's handed over and left to the patient. No. They have to take it in the presence of blues and the indefatigable Herod.

'Powders!' the latter says curtly and importantly, but he doesn't hand it out himself, one of the blues does that. You silently take the packet and place it on the table.

'It has to be taken now', Herod elaborates, perplexed at how such simple precautions can be misunderstood.

'I can't take it now', replies the patient: 'it has to be taken with food.'

'Take the powders, and leave!' Herod orders severely. The blue instantly seizes the packet from the table, and the door again crashes shut.

'What was that comedy all about?' you wonder after such a scene. But after lunch everything is explained. The blue appears again under the direction of that self same Herod. Again the word 'powders' is repeated, and the blue silently follows every move by the patient, who, not understanding, places them on the table as before.

'They have to be taken now,' elaborates the superintendent.

'I'll take them later.'

'Paper cannot be left in the cell!'

That's what it's all about! What precautions! But this is the story not only with powders, but even with drops as well. Vials are not placed in the patients' hands. The gendarmes appear in the cell and measure out a spoonful, – God, what kind of spoon it is! Something like a dredging scoop in miniature – that's how they dole it out. For the healthy it's unpleasant to be in the presence of these hostile characters, but for the sick it becomes simply unbearable. It's not surprising that you hide your illness for a long time, just so as to avoid unnecessary visits from the guards. It's Christmas Eve. Bells ring out from the fortress bell tower. The sounds are indistinct and as if far away – the windows are closed tightly – and yet they transport you to an irrevocable past. Memories are resurrected one after the other. A carefree childhood among family and people who are close to you; youth, full of cares, privations, hope; the revolutionary life, with its light and shade...

Friends: some have already long since left us, they perished in the struggle. Who is still alive? There's no answer, and you don't expect one. You yourself are a living corpse. If only books would be given out soon.

It's already two months, and apart from the Gospels and Old Testament, you've seen nothing. Tomorrow's Christmas, perhaps they'll distribute some for the holiday?

But Christmas brings nothing with it, even the usual food is given out: borscht with cured pork fat and some indigestible pieces of meat, and *kasha*. Only the blues and Herod, dressed in ceremonial uniforms with aiguillettes, clink their spurs loudly: Pilate's servants rejoicing in Christ's memory!.. But in the cells the same sepulchral silence. If only this day would pass more quickly, it awakens so many memories. What good are they? Evening comes. Dinner is distributed. Herod's harsh words are heard: he's issuing rebukes for tapping. And what's for dinner? Meatless borscht – leftovers from lunch. The prisoners are permitted not to accept it. And many indeed do not accept it. But the distribution of dinner is accompanied by one pleasure. Beds are unlocked at this time. How pleasant to take one's ease, lie down after a day of walking from corner to corner.

Myshkin's cell is opened. The noise of an empty plate reverberates, then commotion, noise, knocks and cries from all sides. The prison resounds with inhuman sounds. There's a brawl going on in Myshkin's cell. Gendarmes throw themselves at him like madmen, forgetting that they're breaking the silence (!). 'No need to beat him!' shouts Herod (thus one of Myshkin's closest neighbours heard).

'What are you doing in there, you scum!' a cry from the other corner is heard down the whole corridor.

'What are you doing in there?'

'Scum! Scum!'

Then hysterical female voices. Tapping on the doors. The whole prison has turned into some sort of torture chamber where groans mixed with desperate screams and noise. But then everything stopped dead for a few minutes, only in the corridor there's a whisper like a snake hissing: Herod is giving out some sort of instructions and orders. None of the prisoners knows what all the noise was about, what has happened. But the thought that anything can be expected from the gendarmes overcomes you so strongly that you can't drive it away.

You tap on the window, call the superintendent.

'What were you doing in there?' you naively ask the latter.

'Nothing! There's a madman in there!' He's lost his head, and replies before he's managed to recover.

'Then he should be taken to hospital. This is a prison.'

'There's no hospital yet, it'll be built soon,' he lies. And the window swings shut. He hurries to another window, to hear the same questions and give the same mendacious answers.

The night passed painfully. The sound of prisoners pacing round the cells could be heard for a long time, and in the corridor from time to time there were groans, and some sort of cry.[27]

The next day during lunch the same incident was almost repeated. And no food was given out, without any explanation why. Apparently a completely involuntary cry had burst from someone: 'why haven't I been given any food?' Instead of an answer, a commotion was heard in the corridor, and I.'s cell was opened.[28] Five blues burst in and threw themselves on I., seizing whatever they could get hold of. Two of them gagged him with a towel, so that he could barely manage to get out some sort of indistinct cry. Something heavy was dragged down the corridor – it was I. being taken to the old prison, to a punishment cell, where he was thrown onto the cold, asphalt floor. On the way he acquired a lot of bruises. The next day the doctor went to see him, examined his bruises and acknowledged that they were the result of the gendarmes' zeal. Subsequently, when Orzhevskii visited, I. complained to him about the brutal treatment, referring him to the doctor as Orzhevskii didn't want to believe him. The doctor cringed, straightened up, and failed to confirm I.'s word. To the contrary, he said he had seen nothing (!).

Five days later I. was returned from the punishment cell. He said what had happened to him. The rumour was going round the prison that he had been beaten. Even grim details were doing the rounds: when I. was being carried across the yard, one gendarme in a vest had jumped out and, punching him on the side with his fist, said, 'and that's my hand'! [sic]

But no general protest was raised on this occasion, although the incident was so important that one ought to have been sparked. This is why it didn't happen. Many were absolutely distressed by solitude, strict solitude, and rest was their only desire. Others were suffering physically and could barely drag themselves from day to day. It was at this time that Klimenko died by suicide and Tikhanovich tried to kill himself, and although he was saved by the blues, very soon afterwards he was no longer with us.

Handles were removed from the windows, evidently as a precaution.

Orzhevskii appeared again. Again he went round everyone with the usual questions: are there any complaints or requests? Some protested to him about maltreatment, the lack of books, correspondence with families. On the first two he made a commitment… of the last, he replied that it was impossible.

Some months later, however, some – the sickest, and even two or three of the healthy – were given meetings during exercise periods. These meetings took place on alternate days or every three days. But did they save many? Of those who received meetings then, only three are now alive. Tuberculosis was rampant in our prison. In March Malavskii, who had not been out to exercise all winter, finally took to his bed. For some reason he hadn't been given books for a long time. 'If you need something, tap on the door', Herod said to him a few days before his death. But no-one heard his voice even once. He died a few days later.

Whether he was dead or alive, however, was difficult to find out. We judged this by whether the door to his cell was opened when lunch and tea were being distributed. When a cell was skipped, it meant someone had died.

'What's happened to Malavskii?' One of my neighbours asked me.

'Seems he's died', you reply hesitantly. 'He's not had any lunch or dinner taken in.'

'It's said Butsevich is very weak as well, close to madness', the neighbour continues. 'Isaev has TB, he's exercising with Frolenko', he tells me his news. 'Find out about Iurii (Bogdanovich) and Grachevskii.'

About three weeks later the same neighbour advises about Butsevich: 'Seems he's died too. Today Morozov was exercising alone. But the gendarmes never say anything. Our friends are dying like flies.' All topics of conversation are exhausted, and the sickly condition of our comrades induces despondency in everyone. Something ominous is plaguing the prison. You just keep waiting for death to carry someone else off. In vain you try to lose yourself in a book. But what books? Nothing alive, to refresh the mind. Just a few travelogues that occasionally transported you to the fabled primitive world of the east. Or a mathematical formula that will absorb a hungry mind for a short time. Many of us studied mathematics or learned languages; but the latter does not require particular intensity of thought, and because of that some found this occupation annoying. And then there's the fate of one's comrades. 'Doesn't that fate await us too? What's all this for? You don't need knowledge in the grave!' they said.

But a week or two passes, and they pick up their abandoned activities again: living with your own thoughts is even more boring; it increases melancholy even more.

The fast ends. Easter is already close. The corridor is being cleaned: the blues are mopping the floor, dusting the walls, laying new carpets. We are taken out one by one to bathe – to the bath tub. How boring and endlessly long bath days are! We're not taken out for exercise on either day – Friday or Saturday.

'Wash!' says Herod, opening the cell door and admitting the three gendarmes who accompany everyone to the bath tub.

You take your towel silently and follow them.

'You have to sit down – to be shaved', Herod proclaims again, sitting on a chair and keeping a sharp eye on every movement of all those present.

You sit on a stool. One of the blues takes a huge pair of scissors and begins to 'tear out' your hair, unconcerned not only with aesthetics, but even the integrity of the skin.

'Be careful!' you scream, when the scissors graze the skin, but not so much out of pain as the humiliation you're experiencing. You sit the whole time as if on needles, and barely restrain yourself from punching him in the face.

'No shouting', Herod objects impassively. 'You have to tell me, and I will order you to be shaved more carefully.'

'That order should have been given earlier, not waiting until my skin's snipped', you reply.

'Done, you may wash', he ducks out of further deliberations.

Meanwhile the docile blues are constantly walking round, pouring water, throwing wood under the boiler, inspecting the underwear, supplying basins. But don't think they've forgotten about you! No, each of them has one eye keenly trained on you.

You hurry to wash your hair just so as to finish this ceremony more quickly.

'The first time you're greeting Easter here', a comrade from the Ravelin taps to me. 'In the Ravelin we were treated to an excellent dinner, and even given cakes. I think it was mockery; the next day the food was so disgusting it was impossible to eat! Unbelievably stupid malice! They thought of persecuting us with food. Here they're really torturing us with spiritual food! Besides the scriptures, we've been given nothing. I read the lives of all the saints. Shchedrin appears to be going out of his mind. It was him screaming today', he suddenly changes the topic of conversation. 'He was asked why he was shouting: "Anxiety," he says, "I had to let it out." Ignatii Ivanov will soon die, I think. He no longer leaves his bed.'

And again conversations on this theme…

Easter morning. The sound of bells never ceases and irritates us dreadfully. There's a commotion in the corridor. The gendarmes run and place something by the door of every cell in use. Again the sound of spurs can be heard.

Then the door opens. The blues bring in a plate with pieces of Easter cake and curd pudding, and a piece of roast veal; another carries in a mug of tea, a piece of sugar and some decorated eggs.

But what's this curd pudding? Where's it been? There's sand on it, and it's on a dirty plate... Behind the backs of the gendarmes, Herod is carefully observing what impression the festive treat makes, as though he's anticipating something. But none of the prisoners made a sound. Disgruntled, Herod slammed the door shut.

'Christ is risen!' a comrade taps to me. 'Where did you spend this holiday last time? For some reason it always reminds me of my childhood... My poor mother! Will she ever see me again? I'm afraid for her; you know, the doctor was wrong about her eyes. I used to read her books at one time. You'd read, and she'd lie there.'

'"Mother dear, are you asleep?" you'd ask her. "No!" Precious childhood! How many bright, warm memories! How much inexpressible tenderness there is in you! Even in this living crypt you find respite in yourself, and awaken suppressed feelings.'

'You're probably sad now! After all, aren't you used to a better life', I ask my comrade.

'I wasn't pampered... Tell me about your life!'

But there had been little joy in my life. My stories would probably bore him.

'I recently read about Archpriest Avvakum.[29] "Abide, Markovna," he said to his wife, remember?'

'What a strong nature!' he interrupted me.

In the evenings I had long conversations with him about what we'd read.

'Why are you silent? What are you doing?' another neighbour taps nervously, constantly running round his cell.

'I'm studying maths.'

'Damn your maths! The well-fed don't understand the hungry.'

'Sorry', you answer him, 'outside there was no time to study, so I've jumped at the chance here. Why didn't you call when you wanted to talk?..'

It was difficult and bitter to hear such reproaches, especially since I'd tapped a great deal, as I knew very well the mental condition of my comrade, who had been deprived of his freedom many years before me and had already had time to lose his health and his emotional equilibrium. And then the sound of the bells prevented you from hearing a barely perceptible tap. If you don't immediately understand, you have to ask again, and that causes even more exasperation. It's no surprise that even modest conversations end in an outburst. But fortunately, everything calmed down once the outburst had passed.

'Don't take offence at him', persuaded the first neighbour. 'He's decent, it's just his nerves.'

'In fact we've already made up.'

'That's great. Morozov has been given meetings with Iuvachev. He reported that Iuvachev says incongruous things. Wants to go to a monastery. Not tapping with anyone.'

'So he's mentally unhinged?'

'It's good that he's been given meetings. Perhaps he'll recover. Listen, something's knocking in the yard, being dragged.'

'Aren't they building a hospital? The superintendent told me a long time ago that they were going to build a hospital.'

In the yard, right opposite our windows, some kind of feverish work really was going on. Hammer blows, the clatter of saws, the constant movement of people could be heard.

We gave ourselves over to speculation. What were they doing there? I tried to shin up to the window and look out of the ventilation pane, but couldn't: the window was opaque, the ventilation pane high and closed. Meanwhile everyone was interested in what was being built. It was, as we later found out, allotments that they were 'building'. The strict administration command was carefully hiding from us the humane intentions they were already putting into action for us. And how quickly the work was carried out! Evidently they were hurrying to save by means of the allotments those they themselves had tormented and destroyed...

'Today I saw a worker in a red shirt. Oh, how the gendarmes ran him off his feet. He was just like a mouse, confused, not knowing which way to turn. He started running like he'd gone crazy. Herod was beside himself.' I tell my comrade how I ran into the worker when I was being taken out for exercise. Herod was in a terrible rage. Still: I'd seen a free man. Now the gendarmes were getting it in the neck. And again speculation and guesswork on account of what was being built there.

But soon everything became clear. As soon as the building work was complete, that is, they'd constructed fences for the convicts and a platform for surveillance, and brought in earth from the forest, all the allotments were immediately distributed between those who were allowed meetings. Seeds and iron shovels were distributed, and water tanks installed.

How many conversations, how much tapping was there on account of this! How many amusing incidents there were with inexperienced gardeners! One sowed all his seeds in a space of two or three square yards, another only knew to pour water onto the bed, creating a swamp. So Herod had to intervene and give instructions.

Chapter III.

The allotments were a small thing, but how much material for conversation they supplied us with! Every day, returning from exercise, our gardeners reported something new about the condition of their crops. When the first shoots started to appear, the walls rattled as if something extraordinary had happened. Yet it couldn't be otherwise in such god-forsaken circumstances: where there's no life, no food for either mind or heart, any insignificant change will produce an exaggerated reaction. Amid such monstrous deadness, each person tries to create for themselves some sort of activity, seizing one thing or another, to save themselves from being devoured by inertia. It's true that at first the allotments were given to very few. But this novelty affected everyone; everyone was revived. Soon meetings and an allotment were given to our ladies: Vera Nikolaevna Figner and Liudmila Aleksandrovna Volkenshtein. And it was entertaining to see them set about gardening: they dug the beds, of course, in the most industrious fashion; but when it was time to sow, they threw almost a whole handful of seeds into a single hole, and the distance between the holes was so small, that if Herod hadn't interfered in their husbandry, everything would have died.

When Vera Nikolaevna came back from her first meeting, she was asked: how did it affect her?

'We both started weeping, and cried the whole time', she replied. 'But what were they tears of? Joy? Grief? It's impossible to answer. It's a kind of welling up of feelings that have been concealed for a long time, then suddenly flood out. How profoundly, and how much you experience in the short minutes of a first meeting! The closeness of a comrade living in the same circumstances as you yourself awakens memories of the past with such strength, it's as if you're experiencing them anew, but you experience them somehow differently. All the pictures, all the images are suffused with a quiet, gentle, almost childish feeling, as if there, in the depths of this past, there wasn't a single dark cloud.'

But after every meeting – and at first they weren't given every day – V. N. would return sad and preoccupied with something. Returning from her walks, she often talked to Herod.

'What did Herod say?' she was asked.

'Nothing, it's not important!!' she'd answer abruptly.

But such a reply didn't satisfy us. It seemed something was afoot, and one feared that she might refuse meetings, as she had previously hinted she would do so as to demand meetings for everyone. Or perhaps the death of many comrades had unsettled her, neighbours thought.

At that time death really was mowing us down in the prison. We got by so miserably, our mental state was such that every day you were waiting for another one to be taken away… Once V. N., returning from a meeting, called one of her comrades and emphatically said that meetings were starting to poison her life: 'I can't make use of privileges when comrades don't have them… Liudmila and I have decided to refuse meetings until they're given to everyone…' In vain comrades tried to dissuade her, pointing out that many were sick, and that refusal would be bad even for those who weren't allowed meetings.

'No, we mustn't allow any Herod or commandant to judge us morally, to create divisions between us…' she nervously interrupted, and was even aggrieved.

A few days later some comrades really did refuse meetings and allotments, and informed the administration of the reasons for their refusal.

You can imagine how much our Cerberuses disliked our action. I bet they thought that their cruel regime had squeezed the whole spirit of protest out of the victims, turning them into submissive sheep, but their bad management and unfair treatment were being pointed out to them, with demands for equality for all! 'Not content with this, they're still kicking up a fuss, trying to force us to act differently! It's too much.'

One comrade, Shebalin, after unsuccessfully trying to reason with the commandant, started tapping loudly on the door; then others joined in. A commotion was raised in the corridor, blues ran in… The little window opened in the cell of the first tapper. 'Shut up!' the commandant cried disrespectfully. 'Shut up yourself!' our comrade answered him even louder and, grabbing a metal basin, banged it so hard on the table that it was flattened into a plate. Almost immediately two were taken to the punishment cells.

Fierce persecution for tapping began, apparently in retaliation for the protest. Another pair were taken away… and reprimands for tapping became more frequent. Petty revenge reached stupid heights: if you handed in a book to exchange it for another, the new one wouldn't arrive for several days, and they'd say nothing, whereas previously they were handed out the next day. All this is trivial, of course, but there were so many of these little things that they tried our patience… Or sometimes medicine wasn't distributed…

Conflict grew, altercations between prisoners and staff, which had been infrequent, occurred more and more often… Several more people were taken to the punishment cells, allegedly for tapping, and for correction… But alas, stepping up the persecution only led to more obstinacy. In the punishment cells the tapping was so loud that Herod installed gendarmes in the empty cells with wooden logs that they used to hit the walls, so that the tapping couldn't be heard, while in the corridor other blues worked on metal shutters that had been specially constructed to make a diabolical sound. It turned into a truly hellish Sodom. Of course, Herod appeared.

'When will you stop tapping?' he screamed at one of the prisoners, beside himself.

'When you stop playing tricks on us', you answer. 'I'll never stop tapping, understand, even if you hang me…'

'We will hang you… a document's on its way', he says, calming down a little.

'And you'll be the executioner, no doubt', somehow escaped from our comrade.

Don't think that this phrase offended him – no, he began to talk even more calmly, standing behind the backs of three lackeys in blue. And he limited himself to just giving his interlocutor an extra week in the punishment cell on bread and water, removing the screen and lampshade from the lamp,[30] and not allowing the doctor to see him for several days. The comrade suffered from eye pain, and the doctor was treating him.

'I need to see the doctor', the comrade announces to Herod.

'There's no doctor, he's left', Herod replies each time.

'Well, I'll call him today', says the comrade, and when the doctor appeared in the corridor, he starts shouting:

'Doctor, I need to see you!..'

And the doctor appeared. Herod apparently wasn't ready for this.

'Please excuse an incidental question', the comrade addresses the doctor, 'but answer frankly: have you been here this week?'

'I have', the other answers, surprised.

'So have a good look at this bugger – I've been such a moron that I expected the truth from Herod, who only tells the truth by mistake. He's been lying to me all week, telling me you'd left.'

Herod stands there, goggle-eyed. The doctor is silent.

'Did you give an order for the lampshade to be taken off my lamp?' the comrade asks, continuing.

'Has it really been removed?'

'Yes!'

'Well, I can't allow that', the doctor says, going pale. 'And how are your eyes?.. Replace the lampshade and don't remove it from his cell', he addresses Herod bluntly.

The latter loses patience, and seizes the doctor by the arms in the most presumptuous manner.

'Get out, I don't have time!' shrieks Herod.

'What a refined, delicate way of addressing people this man has, wouldn't you say, doctor?' the comrade shouts after them.

But the door has already slammed shut, and whispering can be heard behind it. Apparently, Herod very much disliked the comrade's prank. He resorted to a new method: making the blues fire up the iron stove at night (?) [sic]. It made such a racket in the corridor, just as everyone had gone to bed, that it could have raised the dead. The only thing you could do to oppose it was scream. As soon as it starts to rumble, one fellow prisoner begins screaming for it to stop, although it's clear beforehand that this won't happen, but Herod appears with false explanations. In the end he himself found it unpleasant to get up every night and run to the prison to restore peace and tranquillity, and the night-time 'idylls' stopped. But for all that it was as though books, exercise and beds didn't exist. It's true that sleeping on a bare, damp, asphalt floor wasn't especially soft or warm, but it seemed trivial compared to being deprived of books for many months. A comrade would wander, wander from corner to corner, and invent various activities. He managed to break a piece of grouting off the stove, and that's how doing maths on the black floor came into vogue. He sits and draws figures from geometry, or works out algebraic formulae using the grouting. But then the door opens.

'Take that stone off him, or whatever he's got', Herod commands.

'Take it!' the grouting is hurled at his feet.

'Why can't you just sit quietly. Ugh, you've smeared the whole floor. I'll put you in fetters', Herod says.

'And then what?' the comrade asks him mockingly. Sometimes at such moments a terrible malice takes control of you, but sometimes all this petty exactitude becomes simply absurd.

The door slams shut until the next occasion.

I don't know, perhaps this is an explanation made with hindsight, and perhaps it's not entirely correct, but I think that despite all the moral torture I endured, it was thanks to the almost constant conflict, the constant petty battles – and there was no question of anything major there – that I survived, stayed alive and almost healthy, precisely as a consequence of these battles, these discharges one allowed oneself, which were always accompanied by some sort of release. Resentment sometimes accumulates, and then suddenly it spills out. I remember all our comrades, and you know what? I find exactly the same thing: of those who were more restless, aside from a few, almost all survived; those with more even-tempered characters, or quieter temperaments, died more quickly.

Indeed for me it was clear how much physical and mental health had to be spent on suppressing feelings of anger and resigning myself to all this persecution. Although I should clarify that no-one managed complete indifference: outbursts of indignation materialized in everyone, just not all at the same frequency. In some it was rare, and took a mild form; in others, it was at its most extreme, as in the cases of Myshkin, Minakov and Grachevskii.

Exaggerated retaliatory measures led to tapping more and more acquiring the right of citizenship: we started tapping not only on the walls, but also on the heaters, so as to be heard on the other side of the corridor; then during exercise we tapped on the fences, and later, when they began to withdraw exercise for tapping, we used shovels. (At that time shovels were distributed to all and sand brought to the pens, so it was as if you were doing something, which at least warmed you up.)

Herod was indisputably fulfilling a higher will: he didn't take away our shovels, which were permitted by the Police Department, even though he could see perfectly well that they were being abused – used for tapping. He tried withdrawing exercise, but that proved not to be entirely convenient. Then he thought up another way: between the tapping prisoners he placed a blue in an empty pen, arming them with shovels too. As soon as tapping began, the blues began their cannonade, in order to interrupt us. And sometimes it would raise enough of a racket to test the patience of a saint. Herod would stand on the tower and contemplate it, infuriated. In the end he'd quickly come down from on high and remove the tapping prisoners.

'You all tap in your cells!' he says bluntly. 'What else do you need? The law does not allow tapping!'

'Well, I didn't make any promise to obey every absurd law.'

'But you're a man, and I'm a man, and they're people' – he points at the blues, who somewhat unexpectedly find themselves standing on this unusual ground. 'You should take pity on them (!). Tap, but so that you're not seen, and not heard.'

'But am I asking anyone to listen? Don't listen…'

'You do all this just to spite me', Herod interrupts. 'There's a few of you people, I'll separate you. You think I won't take care of you?..'

'Take care!..'

'I have my orders… if I'm ordered to feed you hazel grouse, the next day you'll be eating it…' he changed his tone even more and tried to appeal to the prisoners' feelings.

Apparently he thought he was speaking very delicately, but we saw only cynicism. When threats didn't help, Herod turned to all sorts of tricks: food lovers were promised 'full plates' of *kasha* and *shchi*. Or he'd go to someone with warnings about their neighbour: 'There's no point tapping with him: he's sick, a madman!' – he'd say this in the most serious tone. But nothing helped, of course.

In May 1887 a new group of seven men was brought in,[31] of whom five were executed on the same day.

Then another five arrived.[32] Material for conversations increased. They brought news from outside, but it was very sad news…

Shortly before this our cells were made more presentable: the floors were painted yellow, the lower third of the walls lilac. Besides that, exercise increased, and many of the sick were allowed two shifts of walks, that is, around 3½ hours. But I don't know if that worked out well for everybody.

Our shoes and clothes were poorly suited to the damp climate: we wore fur slippers unchanged in winter and summer. Of course, our feet were soaked and frozen. Many had colds, and refused to go on double walks. Having said that, the ventilation windows could now be opened as desired, even for the whole day, whereas previously they'd only been opened during the walks. But how attentively (!) Herod safeguarded our lives. Sometimes, during storms, he'd fly in headlong to close the windows.

'I want the window left open', you'd tell him.

'And if you're killed by a thunderclap, I'll have to answer for it! No!' he'd reply cynically, and wouldn't leave the window open for anything.

Soon Shebeko (Deputy Minister of Internal Affairs, Chief of the Gendarmes) appeared on our horizon. It was amazing how much he resembled Nozdrev.[33] However, the first time he behaved quite tolerably, assuring several they wouldn't be punished for tapping. But at the same time he started telling one comrade that the administration had complained about his misconduct. And when the comrade retorted by asking whether the administration itself was behaving properly, Shebeko cut short the conversation, saying 'I've no time!' V. N. stated that she would like her own books brought in for the library, and he permitted this. Others were allowed to do the same, and our library grew considerably. This was quite an event in our lives.

This was the year our poetry blossomed. So many poets were born among us that almost everybody was composing verses – such as they could, of course.

The reigning mood was somehow gentle, melancholic; the feeling of comradeship seemed to have become deeper, and each person tried to pour this into poetic form. But alas, only very few managed to do this. The majority were writing the clumsiest verses. The writer of the present lines belonged to the latter ranks of poet. Later, when this mood had passed, when I analysed my verses with the benefit of hindsight, I was often surprised at their audacity, and often asked myself: where did this boldness come from? How did that rhythm appear? The solution was very simple: I lived in a very lively spot, and nearly every poem had to pass through me, and I had to tap them out letter by letter. It was this mechanism, obviously, that engendered in me a weakness for assonance.

In content our poems were quite varied: we sang the praises of our past life, of dead fighters... We 'glorified' the prison administration; the weak appealed for courage and endurance, and so on, and so on. Verses were also written for days of celebration: for comrades' birthdays and name days, instead of gifts, and for New Year. Some poets wrote only humorous verses.

The very best poems were by Morozov, V. Figner, Polivanov and Sergei Ivanov.

Our poetic mood was often interrupted by the prose of monotonous life. One comrade had only just returned from the punishment cells when he was sent there again for tapping. Another comrade demanded either that the first be returned, or that he be taken there as well. The latter desire was fulfilled. A third comrade demanded the same, but was categorically refused, perhaps because he was sick. He began to shout, so that he'd be taken to the punishment cell, or the prisoners released.

'I won't take you!' said Herod, and disappeared.

The comrade began to sing, and achieved his aim. This happened late one evening, in summer. And so the comrade being taken away after a long time in the prison, managed for the first time to see a pure blue sky,[34] awash with stars. One of those taken away later conveyed his impressions to me as follows. 'A sort of solemn silence filled the air. I was simply intoxicated, I forgot that I was in the middle of a crowd of blues, I stopped and just looked at the sky. Not even Herod was in a hurry. Could this brutish man really have guessed the condition of his victim? I so didn't want to be separated from this blue dome, and go into the god-forsaken, damp cell!..' Another comrade later told me that night made the same impression on him. A third comrade for a very long time used to reminisce about it. The next day Grachevskii hit the doctor so that he would be executed. One of his neighbours confirmed that he was psychologically ill. Behind a wall it's difficult to judge. It was known only that Grachevskii's nerves were greatly shaken, and apparently life had become unbearable for him. The previous evening Bogdanovich had tried to persuade him, suggest that he postpone, but he hadn't listened... He was also transferred to a punishment cell, but very far away, and didn't want to reply to anyone. What was going on with him right up to his death, nobody knows. Even later, when others were taken there, he didn't respond. What was he enduring at that time!

Those taken to the punishment cells were completely isolated, and all communication with them ceased for several months. This very much distressed the rest. Many thought they were being severely mistreated. This speculation was confirmed when the lamps in our cells were fixed to the walls and started to be locked up so that it was impossible to remove the burners. Had something happened?... The question was raised about demanding the return of comrades from the old prison. But, as usual, where there are many people, and communication between them is only through a wall, it took too long to come to a decision. And the late Bogdanovich, who could no longer stand it, began to sing, other comrades as well. The administration appeared, and that same day everyone was returned. From them we learned of Grachevskii's terrible death. Some of them had smelled the stench of a burning body, but didn't immediately find out what had happened, or to whom. Grachevskii had taken the burner from the lamp, poured kerosene on his mattress, lain down, and set himself on fire... Barely alive, he'd been taken out into the corridor, where he died. A terrible death!

A few days later Shebeko appeared and, it was said, shouted so much at Herod that he was paralysed by a stroke.[35] It wasn't out of pity for Grachevskii that he shouted, of course, but because surveillance of the prisoners had been too negligent. And indeed, it's amazing that Herod's vigilant spirit could have allowed such a thing. The gendarmes must have fallen asleep.

That month our entire administration changed: Herod, the doctor and the commandant were all sacked, others were sent to us. Relations changed: they stopped using the familiar 'you'; the food improved somewhat; invalid portions began to be prescribed more freely; new books were sent, although not substantial ones. Making use of the freer conditions, instead of tapping we thought of using the drains of the internal plumbing, and began to shin up to the windows to look at the world through the ventilation pane. Of course, our world wasn't much to write home about, but it was still variety. For that they began to harass us again. One was reprimanded for it, and he wanted to hit the superintendent, but didn't manage, and instead of hitting him, spat in his face...

Shebeko appeared again, but no longer like he was before. He had obviously decided to catch us out. T.'s cell opens,[36] and Shebeko from the corridor screams:

'You should be whipped, whipped!' and the door instantly slams shut.

T. didn't even manage to make out who was screaming what.

Then Sh.'s door opened.[37]

'Terr-or-ists, you can see it in their faces… we'll whip you!…' and from another door the same thing was repeated. After this Shebeko looked in on another two or three comrades, spewed out the same words, and didn't see anyone else.

Such lack of respect and rudeness outraged everyone terribly. Again the question of a protest was raised, of what to do, how to respond if such-and-such a punishment was employed against anyone. Our agitation was so strong that if anybody really had been punished, the outcome would have been very tragic. In the meantime we decided to tear up and throw out the instructions that were hanging on the wall of each cell. Petersburg was obviously informed of this. Shebeko appeared again, but this time with different intentions. Going into Liudmila V.'s cell, he immediately started speaking about her mother.

'Your mama was in the department.'

'I'd like first of all to know to whom I'm speaking?' Liudmila interrupted him, guessing that this was the very hero who'd pranced before the prisoners last time.

'I'm General Shebeko.'

'So it was you who took the liberty last time of being so rude to my comrades?.. I have no desire to speak to you and no desire to listen to anything you have to say. Leave…' she said, and turned her back.

He didn't go to see anyone else after that, and never visited us again. But the result of his final visit was that our cells were made even smaller, with two corners blocked off so that the cells were six-sided. The plumbing was also altered so that it was impossible to use it for conversation; but we contrived to use the new arrangement as well. At this point Bogdanovich died. His health had already been totally shattered in the Ravelin, but he always kept himself going and played a lively role in all our protests. Just before the fatal event he was in a feverish state. On his request he was transferred to the old prison, where he hoped to recover his health in isolation. But it got even worse. The patient was taken for a cold bath, where he contracted pneumonia. When he was returned to us, his throat was bleeding. He was treated quite attentively. But what was this treatment even for? He fell into unconsciousness because of the loss of blood: he frequently cried out and moaned. How agonizingly these cries resounded in the prison, as if a shroud hung over everyone, as if a piece had broken free from his chest, the place where the most precious feelings were kept... Conversation revolved only around what had been heard about Iurii, what the doctor said, what the superintendent said about him... Soon he was no longer with us.

For several days a deathly silence prevailed. Nobody even felt like tapping. It felt like we had lost a friend and comrade who was first to go on the attack and last to retreat, who knew how to love his comrades, defend them and sacrifice everything for them. The spirit of protest also died away for some time. Some sort of nightmare hung over the prison right until Karaulov's removal.

At first everyone doubted that Karaulov would be taken away at the end of his sentence, that is, in November '88. But two or three months before this he was informed that his wife had finished her medical course and was living in Petersburg. On the day of Karaulov's departure the first carpentry workshop was opened, but the only person allowed to work in it was Waryński, who was in the last stages of tuberculosis, and died three months later.

On 8 November Karaulov was walking with Morozov. Suddenly the blues come up to him and say, 'Come with us, please!' That's how our Karaulov disappeared. Although there had been few hopes for his departure, we had nevertheless given him instructions beforehand for contacting our families, and had even foisted poems on him.

In February Waryński fell seriously ill. He often had clashes with the doctor because of the medicine. He was no longer able to go out for walks, although sometimes the blues led him out, supporting his arms.

But the presence of these people just irritated the sick man. We tried to ask the administration for one of his comrades to be allowed into his cell to help him, but received a categorical refusal. An inspector, some civil servant or other from the Police Department, came, and to the same request answered one of us with the most cynical phrase:

'Perhaps you want angels of mercy assigned to the sick?' he said, and cleared off.

The late Waryński was an extremely amiable man and an outstanding personality, but few of us knew much about him, because he had worked in Poland.

In March '89 Orzhikh was brought in. Evidently, the last two deaths had made an impact on the higher administration. Soon more work was permitted: bookbinding and fretwork. Then everyone was given meetings and allotments. Our mausoleum came back to life. We tried to expand the allotments, planting vegetables and flowers in the exercise pens, but the blues destroyed our new nurseries in the most ruthless manner, digging up all the sand and earth.

I remember that someone spoke out to the superintendent about this, who replied: 'the authorities didn't permit it!' More books were sent, but mostly specialist and few of any interest, to my mind. Nobody liked this at all. We decided to strive for books to be sent according to our lists. But before we could achieve anything new, we had to defend the old. In autumn '89, the director of the Police Department, Durnovo, took it into his head to check up on us. As befitted the true owner of the mausoleum, he went round us all, and tried to peep into every corner of every cell to boot. He spoke discreetly and politely, but something petty and malign shone through his politeness. Then he goes in to see S. Ivanov.

'Hello! How is your health? What are you doing?' he asks, persistently eyeballing the table.

'You're reading... What?' – and this little gnome approaches the table, on which is lying Quinet's *History of the French Revolution* in French.

'Hm! Quinet? Where did this book come from?' he asks meaningfully, hiding his displeasure. Sergei replies that it is one of our books, taken from the library.

'You don't have any statements, complaints to make?' Durnovo continues, and leaves, but where does he go? Straight to the library. He demands the catalogue and makes an order to withdraw all the books that had been brought in by us. But the local administration didn't set about fulfilling this order immediately, they must have foreseen the consequences, because they knew how much we valued our books.

The commandant ran round all the cells berating our complacency, trying to prepare the blow, but he did so very awkwardly, and just irritated everyone. And then it was declared straight away that we had to hand all our own books back to the library, and those who didn't would have them removed. The latter could easily be done during exercise or baths, when the inhabitants weren't in the cells. And all our books were withdrawn from the library. There was no end to our resentment.

We were still being protected from harmful literature like school children. But wasn't this just mockery? They had allowed these books themselves several months ago, and now they were removing them all again without any debate... We had to demand the return of our books... But how to achieve that! Various suggestions were made: some advised refusing exercise, others a hunger strike. Those who suggested the latter method understood that it wouldn't be possible for everyone, because it requires a lot of strength and health, and there were almost no healthy people among us. But other forms of protest were ineffective, so the hunger strike went to a vote. The majority voted in favour, and only four refused to take part. But it was decided that only proponents of the hunger strike would participate. Of those, the weaker ones were given the right to join later, that is, to start the strike four days after the healthy ones. And this was accepted. The protest began.

The blues bring lunch.

'Not required!' rings out from one window.

'Not for me either!' is heard at another, and so on, and so forth.

The opponents of the strike also soon joined in. And all conversation and controversy ended. Indeed, what is there to talk about once the business has already begun?

The first day was even light-hearted. We talked a lot via the plumbing, even sang, read various stories, our own poetic works, cracked jokes. The second day was harder. On the third day and the fourth, the feeling of hunger intensifies greatly. One of the sick people, K.,[38] admitted that he found the fourth day so difficult that he ate the tiny chess pieces he had made out of bread the year before.

'And they were so hard, God dammit, they almost broke my teeth!' he joked.

'So, what, you're full now?'

'What the hell? The hunger's even worse now...'

'You messed up, brother: you should have made them bigger and heavier.'

But jokes are jokes, and this state of mind was not especially significant. The mood changed. General conversations became rarer and rarer. The best thing was to lie down as much as possible and move as little as possible. In a situation like this time passes in a sort of half-asleep state, and even sometimes with indistinct hallucinations. But all the same it's relatively easy. I remember, I lay down for almost the whole of the fourth day and suffered very little from hunger as such.

The commandant appeared. He visited a few people and enquired why they weren't accepting food. He was told...

'But you'll never win this. It doesn't depend on me. The department ordered the books to be withdrawn...'

'It's all the same to us...'

'But, after all, you're torturing yourself...'

'We've been forced into it...'

'I can't help at all', he finished, and left.

On the seventh day some started with bloody diarrhoea and signs of extreme weakness. This forced us to start talking about ending the hunger strike. 'Not unto death…' The pretext for such sacrifices was too small, one person said.

'This is too cruel', added another.

The protest was nearing its end. Several simply declared that continuing the strike was beyond them.

'We'll start accepting food!'

'Let them eat. Then they can continue', someone said, I don't know whether seriously or joking.

Our strength and patience weakened every day; every day demands were repeated even more insistently – give up the protest because it's not worth dying for such trivial things, they say, indeed it was impossible that we'd die, and so on, and so forth.

The administration obviously had no intention of conceding. And so after a ten-day hunger strike we decided to give up… However, a few, including V. N. F., continued, and starved for a few more days. And one opened up an artery in his arm on the eighth day, but a gendarme noticed and took him away to the old prison.

The mood afterwards was dreadful… Fault-finding began, diagnosis of everything. Relations between comrades were out of kilter: there wasn't the same warmth, trust or tenderness. Grievances mounted. On the whole, life and feelings in the first days after the hunger strike were completely and utterly miserable. And then the commandant appeared again and read out a document received from the Police Department, which said that our books wouldn't be returned, but our notebooks, which had been confiscated at the same time, could be returned. Thus the administration announced its victory to us, which made our state of mind even worse.

Again there was chit-chat and quarrelling about what to do and how to respond. But then first one, then another, misfortune befell our fellowship.

Konashevich became mentally ill: he refused to go out for walks with comrades and began to isolate himself. In vain we tried to save him, to draw him into conversation. He began to kick up a fuss, and was taken away to the old prison where, however, he didn't stay long. But when he returned, even meeting others had a very bad effect on him.

This terrible misfortune distracted our attention from the protests. Moreover, after two months, or a month and a half, they sent us new books – not ours, of course. Our commandant was replaced and the new one appointed in his place was more intelligent and diplomatic. A few more workshops were opened and work was promised for us all before too long.

This belated concession, although noticed by everybody, did little to change our mood, and couldn't restore our previous relations... What a shame that was!... How much light and warmth there had been!... Now everything seemed to be covered by some sort of cold shroud.

Another comrade went out of his mind. He began to say god knows what, and regarded almost all his comrades with terrible mistrust. He also wanted to seclude himself, but didn't manage to do so; we persistently and even officiously took him for exercise. These meetings often represented an unbearable torture: almost every time it was possible still to see glimpses of consciousness in him…. But tears, despair, frenzied laughter, a wild, terrible laughter, alternated at short intervals... The administration, apparently, itself guessed that the regime had to be changed, allowing everyone to work. We all jumped at the chance!

A true craze for work ensued. There were few workshops, but many wished to go to them, and besides, at first we worked alone. The majority still had to learn, and listened to lectures through the walls... Evenings were the most restless time: loud tapping often rang round the entire prison. One person announces he's going to the turning workshop the next day, another says he is; it's his turn, he says; a third is planning to go as well, because he hasn't finished his work. Wars of words and disputes begin, and so on. Others tap to express their wish to go to the carpentry workshop, and because of the latter the same sort of duel begins. Everyone wants to work, and ease their nerves through work, but the gendarmes assign work. This is accompanied by a whole load of annoyance, confrontation and discontent. The idea is conceived of taking the allocation of workshops, ordering of materials, tools, and so on, and so forth, into our own hands. And really, what kind of work is it, when the materials you need aren't assigned to the workshop where you want to work, or when you want to entertain yourself or stretch your legs. Again there was recourse to reasoning with the administration, to whom it was proved that the workshops would only have meaning when the management of them was put entirely in our hands.

'Just as we thought', replies the commandant, 'the more concessions you gain, the more your demands increase. We can't allow this.'

'Then why were the workshops opened? It's impossible to work in these conditions, because it's just an aggravation…'

'Ask the higher administration. An inspector will be coming soon', the commandant tried to appease us.

But before the inspector appeared concessions had already begun. Materials bought by the gendarmes aren't accepted [by the prisoners], they say they're unsatisfactory. They insist on everything being bought from our own lists. They demand to be allowed to work in pairs, so that those who have skills can help those who don't. They insist on the mentally ill also being allowed to work in pairs. Particular pressure is applied on the latter point, seeing the positive effect of physical work on the nerves. It was necessary to appeal to the doctor as well.

'Can we really give tools to the psychiatrically ill, and leave them with others in the workshops to boot? What if they kill someone? We'd have to answer for that', the doctor refuses.

'Don't worry. Nothing like that will happen.'

'You say it won't happen,' interposes the superintendent, the stupidest of all the stupidest people in the world, 'but prisoner no. 28 is always rowdy.[39] No, no… I'm afraid, afraid…' Hunched over, he retreats to the door on his thin little stick legs.

But in the end they still give in. New workshops are built. The sick go to work in pairs. One of them is so enthusiastic he works like a galley slave. He returns to the cell as if he's been ducked in water, tired, but calm and in a good mood. His health is noticeably improving: he no longer speaks the same nonsense as he used to, and doesn't descend into agonizing hypochondria. A joyful hope arises in everyone – of saving him. But was he the only one saved by working? Some people did live solely through work for some time, were only supported by that. They worked day and night, taking their work to their cells. You'd sometimes hear filing, scraping, hammering here and there.

The general mood and nervous state improved for everyone. It was like a restless anthill was beginning to stir in the prison.

Our ladies were also allowed to work in the carpentry and turning workshops. There was no end to good-natured jokes, especially directed at V. N. F. After all, she was so small, graceful and fragile in appearance.

'Vera, there are some logs that need sawing and cutting', one comrade, who was always assuring everyone that V. N. would not refuse any kind of work, would say to her wickedly.

'Send it to me, I'll cut it, and we'll saw it when I'm on exercise with Liudmila', she'd reply seriously.

'I knew it… ha-ha-ha', our comrade would laugh.

And Vera obstinately requests logs for herself. She hacks, saws, hews, of course, not as fast, but she doesn't want to fall behind the others. The work had an extremely beneficial effect on her. Her nerves settled down, and her physical condition improved.

But as always happens in god-forsaken prisons, festive moods do not last long. Butsinskii was gravely ill: he developed oedema. Everyone felt that death would soon carry away yet another comrade. Our merriment started to wane, and if it did at any point reappear, then it was always with hints of deep, silent grief.

A few days before Butsinskii's death we were allowed into his cell to help him. He could barely stand, but in spirit he was buoyant and extremely cheerful. The night before his death one comrade went and sat with him for around five hours.

'Sing something!' he said to him.

Butsinskii was a great lover of singing. We knew that singing always made him feel better. And although it was painful and sad, our comrade sang Butsinskii's favourite song: 'Isn't the snow white'.[40] With some sort of special feeling he began to echo his comrade with half open eyes. His comrade couldn't carry on; he fell silent. I don't know whether Butsinskii noticed his comrade's face, but he suddenly said jovially: 'Don't be afraid, I'm perfectly well. Sing something more cheerful'…

But the next morning it was all over…

Chapter IV.

Although he was very much loved by everyone, Butsinskii's death didn't leave such a deep and painful trace as usually remained after the death of other comrades: he died at a time when the life of those who remained was especially hard, and we looked upon his end as more of a release from long and painful suffering. Not long before Butsinskii's death, all our anticipation and hopes of at least someone emerging from this sepulchre were dealt a cruel blow. In 1890 Lagovskii's term ended, as he had been sent to us administratively in 1885. Everyone relied on him being released, and for some reason we were all so certain of this that long before the end of his sentence we started giving him all sorts of errands. For a few months he was fully occupied with accepting these missions: he learned poetry by heart, addresses of families, and so on. Everybody's mood was abnormally elevated, and the originator of all this himself couldn't sleep at night, and kept flitting from corner to corner…

But then the last day of his sentence arrives: no hint of Lagovskii's removal. Everyone's taken out for exercise: still nothing! Lagovskii runs nervously about his cell. The rest stop in their tracks, listening for the slightest rustling in the corridor. 'Surely they'll take him?' my neighbour asks, somehow timidly. 'We're prisoners – they can do anything to us,' I reply, not without some malice.

Finally, a clatter of spurs in the corridor headed straight for Lagovskii's door.

'Who was it? What was said to Lagovskii?' Questions poured out from all sides, as soon as the spurs once more clattered along the corridor.

Lagovskii didn't answer immediately. And we already believed he'd been taken away. But what cruel disappointment! Suddenly he taps.

'The commandant read out a document... by decree... They're leaving me here for another five years!'

'What for? Why? That's vile! We have to demand –' rang out from all sides. That last battle-cry died in the corridor and only reminded us of our recent failure, our impotence, which was even painful to recall. Indeed, it was painful... But it was still more painful to endure this despotism that was in no way justifiable, this incomprehensible outrage. Everyone recognized that a response was imperative, but as soon as the question of the method and form of the response was raised, feelings of irritation and despair began to boil over.

'We have no resources... We're victims of abuse, and suddenly we want to seek its destruction?! It's naive!' some said.

'It's time to abandon all protests. One was enough... We've determined our strengths, learned about each other: haven't our internal relations suffered enough?' added opponents of all protests.

'Aren't we in fact slaves, if we put up with every single arrogant insult!' countered the proponents of protest.

'A protest will give you nothing apart from destroying your nerves!' replied the opponents.

These arguments were hardly sincere – I'd more than once had to listen to and see terrible resentment on the part of the opponents of protests – but I don't think they were obstructing protests out of cowardice. No. In prison the soul festers too much, and explaining one act or another by whatever motive is impossible. The constant strain on the nerves so wears one down, overwhelms the will so strongly, that the calmest people crack, thrown off course by trivial things when they ought to have shrugged their shoulders. And then suddenly the most strident protesters endure the sort of insults to which it seemed there could only be one answer... In such situations everything depended on the moment, on the need for peace of mind or a 'discharge of nervous energy', as we put it.

The incident with Lagovskii happened at exactly the sort of moment when the majority needed rest. And the proposed protest didn't take place, although the idea of answering 'personally' wandered into some minds. And if anyone had appeared before us soon after that, it wouldn't have ended without a drama.[41] Lagovskii went around for several days like a madman. Everybody feared for him. We tried to distract him in all sorts of ways. Gradually he was reconciled to his fate, but he was changed beyond all recognition: he went grey, his face was covered in wrinkles, even his temperament was different. He became steadier, calmer. And our last hope of at least those with fixed sentences getting out disappeared.

'Now it's clear, nobody will get out of here', some said. 'There's a reason why one of the inspectors said, 'this prison is your coffin'.

Coffin or not, there are still living people in it. Its stuffy atmosphere is too unbearable; if it's not refreshed, it will very likely suffocate you. That refreshment began with our 'journals' being established, and chess games spreading. It was precisely in this period that our first illustrated journal, *Vinaigrette*, appeared. Its very title tells you what it was like. Several people edited it; the editors were also its invariable contributors, artists and so on.

The first issue was published in the form of a small, bound book in a single copy. The articles were, of course, handwritten, but quite varied in content. The editorial dealt with the youth of 1887, and for us it was sad news, since the young people it described were not a particularly pleasant sight. Then followed a rather bad story, memoirs, articles about mathematics, on statistics and industry in Russia and Poland, poetry. And between the articles were pasted watercolours and caricatures. One illustration featured an enormous table piled with various treats; around it sat gourmands, trying the dishes. Among them it was easy to recognize one of our fat comrades (a man with an enormous appetite), with his mouth open almost to his ears. The next picture was of the superintendent appearing in a cell with the blues; then a Zaporozhian Cossack, sitting in a mowed cornfield and 'patching up' his attire.[42] Under all the illustrations there were cheerful, ironic inscriptions, which were usually done by G.[43]

The journal exerted an influence on everyone like a contagion. For the next issues almost our entire world turned into writers. Who among us was not writing!.. It was impossible to place all the articles in a single journal, not only because it would have been too big, but also because of partisanship and personal antipathies!.. The birth of a new journal was inevitable. *The Dawn* appeared, published by a small group.

Many were severely displeased by its appearance, partly out of caution, mainly because the journal seemed to reinforce the schism in the prison that had happened for completely different reasons and, it had to be admitted, the most trivial ones. Journals were delivered to each other at meetings and over the fences.

Two literary camps were formed. In terms of number of participants, style and illustrations, *Vinaigrette* remained in first place. But the first issue of *The Dawn* had much better articles, and made a splash particularly with its stories. S. Ivanov's story 'The Ferry' was an uncontrived artistic thing; Popov's story of the life of street toughs was good; N.'s story of peasant life not bad at all.[44] The journalistic articles of the second journal were not as successful and, like *Vinaigrette*, had a strong whiff of 'patriotism', dealing, for example, with the 'superiority' of Russian industry over Polish. Each journal had its own form of 'patriotism': the Russian patriots gathered around *The Dawn*, and the Polish around *Vinaigrette*.

A bitter polemic began. *Vinaigrette* contended that Polish industry was incomparably better than Russian; *The Dawn* asserted the opposite. And on each side figures drawn from Vasil'chikov, Ianzhul, and an ancient Suvorin calendar, and so on, were cited as evidence.[45] To our participants' credit it must be said that no matter how ardently they argued their opinions, they always maintained a decent tone in their polemics. In the end the *Dawn* patriot went too far: he asserted that Russia needed to conquer all the straits, India, Persia, invade Constantinople and stand at the head of all the Slavic peoples. In response his opponent just chuckled discreetly, and, apparently, suggested the idea for a caricature with the following content: the Pamir mountains rise sky high; at the foot of them on the Russian side our patriot with an enormous portfolio under his armpit, on which is inscribed '1000 projects', struggling to drag himself and his burden over the mountains. And a lion waits for him there with a wide open mouth.

We all joked about the patriotism of our publicist S.[46] One old hand – good nature incarnate – A., often cracked witticisms about his friend:[47]

'So, what, N. P. – after all, you haven't seized everything yet. Don't you need to give the Germans a good thrashing? First you need to rough them up. Otherwise they'll never give you anything.'

The latter would smile phlegmatically, but didn't get angry.

In another area the polemic took on a completely different, pugnacious character. It started, as usual, with criticism, which was at first quite mild, but soon two fiery temperaments clashed, neither wanting to give in to the other's opinions. Time and time again harsh words would appear in articles. Outsiders were drawn into the controversy. Aggravation grew, and threatened the total termination of the journals. Meanwhile the contributors had only just started to acquire and polish their literary skills, so to speak. Indeed the content of the journals had become richer and more varied. Stories from prison and working life appeared; a fantastic narrative in the style of Flammarion was published.[48] But the controversy spoiled everything. The question was raised about even stricter 'censorship' – otherwise many threatened to take the journals, which were now being published regularly every month – into their own hands. For their part, the contributors – and there were those who were very much valued among them – insisted on clearing up the controversy. Vera Nikolaevna tried harder than anyone in this respect. For a long time she hadn't even wanted to participate in either journal, and only later did they feature first her poetry, and then a very good story from her youth, 'The Nanny'.

Finally, the censor furrowed his brow, and made several amendments to the criticism section, which was run by G. under the pseudonym 'Cyricus'. The author was absolutely incensed. Fierce representations with the editors followed.

'What is this? Am I, an old man, supposed to wear a muzzle? Do you think I'm unfamiliar with literary devices?' Cyricus huffed and puffed.

'But where is this debate going?' they countered.

'That's not the issue. Why was it pasted over without my knowledge? It should have been on my say so, not behind my back. You knew my article, you read it', contended Cyricus, completely justifiably.

A formidable article appeared in *The Dawn*, directed straight against Cyricus.

The latter in his turn broke free in a thunderous response, which was first accepted for *Vinaigrette*, but later pulled...

After this both journals became thinner, lost many contributors and readers and, finally, ceased to exist entirely.

For some time a lull in journal activity set in, but writing did not cease: the majority were turning out articles and stories. The blues were astonished at us taking such large quantities of writing materials, especially paper, and started to clamp down, that is, they were unwilling to issue it. But we managed to put our foot down here as well. Not only that: as if in consolation, we were given journals: *The Grainfield* for 1887–1889, and the *Pilgrim* for 1887.[49] On this dreadful literature we pounced as if it were nothing less than some sort of spiritual delicacy: we read them virtually from cover to cover. The review of political events gave us some material for conversation and, believe it or not, for our own journal articles (!). One comrade compiled from this material a long series of sketches, in which he tried to depict the political and economic life of Europe. And the statistics! Oh, they brought more than a few challenges and new data for our polemicists. Amendments had to be made, and additions to the old figures. This was all done in the most serious fashion.

If at this time some complete newcomer had glanced at us through the 'peephole', he would surely have taken us all for madmen. So carried away were we, so completely did we abandon ourselves to every new development; and we soon had the idea of repeating and expanding this novelty, as it were. Once we'd been given journals for 1889, why not for 1890 as well?

'Ladies and gentlemen, we have to call the commandant and speak to him about being issued the next year of *The Grainfield*', someone tapped.

'Not *The Grainfield*, fat journals. Are we still being protected from harmful influences? We're not school children', grumbled P., who always put the question point blank in these situations.[50]

Everyone agreed with him. But nothing good came of our discussions with the commandant.

'Ask the inspector about this. I can't do anything on my own account, although I'd be prepared to give you journals for the current year', replied the commandant.

We decided to wait.

Meanwhile our own material was mounting up. Several collections were produced. And Vera Nikolaevna published one issue of the journal *The Cobweb*. But publishing became rather tense, precisely because of *The Cobweb*'s programme, which set itself the aim of uniting all the polemicizing elements. The title page of the first issue even had such an illustration: a little spider carefully spinning its web, in which are caught flies, bees, wasps, and so on, in a word insects of various families and orders. But the trouble was that in the illustration they were all sitting quietly, whereas in real life they were horribly struggling, floundering and trying to set themselves free... For that reason it didn't manage to achieve its desired aim. Some were even especially unhappy with the editor of *The Cobweb* because it dealt the final blow to the previous journals, with its proposal to treat personal attacks more strictly, and not allow particularly strong language. Of course, everyone agreed to this, but the vanity that especially develops in captivity did not allow for reconciliation with 'reforms'. And our journals shut down completely.

In their place appeared a passion for greenhouses and horticulture.

Several people had made themselves small cold frames in the allotments, using oiled paper instead of glass. Despite these primitive adaptations, the seedlings turned out well. The flowers, transplanted to the flowerbeds, bloomed two or three weeks earlier.[51] Competition arose, but it was competition of the most innocent kind. We began to make boxes for early seedlings, which were planted in February and kept in the cells until they were ready to plant out in the flowerbeds. The cells were filled with boxes, the windows laden with them as well. Of course, the air quality suffered a great deal because of this. Our doctor even remarked that all this should be removed – it was impossible to breathe: there were boxes with damp earth under the beds, on the windows, and on the heater as well.

'So let us have real greenhouses, let us have panes of glass, fertilizer', we replied to him.

'I think this will be allowed.'

And we really were soon given panes of glass.

In the workshops there was feverish production of greenhouse frames, subframes and timbers. The new commandant was apparently very well disposed to this mood of ours. He obtained permission for us to install shelves in our cells: he must have wanted to give them the appearance of furnished rooms. The construction of these shelves was turned over to ourselves. Work was in full swing. Some rubbed down uprights, others glued screens, others shaved them or prepared and varnished them. But discontent arose because of the quality of the materials, which was very bad.

'They've bought some sort of trash, not wood, and you can't make anything out of it', many complained, especially the unskilled. 'We need to order the materials and take delivery of them ourselves. It would be best of all to take the whole task in our own hands.'

Time and time again there was conflict with the gendarmes because of this. Finally the commandant agreed that we ourselves could compile a list of materials, arrange work and visits to the workshops, and assign who wanted to work and exercise with whom, and where. In this way the opportunity presented itself for us to run the show ourselves.

We needed official representatives in the form of an elder and a 'promenade-master'. The first was in charge of ordering materials, assigning workshops and distributing work; the second only had to assign exercise. The schedule for the workshops was passed to the gendarmes by the elder, and for walks by the promenade-master. At first both positions were elected; but later an order for doing these jobs for a specified period was ascertained. The elder was entrusted to conduct all conversations of a general nature with the commandant. Under the pretext of helping the unskilled, we began to insist on being permitted to work in pairs. At first we received a refusal, but later succeeded. Even the mentally ill began to be allowed in the workshops with someone else. Thanks to this one of them fully recovered.

A carpentry order was received: a fence for the mass grave of those who died capturing the fortress in which we lived. We were promised 50 rubles for the work, and the money could be used for buying books. How eagerly that work was done! Many sacrificed their walks and went straight from the first shift to the workshops, that is, from 10 in the morning. By that time we were already exercising in two shifts, that is, from 8 or 8.30 to 11.45. But we soon cooled down: the department issued a prohibition on us buying books with this money, and ordered that no paid work be given in future. On this occasion we were allowed to use the earnings to purchase edibles.

A strange mood reigned on high at this time. On the whole, there was a marked propensity for 'economic reforms'. Our food changed completely. *Kasha* was banished definitively, and tea and sugar were now given directly to everyone – half a pound of tea and three pounds of sugar each per month. Our domestic inventory increased, as we were each given two teapots. Mustard, pepper and vinegar began to be distributed. Those who wished to could exchange black bread for white. Dinners became more varied, and meals on religious holidays had three dishes. On the walls of every cell instead of the instructions there appeared... a menu for every two weeks! Witticisms on account of these reforms rained down from all sides. Some of us couldn't eat meat, and one didn't even drink tea; so in view of this they were allowed to exchange meat dishes for dairy ones, which led to misunderstandings with the gendarmes. Then composition of the menus was turned over to us. Another duty appeared, the most unpleasant: 'menu-master'.

But the reforms were not limited to economics alone. Some were given news about their families – true, only the barest bones. But all the same we learned it was possible to receive at least something. When the commandant brought the first memorandum, we asked him whether we could communicate with our families, at least in the same way.

'Of course you can!'

'But we don't even know where our relatives are living...'

'That doesn't mean anything. The department will track them down', the commandant reassured us.

But this final phrase confused many and for a long time prevented them from resolving to write to their families. Meanwhile memorandums were received more frequently. Here is a sample of one of them. 'Memorandum no. 31, 15 January 1894. Arriving for a brief spell in SPburg and now staying with X.'s brother, his mother and sisters also send name day congratulations, bow, bless, and wish him health.'

Often these notes not only failed to satisfy, but directly tormented us. The extreme brevity, the bureaucratic, wooden turn of phrase, poisoned any familial feelings. Again the question of correspondence with our families arose. And, as previously, ended unsuccessfully. Minister Durnovo appeared and visited everyone. His affability verged on mawkishness. He promised whole mountains: journals, books, correspondence, taking away the mentally ill. But he did nothing.

Our internal life was however becoming more and more complicated. Our relationship with the administration had completely changed. The previous disrespect had receded into the past. Someone had the idea of cultivating tobacco (many craved tobacco terribly). Using the Latin name, we placed tobacco on the list of seeds. The seeds were received and planted. Something like tobacco came up.

These plants were tended exactly as if they were children. The tobacco-growers dried out leaves, tried them, and found the product of their cultivation 'outstandingly good' (?) [sic] But the gendarmes expressed a desire to stop this new production. The superintendent came, and tried entreating and inducing us to cease tobacco production and smoking in particular.

'It's banned by the instructions. I might get into trouble if they think I allowed it', he explained timidly.

'The instructions were written in Catherine the Great's time... Now it's completely different!'

'But what if an inspector comes? He'll see, and then I'll be blamed', continued the superintendent. 'At least be more careful', he added.

This superintendent was unbelievably stupid, but the most zealous informer: once he even informed on himself.

In conversation with V. Iv.[52] he accidentally let slip – he liked a chat – and said something, I don't remember now, but I think about something happening outside, all of a few words. Then he forgot about it. The next time V. Iv. again wanted to squeeze something of the same sort out of him, and started talking about the previous disclosure.

'And where do you know that from?' the superintendent asks tartly.

V. Iv. didn't answer him, and started talking about something else. The superintendent went straight to jot down a denunciation to the department. From there all the blues were issued with the strictest reprimand. The superintendent appears, angry, frightened, and with his usual stupidity talks about the roasting. He laments and quails.

'Please tell me who told you about that?' He's trying to find the culprit and work his frustration off.

'But you told me yourself. Have you forgotten?' V. Iv. replies, and clarifies the details.

'Oh, I'm such a so-and-so!' In despair he slaps himself on his large, but apparently completely empty, forehead. 'And I thought the doctor must have told you.'

He didn't get on with the doctor. They both schemed against each other and even complained to us about each other.

Tobacco production blossomed. We managed to order a variety of seeds. Despite the unsuitable climate, the frequent rain, and so on, the tobacco plants grew so tall that the blues could hardly see the prisoners exercising. The beds were as if covered by a young wood with enormous leaves. Even the non-smokers planted tobacco. The sight of the mighty plants seduced everybody and somehow gladdened the eye. When they bloomed, large, pink, bell-shaped flowers appeared on top.

Harvesting the leaves and preparing the tobacco began in earnest, that is, it was cured, after being tied into bundles and wrapped in dressing gowns. Then it was dried. Both operations, of course, took place in the cells. The air became unbearable, because curing tobacco gives off an extremely unpleasant smell. Some had so decorated their cells with leaves, hanging them on threads from the walls and ceiling, that they had to stoop in order to walk.

'What are you doing? You're poisoning yourselves!' the doctor was outraged. 'It's unbearable to breathe.'

'Well, let them allocate us a room for this', we replied.

'That's not my business. But I would advise you to remove it. You're dying in this atmosphere. You already have only one functioning lung anyway. In these conditions I can't treat you. I refuse', he asserted to one of the sick.

'It's your duty as a doctor to talk to the commandant, so that we may be given a bright room in the old prison for tobacco.'

'But I can't be your advocate in this. Here's the superintendent – let him pass on the message to the commandant.'

The matter reached the commandant. He also appeared in exactly the cell where most tobacco was hanging. Opportunely, he had hardly stepped into the cell and said hello when threads broke and wet, unpleasant smelling leaves fell on him. The owner of the cell fussed and rushed to correct the misfortune, but only managed to magnify the disaster, and the remaining bundles fell from all the nails. The commandant could only clear out. The result was the concession of a light room, but with the condition that not a single leaf would be hung up in the cells again.

Apparently the commandant didn't foresee where such a concession would lead, otherwise he would never have agreed to it. Subsequently he expressed his regret more than once. In November 1894 for the first and last time in the broadest sense we took the opportunity to spend two or three hours all together. There was a very convenient excuse – the name day of several comrades. We decided to celebrate like normal people. In the morning our cooks took up cookery in their cells, using left over sugar, milk and white bread, and turning it into rusks, fudge, tarts and biscuits. Antonov and Martynov contrived to make some wine. P. kept hold of the harmonica the gendarmes had given us for repair.[53] Frolenko and Popov removed everything superfluous from their workshop, covered the benches in sheets and some sort of other coloured scraps. That day, 8 November,[54] we got everyone to go to the workshops. By midday everyone had done so, except Lopatin, who for some reason refused. After lunch had been distributed we asked for the doors to be opened. The officer, not suspecting the later consequences, did what we asked, but refused to let the ladies out. However much we reasoned with them, nothing helped.

'Bring the officer to me!' Vera Nikolaevna's peremptory voice rings out from the workshop.

The officer appears before Vera Nikolaevna. Discussions began.

'I can't open the door for you', the officer declares.

'But I demand it', Vera Nikolaevna asserts firmly. 'What sort of barbarism is this? The men have been let out, but not us.'

The officer surrenders. Both Vera Nikolaevna's and Liudmila Aleksandrovna's doors are opened. They are both with us, in Frolenko's workshop.

'Bravo! To the ladies' health!' cries Antonov, pouring wine into some sort of tin cans.

'To the guests of honour!' rejoined the ladies. 'However, you've already clinked glasses without us', adds Vera Nikolaevna.

The noise and din surges. Everyone is talking, bustling.

'Pan, where's your harmonica? Drag yourself over here! We'll waltz with the ladies', says T.[55]

The harmonica appeared and squealed into life. And our 'milord'[56] spun into a rapid waltz with Vera Nikolaevna, Shebalin with Liudmila Aleksandrovna. Applause rang out.

'Singers, over here! Choir! Choir!'

Confused, out of their depth gendarmes tore about near the open door, as if afraid that the higher administration would appear and give them a slap on the wrists.

At 4 o'clock our festivities ended and we were taken off to our cells, not suspecting reprisals. The gendarmes themselves denounced us that night to the commandant, who ordered we be deprived of all the liberties won by so many efforts. He ordered the windows in the workshops to be closed, and no more than one person to be allowed in the corridor. He even tried to take away our right to go to the light room. But he didn't succeed. Everyone firmly held on to newly acquired rights, particularly the light room, where it was sometimes possible to get together in groups of six, chat or form a choir. Although our singing was far from perfect, it always had great feeling.

Even the blues listened to us with pleasure which, however, didn't deter them from denunciations. Congregating in groups of three or four started to be forbidden, but we always found excuses to violate this order. Next to the light room was the kitchen, where glue was heated, wood dried out, and so on. At first when work was established, the gendarmes did everything: heating glue, drying wood, delivering tools. But as they did everything carelessly and inefficiently, and caused dissatisfaction, they began to let us into the kitchen ourselves, at first one by one and only for short periods, then in pairs as well. Of course, it was there that the tobacco-growers met the carpenters and the 'greenhouse workers'. The latter contributed most of all to the expansion of our freedom. Their production flourished; they supplied early seedlings not only to us, but also to the administration who, infected by us with the horticulture bug, tried to grow flowers in their own yard. The blues were amazed at our market gardening.

'There aren't even any radishes or cucumbers in town yet, but yours are already ripe', they'd say.

'And they'd ripen even sooner if we were given the old yard for greenhouses, if the fence was lowered and we were given freer access to the cold frames in the yard. There's not enough light, and the cold frames are almost always covered by screens', the most energetic cold frame workers would reply.

'Yes, we care more about the plants than ourselves: up to now we've had opaque glass.[57] It's time to replace it with transparent', rejoined the nonchalant market gardeners.

A request to replace the opaque glass with clear had already been made long ago: we had received a refusal and had fallen silent. But the authorities apparently themselves remembered, and the doctor made representations about the inadequate light to boot, which partly explained the mental disorders of some of the sick. And we soon had clear glass installed. How much the light increased! How cheerful it made the cells look! Something festive illuminated them. At night the stars and moon were visible...

'Which stars are they? Which constellations?.. And now maps of the starry sky were needed. And they appeared in nearly every cell. Our astronomer N. Morozov supplied them.

As soon as it got dark a few people would shin up the windows and tell their neighbours what stars they could see. But on the south side observations were made in the sunlight as well – not of the stars, of course, but the inhabitants of the gendarmes' courtyard. From some windows all the internal buildings were visible: the church, the communal grave, the main quad. During festivities, especially in summer or at Easter, this yard was brought to life by a crowd, of government employees, of course. The children born and raised in our presence ran about. Soldiers either played *lapta*,[58] or sang songs, and the guards' wives, dressed up like dogs' dinners, sat with an air of importance on benches next to the barracks. Strangely, they also had a soldier's bearing: if someone from the higher ranks passed by, they stood up to attention as if on command. In the evenings children sang songs taught to them by the wife of one of the doctors. And from the officers' apartments sounds of pianos were heard. All this awakened and unsettled memories of a past long gone, ignited the imagination and perturbed us.

Windows on the north side faced the lake, but it was impossible to see: it was obscured by the high wall, along which sentries with guns were constantly wandering. Many of those in cells on the north side (the 'northerners'), of course, wanted to transfer to the south, to see how our opposite numbers lived behind our yard. But not everyone could fit on the south side, and changing places was too unpleasant.

For us this was a period of enthusiasm for work, horticulture and gardening. Although only a very small sum was allotted for all this (25 rubles a month), somehow we managed to make do, despite the fact that the blues made all our purchases, and at high prices. Our ladies in no way lagged behind us, even in carpentry work. A school for the children of gendarmes on our island was organized. It was proposed that we make the furniture. It didn't happen without arguments about whether to take on such commissions, of course. Some were against it at first, saying that facilitating the development of future guards and persecutors of free thought was not our business. But the majority were in favour, and the contract was accepted. Work heated up. We made desks, benches, tables, lecterns, blackboards. We were more at liberty to approach the windows, and not only on work matters, but more generally for conversation At first this was only allowed one at a time; but later, when the greenhouses were expanded and the gardeners had to go out to them repeatedly, they would stop by the ladies in passing, so that sometimes three people would congregate there. The blues would impatiently beg us to disperse, but weren't paid much attention. Little by little this liberty acquired the right of citizenship and expanded.

The women also wanted to work in the greenhouses, because that work gave the opportunity to spend more time in the fresh air and in the corridor. Our greenhouses at that time became real, with transparent glass, and everything sprouted very successfully. We even grew sweet melons and watermelons, which totally amazed our blues.

But then summer arrived, and botany, collecting herbariums and breeding new plants came into vogue. Despite the limited space of our domains, the flora was quite varied. In addition it could be supplemented by asking the blues to bring from the forest as many grasses, mosses and flowers as possible. The most precious plants we grew ourselves, with seeds bought in Petersburg. In this regard there were no restrictions; quite expensive bushes were bought from our lists, such as roses, azaleas, and so on. Of course, every plant was cared for like favourite offspring. But alas! A desperate enemy appeared among our favourites: slugs, which developed in myriads. Nothing helped. How much grief was there when you'd go out into the allotments after rain and discover leaves eaten to a sieve!

Our mental activities were interrupted most often of all by one-sided excitement: three mentally ill comrades had too much influence on us. It was probably due to this circumstance that we so easily achieved various benefits.

When another fell mentally ill, even such a coarse, poorly developed man as our doctor, whom we called Sobakevich,[59] blurted out the phrase: 'yes, the atmosphere needs defusing'. Perhaps he wouldn't have said that if the sick had been more tranquil. But they sometimes put on such performances for the administration that patience ran out. And the healthy? In their tantrums they differed little from the sick. With the exception of two or three, everyone from time to time unloaded their nerves onto the gendarmes, who for a long time couldn't understand how people could lose their tempers for the most insignificant reasons, and create a hue and cry as if a profound insult or injury had been inflicted on them. It was good that opportunities appeared to 'unload' in other, healthier, more innocent ways.

Thus, for example, one day a blue 'presented' Vera Nikolaevna with a tiny swallow chick that had fallen out of its nest. V. N. attentively raised the little creature, which became so attached to her that the nurse started to hope her charge would stay with her forever. But the swallow's impulse for infidelity became apparent as soon as its wings started to grow. Once V. N. was carrying her in a little nest during her walk when the traitor spread her wings, soared up and vanished in the blue of the sky.

'Oh!' cried V. N. 'Gendarmes – catch her!' she added.

A blue spread out his arms, but in vain. All day V. N. was very distressed. And who could have imagined that after all the affection the traitor had shown to her nurse, the matter could end in such disloyalty? The little bird had never left her mistress: she ran after her during walks, and in the cell always sat on the table and watched her every move. And food! Where would she get food like this? Flies, eggs, meat…

Soon nature itself supplied us with many such little birds. One night a terrible storm ripped the entire roof off the barracks and tossed it into the lake, destroyed chimneys, tore up trees, and so ruined the rendering on the old walls that all the swallows' nests crashed to the ground with their entire populations. The survivors from the wrecks were, of course, gathered up and raised. In many cells cheeps were heard all day long. It was interesting to observe the ways of these little birds. They very quickly get used to human beings and treat them like their own parents, demanding food, attention. Children would envy their cleanliness, and their sociability is simply astonishing: as soon as you leave them alone they raise such a cry that you have to move them closer to you. Then they immediately calm down. Sometimes, however, they fight over whose hand they want to sit on. The lucky one who is first to settle on a hand then doesn't want to let any of her brothers or sisters anywhere near: she'll hiss and snap, and if you try to pacify her, start to peck at you. Bold, graceful birdie! But not a single one of them was tamed. It was interesting to observe how they banished predators from our yard. As soon as one appeared, they'd pounce on it with a special cry and great daring, and force its retreat. However, like pigeons, sparrows will seek shelter just anywhere.

Later the birds also wound up in our zoological collection, which in truth was very poor, in the form of taxidermy.

For us, the psychologically healthy, life was varied, one way or another; but it wasn't the same for the mentally ill: for them everything remained as if unchanged. They lived exclusively with their inner worlds; our visits afforded the mentally ill a little entertainment and pleasure.

It should be noted that our jailers were always very suspicious of the mentally ill. They long asserted that Shchedrin, who suffered from delusions of grandeur, was faking. However, when Shchedrin disturbed the peace and comfort of the heartless gendarmes, they didn't hesitate to go to one of the prisoners and ask them to pacify the sick man. That often happened with Shchedrin, who sometimes refused everything, so as not to be obliged to anyone or anything. At such times he wouldn't eat anything for whole weeks and would lie on the asphalt floor stripped stark naked. No reassurance or persuasion from the jailers or doctor helped. Moreover, in fits of malice and revenge our administration thought nothing of punishing the sick. In 1895 Konashevich slept through dinner, woke up at around four in the morning, and demanded his food. The superintendent appeared.

'What do you want?'

'Dinner. Why wasn't I given any dinner?' the sick man asked, obviously meaning to say, 'Why didn't you leave my dinner?'

'How can you have dinner now? It's almost time for morning tea.'

'I haven't eaten. Give me my dinner,' Konashevich asks persistently.

'There isn't any now.'

'That's not my problem. Give me my dinner!' Konashevich shouts testily.

Hiding his anger, the superintendent orders a mug of milk and piece of white bread to be brought. The duty non-com leaves and, returning quickly, places the bread and milk on the table. Konashevich looks at it in silence and, suddenly approaching the superintendent, says perfectly calmly: 'all this is nonsense' – and goes back to sleep. The next day when we're being taken out for exercise, one comrade says that he'd like to go and see Konashevich.

'I've deprived him of everything today, even exercise', replies the superintendent.

'What for?' the comrade asks.

The superintendent tells him of the night's events, and does so angrily, seriously.

'What the hell…? Have you gone out of your mind yourself? Aren't you ashamed? Get me the doctor and the commandant', declares the comrade. And after long discussion the superintendent concedes. I don't know whether Konashevich himself would have embarked on any of this if he knew about the wise and humanitarian disposition of the superintendent. Konashevich was extremely persistent and knew how to get his own way when he was healthy. In the period of his sickness this perseverance manifested itself even more strongly. Thanks to that, we managed to get him a guitar, and the administration agreed. Sometimes he would sing and whistle all day and even all night, giving peace to neither the jailers nor us. The guitar replaced his singing and he strummed it for whole days, without getting on anyone's nerves. But the administration began to make all these concessions only from 1894. Before that the mentally ill were kept in exactly the same conditions as the healthy.

At one point a rumour spread about an amnesty. Somehow and from somewhere the superintendent found out it would be applied to us in the broadest terms.

'Soon you'll all be taken away from here', he anxiously informs Pokhitonov and Orzhikh.

'Where? Why?'

'An amnesty, an amnesty! They're releasing people in Petersburg' – he adds the last phrase to be more persuasive (he has noticed perfectly well that he is little believed on the whole and considered a liar). The sick Pokhitonov and Orzhikh hurry to inform their comrades of the news. Everyone is nonplussed: it's difficult to believe such a liar as the superintendent, but why on earth would he invent such a thing? There had to be something in it. And how down in the mouth the gendarmes were!.. What are they talking about? 'Where will we be transferred? Will we have to look for new jobs?' they whisper quite loudly, looking at us with a sort of malice. The only conversation among them was about where to go when we were transported. They were literally down in the dumps. Losing such a cosy spot – where, without doing anything, they receive 35–45 rubles a month each, with a furnished apartment, uniform, not to mention an annual bonus and a lifetime pension ahead of them to boot – is a distressing prospect! At this point they treated us with a kind of spite.

Very few believed in the blues' fears, but nevertheless assumed something would happen. Speculation and rumour were followed by fantasy – involuntary, however. But who wouldn't want to break out into god's world from this living crypt?

A few days later one of the very same gendarmes informed the department about the rumours regarding the amnesty. And that led to a reprimand for our administration. There seemed to be a phrase in the reprimand that suggested the department itself would know how to act and when to make this arrangement, but in the meantime demanded that all discussions about it with us cease. So the superintendent, who took no end of fright over such things, said later.

'I mustn't talk to you about it! It's caused ructions. Now, oy, oy, we'll catch it!' he said, pointing from habit to the back of his head.

And everything carried on in the usual rut. Weeks went by, months, and there was no hint of what the commandant had said, and we even began to forget about the promised concessions. The blues cheered up:

this showed us that nothing special was going to happen and there was nothing to anticipate.

But how heavily the disappointment impacted on Pokhitonov! After that his illness progressed terribly, and took on a more aggressive form. Not a day went by without a clash with the gendarmes or one comrade or another. He was also writing endless projects, making written instructions, and almost stopped understanding others. Sometimes he wept hysterically, other times he laughed for no reason. Our sepulchre became even more like 'Bedlam'.[60] Again the question was raised of demanding a transfer for the sick prisoners. But how to demand that? There was only one answer to that: we're powerless! The local administration wasn't in a position to do anything; and higher up, everything happened slowly and extremely reluctantly. But when the sick began to make themselves known to the gendarmes, causing them a whole load of trouble and anxiety, they then began to complain to the department about the burdens of their service.

As if in consolation or to calm us down, they sent us books. But what books? From a list drawn up by the sick Pokhitonov!.. Expensive books, but no use to anyone: ballistics, advanced mechanics, and so on. It turns out that 'up there' they look upon us all as if we've gone off our heads, or they consider the sick to be healthy. We decided to speak to the commandant about these useless books. But soon, Zvolianskii, the director of the department himself, appeared. He went round to see everyone cheerfully, behaved civilly, chatted, agreed with our suggestion that it was impossible for the sick to remain in our crypt any longer. But it was all just words, words and feigned courtesy.

He drops in on one of our ladies (V. N.) and cheerfully bows.

'Hello! How is your health? I know your brother', prattles Zvolianskii. 'Do you have any requests?..'

'I'd like the sick to be taken to hospital. And to receive books from the lists of the healthy, not the insane', V. N. replies severely.

'What books would you like? What was sent?'

'Ballistics, which cost a great deal of money and nobody needs.'

'So you're no longer studying ballistics?' Zvolianskii's witticism falls flat.

'That's not what I'm saying. Please drop the inappropriate jokes', V. N. interrupts him.

'What books would you like? Write them down', Zvolianskii turns to his adjutant and again launches into chatting about brothers.

With Lagovskii he sounds out his soul.

'Your sentence will end soon. How do you feel? How is your moral condition? Your convictions and views have probably changed, you've been convinced that you were mistaken...' and so on, he interrogates Lagovskii.

The latter turns a deaf ear to all these questions. Posing such questions after ten years is stupid and bizarre. But the hope that Lagovskii would be taken away was nevertheless reborn among us: after all, higher up everything had changed, that is, the people were different. Lagovskii would barely survive a second blow. Recently he'd changed terribly, become unsociable and overly irritable.

On 5 or 6 November 1895 gendarmes appeared before him, and he disappeared.

'Where is he now? How does he feel? He's probably gone back to life!' we reasoned.

'That means Manucharov will be taken away soon. How much time do you have left, Manucharov?' asked B.[61]

'I don't want to leave... I'll stay. I'll submit an application.'

'You're talking utter rubbish.'

'Rubbish, rubbish? I'll prove it's not rubbish!' Manucharov huffs and puffs.

Manucharov doesn't give up. He becomes totally absorbed in his plan. The more he's discouraged, the more insistent he becomes. He writes a document, a statement. Gives it to us to read. It's in the most impossible form.

'Listen, they won't accept an application like that, and the commandant doesn't have the right to send it. After all, you're directly insulting them. You've decided you're not going to be persuaded by your comrades, so at least do it right.'

'None of you understand me, or you don't want to understand', Manucharov objected.

'So why did you give it to us to read? Why refer to us, if you've decided not to listen to your comrades' voices?'

Everyone expressed themselves in the same spirit. But Manucharov didn't change a word of his document. He submitted it just like that. Of course, it was withheld. And at the end of his sentence gendarmes appeared and took Manucharov away. He just had time to shout out that he was being taken to Sakhalin. He was taken away somehow unexpectedly, and it really blindsided us. Everyone had wanted to say goodbye to a comrade with whom they'd lived for ten years and whom they might never see again. It was just as if he'd been stolen from us – that was the impression left with us. However, everyone's mood improved: at least now there was the hope that those with fixed sentences would leave; two years later another two were due, and then others still. Of course, the prospect of Sakhalin was not a particularly happy one, but all the same it was freer there… Perhaps relations with the living world would be possible. Even if news came late, you'd know what was going on in the world. Sometimes we were afraid for Manucharov: they might lock him in some other crypt because of his application. But of course we didn't manage to find out what happened to him.

Not long before Manucharov was taken away we had electric lights installed. Workers from Petersburg toiled for almost the whole summer, but we didn't manage to see a single one of them; they were always led away when one of us went into the corridor.

Our administration preened at such civilized innovations: they demonstrated with particular eagerness the superiority of electric lamps over kerosene, apparently without suspecting that all this was just gilding a cage.

The superintendent went on leave temporarily. He was replaced by another, a young dandy. This one had to be driven out.

One night, when many were covering the lamps, using books as lampshades so that the bright light wouldn't disturb their sleep, he suddenly appears, opens the doors and orders the blues to remove the improvised shades.

'I'll just cover it again', one protested.

'How dare you burst into my cell?' cries L.,[62] and drives out the gendarme and new superintendent.

'The sentry can't see anything with lighting like that. Lights cannot be put out at night.'

'Get out of here!'

He retires. The next day complaints are made to the commandant about the dandy's behaviour.

'He's inexperienced. Don't attach any importance to his actions', the commandant absolves his subordinate.

'No, you remove him if you want to avoid trouble. Next time he won't get away with a stunt like that without punishment.'

'You're fussing about nothing', the commandant pacifies us, but all the same he removes the dandy.

The latter, however, saw it as his duty to appear before L. and apologize. A 'polite chatterbox' was appointed. But someone among the personnel immediately dashed off a denunciation.[63] That is a right granted to every gendarme, even without the knowledge of his superiors they say.

And then suddenly, quite unexpectedly – as much for the administration as for us – an inspector appeared and conducted a search. Caught off guard, a great deal was confiscated, including books. The library was ransacked, its catalogues reviewed. Management of the library was taken away from us, and an officer was dismissed. The commandant was reprimanded, in a word given a good dressing down. The stupid superintendent was so scared that he submitted a request for retirement, fearing losing his pension, for which his main excuse was disturbance of his mental faculties, as if he'd ever had any in the first place. His request was honoured. In his place someone new was appointed.

Relations with the commandant changed markedly: he no longer appeared of his own accord, but always waited to be summoned.

A period of restrictions began: the administration decided to remove all our concessions in the workshops, even ordered all the windows to be closed. No more than one person was allowed in the corridor at one time. This reaction was carried out without saying a word. We appear in the workshops – and the doors are slammed behind us, the windows as well. 'What's the meaning of this?' 'It's an order', replies the gendarme. 'I don't know anything.' The usual excuse.

'We have to go home,[64] we cannot allow such tricks,' we said among ourselves. But at that moment a significant conversation was already going on in the corridor between L. and a gendarme.

'I won't go into a workshop until the window is opened', says L.

Taps echo from several doors... And there are several people in the corridor again. The superintendent is called.

'Gentlemen, go into the workshops, the superintendent is on his way', a gendarme implores. 'It wasn't my order.'

'It doesn't matter who ordered it. But let the superintendent come.'

The messenger sent to the latter told him everything, of course, in over-inflated terms. The novice superintendent, who had not had time to settle in, didn't know whether he was coming or going.

'What is this innovation?' L. tore into him. 'Our windows have always been open.'

'We won't leave the corridor until you rescind your orders', others say.

'I can't, it's orders. As it wasn't my order, how can I reverse it?' the superintendent asks.

'In that case we're staying here.'

'You're to blame yourselves, gentlemen: you don't stick to the limits, you're always trying to go further and further. You're allowed out in groups of no more than two, but you get together in threes and fours. And we get reprimanded for this... Very well, I'll order the windows to be opened, but I ask you not to abuse...'

Thus ended the whole incident with the windows. The question of the corridor remained unresolved: they stopped letting us into the corridor even in twos. However, it was difficult to work in the workshops in these conditions: if we needed to saw wood, or go out to open the greenhouses, one person on their own struggled. Of course, with some effort it was always possible to achieve one's goal, which indicated the possibility of returning to the previous situation. Every day the superintendent appeared before our elder with complaints about rule-breakers.

'Why do you force us into this?' the elder replied. 'Stop viewing us as automatons who must fulfil your every order. We're living people, we can't put up with this. All your harassment aggravates us.'

'Take it easy. The whole problem is that you can't restrain yourselves, you offend my subordinates, and they constantly complain', counters the superintendent.

'Complaints are the only way they can express their concept of diligent service: they don't have anything else to do. And you'd do better to stop just accepting their complaints and start paying them attention. If relations continue like this, you'll have to deal not with me alone, but all of us… Taking on a role such as mine in these conditions is extremely unpleasant, you must agree', explains the elder, whose position is indeed horrendous.

He constantly has to deal with the gendarmes, conduct discussions, and what's even more unpleasant, listen to complaints about comrades, vindicate them, write reports, produce 'posters' on various questions, collect votes, accept complaints and comments from comrades, and so on, and so forth. In the end it got to the point where everyone started refusing to serve as elder. It became necessary to resort to coercive methods and introduce a paragraph into our constitution about obligatory service for everyone who had not yet served. Without that there would have been anarchy or an interregnum.

The administration was so used to our designated officers (even more than that: dealing with one of us or dealing with all of us are not the same things at all!), even though they changed frequently, that they feared an interregnum, and tried in all matters – even those that didn't have a communal dimension – to conduct all business through the elected people.

The elder's threats had their effect: the superintendent gave in, agreeing to allow two people into the corridor and one to go to the greenhouses.

The elder set the results of his negotiations down on paper and publicized them. The audience – granted, not all of it – did not react particularly favourably.

A minority stood up for the elder: he had done everything he could; we would gradually return to the old ways; there was no need to exaggerate the incident.

But an incident arose of its own accord.

One day, just after we had eaten lunch and gone back to work, Martynov appeared at reception, pale and agitated, with burning eyes.

'Gentlemen, Pokhitonov's being beaten!' he cried.

'Who? What for?' the people in the corridor asked him in alarm.

'Open the doors!' voices rang out from the windows.

The gendarmes somehow unwillingly unlock one, then another door, and several people shoot out into the corridor.

'Who? Who's beating him?'

'The gendarmes are beating Pokhitonov', replies Martynov.

'What are you making up', one offended gendarme interrupts. 'Who would touch a sick man? It's him who's beating us.'

'I heard a commotion in his cell myself. I called the superintendent, they didn't bring him to me,' Martynov explains incoherently.

'What is this? Beating the sick? We'll find a way to retaliate… We won't stand for this!' Everyone is agitated.

The gendarmes had sent for the superintendent on the quiet.

'Let's go to the cells', someone suggested.

'I won't allow it', said a gendarme, blocking the way.

'How dare you! Out of the way!'

'Not allowed! Not allowed! Ring the bell!' screams the gendarme, losing his head.

'What is this disrespect? It means they really are beating him.'

'Let's go home, home!' voices ring out.

'We won't let anyone through!' the gendarmes reply.

One of them tugs on the bell, and a moment later 12 soldiers appear at the doors with bayonets at the ready. Seeing so many people in the corridor, and hearing the noise and shouts of the gendarmes, the soldiers quickly jumped into the corridor, and it looked as though a free-for-all couldn't be avoided.

'Stop!' the gendarme who had given the warning sign, and who had himself turned as pale as a sheet, suddenly screamed, coming to his senses.

The soldiers stopped.

'Scum!' cried one comrade, while others rushed to the round timbers lying in the corridor, so as to have something to defend themselves with.

For a moment everything went quiet. The gendarmes stand by the doors; behind them bayonets flash… The soldiers wait, silent. Our lot are silent as well, but drop the timbers.

The superintendent appears and is astonished: soldiers with bayonets at the ready, gendarmes lined up against the wall by the doors, all the workshops unlocked, a whole crowd in the corridor. The sight even scared him.

'What is this?' he asks. 'What's happened? Why were the soldiers called?'

'Your honour!' reports a gendarme.

'Restrain your subordinates!' I. interrupts him.[65]

'An all-out brawl nearly happened!' added another.

'I wanted to go home, wasn't allowed, and they're taking liberties', I. continued.

'Pokhitonov's being beaten.'

'Who said that? I've just been to see him with the doctor', the superintendent interrupts.

'But why didn't you come when I called you? I'm right in the next cell. I heard Pokhitonov's frantic cries and a terrible commotion in his cell', asks Martynov.

'So you thought. Instead of waiting to find out what was going on, you ran and incited your comrades for no reason. I couldn't come straight to you, I was in number 15's cell', the superintendent justified himself. 'You all look on my subordinates as if they're animals. They're human beings.'

'But they're capable of anything. We've had examples', notes P.

'Why say that?' interrupts one of the blues, hurt by the phrase.

And it was one of the ones who, in the earlier, strict period, had indeed done all sorts of nasty things. P. stops him.

'Shut up!'

'Calm down, why are you getting so angry? You're only working yourself up', the superintendent appeases him. 'You can go and see Pokhitonov right now and satisfy yourself that nothing's been done to him. He needs taking away from here, isolating. Otherwise he's only going to worry you.'

'But we can't trust your subordinates. They might offend or humiliate him as a sick person.'

'To avoid any misunderstanding, we want one of us to keep watch of him', says V. N. from the window.

'Otherwise we won't allow him to be moved', another adds.

'Very well, I'll talk to the commandant and the doctor', the superintendent agrees.

When everything had settled down we found out that Mart. really had 'jumped to conclusions' and almost caused a bloody brawl. There was just a commotion in Pokhitonov's cell when some gendarmes had gone in and tried to take something. He raised a cry, they tried to calm him down, and it seems, a blue got a crack on the head. Subsequently he even hit one of the gendarmes so hard on the head with a copper bowl that he crushed it. But I have to give the proviso that I wasn't witness to the scene, so it's difficult to know the truth, particularly with regards to the mentally ill. In any case, Pokhitonov showed no signs of any beating, and himself did not complain.

The one guilty of 'jumping to conclusions' was deprived of the workshops for a month as punishment for inciting his comrades. For using the word 'scum', another also had a month without work.

But every cloud has a silver lining. This incident gave us the right to monitor the gendarmes' behaviour with the sick.

When Pokhitonov was transferred to the old building, the administration agreed to all our demands: they allowed one comrade to stay there with him permanently and, most importantly, without this comrade blues could not enter Pokhitonov's cell. At all times we went to see Pokhitonov and sat with him until we no longer had the strength or he himself was tired of us. Thus both 'jumping to conclusions' and the blues' brutality were eliminated.

Pokhitonov's illness meanwhile was progressing unbelievably quickly. In the space of a month he turned into a non-person: he understood nothing, heard no-one, and barely knew who he was. From time to time he was seized by violent impulses – then he would break glass, break anything that came to hand. Thick, mirrored glass had been installed for him, but he smashed that to smithereens as well.

Sometimes he was seized by a sort of childish feeling: he'd cry, scream, call for his mother, and believed she was with him; he'd fall to his knees before her. Sometimes he'd write reports, orders to execute the priest, the commandant, and so on, or he'd dispatch plans for the construction of mechanical plants of the very grandest size. Seeing or hearing him became quite hair-raising. Luckily for us he was transferred. He couldn't be saved, and the healthy needed to be cared for. And there were many more scenes we witnessed.

Such incidents were difficult to endure. Again we began to demand the transfer of the sick. We asked the doctor to explain to the department the impossibility of leaving the sick with us any longer. Of course, the commandant and the doctor did all this, but without particular urgency, because they didn't have to experience 'up close' the condition of the sick for themselves.

One evening the sick Konashevich taps on his door.

'What do you want?' asks the sentry.
'Call the superintendent!'
'He's coming soon.'
'Call him now!'
'I'll send for him soon.'
'Call him now! I'm telling you!' Konashevich rattles on the door with greater force and screams.

The sentry retreats from the door. But that maddens Konashevich even more. The comrade in the next cell calls the sentry.

'What's Konashevich asking for?'
'The patient wants the superintendent, but he's at church, preparing for communion.'
'You need to send for him.'
'I've sent for him. He'll come soon.'

A few minutes later footsteps and the sound of spurs is heard in the corridor. Konashevich's door opens. The comrade in the next cell listens with bated breath, but he's unable to hear through the thick walls.

'You're all lying!' Konashevich cries out, and at that very moment something heavy thudded against the door.

A commotion, stamping, wheezing and muffled voices are heard in Konashevich's cell. His neighbouring comrade automatically taps on the door and shouts: 'what are they doing? Why are they beating him?' Other doors also start hammering, and our crypt turns into hell.

The superintendent doesn't put in any appearance, which increases our suspicions of horrendous misbehaviour by the gendarmes.

'Let go, leave me, I'll put the shirt on myself!' Konashevich shouts loudly. Everything falls silent in his cell.

'Why was my tobacco taken? Why were my notebooks taken? Damn it! Bring them back!' Konashevich shouts again.

'Leave them with him!' the commandant's order issues from below.[66]

He's also got round to appearing.

'What's being done to Konashevich?' he's asked.
'Nothing, he's been put in a straitjacket: he hit the superintendent.'
One comrade asks to be allowed to see Konashevich.
'Very well.'

The comrade goes in. Konashevich is lying in a straitjacket and looks angry.

'Are you alright, Vasilii?' his comrade asks him.
'It's okay, they wanted to put the shirt on me, I wouldn't let them', he replies unwillingly, and suddenly, completely changing his tone, screams.

'Get out!'

'Am I really upsetting you?'

'Get out, get out, I tell you.'

The comrade tapped, and was taken out.

After that Konashevich began to shun us completely as well.

The superintendent asked for a transfer to a different post, but was refused.

Chapter V.

The incident with Konashevich wasn't succeeded by any reprisals. On the contrary, it only hastened the transfer of the sick. It's true that for a few days utensils and some tools were taken off him as dangerous weapons. But then everything was returned, only the superintendent became more careful and satisfied his demands more quickly. Konashevich's condition had changed radically: it was as if he'd expended all his energy on the previous incident. It made him calmer, and at the same time antisocial. He spent his entire time whistling and singing, upsetting everybody's nerves.

A new incident occurred. Our administration was expecting the new Minister of Internal Affairs and, as usual, trying to rectify the various liberties we'd won in the workshops. Again there was an attempt to 'curb' us. Clashes with the gendarmes became more frequent. On orders from higher up they stopped allowing us into the corridor in twos.

'What's going on?' asks our elder.

'It's an order. I don't know anything', answers the sergeant-major.

'You have to call the officer!'

'Very well.'

An officer who's only just been appointed appears.

'What does this mean? Every time an officer changes, we get a new regime!' the elder complains.

'The previous officer infringed the instructions.'

'Please keep your instructions out of it', interrupts the elder.

'Leave that right to me', counters the officer in a superior tone. L. hears this final phrase.

'P.! are you going to allow him to speak to you in that tone of voice!' he shouts through the window. 'What sort of conversation is this? It's disrespectful!'

The officer flies to his window and utters something. L. shouts at him. Others hear this shout. S. Ivanov and several others appear, accidentally released from the workshops. Heated representations are made. Gendarmes gather as well.

What was said after that is difficult to remember, of course, but one phrase was burned into my memory and, I remember, it angered everyone present.

'Take him to the cell', the officer commanded the gendarmes, pointing to S. I.

'We won't allow that,' those present replied, standing between S. I. and the gendarmes.

'Then I'll call the soldiers,' exclaimed the officer, rushing towards the bell.

But then one of the prisoners grabbed his hand and stopped him. The officer was confused, and started mumbling something. Gradually everything settled down. We announced that we would all leave the workshops, and we did. The officer immediately reported the incident to the commandant and superintendent, painting events in his own colours, of course. We also raised the question of ceasing all relations with this officer and demanding his removal. Paper was given out for a vote, but what ensued was not a vote, but a discussion: the paper was covered in all directions with various notes and considerations, and so on. The issue dragged on. But how to bring it to a solution? After all, the officer met the elder every day on business. The latter's position was unbearable, because of uncertainty about the decision. We agreed for the time being to avoid contact with the officer, and if he put in an appearance himself, to avoid conversation with him as well. As the elder's term of service was finishing, and he himself hurried to declare he couldn't serve any longer, another question was connected to this: who to elect?

When the new elder was chosen, he was given definitive instructions to tell the superintendent that the officer should not appear before us for any reason, and that no-one wanted to have anything to do with him. This was a rather delicate duty, but fulfilling it was unavoidable, so as to avoid making things worse.

All our discussions took place more or less openly for the gendarmes, so they knew beforehand what we had decided, and had informed the proper authorities. The officer didn't hesitate to run to see some of us, and at least say something to justify himself, but was unsuccessful. When he tried to start conversations the reply was silence or the phrase: 'deal with our elder'. The latter declared he couldn't talk to him and wanted to see the superintendent.

'You called for me?' the latter asked.

'Yes, I wanted to announce that after the way your officer behaved in the workshop, I cannot deal with him on any matter whatsoever. Nothing can be expected of it apart from misunderstanding and conflict.'

'But you could after all say the same about everything and not wish to talk to anyone', the superintendent countered.

'There were officers before and we didn't make statements like this.'

'But where can I get you another one from? I don't do things like that myself!'

'That's your business. Mine is to notify you and warn you.'

'You're acting unfairly, blaming one officer for everything. After all, your comrades are not completely right... they get worked up about trivial things.'

'I'm speaking to you not as a judge of my comrades or your officer, but as a man who wishes to avoid any kind of incident.'

'But as the elder, you must restrain your comrades, deter them.'

'I won't take on a political role like that, it's too humiliating. You'd better try and make sure your subordinates don't upset us. You said yourself that my comrades are quick-tempered – all the more need then to be careful with them, but your officer is not capable of that, and I repeat, I won't have anything to do with him, and ask you to tell him not to show his face.'

'I don't know whether the commandant will agree, I'll check', replies the superintendent. 'We don't have any free officers.'

'As you wish: if you don't want any incidents, then of course you'll remove your officer.'

The superintendent went away very dissatisfied. The officer appeared to some of us several more times but, encountering a hostile reception, stopped his visits and soon disappeared off somewhere.

A rumour spread about Pokhitonov's removal to hospital, which both the superintendent and the doctor confirmed before long. The latter had the predicament of how to get him out of his cell: Pokhitonov refused to leave it, and it was as if he guessed that they wanted to send him to a hospital for the insane. But this was difficult to believe: he had progressive brain paralysis, and the process was moving extremely fast.

'I think he sometimes has glimmers of consciousness', the doctor says. 'Taking him away directly won't work. We'll have to trick him.'

'It doesn't matter. He'll probably calm down quickly, once he's sitting in the wagon', says one of the duty officers.

And indeed when they came to Pokhitonov and told him he was going, at first he refused, but then they managed to bring him out on some pretext, and the patient willingly went and sat in the wagon. How he was taken and arrived at the hospital isn't known. The doctor only informed us he was calm for the whole journey. The gendarmes said that Pokhitonov had been placed in the best hospital, and his family informed.

The present writer heard that the patient's brother and sister did indeed go to see him, but he no longer recognized them, or understood anything.

Pokhitonov's transfer made a sort of ambivalent impression on everyone: grief and joy. There was pity for our unfortunate comrade, whose future fate we wouldn't know. Here he was within sight of comrades, who wouldn't allow anyone to treat him roughly. But there… amid such sick half-people, unknown to everybody and without a single soul dear to him! These thoughts worried us terribly. But either egoism or a sense of self-preservation lived in us: we were glad he wasn't here, that our nerves would gain some respite, and justified this feeling with the dubious hope that he would be better there, that it wasn't a living grave, but a hospital with every facility. This feeling progressed, and we grew confident that two others would also be taken away. We decided to petition the inspector about this at the first opportunity. Now there was something to make reference to, especially as even the nerves of those who'd always seemed immune from this point of view began to give way. Fears for some of them grew so much that if the sick were to be kept in the prison for another year or two, two or three new ones would probably have been added to their number. 'Better to die or kill yourself than go out of your mind', several said. 'Yes, as long as you know when it's happening to you.'

In summer '96, Goremykin, the new Minister of Internal Affairs came to the prison, of course with the director of the State Police Department Zvolianskii. Our sepulchre was cleaned and tidied, and the gendarmes themselves were decked out in their dress uniforms. Spurs rang out in the corridor, doors slammed. Our new boss visited everyone and seemed a terrible bear, clumsy and slow-witted: besides greetings and questions about statements and complaints, he asked the most inappropriate questions. He didn't even want to visit the sick. But Konashevich tapped persistently on the door and demanded to see the inspector. The occupant of the cell next to Konashevich's heard some of the latter's words.

'No, you sit down, I'm going to read to you', Konashevich eagerly stopped Goremykin and, as the superintendent said later, began to read his philosophical work, in which there wasn't a single coherent phrase. Several times the inspector tried to sneak out, but the persistent patient stopped him, grabbing Goremykin by the arm and sitting him down on the bed.

'Quarter of an hour more: you'll learn the most important thing!'

'No, you'd better give me the notebook, I'll read it myself', said Goremykin.

Thus was Konashevich's most cherished dream realized. Several times he had given his notebooks to the superintendent to be sent higher up, but each time he had been given them back without any result, and he suspected that they had never been sent to their destination.

The inspector left.

'Huh, what an oppressive atmosphere', Goremykin muttered when he landed in the corridor.

I don't know whether his words related to the moral or physical atmosphere.

'It smells of tobacco', explained the superintendent.

'What tobacco?'

'Well, they (the prisoners) grow their own tobacco and smoke it.'

'Hm!'

Goremykin was asked about journals, correspondence with families, transfer of the sick, and even about tobacco. He replied to everything with vague promises that resembled earlier promises, so we expected nothing to come of this inspection. But it turned out we were mistaken.

Two comrades were approaching the end of their sentences. As usual, all sorts of speculation went on, particularly in relation to one of them, who some years previously had assaulted the superintendent: everyone thought he'd get an extra five years. But suddenly the prisoners were informed that notification of the transfer of the sick had arrived.

The gendarmes smiled broadly: they were already fed up of having to mess about with them, and fears for their own lives had already gone too far as well.

'Thank God!' one blue crossed himself, removing his cap. 'We've suffered with them. How they fight... Once he slapped the superintendent!.. I would have died. I've got children, a wife.'

'But what if they take them all away?' another interrupts fearfully.

'God forbid! Where will we end up! It's good for them (the prisoners) and us here now.'

Such conversations were heard frequently on the watchtower and in the corridor. The gendarmes were afraid of the idea that all the prisoners might be transferred, and then they'd be deprived of cosy, well paid positions. But their apprehensions were unfounded. At that point only the sick were transferred.

On the day of the transfer we were warned not to make a fuss if the sick prisoners started to struggle or shout. We weren't concerned about Konashevich: he'd be delighted. But Shchedrin would surely refuse. And in fact, when the doctor and superintendent came to him to tell him to dress, he refused flat out.

'I'm not going anywhere!'
'Please! You're going on a steam ship.'
'What does that mean? To a mad house?'
'No, to Petersburg', the doctor deceived him.

The argument continued for a whole half hour. And finally he was persuaded.

Konashevich was as if totally reborn. When he was told to dress and collect his notebooks and tobacco, he replied:

'Devil take them! I'm being transferred? At least to hard labour. I'll work 12 hours a day as long as I'm taken away from here.'

What was this? Glimmers of consciousness, an irrepressible thirst for change?..

Our crypt grew silent. The presence of comrades who'd turned into half-people had been hard, but we also felt their absence. In the first period after their transfer we talked only about their fate. We asked the doctor, the superintendent, about their transfer, where they'd been left, where they were placed. They lied to us endlessly, but we naively believed them, deceiving ourselves. In fact it turned out that they both spent more than a month in Kresty,[67] where, it seems, they were experimented on, to make sure they weren't simulating... Later they were allegedly taken first to Kazan', and from there to Vinnitsa (?).[68]

Our crypt was gradually emptying, although life was becoming more tolerable. Soon we were allowed to buy tobacco from public funds, and then fat journals from previous years. With what greed the prisoners attacked them! We read them from cover to cover, trying to spot social movements. We got a whiff of something living. The past was resurrected. We compared contemporary literature with literature from the past. What a difference! The past had retreated into eternity. The former literature was obsolete, and its readers were obsolete too. Now there was something new that was quite alien. Alien because it contained more reason and less heart, feeling. The old ideals by which the prisoners had once lived were called utopian. A fierce polemic between two tendencies caused annoyance and bitterness, although they had much in common. Instead of fighting the enemy with our combined efforts, we began to bait each other. How many arguments there were, every kind of speculation was engaged in about whether the literary tendency really reflected a contemporary movement or was just floating above its surface. In the prison there were proponents of the new trend which, of course, they celebrated, but the majority were against it.

We speculated about the real authors behind many pseudonyms…

Alongside living literature, lectures began again on zoology and palaeontology, with the accumulation of collections, of course. Palaeontology especially confused the prison guards: prisoners rummaging round everywhere, picking at the outer walls, seeking ancient shells, trilobites, and so on, and so forth. The prison island was formed of rock dating to the Silurian period,[69] and in that there was many a good thing.

'No, please, don't break the walls', the superintendent tried to reason, when the prisoners got particularly carried away.

We were given permission to buy missing specimens with the money allocated for the workshop. The prison museum in particular was significantly enlarged and became more varied. The prisoners made the cabinets and showcases themselves, of course. But alas, they couldn't save the collections they had accumulated: bark beetles decimated and spoiled the insects. Instead of complete specimens only debris remained, or rare butterflies lying at the bottom of a case with eaten wings and legs. V. N., as the main custodian of the museum, was driven to despair.

We were allowed to subscribe to two foreign journals, *Revue de Revues* and *Cosmopolis*.[70] From these we extracted rather scanty political information; but all the same they provided an important service, helping us not forget foreign languages. On the contrary, they even forced us to take them more seriously. Readings in English became more frequent, and the passion some had for learning languages reached an unhealthy point. However, in such circumstances everything happens in bursts, with great enthusiasm: an empty life has to be filled somehow!..

We subscribed to one of the Petersburg museums, from where we were brought paleontological collections. So our interest in palaeontology increased. Those who had previously reacted ironically to the hobby themselves started to get involved. In summer, lectures on this subject were a real pleasure. In two or three neighbouring pens or allotments, the prisoners exercising in pairs would gather, taking up position by the fences on the scaffolding, and would take turns to examine the collections while the lecturer explained. But in winter standing still in a frost of −10 to −15° was too uncomfortable and tiresome. Despite that, however, lectures carried on in winter as well. Before he left the prison the present writer was planning to arrange new readings on electricity and mechanics. There were also group readings of various journal articles on social questions. But these regularly ended in aggravation. Debates became far too heated, and for that reason this sort of reading soon slipped off the horizon: was it worth spoiling relations and making life miserable over words, all the more so as there was no hope of bringing each other round? Had conditions been somewhat better, if we'd been able to get together even just twice a week to study, we'd have learned a great deal, and even sitting alone plugging away at a book you could still make a little progress. Although for some, isolated studies were a struggle; they quickly got bored, and the desire vanished...

But after the transfer of the sick there was a notable uplift of spirits: candidates for exit diligently set about studying various subjects: some medicine, others maths, and so on. Unfortunately, a devastating gloom again descended over our prison.

Iurkovskii fell sick, and hopelessly so. He had previously suffered from bowel and bladder disorders, but they were now accompanied by oedema. For a whole month it tortured him, and day in, day out we awaited his death. The administration allowed us to attend him day and night: he couldn't bear the presence of the gendarmes; we held him under the arms to take him out for exercise. The doctor said that under no circumstances would he recover unless he was transferred. Our hopes rested on that. The superintendent told someone that Iurkovskii's mother was in Petersburg and making efforts on his behalf. We knew that she had significant connections, and also that there would be a coronation, so perhaps he'd be taken away. Iurkovskii himself relied on this as well, and often said that he'd have to be transferred. But this was already in his final days, when he was suffering terribly: he could neither stand nor lie down, he was choking, and on the eve of his death, when the attacks of swelling intensified, he asked his comrades to come and say goodbye to him. The women were allowed as well. In the morning, at around four o'clock, he died in the arms of the two comrades on duty. They washed and dressed him with the help of the gendarmes. One of the latter even got all emotional as they put the deceased in a box.

'Well, Fedor Nikolaevich, I served you when you were alive, I'll serve you one last time.'

His body lay in the cell for almost 24 hours, and the administration themselves suggested we go to say goodbye to him... Difficult moments, although everyone had been prepared for this ending.

From the windows a few comrades saw the soldiers take the coffin out of the external gates on a barrow. Besides blue uniforms not a single kindred spirit was able to accompany the deceased. Does such an outcome await us all?..

Again a shroud hung over our crypt for several months. But if only Iurkovskii had lived a little longer! Two or three months later, when the prisoners were preparing to send two comrades to liberty, suddenly everyone was called out from the workshops at an unusual time. Why?

What for? Some quick-wittedly glanced at their comrades through the windows as they passed, and said farewell just in case: evidently, they guessed, they were going to be transferred. After all, previously people had been taken away unexpectedly, as if they'd been abducted, without saying goodbye.

They installed all the prisoners in their cells and locked them up. In the heat of the moment one flared up about this being done without any explanation, tapped on the door and demanded to be returned to the workshop.

'The commandant's coming', the sergeant-major answered him.

Doors slammed, and there was some sort of commotion in the corridor. Then the door on Janavičius's cell slammed.

One neighbour taps.

'What's happened?'

'I'm being transferred... they told me... to Irkutsk governorship-general', he replies somehow incoherently, excitedly.

'What's up?' another neighbour, G. L., repeats the question.

But the answer is even more vague. The prisoners are starting to get angry. But then another door opens. The commandant goes in with a piece of paper and congratulations. The prisoner is silent. Then the commandant reads the document: 'On the order of the Min. Int. Af. etc.... the sentence is shortened by one third, so-and-so will remain in this fortress until the end of the sentence.'

'And other comrades?' asks the prisoner.

'The same', replies the commandant, showing the prisoner the document. The entire corridor's rattling, you can't make out the taps. Everyone's interrupting everyone else. Then we're taken to the workshops. On the way one of the gendarmes, who at some point had been present during a conversation between General Orzhevskii and one of the prisoners concerning his conduct, says to him:

'So, Mr X., your words haven't come true. Remember, you said to General Orzhevskii that you didn't expect to get out of here, that you wouldn't survive. Well, you see. He was right to convince you to behave differently. Congratulations.'

The prisoner remained silent. He didn't understand anything and had other things on his mind. Like all the others, he was more concerned with finding out about the others. A fantasy was developing. It had looked as though the amnesty would be applied to everyone. How soon disappointment would come, however!..

The workshops were full of people. There's a crowd by V. N.'s window: laughter and tears, animated conversations.

'Pankratov, what about you?' V. N. asked one of those arriving.

'Me as well. And you?'

'Hurrah! Pankratov!' she cried.

'And you, Vera?' Pankratov asks her.

'No. We'll see the young off first. Hurrah! Pankratov!' she repeats, wanting to drive away the disappointment that the amnesty doesn't apply to everyone, but only to eight people.

'Who?' asks one of those present.

It turns out that five will be transferred shortly. Their sentences have already finished. Three had been moved from life terms to fixed sentences, and one more had a 20-year sentence reduced by a third.

'Pankratov, we'll arrange a send-off', V. N. rejoices.

'Liudmila, why are you crying as though you're at a funeral?' she consoles her friend.

'I'm outraged. Why not everyone?'

'Well, that's their business; we have to be glad all the same that at least you're leaving.'

It was impossible to agree with such an argument. To depart yourself, and have to leave your comrades and friends behind because of some caprice of fate was too hard and shameful.

We began to discuss the motives governing the application of the amnesty. None of them fitted. Good, meek behaviour couldn't serve as a pretext: it was countered by the behaviour of one of the prisoners, considered practically the worst by the administration. Past activity? Why in that case was it applied to Starodvorskii, but not S. I. or A.?[71] In a word, who knows what they were guided by. Soon the administration started a rumour that it was going to be applied to the rest. The first days of grief passed. Five people were leaving. Three of them felt as they never had before: they became brighter, cheered up, and went around in a sort of festive mood, awaiting their transfer impatiently. The rest continued to rejoice, preparing their comrades for the journey. Dear V. N. tried particularly hard, as if she were leaving this crypt herself. She brewed up a farewell meal, cooked, sewed and knitted day and night. She called the administration and asked that our comrades wouldn't be taken away on the sly, as had happened previously, but we'd be able to say goodbye. The administration itself was in some sort of peculiar state and promised to fulfil this small request.

Dispatch was delayed from day to day. Travelling caps had already long been distributed and our prisoners were already exercising in them. A strange custom: whenever someone was being transferred, they were awarded with coachman's hats with plush blue tops and blue sides. The rest of the uniform remained the same. These hats were known in the prison as 'boyar-caps'.

Pending the transfer all intellectual work was abandoned. Did anyone feel like doing it? There hadn't been such an event in the prison: five comrades were being seen off to freedom at once! We wanted to bid them farewell properly. Pies and biscuits were cooked, reserves of vegetables used up, and the forward-thinking A. made a myrtle fizz and wrote an announcement: 'Farewell concert. On the occasion of the departure of our soprano, with the participation of Ms. V. Figner and a guitar accompaniment'. He decorated it splendidly. Everyone was doubled up with laughter. But it wasn't a joke. On the morning of the transfer all the singers gathered in adjoining pens during exercise: everyone was on form, as they say, and sang our favourite songs beautifully: 'You're not alone in the field, my dear', 'Oh, the Cossacks are many' and a duet: 'Don't tempt me'.[72]

The audience applauded feverishly from the other pens and allotments.

'Farewell, soprano! Who are you going to sing with now?' says A.

'With M.[73] After all, he'll be there', V. N. replies happily for Liudmila.

'I'd willingly stay here with all of you', Liudmila demurs sadly.

She is the saddest of all. She's an extremely affectionate person, a gentle and wonderful comrade.

'Liudmila, it's time to give that up. It would be harder for us if it were as you want it.'

'But we're sorry to part with you all the same. We may not see each other again', one of her neighbours was overcome with emotion.

'Hey, gypsy, you'll soon be leaving yourself. I'll see you soonest of all', she counters me.[74]

'Then you'll sing a duet together. He'll teach you to play the guitar. My children, singing's better! Why all the conversation?' cries V. N. And the concert resumes.

In the workshops the cooks have already prepared a lunch so refined it might have been real food from the free world.

After two o'clock everyone went back to their cells. The administration appeared. Those being transferred changed their clothes and began to go round the cells to bid the comrades staying behind farewell. Liudmila also went round to see everyone, and cried with everyone. Parting was much more difficult for her than for the others…

When they were being taken out of the prison, whoever was able climbed up to their window and for a long time followed them with their eyes. As they went through the yard, they turned round and bowed deeply. All this was just like a dream: it was hard to believe you were parting with them forever. We waved at them through the windows with handkerchiefs. What did they experience as they looked round at this living grave, where there remained so many dear friends, dead and alive, where they had endured the most difficult years of their lives!.. You'll only understand when you have experienced these moments yourself. It's scarcely possible to find the words for such a condition.

Chapter VI.

Soon after the transfer a rumour spread among the comrades that our crypt was going to be wound up. This rumour was begun by the local administration itself, and gave the prisoners an excuse to construct various hypotheses: some said everyone would be sent to Sakhalin, others to Kara, and so on. There were also some, incidentally, who wished only for the Caucasus, far-off places being preferred to the crypt.

'I know life in Iakutsk: it's worse there than here,' P—ov said testily.[75] 'It's also a prison, just without walls, but for all that a person is bound and feels all the more morally oppressed. What sort of freedom is that? You don't dare do anything, don't dare go anywhere …'

'Well, brother, you only argue like that while you're here. You're joking, of course!' Tr. replies with good-natured irony.[76]

P. gets cross. He's talking absolutely seriously.

'It's a good job you've been tamed here!...'

But then signs of disappointment regarding a prompt transfer appear. V. N. is brought a genuine letter from her sister, and it's added that correspondence will soon be permitted for everyone.

V. N., without reading the letter, taps to the whole sepulchre about this first swallow, and a tap echoes round the whole prison: hurrah! Questions vie with each other from all sides, you can't make anything out.

'Tomorrow at exercise. I haven't read it yet…'

But the desire to share her joy prevailed, and that evening V. N. tapped some news around the prison.

The next day during exercise she read out the most interesting parts, with the audience standing on one side of the fence and her on the other. There was no end of delight, but it didn't pass without tears… These lines from kin, from a loving sister, so upset the reader that she had to interrupt her reading several times. Something living, bright, breathed on all of us; as if a hole had been broken through these walls, and behind them a new world opened up to us; we had returned to the distant past.

If the author of the letter had witnessed all this, they would have considered themselves the happiest of people.

In February 1897 all the prisoners were assured that they would be allowed personal correspondence with close family, but no more than twice a year; in addition we were allowed to receive all periodic publications for previous years, and assigned a specific sum for subscriptions to them and for buying books, to the amount of 144 rubles a year.

Many immediately asked for writing paper and envelopes, and set about writing. What was written was read out loud in advance to closest comrades and friends, and only then sent to its address. Although the monitoring was very tight, frequently missives came out very positively anyway: sincere, simple and cheerful. Communal questions arose about how to use the assigned funds. It was here that arguments and suggestions never ended. Common lists produced by the librarian were annotated all over. Polls and arguments, often the bitterest, continued for more than a week. This all finally shattered the poor librarian's nerves: he was ready to give up his post and hide in his shell. His role is utterly unbearable in such circumstances: he has to listen to everyone, read every comment and suggestion; withstand heated attacks from highly-strung comrades; compile a summary, scribble a new list and again run from one person to another listening to approval and blame. More than once the same person would propose completely contradictory plans on two lists.

'So are you going to figure it out?' the librarian grumbles angrily: 'sick people. The only thing left is to refuse.'

'All the more reason for you not to get angry with them', one comrade pacifies the librarian, fearing that he really will give up.

After all, choosing a new librarian would only complicate matters. And where would we get one from? Suitable people would themselves refuse, and we couldn't pick from the unsuitable – the overly neurotic.

Finally, everyone was, I think, weary of such fruitless disputes, and the question was resolved in line with the first suggestion: part of the money would be pooled for journal subscriptions, and the rest would be divided into equal shares.

We were permitted to subscribe to museums and receive zoological, paleontological collections and suchlike.

Some letters from family arrived, which were read out like communal possessions, like journals or newspapers. It's true that many of them were like obituaries: over 11 years some had lost parents, others brothers and sisters.

There was sometimes a great deal of unpleasantness surrounding our letters: if there was something in them that the administration didn't like, they'd simply shelve them, without even informing us. A letter of S. I.'s sat for four months in the Police Department in that way. When he made an enquiry about whether his letter had been sent, it was returned with an addendum that writing about our life was forbidden…

There were other examples of generosity… Trig. received a letter from his mother, in which she informed him that she had been to the Police Department and requested a meeting, but received a refusal. An order obviously came down from the Police Department to our commandant to talk to Tr. about this. The commandant commissioned the superintendent to carry out this delicate conversation. The latter, giving Tr. his letter, reported: your mama was at the Police Department and requested a meeting with you. The Police Department replied that not only do meetings with your mother depend on you, but also that you might be released in Petersburg. Clear hints of a pardon. Tr. understood it thus, almost exploding at such cheek. A person who has spent 17 years in prison has a thing or two to be angry about. Fortunately the matter ended without incident. Tr. replied quite calmly: the fact that I'm here didn't depend on me, and if I continue to be here it won't depend on me either.

But not everyone had such willpower… On the evening of 7 February 1898, Orzhikh suddenly informs his neighbour, N. Morozov, that tomorrow he'll be transferred from the fortress.

The gentle and gracious Morozov was terribly shocked by this news.

'All at once I felt that next door to me there was a decaying corpse', Morozov conveyed his impression.

Morozov knew that without petitioning for a pardon, Orzhikh could not be transferred: he had a life sentence.

'I'll come to you and explain', Orzhikh said to Morozov. 'I submitted a petition, but there was nothing like that in it.'

'Explanations are superfluous. Tell other people about it', replied Morozov.

Soon the corridor was ringing with taps, and the whole prison already knew what Orzhikh had done.

There was no end to the prisoners' resentment, not least because the petition had already been submitted in September 1897, but he had carefully concealed this from his comrades. However Orzhikh tried to justify his conduct, he could convince no-one, nor lessen his comrades' severity.[77]

The next day, 8 February, he was taken away. And the prison again breathed freely, as if a decayed corpse had indeed been removed from its walls. Even our administration noticed this. The doctor, visiting Morozov the next day, said in passing: 'yes, a weak man.' These words related to Orzhikh, whom we were trying not to recall, so as not to awaken painful feelings and memories.

A month later Gen. Panteleev came for an inspection.[78] Following the example of his predecessors, he chatted and behaved courteously. Addressing the writer of these lines, he probed his mood, intentions, and even his moral wellbeing (?). He even congratulated him on his imminent release and spouted a whole pile of fables about the freedom that awaited him in Siberia. I expressed my doubts, saying that I knew the conditions in exile, and looked upon it as a vast prison without walls.

'That's how it was in your time,' he countered, 'now politicals aren't shackled. They're building a railway, and need people like you; many are already in service there…'

All the same I remained unconvinced and just requested permission for a meeting with family.

On 8 March my sentence finished, but I wasn't transferred on that day. The comrades were agitated. V. N. suggested sending for the commandant and demanding an explanation. I refused.

'There's no need to stand on ceremony with him! What is all this dancing on edge?' said V. N.

'Perhaps they've changed their minds, dammit! I'm not going to send for anyone. After all, they haven't even told me where they're sending me,' I said.

'I'll send for him myself if nothing happens tomorrow.'

But she didn't have to. The next day the superintendent told someone, but not me, that I'd be taken that day, but where – he didn't know. It was all the stranger because everyone else had been told their destination.

Before lunch I said goodbye to my comrades and was transferred to an empty cell, where my old clothes and underwear were removed and I was given everything new, not for the sake of cleanliness, of course, but for a search… Then an officer appeared, stood by the doors and muttered, scarcely audibly: 'on order.. you are freed from Shlissel'burg Fortress…' and that was it. But where? Perhaps to another fortress. Why haven't I been told? I asked myself, and gloomy thoughts flashed in my mind. And then another parting with dear comrades. I asked to return for a final time to V. N.'s door, to say farewell to her. The door opened. Poor V. N.! She had tears in her eyes…

'Goodbye, Pankratov! You'll always remain the same in liberty as you were here, I hope. It's good that you came once more to say goodbye. Little joy awaits you, but let there be even less grief… Goodbye!…

It's hard to remember what I said to these wishes. The door slammed shut again. In the corridor there was a final shout, 'farewell'. Going across the yard, I looked back and saw through the inner fence a handkerchief fluttering and familiar faces nodding at the windows. They were submerged back in the prison!…

After my departure 14 people remained in Shlissel'burg Prison. Of those, five had fixed terms and nine people had life sentences.

Fixed terms:

Trigoni, Mikhail Nikolaevich, finishes his sentence in spring 1902. Arrested in February 1881, until 1884 imprisoned in the Alekseevskii Ravelin.

Polivanov, Petr Sergeevich, also finishes his sentence in 1902, but in autumn, in August. Arrested in 1882. Before his transfer to Shlissel'burg Fortress imprisoned in the Alekseevskii Ravelin.

Ashenbrenner, Mikhail Iul'evich, arrested in 1883. His sentence finishes in 1904, in September.

Ivanov, Vasilii Grigor'evich, sentence ends with Ashenbrenner's, arrested in February 1883.

Starodvorskii, Nikolai Petrovich, arrested in May or April 1884. Finishes his sentence only in 1907, as three years of pre-trial detention were not credited to him.

Life terms:

Antonov, Petr Leont'evich, arrested in summer 1885; brought to Shlissel'burg Fortress in 1887.

Lopatin, German Aleksandrovich, arrested in autumn 1884. Brought to Shlissel'burg Fortress in 1887.

Lukaszewicz, Jyzef, and Novorusskii, Mikhail Vasil'evich, both arrested in spring 1887; brought to Shlissel'burg Fortress in summer of the same year.

Morozov, Nikolai Aleksandrovich, arrested at the beginning of 1881; before Shlissel'burg Fortress imprisoned in the Alekseevskii Ravelin.

Popov, Mikhail Rodionovich, arrested in 1880, at first in Kara, from Kara transferred to the Peter and Paul Fortress, and then to Shlissel'burg Fortress.

Frolenko, Mikhail Fedorovich, arrested in 1881; before Shlissel'burg Fortress imprisoned in the Ravelin.

Figner, Vera Nikolaevna, arrested in February 1883.[79]

Notes

1. This period of his life is covered in: Pankratov, *Vospominaniia: kak prikhodilos' rabotat' sredi rabochikh v 1880–1884 godakh*. See also Pearl, 'From worker to revolutionary', 1996, 17–18.
2. The all-Russian political forum convened in Moscow by the Provisional Government, 12–15 (25–28) August 1917.

3 The period of unrest between 3 and 7 (16–20) July 1917 in Petrograd, when industrial workers, soldiers and sailors demonstrated against the Provisional Government, leading to violence and a crackdown on the Bolshevik Party.
4 See Pankratov, *S tsarem v Tobol'ske*.
5 The anti-Bolshevik conference was held in Ufa in Southern Russia from 8–23 September 1918.
6 Figner, *Zapechatlennyi trud*, 2:140.
7 Figner, *Zapechatlennyi trud*, 2:141.
8 Sorokin, *A Long Journey*, 133.
9 Originally constructed out of letters on Shlissel'burg written to Vera Figner's sister Ol'ga Florovskaia-Figner, Pankratov's memoir was first published in 1902 in Geneva by the Socialist Revolutionary Party Press. It was reprinted in Berlin in 1904 by Shteinits (who also republished Volkenshtein's and Ashenbrenner's memoirs), and in 1906 in Moscow by Molodaia Rossiia (Young Russia), then republished in 1922 in Petrograd with notes by R. M. Kantor.
10 There were 11 men from the Ravelin: Grigorii Isaev, who died in Shlissel'burg Fortress in 1886; Savelii Zlatopol'skii, who died at the end of 1885; Nikolai Morozov; Butsevich, who died in spring '85; Iurii Bogdanovich, who died in summer '88; Aronchik, who died in '86; Petr Polivanov; Klimenko (according to one witness he hanged himself; according to others, he was taken down from the noose still alive, but died soon after); Mikhail Frolenko; Trigoni; and Grachevskii (burned himself to death in '88). *Author's note*. [Aronchik actually died in 1888; see Volkenshtein, note 31, on the date of Grachevskii's suicide. The first transfers to the fortress were actually on 2 (14) and 4 (16) August 1884. *Translator's note*.]
11 On Kara, see Volkenshtein, note 26.
12 Pokhitonov was brought from the Peter and Paul Fortress in October 1884, in the same group as Figner, Volkenshtein and Ashenbrenner. Butsinskii was in another group brought in August 1884, from the Trubetskoi Bastion at the Peter and Paul Fortress, that had previously been serving hard labour sentences in Kara, hence his reference to returning there.
13 The Russian here has 'хочь гирше, та инше', though the proverb is in fact Ukrainian: 'хоч гірше, та інше'. My thanks to Uilleam Blacker for clarifying this meaning.
14 All the prisoners were issued with grey prison robes with yellow diamonds and letters on the back, grey caps with black crosses, grey jackets with black sleeves – our ladies, V. Figner and L. Volkenshtein, wore the same jackets – and grey trousers, though the ladies were given grey skirts in prisoners' fabric. Subsequently these motley costumes were replaced by plain grey, and in summer light clothes in white canvas were offered. Instead of boots we were given fur slippers. *Author's note*.
15 The first inhabitants of Shlissel'burg Prison, besides the Ravelinites, were brought there from Kara. There were 11 people from Kara: Minakov, Ignatii Ivanov, Nikolai Shchedrin, Gellis, Mikhail Popov, Dmitrii Butsinskii, Malevskii [sic], Myshkin, Kobylianskii, Dolgushin and Iurkovskii. Of the 11 men only two remain among the living: Popov and Shchedrin, but the latter had already gone out of his mind by '85, and in '96 was transferred to Kazan' hospital. *Author's note*.
16 This is precisely the same formulation that Ashenbrenner (Chapter II) uses to describe Sokolov.
17 General Aleksandr L'vovich Potapov (1818–86), Chief of Staff of the Special Corps of Gendarmes, 1861–4, Chief of Gendarmes and Executive Head of the Third Section of the Imperial Chancellery 1874–6.
18 Sergei Gennadievich Nechaev (1847–82), opportunist Russian revolutionary, author of 'The Catechism of a Revolutionary' and responsible for the murder of a student as part of his plan to foment a revolutionary conspiracy, an incident that Dostoevskii used as the basis of his 1872 novel *Demons*.
19 On Sudeikin, see Ashenbrenner, note 8.
20 Sapernyi Lane is in central St Petersburg.
21 The Decoration of the Military Order of St George was awarded for bravery, initially among the lower ranks, between 1807 and 1917. It was reinstated in 1992.
22 The food, as has already been said, was grim and insufficient in quantity. For lunch there was *shchi* with five or six small pieces of rotten meat and sinew, and some *kasha* – buckwheat or barley, with oil; morning and evening there was a mug of tea each. Only black bread was distributed. All fast days were strictly observed. *Author's note*.
23 Russian: 'узник'.
24 Baron Shtromberg, Rogachev, V. Figner, Tikhanovich, Nemolovskii, Vasilii Ivanov, Iuvachev, Pokhitonov, Surovtsev, Liudmila Volkenshtein and Ashenbrenner. Of these two died:

Nemolovskii and Tikhanovich. It was said of the latter that he hanged himself, and that is quite possible, because he was mentally ill and, according to rumours that were circulating, had more than once attempted suicide. Pokhitonov went out of his mind in '94 and was only sent to Nikolaevskii hospital in Petersburg in '96, where he apparently died in '97. Baron Shtromberg and Rogachev were executed. *Author's note.*

25 Martynov, Shebalin, Karaulov and Pankratov. *Author's note.*
26 Russian: способы, that is, methods of dying by suicide.
27 The further fate of Myshkin. He was tried in the fortress. Subsequently, many, many years later, the writer of the present lines managed to find out from someone who was present at the trial, that Myshkin 'berated the judges severely', and gave such a powerful speech that even the gendarmes were moved. I don't know what the speaker meant by these words, but I could see that he was very gratified by Myshkin's speech. He probably spoke of the brutality of the administration, from which the gendarmes suffered as well. That's where their sympathy for Myshkin came from. Where Myshkin was executed is unknown. Probably in Shlissel'burg. *Author's note.*
28 On the basis that Pankratov tends to name in full fellow prisoners who died in Shlissel'burg, it seems likely that this is Vasilii Ivanov.
29 Avvakum Petrov (1620/21–1682) was the priest who led opposition to the reforms of the Orthodox church introduced by Patriarch Nikon that resulted in the schism between the mainstream church and the Old Believers. Imprisoned and exiled to Siberia with his family, Avvakum was recalled to Moscow and then imprisoned again, before being burned at the stake. His *Life of the Archpriest Avvakum, Written by Himself* is a masterpiece of early modern Russian literature, representing one of the earliest autobiographies written in vernacular Russian, and one of the first Russian memoirs of imprisonment and exile.
30 That is, to make the light harsher. As Ashenbrenner (Chapter IV) attests, lights were kept on all night in cells, a practice that continued in Soviet-era prisons.
31 They were brought in from the trial of 2 March: Shevyrev, Generalov, Andreiushkin, Osipanov, Ul'ianov, Novorusskii and Lukaszewicz. The first five were executed straight away, but the last two lived on in Shlissel'burg Prison. They've now left. *Author's note.*
32 From Lopatin's trial: Lopatin, Starodvorskii, Antonov, Konoshevich [sic] and Sergei Ivanov. Konoshevich went mad in 1890, and in '96 he and Shchedrin were sent to Kazan' hospital. In the period between 1885 and 1887 the following were sent to Shlissel'burg Prison: in '85, Lagovskii, without a trial, by administrative order, for five years, and when it expired he had another five years added on, so that he was locked up with us until '95, after which he was sent to the Steppe Governate-General [in Central Asia] for three years. After Lagovskii, in '86 Manucharov was brought for 10 years, after a trial. In '92 [in fact 1896 – *trans.*] he was taken away to Sakhalin. In '86 after the trial of the [Polish] proletarians, Janavičius and Waryński were brought. Of those two only the first survived, nowadays he's residing in Srednekolymsk. *Author's note.* [Janavičius died by suicide in 1902. *Translator's note.*]
33 Nozdrev, one of the landowners in *Dead Souls*, by Nikolai Vasil'evich Gogol' (1809–52), is the archetypal cheat, liar and bully of Russian literature.
34 Due to the northerly latitude of Shlissel'burg Fortress, this would be during the White Nights.
35 According to Volkenshtein, it was Petrov, rather than Shebeko, who upbraided Herod.
36 This must refer to Mikhail Trigoni.
37 Mikhail Shebalin.
38 Vasilii Konashevich.
39 Each prisoner was assigned a number rather than referred to by name. Sergei Ivanov was no. 28.
40 A popular Russian song with music by the composer Petr Petrovich Bulakhov (1822–85).
41 That is, if an official had visited for an inspection.
42 Russian: 'латающий' свой туалет. The Zaporozhian Cossack Sich territory, beyond the Dnieper Rapids in Central Ukraine, was a well-established political entity from the fifteenth to the eighteenth century, with a parliamentary system of government. The significance of the image described here is unclear.
43 Probably German Lopatin.
44 The letter N is in Latin script in the original. It probably refers to Mikhail Novorusskii, or possibly Nikolai Morozov or Nikolai Starodvorskii.
45 Aleksandr Illarionovich Vasil'chikov (1818–81), prince and academic, who published treatises on agriculture, land tenure and self-government in Russia. Ianzhul: see Ashenbrenner, note 100. Aleksei Sergeevich Suvorin (1834–1912), publisher and journalist, who produced an annual statistical journal from 1872.

46 Nikolai Petrovich Starodvorskii, as the subsequent initials make clear.
47 Probably Petr Antonov, who was tried alongside Starodvorskii.
48 Nicolas Camille Flammarion (1842–1925), French astronomer and writer, author of science fiction works that featured extra-terrestrials and metempsychosis. The story mentioned here is presumably one of those written by Nikolai Morozov.
49 The *Russian Pilgrim* [*Russkii palomnik*] was an illustrated pre-revolutionary Russian journal, published in St Petersburg between 1885 and 1917. Its focus on ecclesiastical issues would have been far from the interests of most of these prisoners.
50 As the author has used this phrase previously, this is most likely a reference to Pankratov himself.
51 That is, earlier than those plants that had not benefitted from the cold frames.
52 Vasilii Ivanov.
53 Again P. refers to the author, as the subsequent use of the shortened version of his surname, Pan, indicates.
54 The Orthodox feast day of the Archangel Michael. Seven of the prisoners alive at this time were named Mikhail.
55 Mikhail Trigoni, one of those celebrating his name day.
56 'Milord' was Trigoni's alias in the revolutionary underground.
57 That is, in the cell windows.
58 *Lapta* is a bat and ball game resembling baseball or rounders.
59 A character in Gogol"s *Dead Souls*, associated with calculation and philistine conservatism.
60 The Bethlem Royal Hospital, a London psychiatric hospital, was located in Southwark from 1810–1930, in the building that now houses the Imperial War Museum. Founded in 1247 and the oldest psychiatric hospital in continuous use in Europe, its reputation was notorious, leading to the nickname 'Bedlam' that became synonymous with madness and chaos.
61 Boris Orzhikh.
62 Probably Lukaszewicz, as Pankratov tends to use the initial G. to refer to German Lopatin.
63 Personnel: Russian: служащие.
64 That is, back to their cells.
65 Vasilii or Sergei Ivanov.
66 That is, from the ground floor of the prison.
67 Kresty is the main prison in St Petersburg, reconstructed between 1884 and 1890.
68 Vinnitsa is a city in central Ukraine.
69 The third period of the Paleozoic era, from 443 million to 416 million years ago.
70 *Cosmopolis* was a monthly, multilingual literary magazine published between 1896 and 1898 in London, Paris, Berlin and St Petersburg.
71 Probably Petr Antonov, who arrived in the same group as Sergei Ivanov and Starodvorskii in July 1887.
72 Popular folk songs. 'Oh, the Cossacks are many' has music by Ukrainian composer Nikolai [Mikola] Vital'evich Lysenko (1842–1912). 'Don't tempt me for no reason' has lyrics by poet and translator Evgenii Abramovich Baratynskii (1800–44) and music by Mikhail Ivanovich Glinka (1804–57), the influential composer credited with the development of a specifically Russian style of classical music.
73 Ivan Manucharov.
74 Vera Figner notes that Pankratov described himself as a 'real gypsy', due to his swarthy features and black hair and eyes. *Zapechatlennyi trud*, 2:141.
75 Mikhail Popov was the only survivor of the group that had been transferred from Kara hard labour.
76 Mikhail Trigoni.
77 Other Shlissel'burg memoirs do not mention Orzhikh's petition, but it is notable that beyond the present work, his name appears only in the texts that aim to document the names of all the prisoners for posterity: the memoirs of Figner, Iuvachev, Novorusskii and Volkenshtein. Petitioning for clemency was considered a betrayal by the revolutionaries, because it entailed both an admission that one's actions had been a crime, and acknowledgement of the state's legitimacy, which revolutionary groups rejected. Iuvachev's early transfer from the fortress tends to be viewed more leniently on the grounds that he was suffering from religious mania, even if he later recovered.
78 Infantry General Aleksandr Il'ich Panteleev (1838–1919), Commander of the Special Corps of Gendarmes, 1898–1900.
79 Sergei Ivanov is missing from Pankratov's list of those remaining in the fortress.

Appendix: Shlissel'burg's inmates, 1884–1906[1]

Andreiushkin, Pakhomii Ivanovich (1865–87) Born on 15 (27) May 1865 in the Caucasus and educated at Ekaterinodar Gymnasium, then in the mathematics and physics faculty of St Petersburg University, where he joined the People's Will, participating in the attempt on the life of Tsar Alexander III. Arrested on 1 (13) March 1887 and sentenced to death, he was transferred to Shlissel'burg Fortress and executed on 8 (20) May 1887, alongside Aleksandr Ul'ianov and others.

Antonov, Petr Leont'evich (1859–1916) Prisoner no. 31.[2] Born on 21 December 1859 (3 January 1860) in Nikolaev (Ukraine) to a cantonist non-commissioned officer, Antonov went to vocational school and worked as a machinist in Kharkiv, where he led strikes, and then in a railway workshop in Poltava, where he joined the People's Will. As a member of the Southern Russian battle organization of the People's Will, he took part in a robbery of the Poltava mail, killed a worker suspected of being a police informer, and organized an illegal printing press. He was arrested on 1 (13) May 1885 in Kharkiv and transferred to Petersburg where, after two years in the Peter and Paul Fortress, he was sentenced to death, commuted to lifelong hard labour. He was transferred to Shlissel'burg on 23 June (5 July) 1887, and was freed on 28 October (10 November) 1905. He died of cancer in Odessa on 18 June (1 July) 1916.

Aronchik, Aizik Borisovich (Itsok-Aizik Berovich Aronchik) (1859–88) Cell 28. Born on 28 December 1859 (10 January 1860) in Zhitomir (Ukraine) and educated in Odessa and at the St Petersburg Institute of Engineers, Aronchik abandoned his studies for revolutionary work, and kept safe houses used in attempts on the life of Alexander II. He was arrested in March 1881, convicted in the 'Trial of the 20', and sentenced to lifelong hard labour. Aronchik was already suffering from mental illness when he was transferred to Shlissel'burg Fortress on 4 (16) August 1884, where he also fell victim to paralysis. Memoirs record that he never left his cell or spoke to other inmates. His presence was unknown until some time after his death in the fortress on 2 (15) April 1888.

Ashenbrenner, Mikhail Iul'evich (1842–1926) Prisoner no. 14, cell 40. Born on 9 (21) September 1842 in Moscow to a family of Russified German nobility, Ashenbrenner was an officer in a guards' regiment. He served in Turkestan for five years after refusing to participate in the suppression of the Polish uprising in 1864. In the 1870s he became involved in propaganda work, and in 1881 joined the military centre of the People's Will. Arrested in 1883 and convicted in the 'Trial of the 14' alongside Vera Figner, Liudmila Volkenshtein and others, Ashenbrenner's death sentence was commuted to lifelong hard labour. He was transferred to Shlissel'burg Fortress in October 1884, and was imprisoned there until September 1904. He was transferred to exile in Smolensk, where he returned to revolutionary work. He died in Moscow on 11 November 1926.

Balmashev, Stepan Valer'ianovich (1881–1902) Born on 3 (15) April 1881 in Arkhangel'sk province to a Populist family that had been exiled there administratively, Balmashev studied at the Taras Shevchenko National University of Kiev and was first arrested in January 1901 as a leader of student unrest. Later that year he made contact with revolutionaries, and operated in both Marxist and Populist circles. In 1902, as a member of the newly-formed battle organization of the Socialist Revolutionary Party, Balmashev assassinated Minister of the Interior Dmitrii Sergeevich Sipiagin, for which he was sentenced to death. He was transferred to Shlissel'burg Fortress, and hanged on 3 (16) May 1902, the first execution carried out there since 1887.

Bogdanovich, Iurii Nikolaevich (1849–88) Cell 22. Born on 1 (13) April 1849 to a noble family in Toropets district (Tver' Governate), Bogdanovich studied at Pskov Gymnasium and qualified as a tax inspector. After working as a land surveyor, he began studying at the St Petersburg Medical-Surgical Academy, but left in 1873 to participate in the 'Going to the People' movement, conducting propaganda among the peasantry in Saratov province alongside Vera Figner. In 1879 after the split in the Land and Liberty Party he joined the People's Will, becoming a member of the Executive Committee the following year. Bogdanovich opened the cheese shop on Malaia Sadovaia Street in St Petersburg from where the group tunnelled under the street as part of the final and successful attempt on Tsar Alexander II's life. He was arrested in May 1882 and sentenced to death the following year in the 'Trial of the 17'. His sentence was commuted to lifelong hard labour and he was transferred to Shlissel'burg Fortress on 4 (16) August 1884. He died there of tuberculosis on 18 (30) July 1888.

Butsevich, Aleksandr Vikent'evich (1849–85) Cell 19. Born in Pskov to a civil servant's family, Butsevich studied at the St Petersburg Naval Institute and gained the rank of midshipman. He worked in the Ministry of Transportation and in 1880 joined the military centre of the People's Will, participating in organizing a dynamite workshop. At the rank of lieutenant, he was arrested in July 1882 and was a defendant in the 'Trial of the 17' in 1883. His death sentence was commuted to lifelong hard labour and in August 1884 he was transferred to Shlissel'burg Fortress, where he died of tuberculosis on 17 (29) May 1885.

Butsinskii, Dmitrii Timofeevich (1855–91) Cell 20. Born on 9 (21) February 1855 to a priest's family in Kursk province, Butsinskii studied at theological seminaries and in the medical faculty of Kharkiv University. In 1878 he was expelled from university for participating in student unrest, and joined the People's Will. He was arrested in 1880, tried in Kiev, sentenced to 20 years' hard labour and sent to Kara hard labour system. He was transferred to the Peter and Paul Fortress in 1882 and to Shlissel'burg on 4 (16) August 1884, where he died of stomach cancer on 16 (28) July 1891.

Chepegin, Nikita Koz'mich (1882–?) Born on 28 May (9 June) 1882 to a worker's family, Chepegin studied at a village school and worked as a carpenter. He took part in the attempted assassination of retired General-Lieutenant Weis in Kiev in May 1902, for which he was sentenced to 20 years' hard labour. He was transferred to Shlissel'burg Fortress in July 1902. In January 1904 he was transferred to a transit prison, and the following year was moved to Vilensk (Vilna District) psychiatric hospital. His subsequent fate is unknown.

Dolgushin, Aleksandr Vasil'evich (1848–85) Cell 37. The son of a civil servant from the nobility, Dolgushin was born in Tara in Tobol'sk Governate and studied at the St Petersburg Technical Institute. Acquitted in the Nechaev trial of 1871, he formed his own revolutionary circle, and was arrested again in 1873. In 1874 he was sentenced to 10 years' hard labour. In 1881 he was given an additional 10-year sentence for participating in an uprising at Krasnoiarsk prison. In 1883 he was transferred from Kara hard labour back to St Petersburg, and on 4 (16) August 1884 sent to Shlissel'burg Fortress, where he died the following year, on 30 June (12 July) 1885.

Figner, Vera Nikolaevna (1852–1942) Prisoner no. 11, cell 26. Born in Kazan' Governate to a noble family on 24 June (6 July) 1852, Figner studied at the Rodionovskii Institute for Noble Girls in Kazan'. She then enrolled at Kazan' University, but wanted to study medicine, which at the time was not open to women in Russia. When her father forbade her to travel to Zurich to study, she married court investigator Aleksei Viktorovich Filippov, and travelled to Switzerland. She was enrolled as a student in Zurich University's department of medicine from 1872 to 1875. In 1873 she joined a circle of radical young Russian women. A directive forbidding Russian women from further study of medicine was passed, but Figner remained in Switzerland, hoping to finish her course. However, she returned to Russia in 1875 without gaining a degree, began work as a paramedic, and joined Land and Liberty. In the late 1870s she conducted revolutionary propaganda around Saratov and Samara, while working as a doctor's assistant. Following the 1879 split of Land and Liberty over the question of terrorist tactics, Figner joined the People's Will, and became a member of its Executive Committee. She was involved in planning the attempt on Alexander II's life in Odessa in 1879, and in the successful assassination on 1 (13) March 1881. Following the arrest of other members of the Executive Committee, Figner as de facto leader was responsible for restoring the organization's network, including setting up a new printing press and returning to propaganda work, as well as organizing further assassination attempts on high-profile government figures. She was betrayed by police agent Sergei Degaev, arrested in February 1883, and held in the Peter and Paul Fortress until September 1884. A defendant in the 'Trial of the 14', her death sentence was commuted to lifelong hard labour, and she was transferred to Shlissel'burg in October 1884. After 20 years' incarceration she was released to exile first in Arkhangel'sk Governate, then Kazan', and finally Nizhnii Novgorod. In 1906 she was allowed to go abroad, where she conducted an extensive campaign for political prisoners in Russia. She joined the Socialist Revolutionary Party, but left in 1909 after the Azef affair.[3] She returned to Russia in 1915, and published her celebrated memoirs in 1921–2, which were translated into many languages. She was a key figure in the establishment of the Society for Former Political Prisoners and Exiles, and its journal *Hard Labour and Exile* (*Katorga i ssylka*). She opposed the October Revolution of 1917, and remained unreconciled to the Bolshevik government as its repressive nature became more apparent. Figner died in Moscow on 15 June 1942.

Frolenko, Mikhail Fedorovich ('Mikhailo') (1848–1938) Prisoner no. 2, cell 6. The son of a retired sergeant-major, Frolenko was born in November 1848 in Stavropol', and educated at a district school, Stavropol' Gymnasium, St Petersburg Technical Institute and Petrovsk land-economy academy. He was a member of the Chaikovskii Circle in 1873–4,[4] and participated in the 'Going to the People' movement. In 1878 he joined Land and Liberty, and on its split became a member of the

Executive Committee of the People's Will. He participated in the unsuccessful attempt on the life of Alexander II in Odessa in November 1879, and his assassination on 1 (13) March 1881. He was arrested two weeks later in St Petersburg, and convicted in the 'Trial of the 20'. His death sentence was commuted to lifelong hard labour, and he was held in the Alekseevskii Ravelin until August 1884, when he was transferred to Shlissel'burg. He was freed in October 1905 under the terms of the amnesty of that month, and worked as an editor of the revolutionary journal *The Past* (*Byloe*), where many memoirs of Shlissel'burg Prison were published. Frolenko's own memoirs appeared in 1927. From 1922 he lived in Moscow. He was a member of the Society for Former Political Prisoners and Exiles, and an editor of the journal *Hard Labour and Exile* (*Katorga i ssylka*). He joined the Communist Party in 1936, and died in Moscow on 18 February 1938.

Gellis, Meier Iankelevich (*Iakovlevich*) (Girsh Izrailovich Gellis) (1852 (or 1857)–1886) Cell 8. Born in Odessa to a Jewish tradesman's family, Gellis studied at the Odessa Jewish Institute and Commercial Institute. He fled abroad to escape military conscription, and worked as a printer in Geneva and Zurich. He returned to Odessa in 1878 and organized revolutionary circles, and in February 1879 took part in the murder of a police agent. Arrested in May 1879, he was sentenced to death at the Odessa 'Trial of the 19', subsequently commuted to lifelong hard labour. In October 1880 he was transferred to Kara hard labour, but in 1882 transferred to the Peter and Paul Fortress, before being moved to Shlissel'burg on 2 (14) August 1884, where he died two years later, on 10 (22) October 1886.

Generalov, Vasilii Denisovich (1867–87) Born on 8 (20) March 1867 to a Don Cossack family, Generalov studied at Novocherkassk Gymnasium and matriculated in the law faculty of St Petersburg University, but abandoned his studies to join the terrorist faction of the People's Will. He participated in the attempt on Alexander III's life in March 1887, and was sentenced to death. He was transferred to Shlissel'burg Fortress and hanged alongside Aleksandr Ul'ianov and Pakhomii Andreiushkin on 8 (20) May 1887.

Gershkovich, Girsh (*Khaim*) *A.* (1886–1905) Born to a poor Jewish family, Gershkovich was a member of the battle organization of the Socialist Revolutionary Party, and an associate of Boris Savinkov.[5] He was arrested in June 1905 and sentenced to death by the Petersburg military tribunal the following month. He was transferred to Shlissel'burg Fortress on 19 August, and hanged on 20 August (2 September) 1905 alongside Aleksandr Vasil'ev.

Gershuni, Grigorii Andreevich (Isaak Tsukovich Gersh) (1870–1908) Born on 18 February (2 March) 1870 in Kaunas, Lithuania, to a Jewish petty-bourgeois family, Gershuni studied pharmacy at Kiev University and was arrested for activities in the student movement. After graduating he opened a chemical-biological factory in Minsk. Alongside Ekaterina Breshko-Breshkovskaia, Viktor Chernov and others, including the police spy Evno Azef, Gershuni was a founder member of the Socialist Revolutionary Party in 1901. The following year, Gershuni founded the battle organization of the SRs, which carried out the executions of Minister of the Interior Dmitrii Sipiagin (killed by Stepan Balmashev, who was executed at Shlissel'burg Fortress) and Governor-General of Ufa M. N. Bogdanovich. Gershuni was arrested in May 1903, transferred to the Peter and Paul Fortress, and convicted in 1904. His death sentence was commuted to lifelong hard labour, and he was transferred to Shlissel'burg on 31 August (13 September) 1904. In January 1906 he was transferred to Nerchinsk hard labour system, but escaped to China and travelled to the United States. Returning to Europe, he defended Azef against the charges that he was a police spy. Gershuni's memoirs detail his imprisonment in both the Peter and Paul and Shlissel'burg Fortresses. He died in Zurich of tuberculosis on 29 March 1908.

Ginsburg, Sof'ia Mikhailovna (1863–91) Born on 20 March (1 April) 1863 in the Ekaterinoslav Governate (present-day Dnipro, Ukraine), possibly to a Jewish family, Ginsburg studied at Kerch Gymnasium, then took an obstetrics course. In 1884 she joined the People's Will and kept a safe house in St Petersburg. She travelled in Europe and studied medicine from 1885, and joined the 'Allied Terrorist Circle', formed in Switzerland in 1888 by remaining members of the People's Will. She returned to Russia, converting to Orthodoxy to marry. In 1889 she participated in plans for an attempt on the life of Alexander III, for which she was briefly arrested. Intending to escape abroad again, Ginsburg travelled to Kharkiv and then Sevastopol', but was arrested on 31 May (12 June) 1889. On 31 October (12 November) 1890 she was sentenced to death, but after a plea for mercy the sentence was commuted to lifelong hard labour. She was transferred to Shlissel'burg Fortress on 1 (13) December 1890, and incarcerated alone in the old prison. She obtained a pair of scissors for sewing and used them to die by suicide on 7 (19) January 1891.

Grachevskii, Mikhail Fedorovich (1853 (or 1849)–1887) Cell 11. Born on 6 (18) November 1853 (or possibly 1849) to the family of a sexton in Saratov Governate, Grachevskii was a student at Saratov Theological Seminary before working as a machinist in a railway workshop. He was first arrested in 1875 for spreading revolutionary propaganda, convicted in the 'Trial of the 193' and given a short sentence. He escaped from exile in Arkhangel'sk Governate, and played an active role in the assassination of Alexander II. He was arrested in June 1882, and convicted in April 1883 in the 'Trial of the 17', alongside Bogdanovich, Butsevich and Klimenko. His death sentence was commuted to lifelong hard labour, and on 2 (14) August 1884 he was taken from the Alekseevskii Ravelin to Shlissel'burg Fortress. As many of the memoirs record, Grachevskii assaulted the prison doctor in an attempt to provoke a death sentence, but was declared insane and incarcerated in the old prison, where he set fire to himself using a kerosene lamp, and perished on 26 October (7 November) 1887.

Isaev, Grigorii Prokof'evich (1857–86) Cell 3. Born in Mogilev (present-day Belarus) on 10 (22) January 1857 to a postmaster's family, but raised in Mogilev orphanage and educated at the local gymnasium, Isaev enrolled in the mathematics and physics department of St Petersburg University in 1876, before transferring to the Medical-Surgical Academy. In 1879 he joined the terrorist group Freedom or Death, and became a member of the Executive Committee of the People's Will. He organized a dynamite workshop, and participated in attempts on the life of Tsar Alexander II near Moscow and Odessa, as well as the successful attempt in Petersburg. In February 1882 he was convicted in the 'Trial of the 20' and sentenced to death, commuted to lifelong hard labour. In August 1884 he was transferred to Shlissel'burg Fortress, where he died on 25 March (6 April) 1886 of tuberculosis.

Iurkovskii, Fedor Nikolaevich ('Sashka-Inzhener') (1851–96) Prisoner no. 10, cell 39. Born in Nikolaev (Ukraine) to a military family, Iurkovskii studied at Nikolaev Gymnasium and the St Petersburg Naval Institute, but also attended courses at the Technological Institute and the Medical-Surgical Academy before turning to revolutionary activities. He was arrested on 7 (19) March 1880 for his part in a plot against the Kherson Treasury Department, and tried in Kiev. Sentenced to 20 years' hard labour, he was sent to Kara hard labour in February 1881, but escaped in May the following year. He was captured on the Chinese border, and his sentence was increased by 10 years. After participating in further disorder in Kara, Iurkovskii was returned to St Petersburg, and on 4 (16) August 1884 transferred to Shlissel'burg Fortress. In the prison he wrote a novel, *Bulgakov*, based on his revolutionary experiences, but this remained unfinished when, after a long illness, he died on 30 August (11 September) 1896, the last of the long-term prisoners to perish there.

Iuvachev, Ivan Pavlovich (1860–1940) Cell 23. Born on 23 February (6 March) 1860 to the family of a palace floor polisher who worked at the Anichkov Palace in St Petersburg, Iuvachev was educated at the Kronstadt Admiralty Technical Institute, qualifying as a navigator and achieving the rank of warrant officer. He served in the Black Sea Fleet, and in 1881 met Mikhail Ashenbrenner in Nikolaev and became involved in revolutionary activity. One of the members of the People's Will betrayed by Degaev, he was arrested in Petersburg in March 1883. Convicted in the 'Trial of the 14' in September 1884, Iuvachev was sentenced to death, commuted to 15 years' hard labour. He was transferred to Shlissel'burg Fortress on 16 (28) October 1884, where he underwent a religious conversion (memoirs record him as suffering from religious mania). On 23 November (5 December) 1887, he became the first of the long-term inmates to leave the prison when he was transferred to exile on Sakhalin Island. He was released in 1895 and returned to St Petersburg two years later. In addition to his 1907 memoir-history of the fortress (translated into English in 1909 as *The Russian Bastille, or the Schluesselburg Fortress*) and a further memoir about his period of exile, *Eight Years on Sakhalin* (1901), Iuvachev wrote a number of spiritual works. He married in 1902 and in 1905 his son Daniil, better known as the absurdist writer Daniil Kharms, was born. Ivan Iuvachev died in Leningrad on 17 May 1940 or, according to some sources, in 1936.

Ivanov, Ignatii Kirillovich (1859–86) Cell 2. Born in Poltava Province to an officer's (or possibly a priest's) family, Ignatii Ivanov studied at Kiev University and joined a terrorist group. Arrested on 25 February (9 March) 1880 with a bomb in his hands, he was tried alongside Fedor Iurkovskii and Mikhail Popov, and sentenced to death, commuted to lifelong hard labour. For participating in the murder in Kara hard labour of Petr Gavrilovich Uspenskii (a member of the Nechaev group responsible for the murder of the student Ivan Ivanov), Ignatii Ivanov was transferred to the Peter and Paul Fortress, where he suffered a mental breakdown. He was treated at Kazan' Psychiatric Hospital, then transferred to Shlissel'burg, where his mental condition worsened. He died in the prison on 21 February (5 March) 1886.

Ivanov, Sergei Andreevich ('Danilov', 'Vasilii Alekseevich') (1859–1927) Prisoner no. 28. A great-grandson of the poet Konstantin Nikolaevich Batiushkov (1787–1855), Sergei Ivanov was born on 7 (19) August 1858 in Iaroslavl' Governate to a noble family, and studied at Iaroslavl' Gymnasium and the St Petersburg Medical-Surgical Academy, where he joined a revolutionary circle. Exiled to Arkhangel'sk Province in 1879 for participating in student disturbances, he returned to the capital in 1881 and joined the People's Will. He was arrested in April 1881 and administratively sentenced to five years' exile in Siberia, but escaped in December 1882 and returned to Petersburg, where he worked on an illegal printing press for the People's Will. He subsequently also ran an illegal press in Rostov-on-Don, and a bomb-making workshop in Lugansk, and organized the local party group in Kiev with Mikhail Shebalin. He left Russia at the end of 1884, but returning the following year, joined the Southern organization of the People's Will, working alongside Boris Orzhikh. He was arrested on 18 January 1886, convicted that year, and sentenced to death, commuted to lifelong hard labour. He served his sentence in Shlissel'burg Fortress, and was released on 28 October 1905. He lived in Livonia (present-day Latvia and Estonia), then Kiev, and wrote his memoirs, as well as sketches of Vera Figner and Liudmila Volkenshtein. He joined the Socialist Revolutionary Party, and was a member of the party's commission that investigated the Azef affair. In 1910 he visited Geneva, and then lived in Switzerland and France for the rest of his life. He worked with a revolutionary group organized by Mark Natanson,[6] but from 1912 he gave up political activity for charitable work. He died in Paris on 12 February 1927.

Ivanov, Vasilii Grigor'evich ('Mitrofan') (1857 (or 1859)–1917?) Prisoner no. 13, cell 10. Born in Kiev to a merchant family, and educated at Kiev University, Vasilii Ivanov joined the People's Will and was arrested in 1882 for spreading propaganda among workers. He escaped with the help of Aleksandr Tikhanovich, a member of the military centre of the People's Will and subsequently also imprisoned in Shlissel'burg. Arrested again in 1883 and tried in the Kiev 'Trial of the 14', he was sentenced to lifelong hard labour and transferred to Shlissel'burg Fortress in October 1884. After 20 years' imprisonment he was transferred to exile in Tashkent in 1904, and joined the Socialist Revolutionary Party. Sources suggest he died in 1917, but Venediktov-Beziuk records the rumour that Vasilii Ivanov was shot by White forces in Southern Russia, which would indicate a later date.[7]

Janavičius, Liudvikas (Liudvig Fomich Ianovich) (1850–1902) Prisoner no. 23. Born into a noble family in Šiauliai district (present-day Lithuania) on 5 (17) September 1859, Janavičius was educated at gymnasiums at first locally, then in Vilnius. He became involved in the Polish socialist movement, and became one of the leaders of the Proletariat Party. He moved to Warsaw University and was arrested in 1884. He was sentenced to 16 years' hard labour, and transferred to Shlissel'burg Fortress on 3 March (15) 1886. In November 1896 he was sent to exile in Srednekolymsk, where he died by suicide on

30 May (13 June) 1902. He left a memoir of his involvement in the revolutionary movement and imprisonment in Shlissel'burg, which remained unfinished at the time of his death.

Kachura (Kochurenko), Foma Korneevich (1877–?) Born in Kiev province on 7 (19) July 1877 to a poor soldier's family, and educated at a village school, Kachura worked in a workshop, and on the directions of the battle organization of the Socialist Revolutionary Party made an attempt on the life of Kharkiv governor Prince N. Obolenskii, who had participated in the suppression of a peasant uprising in the province. He was tried in Kiev, and sent to Shlissel'burg Fortress in January 1903, but recalled to Petersburg several times, apparently to give evidence against the revolutionary movement. In 1904 he was transferred to settlement in Arkhangel'sk Governate. His subsequent fate is unknown.

Kaliaev, Ivan Platonovich ('Poet') (1877–1905) Born in Warsaw on 24 June (6 July) 1877 to a Russian police inspector and a Polish mother, Kaliaev studied at St Petersburg University but was expelled for participating in student protests and exiled to Ekaterinoslav (Dnipro, Ukraine). He first joined the Russian Social Democratic Labour Party, but became convinced of the need for direct action. After his term of exile ended he went to Lemberg (present-day Lviv, then in the Austro-Hungarian Empire) and moved in revolutionary circles. He was arrested in Berlin, briefly imprisoned in Warsaw, and then exiled to Iaroslavl', where he met Socialist Revolutionaries and writers Boris Savinkov (1879–1925) and Aleksei Remizov (1877–1957), and became a member of the SRs' battle organization. Kaliaev was the reserve bomber in the murder of Interior Minister Viacheslav von Plehve on 15 July 1904 (carried out by Egor Sozonov, who was also briefly incarcerated in Shlissel'burg Fortress), and himself carried out the assassination of Grand Duke Sergei Aleksandrovich, Governor-General of Moscow and brother of Alexander III (1857–1905). Kaliaev was arrested at the scene and sentenced to death. He was transferred to Shlissel'burg on 9 May and hanged on 10 (23) May 1905. A volume of Kaliaev's poetry was published by the SR Party after his death, and his execution is the subject of Albert Camus' 1949 play *Les Justes*.

Karaulov, Vasilii Andreevich (1854–1910) Cell 31. Born on 12 (24) November 1854 in Toropets District (Tver' Governate) to a family of hereditary nobility, Karaulov was educated at Pskov's Classical Gymnasium and St Petersburg University. He joined the People's Will, and left Russia to avoid detection by the authorities, but returned in 1884 and was arrested. He was convicted in the 'Trial of the 12' and sentenced to four years' exile with hard labour. He served his sentence in

Shlissel'burg Fortress and on 8 (20) November 1888 was transferred to settlement in Siberia, where he worked variously as a pharmacist, medical assistant, teacher and legal advocate, in Angara and later Krasnoiarsk. He was amnestied in 1905 and joined the Constitutional Democratic (Cadet) Party in Krasnoiarsk. In 1907 he was elected as a deputy for the Third State Duma from Eniseisk Governate, and in 1909 was elected to the Central Committee of the Cadet Party. He died on 19 December 1910 (1 January 1911).

Karpovich, Petr Vladimirovich (1874–1917) Born on 3 (15) October 1874 in Gomel' (present-day Belarus), Karpovich studied at Gomel' and Slutsk Gymnasiums, and in 1895 enrolled in the medical faculty of Moscow University, then studied at Tartu (at the time Iurev) University, but was expelled for participating in student movements. He was the organizer of the Gomel' Committee of the Russian Social Democratic Labour Party, and in 1899 fled to Germany, where he became close to Socialist Revolutionaries. Returning to Russia, on 14 (27) January 1901 he fatally wounded Minister of Education N. P. Bogolepov (1846–1901) and was sentenced to 20 years' hard labour. On 30 April (13 May) 1901 he was transferred to Shlissel'burg Prison, where, as memoirs record, he was the first new arrival for over 10 years, and brought the existing inmates their first real news from the outside world. On 30 January (12 February) 1906 Karpovich was transferred to Akatui Prison, part of Nerchinsk hard labour system. He was released to settlement the following year, and quickly escaped abroad. He joined the battle organization of the SRs, and participated in an unsuccessful attempt on the life of Tsar Nicholas II. He left the SRs following the revelation of Evno Azef's betrayal. Living in London, he worked as a bath house attendant and masseur. He decided to return to Russia following the February 1917 revolution, but drowned on 13 April 1917 when the ship he was travelling on was torpedoed by a German submarine.

Klimenko, Mikhail Filimonovich (1856–84) Cell 26. Born in Bessarabia to a noble family, Klimenko was educated at an Odessa Gymnasium, and at universities in Novorossiisk and Kiev, but was expelled from the latter for participating in student demonstrations. He was arrested in 1880 for belonging to a secret society and sent to exile in Siberia, from where he escaped in May 1881. He joined the People's Will and participated in the attempted assassination of General Strel'nikov. He was arrested on 5 (17) June 1882, and convicted the following year in the 'Trial of the 17'. Sentenced to death, commuted to lifelong hard labour, he was transferred to Shlissel'burg Fortress on 4 (16) August 1884, where two months later he hanged himself in his cell, on 5 (17) October.

Kobylianskii, Liudvig Aleksandrovich ('Poliachok') (1859–86) Cell 34. Born in Warsaw to a noble family, and working as a machinist, Kobylianskii joined the Proletariat Party and was arrested in Kiev in 1879 for his part in the assassination of Prince Dmitrii Kropotkin, Governor-General of Kharkiv. He was sentenced to 20 years' hard labour in the 'Trial of the 16', and transferred first to the Peter and Paul Fortress, then to Kara hard labour in 1882. After an attempt to escape he was moved back to Petersburg and incarcerated in Shlissel'burg Prison from 4 (16) August 1884. He died of tuberculosis on 3 (15) January 1886.

Konashevich, Vasilii Petrovich (1860–1915) Prisoner no. 30. Born into a noble family in Kazan', Konashevich worked as a teacher in Poltava and joined the People's Will. In December 1883 he participated in the assassination in St Petersburg of Gendarme Colonel and inspector of the secret police, G. P. Sudeikin. Arrested in Kiev and transferred back to St Petersburg, he was tried in 1887 alongside Petr Antonov, Sergei Ivanov, German Lopatin and Nikolai Starodvorskii. His death sentence was commuted to lifelong hard labour, and he was transferred to Shlissel'burg on 23 June (5 July) 1887. Suffering from severe mental illness from 1889, he was moved to Kazan' psychiatric hospital on 2 August (14) 1896, where he died in 1915.

Konopliannikova, Zinaida Vasil'evna (1878–1906) Born in Saratov on 14 (26) November 1878 and qualified as a teacher, Konopliannikova taught in a school near Peterhof. Arrested in 1903 for spreading propaganda among the peasantry, she was freed in 1904 and joined the battle organization of the Socialist Revolutionary Party. In August 1906 she shot dead General-Major Grigorii Aleksandrovich Min, Commander of the Semenovsk Imperial Guards Regiment, in revenge for his role in supressing the armed insurrection in Moscow in December 1905. Sentenced to death in the Peter and Paul Fortress, Konopliannikova was transferred to Shlissel'burg, where the sentence was carried out on 28 August (10 September) 1906.

Lagovskii, Mikhail Fedorovich (1856–1903) Prisoner no. 21. Born in July 1856 in Kostroma Governate to a civil servant's family, Lagovskii studied at Orenburg's Military Gymnasium and gained the rank of warrant officer. In 1881 he was sentenced administratively to exile in Tomsk province. He escaped exile in September 1883 after a brawl in which he tore off an officer's epaulets. In 1884 he joined the People's Will. He was arrested in St Petersburg in October 1885, and sent to Shlissel'burg Fortress without trial on an administrative sentence of five years. At the end of his term he was given another five-year sentence. In October 1895 he was sent to exile in Przeval'sk (Karakol in present-day

Kazakhstan). On 29 May (11 June) 1903 he drowned in the Khoper river, west of Saratov.

Lopatin, German Aleksandrovich (1845–1918) Prisoner no. 27. Born in Nizhnii Novgorod on 13 (25) January 1845 to a noble family, and educated at Stavropol' Gymnasium and St Petersburg University, where he was awarded a candidate's (doctoral) degree, Lopatin was exiled back to Stavropol' for forming a revolutionary society. He was arrested in 1869 but escaped and joined the First International in Paris. He became close friends with Karl Marx, translated the first volume of *Capital* into Russian, and was elected a member of the General Council of the International. In between periods of Siberian exile and escapes to Europe, Lopatin made several clandestine returns to Russia. In 1871 he made an unsuccessful attempt to free Nikolai Chernyshevskii from Siberian exile, for which he was arrested. After working with Land and Liberty, he joined the People's Will in 1879, and was involved in the unmasking of Sergei Degaev as a police spy. Convicted in the 'Trial of the 21', Lopatin was sentenced to death, commuted to lifelong incarceration in Shlissel'burg Prison. He was transferred to the fortress in June 1887 and released in October 1905. Due to ill health he took no further part in the revolutionary movement. He wrote a short memoir of his fellow prisoner Vasilii Karaulov, and composed a significant body of poetry in the fortress. He died on 26 December 1918.

Lukaszewicz, Jyzef (Iosif Dement'evich Lukashevich) (1863–1928) Prisoner no. 26. Born on 1 (13) December 1863 near Vilnius to a noble Polish family, Lukaszewicz studied at Vilnius Gymnasium and St Petersburg University, and became one of the organizers of the terrorist faction of the People's Will. He was arrested on 3 March 1887 in connection with the attempt on the life of Alexander III, and sentenced to death, commuted to lifelong hard labour. He was transferred to Shlissel'burg Prison in May 1887, and freed under the terms of the October 1905 amnesty. He took no further part in the revolutionary movement, but worked as a geologist, winning prizes from the Academy of Sciences and the Geographical Society for his discoveries. In 1919 he returned to Vilnius and became professor of geology at Vilnius University (then Stefan Batory University). He died on 19 October 1928.

Malavskii, Vladimir Evgenievich (1853–86) Cell 24. Born in Kamenetsk-Podol'sk to the noble family of a Collegiate Councillor and Gymnasium Latin teacher, Malavskii studied at Kamenetsk-Podol'sk Gymnasium and then in various faculties at Kiev University, before being expelled for non-payment of fees and returning to Kamenetsk-Podol'sk to work as a civil servant. He was arrested in Kiev in August 1877 in connection with the 'Chigirinsk Conspiracy', an attempt to foment an uprising among peasants in Chigirinsk District near Kiev. As numerous sources testify, Malavskii had nothing to do with the conspiracy, but when his flat was searched a number of revolvers and an illegal printing press were found. In 1880 he was sentenced to 20 years' hard labour. In October 1881 he escaped from Krasnoiarsk Prison, but was re-captured the following month, and given an additional sentence of 15 years. He was transferred to Kara hard labour system in October 1882, but after participating in unrest at Kara Prison was returned to Petersburg in April 1883 and incarcerated in the Peter and Paul Fortress. On 4 (16) August 1884 he was transferred to Shlissel'burg, where he died of tuberculosis on 16 (28) March 1886.

Manuchariants, Ovanes Ashotovich (Ivan L'vovich Manucharov) (1861–1909) Prisoner no. 22. Born on 31 July (12 August) 1861 in Tiflis (Tbilisi), Manucharov was a member of the People's Will. First arrested in Kharkiv in January 1884, he escaped from prison, but was re-arrested in Rostov-on-Don in November of the same year. He was tried in Odessa in December 1885, and sentenced to death, commuted to 10 years' hard labour. In January 1886 he was transferred to Shlissel'burg. In December 1895 he was sent to exile on Sakhalin Island, and later settled in Blagoveshchensk, where he worked for the newspaper *Amurskii krai* (Amur Region). He wrote two short memoirs, published in 1906 and 1907. He died on 29 May (11 June) 1909.

Martynov, Kalinnik (Nikolai) Fedulovich (1855–1903) Prisoner no. 17, cell 36. A worker and member of the People's Will, Martynov was arrested in March 1884 and was a defendant in the Kiev 'Trial of the 12' in the same year. He was sentenced to 20 years' hard labour, and sent to Shlissel'burg in December 1884. In November 1896 as part of the coronation amnesty he was sent to exile in Kolyma. He died by suicide in Iakutsk on 13 (26) May 1903.

Mel'nikov, Mikhail Mikhailovich (1878–1917) Born in Seleginsk (Buriatia), Mel'nikov enrolled in the Mining Institute in 1897, but did not complete the course, and in 1898 was arrested for revolutionary activities. After two years in prison he was sentenced administratively, but escaped his place of exile and became a deputy to Gershuni in the SRs' battle organization. He participated in Balmashev's assassination of Interior Minister Dmitrii Sipiagin, and was arrested in January 1903. He was sentenced to death, commuted to lifelong hard labour, and sent to Shlissel'burg Fortress in April 1904. In January 1906 he was transferred along with Sikorskii and Sozonov to Nerchinsk hard labour. He died in 1917.

Minakov, Egor Ivanovich (1854–84) Cell 1. Born on 10 (22) April 1854 to the family of an Odessa civil servant, Minakov was a member of Meier Gellis's revolutionary group, and in February 1879 took part in the murder of police spy and provocateur N. Gofshtof. At trial in Odessa he was sentenced to 12 years' hard labour. He was tried again the following year as a member of Gellis's organization and his sentence was increased to 30 years. With N. F. Kryzhanovskii he escaped from prison in Kara, but was recaptured and given a life sentence. Minakov was returned to Petersburg in June 1883 and incarcerated in the Peter and Paul Fortress, then transferred to Shlissel'burg on 2 (14) August 1884. A few weeks later he assaulted the prison doctor in order to provoke a death sentence, which he duly received. He was executed by firing squad on 21 September (3 October) 1884.

Morozov, Nikolai Aleksandrovich ('Vorobei') (1854–1946) Prisoner no. 4, cell 15. Morozov was born on 25 June (7 July) 1854 at Borok, the family estate near Iaroslavl', the son of a nobleman and a serf woman. After a home education, from 1869 he studied at the Second Moscow Gymnasium, but was a poor student and was expelled. He audited courses at Moscow University in 1871–2. In 1874 he joined the Chaikovskii Circle, and participated in the 'Going to the People' movement, spreading propaganda among the peasantry. He then went to Switzerland, worked on revolutionary journals, and became a member of the First International. Returning to Russia, Morozov was arrested and convicted in the 'Trial of the 193' in 1878, but sentenced to time served, and released. He continued revolutionary work, and joined Land and Liberty, co-editing the party journal with Sergei Kravchinskii. In 1879 when the party split, he became a member of the Executive Committee of the People's Will. He was a member of the editorial board of the party newspaper, and participated in preparations for assassination attempts on Alexander II. In 1880 Morozov left the People's Will and with his wife, Olga Spiridonovna Liubatovich (1853–1917), travelled to Europe, living in Geneva and London. He met Karl Marx, who gave him work translating texts into Russian, including *The Communist Party Manifesto*. In January 1881 Morozov was arrested while attempting to return to Russia. In 1882 he was a defendant in the 'Trial of the 20', and sentenced to life imprisonment. After two years in the Peter and Paul Fortress, he was transferred on 2 (14) August 1884 to Shlissel'burg Prison. He was freed in October 1905 under the terms of the amnesty of that month. While in the fortress, Morozov undertook intensive studies in chemistry, physics, astronomy and history, and wrote several controversial works, notably *Revelation in Storm and Thunder* (published in 1907), and *Song of the*

Stars (published in 1910, for which the author was again arrested), as well as the short story *A Journey into Cosmic Space* (written early in his imprisonment), and a large body of poetry. Following his release Morozov wrote his memoirs, and published the letters he had been allowed to write during his final years in the fortress. At liberty he took little interest in politics, and taught physics and chemistry at St Petersburg University. After the 1917 revolutions he taught at the P. F. Lesgaft Institute of Natural Sciences in Petrograd/Leningrad.[8] In later years he ran a scientific laboratory from his old family estate, and was made an Honorary Member of the Soviet Academy of Sciences. He died at Borok on 30 July 1946.

Myshkin, Ippolit Nikitich (*Nikolaevich*) (1848–85) Cell 30. Born on 3 (15) February 1848 in Pskov to a non-commissioned army officer and a serf, Myshkin was sent to a cantonist school at the age of seven. Five years later he was sent to Petersburg to study at a military-topographic school, following which he worked in the Academy of the General Staff, and then in Moscow as a stenographer at a district court. In 1873 Myshkin acquired a printing press, and began to distribute propaganda, but the press was broken up and Myshkin fled to Switzerland. He soon returned to Russia with the aim of freeing the writer and Populist Nikolai Chernyshevskii, but was arrested in Viliuisk and incarcerated in the Peter and Paul Fortress. He was a defendant in the 'Trial of the 193', sentenced to 10 years' hard labour, and sent to Kara. His sentence was increased to 15 years for delivering a speech at the grave of Lev Adol'fovich Dmokhovskii (1850–81), a member of Dolgushin's revolutionary group who died during transport to Kara, and then by another six years for an attempted escape. In 1883, after taking part in a hunger strike, Myshkin was returned to Petersburg and again imprisoned in the Peter and Paul Fortress. He was transferred to Shlissel'burg on 4 (16) August 1884, and on 25 December of that year (6 January 1885) threw a plate at the superintendent, Sokolov, for which he was tried by a military court and sentenced to death. Myshkin was executed by firing squad at the fortress on 26 January (7 February) 1885.

Nemolovskii, Apollon Irineevich (1855–86) Cell 7. The son of a priest, Nemolovskii was a member of the People's Will. He was arrested in Kharkiv in June 1884, convicted in the 'Trial of the 14', and sentenced to lifelong hard labour. He was transferred to Shlissel'burg Fortress on 15 (27) October 1884, where he died of tuberculosis on 29 March (9 April) 1886.

Novorusskii, Mikhail Vasil'evich (1861–1925) Prisoner no. 25. Born on 28 September (10 October) 1861 in Novaia Russa, Novgorod

Governate, to the poor family of a church sexton, Novorusskii was educated at the local church school and at Novgorod Theological Seminary. In 1882, as a prize-winning student, he was sent to the St Petersburg Theological Seminary on a state stipend. He started reading illegal literature and became involved with student organizations. The dynamite for Aleksandr Ul'ianov's unsuccessful attempt on the life of Alexander III was prepared in Novorusskii's apartment, and he was arrested in 3 (15) March 1887. His death sentence was commuted to lifelong hard labour, and he was sent to Shlissel'burg Fortress in May 1887. He was freed in October 1905 under the terms of the amnesty of the same month. He taught at the Lesgaft Higher Free School in Petersburg (later the Lesgaft Institute of Natural Sciences), at first as director of the agriculture department, then as an assistant in the chemistry department. From 1917 he was director of the Petrograd Agricultural Museum. Novorusskii's memoirs of Shlissel'burg Fortress were published in 1920. He died in Leningrad on 21 September 1925.

Orzhikh, Boris Dmitrievich (1864–1947) Prisoner no. 32. Born on 23 November (5 December) 1864 in Odessa to a Jewish family – his father a lawyer, his mother the manager of a fashion boutique – but raised in Tobol'sk and Tomsk, Orzhikh attended secondary school in Tomsk, where he met Vasilii Osipanov. In 1882 he enrolled in the natural sciences department of the physics and mathematics faculty at Novorossiisk University. Involved in the revolutionary movement from 1880, in 1884 Orzhikh was instrumental in uniting various groups to form the Southern Russian chapter of the People's Will. In the same year he organized underground printing presses in Taganrog and Novocherkassk. In January 1886 the Taganrog press was broken up and Orzhikh was arrested in Ekaterinoslav. He was transferred to Petersburg, and in November 1888 sentenced to death, commuted to lifelong hard labour. He was sent to Shlissel'burg Fortress in March 1890; aside from Sof'ia Ginsburg, who died by suicide before she was moved to the new prison, Orzhikh was the last of the new prisoners to arrive in the second phase of transfers. In January 1898 his petition for clemency was granted, and Orzhikh was transferred to exile in Nikol'sk-Ussuriisk in the Far East, and lived there and in Vladivostok, where he set up a gardening and horticulture supplies business. He returned to political activities in 1905, but in 1906 escaped to Japan, from where he maintained contact with the SRs. In 1910 he moved with his family to Chile. In 1939 he attempted to return to the USSR, but fell seriously ill in France, where he was caught at the outbreak of the Second World War. He returned to Chile, dying in Santiago on 14 April 1947.

Osipanov, Vasilii Stepanovich (1861–87) Born in Tomsk on 21 February (5 March) 1861 to a petty-bourgeois family, Osipanov was educated at Tomsk and Krasnoiarsk Gymnasiums. In 1881 he enrolled at Kazan' University, and began to participate in student revolutionary groups. In 1886 he moved to St Petersburg University, and took part in the attempt on the life of Tsar Alexander III on 1 (13) March 1887, for which he was sentenced to death. Alongside Aleksandr Ul'ianov and others, he was transferred to Shlissel'burg Fortress on 5 May, and executed on 8 (20) May 1887.

Pankratov, Vasilii Semenovich (1864–1925) Prisoner no. 20, cell 25. Born on 26 December 1864 (7 January 1865) to a poor peasant's family in Tver' Governate, Pankratov received a technical education and worked as a machinist. In 1883 he joined the People's Will, and became a member of the armed workers' detachment. In 1884 he was arrested in Kiev, and tried alongside Vasilii Karaulov, Kalinnik Martynov and Mikhail Shebalin. He was sentenced to death, commuted to 20 years' hard labour, and transferred to Shlissel'burg in December 1884. In 1898 he was sent into exile near Iakutsk. He joined the Socialist Revolutionary Party, and became a member of its Central Committee in 1909. In 1917 he was elected to the All Union Constituent Assembly, and in September was sent to Tobol'sk as part of the special detachment assigned to guard the Romanov family. Following the SRs' decision to halt opposition to Bolshevik rule, Pankratov joined the White forces and was expelled from the party. He later became a member of the Society for Former Political Prisoners, and died in Leningrad on 5 March 1925.

Pokhitonov, Nikolai Danilovich (1857–97) Prisoner no. 15, cell 21. Born on 17 (29) March 1857 to the noble family of a high-ranking army officer in Mirgorod (Mirhorod), Poltava District, central Ukraine, Pokhitonov enrolled in the Artillery Academy in 1879, where in 1880 he joined a military group allied to the People's Will. In March 1883 he was arrested, and convicted in the 'Trial of the 14'. He was sentenced to death, commuted to lifelong hard labour, and sent to Shlissel'burg Fortress in October 1884. Memoirs record that he was one of the inmates to suffer from severe mental illness. In March 1896 he was transferred to the psychiatric department of the Nikolaev Military Hospital in St Petersburg, where he died on 4 (16) April the following year.

Polivanov, Petr Sergeevich (1859–1903) Prisoner no. 9, cell 33. Born in Saratov Governate to a rich family, Polivanov's association with revolutionary circles began while he was still at school, when he was involved in spreading illegal propaganda among the peasantry. In 1878 he began studying in the veterinary department of the St Petersburg

Medical-Surgical Academy, but in the same year was sent to exile in Vologda Governate for participating in student unrest. In 1881, he was involved in an unsuccessful escape attempt of a fellow member of the People's Will from Saratov Prison, during which a guard was killed. Polivanov was sentenced to death, commuted to lifelong hard labour. He spent two years in the Peter and Paul Fortress, where he attempted suicide, before being transferred to Shlissel'burg on 4 (16) August 1884. His sentence was reduced to 20 years, and in 1902 he was sent to exile in Akmolinsk (present-day northern Kazakhstan), from where he escaped to France in April 1903. He joined the Socialist Revolutionary Party, but died by suicide on 17 August of the same year. Polivanov left poetry and a short memoir about his incarceration in the Alekseevskii Ravelin and Shlissel'burg Fortress.

Popov, Mikhail Rodionovich ('Rodionich') (1851–1909) Prisoner no. 5, cell 17. Born on 14 (26) November 1851 to the family of a priest in Ekaterinoslav Governate (Dnipro, Ukraine), Popov studied at the Ekaterinoslav Theological Seminary and the Medical-Surgical Academy, from 1875 living near Petersburg. He conducted propaganda among workers and led strikes, as well as participating in the 'Going to the People' movement. In February 1879 he was involved in the murder of police spy Nikolai Vasil'evich Reinshtein. When Land and Liberty split, Popov initially sided with the Black Repartition faction, but then in Kiev working with Butsinskii led a united group of revolutionaries from both the People's Will and Black Repartition. In February 1880 he was arrested in Kiev, and tried in the city in July of that year. He was sentenced to death, commuted to lifelong hard labour. After two years in Kara hard labour, he was transferred to the Alekseevskii Ravelin, then on 2 (14) August 1884 sent to Shlissel'burg. He was released under the terms of an amnesty in October 1905, and died in Rostov-on-Don on 4 (17) January 1909. Popov wrote a short memoir of his incarceration in Shlissel'burg, as well as a sketch about Ippolit Myshkin.

Rogachev, Nikolai Mikhailovich (1856–84) Rogachev was born in Orlov Governate to the family of a landowner. Brother of the Populist D. M. Rogachev, he was educated at the Orlov Military Gymnasium and Pavlovsk Military Institute, from where he graduated with the rank of second lieutenant, serving in the 28th Artillery Brigade. He joined the People's Will in 1880 and became a significant figure in its military organization. He was arrested in April 1883 and convicted in the 'Trial of the 14' in September 1884. Sentenced to death, he was transferred to Shlissel'burg Fortress on 7 October 1884, and executed alongside Baron Shtromberg on 10 (22) October.

Shchedrin, Nikolai Pavlovich (1858–1919) Prisoner no. 3, cell 12. Born to a noble family in Petropavlovsk, Shchedrin was educated at the Omsk Military Gymnasium and St Petersburg Teachers' Institute, where he became a member of Land and Liberty. When the organization split he joined the Black Repartition faction. In Kiev he organized the Southern Russian Workers' Union with Elizaveta Koval'skaia. He was arrested in October 1880, and in May 1881 sentenced to death, commuted to lifelong hard labour, and was sent to Kara, where he was chained to a wheelbarrow.[9] In 1882 he was transferred to Petersburg and incarcerated in the Alekseevskii Ravelin, then on 2 (14) August 1884 to Shlissel'burg Fortress. He fell ill in 1895, and in August 1896 was transferred to Kazan' psychiatric hospital, where he died on 1 October 1919.

Shebalin, Mikhail Petrovich (1857–1937) Prisoner no. 18, cell 4. Born to a noble family in a village in Kazan' Governate on 27 May (8 June) 1857, Shebalin studied at Kamanetsk-Podol'sk Gymnasium and the physics and mathematics faculty of St Petersburg University, where he became involved in the student movement and the People's Will. In 1883 he ran a safe house with a secret printing press. He also set up printing presses in Moscow and Kiev. Pankratov and Martynov worked at the latter. He was arrested in March 1884 and tried alongside Pankratov, Martynov and Karaulov. Sentenced to 12 years' hard labour, he was sent to Shlissel'burg Fortress in December 1884. In November 1896 he was sent to settlement in Viliuisk (Iakutsk). Amnestied in 1905, he returned to European Russia and had links with the Socialist Revolutionaries, although he did not formally join the party. In 1909 he was arrested again, and spent two years in exile in Arkhangel'sk Governate. In 1917 he was living in Astrakhan, working as an authorized representative of the Volga Shipping Insurance Partnership for accident insurance. He joined the SR Party, but left again the following year. In 1922 Shebalin moved to Moscow, where he worked as director of the Kropotkin Museum, and wrote his memoirs. He died in Moscow on 24 February 1937.

Shevyrev, Petr Iakovlevich (1863–87) Born in Kharkiv on 23 June (5 July) 1863 to a merchant's family, and educated at the Third Kharkiv Gymnasium, Kharkiv University and St Petersburg University, Shevyrev, alongside Aleksandr Ul'ianov, was a member of the group arrested for the attempted assassination of Tsar Alexander III on 1 (13) March 1887. He was arrested in Yalta on 7 (19) March, and sentenced to death on 19 April (1 May). On 5 (17) May 1887 he was transferred to Shlissel'burg Fortress, where he was executed three days later.

Shtromberg, Aleksandr Pavlovich (1854–84) A baron, Shtromberg was born on 5 (17) September 1854, studied at the St Petersburg Naval

Institute, and served in the Baltic and Pacific Ocean fleets. Along with Nikolai Rogachev and others, Shtromberg ran the central military organization of the People's Will. Arrested in April 1881, he was sent into exile due to lack of evidence, but in 1883 was returned to Petersburg and sentenced to death in the 'Trial of the 14'. He was transferred to Shlissel'burg on 7 (19) October 1884 and hanged three days later alongside Rogachev.

Sikorskii, Shimel'-Leiba Vul'fovich (1884–1927) Born in the village of Knyszyn near Bialystok in present-day Poland, Sikorskii worked as a tanner from the age of 14. He became a member of the battle organization of the Socialist Revolutionary Party, and alongside Boris Savinkov, Ivan Kaliaev, Egor Sozonov and others participated in the assassination of Interior Minister von Plehve in June 1904. He was arrested immediately, and sentenced to 20 years' hard labour. He was transferred to Shlissel'burg Fortress on 24 January 1905, and then to Nerchinsk hard labour on 31 January 1906. He died in 1927.

Sozonov (Sazonov), Egor Sergeevich ('Avel', 'Iakov') (1879–1910) Born on 26 May (7 June) 1879 in a village in Viatka Governate in the Ural Mountains, Sozonov studied at Ufa Male Gymnasium and Moscow University, in the law, and then the medical faculty. He was expelled for participating in student unrest and returned to Ufa, where he joined the Urals Union of Social-Democrats and Socialist Revolutionaries. In July 1903 he was sent to exile in Western Siberia, but escaped en route and fled to Switzerland, where he joined the SRs' battle organization. Returning to Russia on a fake passport, he carried out the assassination of Interior Minister von Plehve, for which he was sentenced to lifelong hard labour. He was transferred to Shlissel'burg on 24 January 1905, and then to Nerchinsk hard labour on 31 January 1906. Incarcerated first in Akatui Prison and then at Gornyi Zerentui, Sozonov was a key figure in protests against the extremely harsh treatment of political prisoners, following the official abolition of the distinction between political and criminal convicts. He died by suicide in his cell on 27 November (10 December) 1910.

Starodvorskii, Nikolai Petrovich (1863–1918) Prisoner no. 29. Born into a priest's family on 1 (13) May 1863, Starodvorskii attended Kamenetsk-Podol'sk Gymnasium and joined the People's Will. In December 1883, along with Vasilii Konashevich, he was involved in the murder of chief of the secret police Sudeikin. He was arrested in March 1884 in Moscow, tried in the 'Trial of the 21' in 1887 and sentenced to death, commuted to lifelong hard labour. He was transferred to Shlissel'burg in June 1887, and in August 1905, following a plea for clemency, moved to the Peter and Paul Fortress. He was freed in November

1905 under the terms of the amnesty announced in the Manifesto of 17 (30) October 1905. Starodvorskii moved to Paris and joined the Socialist Revolutionaries, but was exposed by Vladimir Burtsev as a police agent and in 1908 tried in a revolutionary arbitration court. He was found not guilty, but documents uncovered following the February Revolution of 1917 revealed that Burtsev's accusations had been correct. Nevertheless when Starodvorskii died in Odessa the following year, he was buried with revolutionary honours.

Surovtsev, Dmitrii Iakovlevich (1853–1925) Prisoner no. 16, cell 32. Born to a priest's family in Vologda Governate, Surovtsev attended Vologda Seminary and Pavlovsk Agricultural Institute, but was expelled from the latter. In 1876 he was arrested and sent to Kholmogory under police surveillance, but escaped in September 1878 and from then on lived in the revolutionary underground. He joined the People's Will and set up the printing press which produced the party's periodical. He was arrested in Odessa in December 1882, and convicted in the 'Trial of the 14' in September 1884. Sentenced to 15 years' hard labour, Surovtsev was sent to Shlissel'burg Fortress in October 1884. In November 1896 under the terms of an amnesty he was sent to exile in Kolyma. He died on 3 March 1925 in Tot'ma, near Vologda.

Tikhanovich, Aleksandr Pakhomovich (1855–84) Cell 13. Second lieutenant and a member of the military centre of the People's Will, stationed at Kiev Prison, Tikhanovich assisted in the escape of Vasilii Ivanov. He was arrested in March 1884, tried in the St Petersburg 'Trial of the 14', and sentenced to lifelong hard labour. Transferred to Shlissel'burg in October 1884 and already suffering from severe mental illness according to reports, he died on 28 December 1884 (9 January 1885), shortly after attempting to hang himself.

Trigoni, Mikhail Nikolaevich ('Milord') (1850–1917) Prisoner no. 1, cell 5. Born in Sevastopol' in October 1850 to a general-major in the guards of Greek origin and the daughter of an admiral, Trigoni studied law at Novorossiisk University and became a lawyer's assistant. In 1879 he moved to St Petersburg and joined the People's Will. He participated in the tunnelling operation under Malaia Sadovaia Street, but was arrested shortly before the assassination of Alexander II. Convicted in the 'Trial of the 20' in February 1882, and sentenced to 20 years' hard labour, Trigoni was transferred to Shlissel'burg in August 1884. In February 1902 he was sent to exile on Sakhalin Island, from where he was amnestied in 1905. He wrote a short memoir of life following his release from the fortress. Ashenbrenner records that he went blind after his release. He died on 5 (18) July 1917.

Ul'ianov, Aleksandr Il'ich (1866–87) The older brother of Vladimir Il'ich Lenin, Ul'ianov was born on 31 March (12 April) 1866 in Nizhnii Novgorod, and studied at Simbirsk Gymnasium and St Petersburg University. He organized the unsuccessful attempt on the life of Alexander III in March 1887, for which he was sentenced to death. He was transferred to Shlissel'burg Fortress on 5 (17) May 1887 and hanged on 8 (20) May, alongside Vasilii Generalov and Pakhomii Andreiushkin.

Vasil'ev, Aleksandr (c.1887–1905) A worker, Vasil'ev killed a police officer in 1905, for which he was sentenced to death. He was transferred to Shlissel'burg on 19 August, and hanged on 20 August (2 September) 1905 alongside Girsh Gershkovich.

Vasil'ev-Finkel'shtein, Iakov Borisovich (Viktor Vasil'ev) (?–1906) A member of the Socialist Revolutionary Party, Vasil'ev-Finkel'shtein killed General Kozlov, whom he had mistaken for General Trepov. Sentenced to death, he was transferred to Shlissel'burg Fortress on 18 September (1 October) 1906, and hanged the next day.

Volkenshtein, Liudmila Aleksandrovna (1857–1906) Prisoner no. 12, cell 35. Born on 18 (30) September 1857 in Kiev to a minor gentry family and educated at the local gymnasium, Liudmila Aleksandrovna Aleksandrova married Aleksandr Volkenshtein, a young doctor, in 1875. Her husband was arrested in 1877 and was acquitted in the 'Trial of the 193' in St Petersburg in 1878, but these events led to Liudmila joining the revolutionary movement. She kept a safe house used to plot the assassination of Prince Dmitrii Kropotkin in 1879, then escaped Russia on a fake passport. Returning to Russia in 1883, she was arrested, and convicted in the 'Trial of the 14' alongside Figner, Ashenbrenner and others. Her death sentence was commuted to 15 years' hard labour, and she was transferred to Shlissel'burg in October 1884. In autumn 1896 her sentence was reduced under the terms of the coronation amnesty, and, reunited with her husband, she was transferred to exile on Sakhalin Island. The couple settled in Vladivostok in 1902, and on 10 (23) January 1906 Liudmila Volkenshtein was shot dead when soldiers fired on demonstrators. Her memoir of life in the fortress was the first to be published by a member of this group of prisoners.

Waryński, Ludwik Tadeusz (Liudvig-Faddei Severinovich Varynskii) (1856–89) Born on 24 September (6 October) 1856 to a wealthy Polish family, Waryński studied at the St Petersburg Technological Institute, but was expelled in 1875 for participating in student unrest and returned to Poland, where he found work as a labourer in a factory and organized workers' groups. In 1880–1, living in Geneva, he founded the socialist group Equality (*Ravenstvo*), and at the end of 1881 returned illegally to

Warsaw to form the Proletariat Party from socialist workers' groups. He was arrested in September 1883 and in December 1885 sentenced to 16 years' hard labour. He was transferred to Shlissel'burg Fortress in February 1886, and died of tuberculosis three years later, on 18 February (2 March) 1889.

Zlatopol'skii, Savelii Solomonovich (Savelii Solomonovich Shlemovich) (1855–85) Cell 14. Born in August 1855 into a Jewish family of traders in Elizavetgrad, Zlatopol'skii was educated at Nikolaevsk Gymnasium and St Petersburg Technical Institute, but left the latter in 1876 and joined the People's Will in 1879, participating in an attempt on the Tsar's life in Odessa. In 1880 he joined the Executive Committee of the People's Will, and from March 1881 was the representative of the Executive Committee on the Central Committee of the People's Will's military organization. Arrested in April 1882 and a defendant in the April 1883 'Trial of the 17', Zlatopol'skii was sentenced to death, commuted to lifelong hard labour. He was transferred to Shlissel'burg on 2 (14) August 1884 and died of tuberculosis on 29 December 1885 (10 January 1886).

Notes

1. In addition to the 68 prisoners listed here, some sources include one further prisoner from this period: Nikanor Fedorovich Kryzhanovskii (1859 (or 1856)–1891). His name is included on the fortress's monument to the prisoners, and he is listed, for example, in the normally reliable Gernet, *Istoriia tsarskoi tiur'my*, 3:231. However, other sources deny that Kryzhanovskii was a prisoner at Shlissel'burg (Venediktov-Beziuk, *Po kazematam Shlissel'burgskoi kreposti*, 86), and some of the prisoners themselves also cast doubt on his presence (Iuvachev, *Shlissel'burgskaia krepost'*, 161). The confusion stems from the fact that in the early days when communication was extremely limited, inmates did not always know who was incarcerated at the other end of the prison, or who died there (Frolenko, *Zapiski semidesiatnika*, 208). In fact Kryzhanovskii was transferred from the Peter and Paul Fortress to Sakhalin Island in 1884, and died in Nikolaevsk-on-Amur.
2. Prisoners were referred to by the number they were assigned rather than by name. Later prisoners were reassigned numbers from inmates who had died. The information is incomplete, but where available both prisoner numbers and cell numbers (for the prisoners transferred in 1884) are provided, as given in Kolosov, *Gosudareva tiur'ma*, 85–7. Figure 1.3, the plan of the new prison, indicates cell assignments of the prisoners transferred in 1884.
3. The 1909 unmasking, following a tip-off to Vladimir Burtsev, of the Socialist Revolutionary Evno Fishelevich Azef (1869–1918) as a double agent working for the tsarist Secret Police.
4. A radical student group, named after one of its founders, Nikolai Vasil'evich Chaikovskii (1851–1926), who gave up revolutionary work when the Populists began to turn to terrorism.
5. Boris Viktorovich Savinkov (1879–1925) was a revolutionary and writer, one of the leaders of the Socialist Revolutionary battle organization, and author of *Memoirs of a Terrorist* (1917) and novels including *The Pale Horse* (1909).
6. Mark Andreevich Natanson ('Bobrov') (1850–1919), Russian-Jewish revolutionary and founder member of the Chaikovskii Circle, Land and Liberty and the Socialist Revolutionary Party. In 1917 he was the leader of the Left SRs.
7. Venediktov-Beziuk, *Po kazematam Shlissel'burgskoi kreposti*, 86.
8. Petr Frantsevich Lesgaft (1837–1909), Russian biologist, anatomist, doctor and teacher.
9. See Volkenshtein, note 52.

Glossary

arshin	An old unit of length, measuring 71.12 cm or 2⅓ feet.
blues	Informal term used to refer to the gendarmes guarding the prisoners, who wore pale blue uniforms.
cantonist	The son of a conscript soldier, registered for service at birth and educated at special 'canton schools' for future military service.
club	Informal term for a group of prisoners meeting with or without official sanction for a particular activity, such as group readings.
commune	(Russian: община) The form of social organization favoured by the Populist revolutionaries, based on the principles of collective ownership, support and decision-making, and inspired by the ancient Russian peasant model of self-governance.
elder	(Russian: староста) The informal but still common position of an elected representative of the prisoners who deals with the prison administration on behalf of all the inmates.
fat journal	The mainstay of the Russian highbrow publishing industry in the Imperial era, usually a monthly publication featuring serializations of literary works and scholarly essays on a wide range of intellectual subjects.
garnets	An old unit of dry measurement, equivalent to 3.28 litres or 5.77 pints, and the round or oval scoop or ladle with a straight horizontal handle, used as a measure.
instructions	The rules governing the treatment of prisoners, the conduct expected of inmates and penalties for infringements.
lenten food	(Russian: постная пища) The calendar of the Russian Orthodox church features over 200 fast days, of which Lent (Russian: великий пост) is the strictest and

	longest: 'only boiled vegetarian dishes are allowed, and meat, fish, milk, eggs, cheese, sour cream, animal and oil butter, fancy cakes, buns are forbidden'. Voronina, 'Fasting in the life of Russians', 2006, 236.
locked bunks	A common arrangement in Russian prisons then and since, hinged iron bedsteads were attached to the cell wall and had to be raised and locked against the wall during the daytime.
meeting	(Russian: свидание) Association between the inmates in exercise yards or allotments. The same word is also used to refer to the possibility (never granted until the very end of the Populists' incarceration) of visits from family members.
sazhen	An old unit of length, measuring 2.1336 metres or 7 feet.
tapping	(Russian: стук, стучать) Communicating with prisoners in adjacent cells via a series of taps on the walls to denote individual letters of the alphabet.
telephone	Informal term for the communication system the prisoners devised by emptying out the water in the toilets in their cells to talk via the plumbing.
thin journal	Weekly, fortnightly or monthly illustrated magazine characteristic of the popular and lower-brow end of the Imperial Russian publishing market.
ventilation pane	(Russian: форточка) Small panes within larger windows that can be opened for ventilation purposes.
vershok	An old unit of length, measuring 4.445 cm or 1¾ inches.
wall alphabet	System devised by Decembrist Mikhail Bestuzhev in Shlissel'burg Prison for communicating with fellow prisoners by tapping on the cell walls.
zemstvo	Institution of local government in the late Russian Empire, set up in 1861 as part of the reforms to emancipate the serfs, consisting of a representative council and executive board, and with powers and responsibilities relating to education, health, welfare, food supply and road maintenance.

Bibliography

Works by Populist prisoners, 1884–1906

Works included in the corpus analysed in the Introduction are marked *

Antonov, P. L. 'Avtobiografiia P. L. Antonova (s predisl. V. N. Figner)'. *Golos minuvshego* 11, no. 2 (1923): 77–96.
*Ashenbrenner, M. Iu. 'Shlissel'burgskaia tiur'ma za 20 let, ot 1884 po 1904 gg: vospominaniia'. *Byloe* 1, no. 1 (1906): 54–93.
Ashenbrenner, M. Iu. *Voennaia organizatsiia 'Narodnoi voli' i drugie vospominaniia, 1860–1904 gg*. Edited by N. S. Tiutchev. Moscow: Izdatel'stvo politkatorzhan, 1924.
*Figner, V. N. 'Shlissel'burgskaia uznitsa Liudmila Aleksandrovna Volkenshtein'. *Byloe* 1, no. 3 (1906): 253–75.
*Figner, V. N. 'Mikhail Nikolaevich Trigoni'. *Golos minuvshego* 5, no. 7–8 (1917): 198–211.
Figner, V. N. 'Sanovniki v Shlissel'burgskoi kreposti: vospominaniia'. *Byloe* 14 (1919): 3–18.
*Figner, V. N. *Zapechatlennyi trud: vospominaniia*. Moscow: Mysl', 1964.
Figner, V. N. *Memoirs of a Revolutionist*. Authorized translation. DeKalb: Northern Illinois University Press, 1991.
*Frolenko, M. F. 'Mikhail Rodionovich Popov'. *Golos minuvshego* 5, no. 7–8 (1917): 171–9.
*Frolenko, M. F. *Zapiski semidesiatnika*. Moscow: Izdatel'stvo politkatorzhan, 1927.
*Gershuni, G. A. *Iz nedavnego proshlogo*. Izdanie tsentral'nogo komiteta partii sotsialistov-revoliutsionerov. Paris: Tribune Russe, 1908.
Gershuni, G. A. *From My Recent Past: Memoirs of a revolutionary terrorist*. Translated by K. Vladimirov. Lanham, MD: Lexington Books, 2015.
*Ianovich, L. F. (Liudvikas Janavičius). *Shlissel'burzhets L. F. Ianovich*. St Petersburg: Obshchestvennaia pol'za, 1907.
Iurkovskii, F. N. *Bulgakov*. Moscow: Akademiia, 1933.
*Iuvachev, I. P. *Shlissel'burgskaia krepost'*. Moscow: Izdatel'stvo 'Posrednik', 1907.
Iuvachev, I. P. (I. P. Youvatshev) *The Russian Bastille, or the Schluesselburg Fortress*. Translated by A. S. Rappoport. London: Chatto & Windus, 1909.
*Ivanov, S. A. 'Liudmila Aleksandrovna Volkenshtein'. In *Gallereia Shlissel'burgskikh uznikov*. Edited by N. F. Annenskii et al., 1: 222–33. St Petersburg: Tipografiia M. M. Stasiulevicha, 1907.
*Ivanov, S. A. 'Vera Nikolaevna Figner'. In *Gallereia Shlissel'burgskikh uznikov*. Edited by N. F. Annenskii et al., 1: 250–97. St Petersburg: Tipografiia M. M. Stasiulevicha, 1907.
Ivanov, S. A. 'Iz narodnovol'cheskikh vospominanii S. A. Ivanova'. In *Narodnovol'sty 80-kh i 90-kh godov: sbornik statei i materialov, sostavlennyi uchastnikami narodnovol'cheskogo dvizheniia*. Edited by B. N-skii and A. V. Iakimova-Dikovskaia, 24–65. Moscow: Izdatel'stvo Vsesoiuznogo obshchestva politkatorzhan i ssyl'no-poselentsev, 1929.
*Lopatin, G. A. *German Aleksandrovich Lopatin, 1845–1918: avtobiografiia, pokazaniia i pis'ma, stat'i i stikhotvoreniia, bibliografiia*. Edited by A. A. Shilov. Petrograd: Gosudarstvennoe izdatel'stvo, 1922.
*Manucharov, I. L. 'Epizod iz zhizni Shlissel'burgskoi kreposti'. *Byloe* 1, no. 8 (1906): 81–2.

Manucharov, I. L. 'Iz Shlissel'burga na Sakhalin'. *Byloe* 2, no. 8 (1907): 31–42.
Morozov, N. A. 'Iz Shlissel'burgskikh motivov: neizdannye stikhotvoreniia N. A. Morozova, posviashchennye tovarishcham po zakliucheniiu'. *Byloe* 1, no. 2 (1906): 121–3.
*Morozov, N. A. *Iz sten nevoli: Shlissel'burgskie i drugie stikhotvoreniia*. Rostov-na-Donu: Donskaia rech', 1906.
Morozov, N. A. *Otkrovenie v groze i bure. Istoriia vozniknoveniia Apokalipsisa*. St Petersburg: Byloe, 1907.
*Morozov, N. A. *Pis'ma iz Shlissel'burgskoi kreposti*. St Petersburg: Izdatel'stvo M. Aver'ianova, 1910.
*Morozov, N. A. *Povesti moei zhizni*. Edited by S. Ia. Shtraikh. 3 vols. Moscow: Izdatel'stvo Akademii nauk SSSR, 1947.
Novorusskii, M. V. 'Kak i za chto ia popal v Shlissel'burg'. *Byloe* 1, no. 4 (1906): 43–64.
Novorusskii, M. V. 'O Shlissel'burgskom arkhive'. *Golos minuvshego* 1, no. 10 (1913): 140–8.
*Novorusskii, M. V. *Zapiski shlissel'burzhtsa: 1887–1905 gg*. Petrograd: Gosudarstvennoe izdatel'stvo, 1920.
Novorusskii, M. V. 'Zhenshchiny v Shlissel'burge'. *Golos minuvshego* 10, no. 2 (1922): 157–64.
Novorusskii, M. V. *Tiuremnye robinzony*. Moscow: Gosudarstvennoe izdatel'stvo, 1924.
*Pankratov, V. S. *Zhizn' v Shlissel'burgskoi kreposti, 1884–1898*. Moscow: Knigoizdatel'stvo 'Molodaia Rossiia', 1906.
*Pankratov, V. S. 'Pamiati L. A. Volkenshtein'. *Byloe* 1, no. 2 (1906): 280–2.
Pankratov, V. S. 'Iz deiatel'nosti sredi rabochikh v 1880–1884 gg.' *Byloe* 1, no. 3 (1906): 230–52.
*Pankratov, V. S. 'Vozvrat k zhizni'. *Golos minuvshego* 5, no. 7–8 (1917): 287–315.
Pankratov, V. S. *Vospominaniia: kak prikhodilos' rabotat' sredi rabochikh v 1880–1884 godakh*. Moscow: Krasnaia nov', 1923.
Pankratov, V. S. *S tsarem v Tobol'ske: iz vospominanii*. Leningrad: Kooperativnoe izdatel'stvo tovarishchestvo 'Byloe', 1925.
*Polivanov, P. S. 'Otryvki iz pisem byvshego shlissel'burzhtsa'. *Byloe* 1, no. 2 (1906): 272–7.
*Polivanov, P. S. 'Koshmar (stikhotvorenie)'. *Byloe* 1, no. 2 (1906): 278–9.
*Popov, M. R. 'K biografii Ippolita Nikiticha Myshkina'. *Byloe* 1, no. 2 (1906): 250–68.
*Popov, M. R. 'Mechti o svobode: iz Shlissel'burgskikh vospominanii'. *Golos minuvshego* 5, no. 7–8 (1917): 257–86.
Popov, M. R. 'L. A. Volkenshtein'. *Golos minuvshego* 6, no. 4–6 (1918): 71–9.
Shebalin, M. P. *Klochki vospominanii*. Moscow: Izdatel'stvo Vsesoiuznogo obshchestva politkatorzhan i ssyl'no-poselentsev, 1935.
Sozonov, E. S. 'I. P. Kaliaev'. *Golos minuvshego* 5, no. 7–8 (1917): 316–32.
Sozonov, E. S. (E. Sazonov). 'Vospominaniia, pis'ma, materialy dlia biografii. S predisl. S. P. Mel'gunova'. *Golos minuvshego* 6, no. 10–12 (1918): 5–100.
Trigoni, M. N. 'Posle Shlissel'burga'. *Byloe* 1, no. 9 (1906): 45–62.
*Volkenshtein, L. A. *13 let v Shlissel'burgskoi kreposti: Zapiski*. Edited by V. L. Burtsev. Purleigh: A. Tchertkoff, Izdanie Svobodnogo slova, 1900.

Other sources on Shlissel'burg Fortress and its prisoners

Annenskii, N. F., V. Ia. Iakovlev, V. I. Semevskii, and V. Ia. Bogucharskii, eds. *Gallereia Shlissel'burgskikh uznikov: chast' pervaia*. St Petersburg: Tipografiia M. M. Stasiulevicha, 1907.
Davydov, Iu. V. *Dve sviazki pisem: Povest' o Germane Lopatine*. Moscow: Politizdat, 1983.
Dobrinskaia, L. B., ed. *Uzniki Shlissel'burgskoi kreposti*. Leningrad: Lenizdat, 1978.
Frumkin, S. 'Evrei – uzniki Shlissel'burga'. *Leningradskii evreiskii al'manakh*, no. 27 (1984): 54–60.
Gernet, M. N. *Istoriia tsarskoi tiur'my*. 5 vols. Moscow: Gosudarstvennoe izdatel'stvo iuridicheskoi literatury, 1960.
Gladilin, A. T. *Sny Shlissel'burgskoi kreposti: Povest' ob Ippolite Myshkine*. Moscow: Politizdat, 1974.
Goncharov, V. F. 'Shlissel'burgskaia katorga: iz vospominanii'. *Byloe*, nos. 25, 26, 27–28, 29, 30 (1924–5): 157–94, 104–38, 183–224, 119–55, 124–45.

Hartnett, L. A. 'The making of a revolutionary icon: Vera Nikolaevna Figner and the People's Will in the wake of the assassination of Tsar Aleksandr II'. *Canadian Slavonic Papers / Revue Canadienne Des Slavistes* 43, no. 2/3 (2001): 249–70.

Hartnett, L. A. *The Defiant Life of Vera Figner: Surviving the Russian Revolution*. Bloomington, IN: Indiana University Press, 2014.

Hoogenboom, H. 'Vera Figner and revolutionary autobiographies: The influence of gender on genre'. In *Women in Russia and Ukraine*. Edited by R. J. Marsh, 78–93. Cambridge: Cambridge University Press, 1996.

Iakimova-Dikovskaia, A. V., ed. *Narodnovol'sty 80-kh i 90-kh godov: Sbornik statei i materialov, sostavlennyi uchastnikami narodnovol'cheskogo dvizheniia*. Moscow: Izdatel'stvo Vsesoiuznogo obshchestva politkatorzhan i ssyl'no-poselentsev, 1929.

Iakubovich, P. F. 'Raskrytyi tainik: iz poezdki v Shlissel'burgskuiu krepost''. In *Gallereia Shlissel'burgskikh uznikov: chast' pervaia*. Edited by N. F. Annenskii, et al. xxix–xlv. St Petersburg: Tipografiia M. M. Stasiulevicha, 1907.

Iakubovich, P. F. *Vmesto Shlissel'burga*. St Petersburg: Knigoizdatel'stvo 'Russkoe bogatstvo', 1906.

Iasiukevich, B. A. 'Malen'kii ostrov: iz zhizni politicheskogo zakliuchennogo Shlissel'burgskoi kreposti 1906–1915 gg'. *Na perevale*, Iubil. nomer (1923): 48–51.

Kolosov, E. E. *Gosudareva tiur'ma - Shlissel'burg. Po ofitsial'nym dannym*. 2nd ed. Moscow: Izdatel'stvo Vsesoiuznogo obshchestva politkatorzhan i ssyl'no-poselentsev, 1930.

Koniaev, N. M. *Shlissel'burgskie psalmy. Sem' vekov russkoi kreposti*. Moscow: LitRes, 2017.

Kropotkin, P. A. 'The revolution in Russia'. *The Nineteenth Century and After: A Monthly Review (London)* 58, no. 346 (December 1905): 865–83.

Kross, J. *The Czar's Madman*. Translated by A. Hollo. London: The Harvill Press, 1992.

Leonidova, K. S. *Na katorzhnom ostrove: dnevniki, pis'ma i vospominaniia politkatorzhan 'novogo Shlissel'burga', 1907–1917 gg*. Leningrad: Lenizdat, 1966.

Nikitina, E. D. *Krepost' Shlissel'burg 1718–1905 gg*. Moscow: Izdatel'stvo politkatorzhan, 1927.

Nikolaevskii, B. I. 'Skorbnye stranitsy Shlissel'burgskoi kreposti'. *Byloe* 7, no. 13 (1918): 76–90.

Nikolaevskii, B. I. 'S. M. Ginzburg v Shlissel'burgskoi kreposti'. *Byloe* 15 (1920): 88–98.

Noskov, N. 'V russkoi bastilii'. *Ogonek*, no. 43 (5 December 1905): 339–43.

Noskov, N. 'Za stenami Shlissel'burga: iz vpechatlenii poezdki v Shlissel'burgskuiu krepost''. *Probuzhdenie*, no. 21 (1906): 617–22.

O'Meara, P. 'Timotheus von Bock: Prisoner of Alexander I'. *The Slavonic and East European Review* 90, no. 1 (2012): 98–123. https://doi.org/10.5699/slaveasteurorev2.90.1.0098.

Popovskii, M. *Pobezhdennoe vremia: Povest' o Nikolae Morozove*. Moscow: Politizdat, 1975.

Prugavin, A. S. *Proshloe i nastoiashchee Shlissel'burgskoi kreposti*. Rostov-na-Donu: Donskaia rech', 1904.

Prugavin, A. S. 'Shlissel'burgskaia krepost''. In *Gallereia Shlissel'burgskikh uznikov*. Edited by N. F. Annenskii et al., 1:v–xxviii. St Petersburg: Tipografiia M. M. Stasiulevicha, 1907.

Prugavin, A. S. *V kazematakh. Ocherki i materialy po istorii russkikh tiurem. Shlissel'burg. Suzdal'skaia tiur'ma. Petropavlovskaia krepost'*. St Petersburg: Tipografiia Pervoi S-Peterburgskoi trudovoi arteli, 1909.

Semevskii, V. I., and V. Bogucharskii. 'Ot Shlissel'burgskogo komiteta'. *Byloe* 1, no. 1 (1906): 315–7.

Simanovich, V. A. *V novom Shlissel'burge*. Moscow: Izdatel'stvo politkatorzhan, 1934.

Sinel'nikov, A. *Tainy Peterburgskikh krepostei: Shlissel'burgskaia pentagramma*. Moscow: Eksmo, 2008.

Sobolev, Iu. *Mucheniki Shlissel'burgskoi kreposti*. Moscow: Izdatel'stvo 'Krasnaia nov'', 1923.

Szwarce, B. *Siedm lat w Szlyselburgu*. Lwów: Towarzystwo im. Stanisława Staszica, 1893.

Szwarce, B. (B. Shvartse). *Sem' let v Shlissel'burge*. Translated by S. Basov-Verkhoiantsev. Moscow: Izdatel'stvo politkatorzhan, 1930.

Trifonov, Iu. V. *Neterpenie: Povest' ob A. Zheliabove*. Moscow: Politizdat, 1973.

Venediktov-Beziuk, D. G. *Po kazematam Shlissel'burgskoi kreposti*. Moscow: Izdatel'stvo politkatorzhan, 1928.

Vladimirov, K. 'Introduction'. In *From My Recent Past: Memoirs of a revolutionary terrorist*, by G. A. Gershuni, ix–xvii. Translated by K. Vladimirov. Lanham, MD: Lexington Books, 2015.

Vladimirov, Z. 'O Shlissel'burgskoi kreposti'. In *Ocherki sovremmenykh kaznei*, 235–68. Moscow: Tipografiia A. P. Poplavskogo, 1906.

Voinovich, V. N. *Stepen' doveriia: Povest' o Vere Figner*. Moscow: Politizdat, 1973.
Wallace, A. 'Horrors of Schlusselburg Fortress: Personal narrative and "human document"'. *The Advertiser*. 12 March 1910.
Young, S. J. 'Isolation, control and resistance: Political inmates in the Shlissel'burg Fortress, 1884–1906'. In *De Los Controles Disciplinarios a Los Controles Securitarios. Actas Del II Congreso Internacional Sobre La Historia de La Prisión y Las Instituciones Punitivas*. Edited by P. Oliver Olmo and M. C. Cubero Izquierdo, 635–48. Cuenca: Ediciones de la Universidad de Castilla-La Mancha, 2020. http://doi.org/10.18239/jornadas_2020.25.44.

Other sources cited

Adams, B. F. *The Politics of Punishment: Prison reform in Russia 1863–1917*. DeKalb: Northern Illinois University Press, 1996.
Akopian, T. V., and M. A. Lukovskaia, eds. *Gazety dorevoliutsionnoi Rossii, 1703–1917: katalog*. St Petersburg: Rossiiskaia natsional'naia biblioteka, 2007.
Badcock, S., and J. Pallot. 'Russia and the Soviet Union from the nineteenth to the twenty-first century'. In *A Global History of Convicts and Penal Colonies*. Edited by C. Anderson, 271–306. London: Bloomsbury Academic, 2018.
Bakunin, M. A. *Sobranie sochinenii i pisem 1828–1876*. Edited by Iu. M. Steklov. Vol. 4. 4 vols. Moscow: Izdatel'stvo Vsesoiuznogo obshchestva politkatorzhan i ssyl'no-poselentsev, 1935.
Bal, M. 'First person, second person, same person: Narrative as epistemology'. *New Literary History* 24, no. 2 (1993): 293–320. https://doi.org/10.2307/469408.
Beer, D. '"Microbes of the mind": Moral contagion in late Imperial Russia'. *The Journal of Modern History* 79, no. 3 (2007): 531–71. https://doi.org/10.1086/517981.
Beer, D. *The House of the Dead: Siberian exile under the Tsars*. London: Allen Lane, 2016.
Boer, R. 'Religion and socialism: A. V. Lunacharsky and the god-builders'. *Political Theology* 15, no. 2 (2014): 188–209. https://doi.org/10.1179/1462317X13Z.00000000074.
Chatterjee, C. 'Imperial incarcerations: Ekaterina Breshko-Breshkovskaia, Vinayak Savarkar, and the original sins of modernity'. *Slavic Review* 74, no. 4 (2015): 850–72. https://doi.org/10.5612/slavicreview.74.4.850.
Code, L. 'Second persons'. *Canadian Journal of Philosophy* 17, no. 1 (1987): 357–82. https://doi.org/10.1080/00455091.1987.10715942.
Daly, J. W. *Autocracy Under Siege: Security police and opposition in Russia, 1866–1905*. DeKalb: North Illinois University Press, 1998.
Daly, J. W. 'Criminal punishment and Europeanization in late Imperial Russia'. *Jahrbücher Für Geschichte Osteuropas*, Neue Folge, 48, no. 3 (2000): 341–62.
Daly, J. W. *Crime and Punishment in Russia: A comparative history from Peter the Great to Vladimir Putin*. London: Bloomsbury Academic, 2018.
DelConte, M. 'Why you can't speak: Second-person narration, voice, and a new model for understanding narrative'. *Style* 37, no. 2 (2003): 204–19.
Dostoevsky, F. *Notes from the House of the Dead*. Translated by B. Jakim. Grand Rapids, MI: Eerdmans, 2013.
Ely, C. *Underground Petersburg: Radical populism, urban space and the tactics of subversion in reform-era Russia*. DeKalb: Northern Illinois University Press, 2016.
Etkind, A. 'Hard and soft in cultural memory: Political mourning in Russia and Germany'. *Grey Room*, no. 16 (2004): 36–59.
Fludernik, M. 'Introduction: Second-person narrative and related issues'. *Style* 28, no. 3 (1994): 281–311.
Foucault, M. *Discipline and Punish: The birth of the prison*. Translated by A. Sheridan. London: Penguin Books, 1991.
Geifman, A. 'Aspects of early twentieth-century Russian terrorism: The socialist-revolutionary combat organization'. *Terrorism and Political Violence* 4, no. 2 (1992): 23–46. https://doi.org/10.1080/09546559208427147.
Ginzburg, E. *Into the Whirlwind*. Translated by P. Stevenson and M. Harari. London: Harvill, 1999.
Goodwin, J. F. 'The afterlife of terrorists: Commemorating the People's Will in early Soviet Russia'. In *Just Assassins: The culture of terrorism in Russia*. Edited by A. Anemone, 229–46. Evanston, IL: Northwestern University Press, 2011.

Grant, K. 'British suffragettes and the Russian method of hunger strike'. *Comparative Studies in Society and History* 53, no. 1 (2011): 113–43.
Gullotta, A. *Intellectual Life and Literature at Solovki 1923–1930: The Paris of the northern concentration camps.* Cambridge: Legenda, 2018.
Haslam, S. A., and S. D. Reicher. 'When prisoners take over the prison: A social psychology of resistance'. *Personality and Social Psychology Review* 16, no. 2 (2012): 154–79. https://doi.org/10.1177/1088868311419864.
Jackson, R. L. *The Art of Dostoevsky: Deliriums and nocturnes.* Princeton, NJ: Princeton University Press, 1981.
Jones, P. *Revolution Rekindled: The writers and readers of late Soviet biography.* Oxford Scholarship Online. Oxford: University Press, 2019. https://dx.doi.org/10.1093/oso/9780198804345.001.0001.
Lorer, N. I. 'Zapiski moego vremeni: vospominanie o proshlom'. In *Memuary Dekabristov.* Edited by A. S. Nemzer, 313–545. Moscow: Izdatel'stvo 'Pravda', 1988.
Massey, D. 'Places and their pasts'. *History Workshop Journal*, no. 39 (1995): 182–92.
Mildorf, J. 'Reconsidering second-person narration and involvement'. *Language and Literature* 25, no. 2 (2016): 145–58. https://doi.org/10.1177/0963947016638985.
Misztal, B. A. *Theories of Social Remembering.* Maidenhead: Open University Press, 2003.
Pallot, J. 'The Gulag as the crucible of Russia's 21st-century system of punishment'. *Kritika: Explorations in Russian and Eurasian History* 16, no. 3 (2015): 681–710.
Patyk, L. E. *Written in Blood: Revolutionary terrorism and Russian literary culture, 1861–1881.* Madison: The University of Wisconsin Press, 2017.
Pearl, D. L. 'From worker to revolutionary: The making of worker narodovol'tsy'. *Russian History* 23, no. 1–4 (1996): 11–26. https://doi.org/10.1163/187633196X00033.
Peterson, N. 'Dirty women: Cultural connotations of cleanliness in Soviet Russia'. In *Russia, Women, Culture.* Edited by H. Goscilo and B. Holmgren, 177–205. Bloomington: Indiana University Press, 1996.
Piacentini, L. *Surviving Russian Prisons: Punishment, economy and politics in transition.* Cullompton, UK; Portland, OR: Willan, 2004.
Polak, L. S. *Bylo tak: Ocherki.* Moscow: n. pub., 1996
Riehl, A. A. *Der Philosophische Kritizismus Und Seine Bedeutung Für Die Positive Wissenschaft. Zweiter Band. Zweiter Theil (Schluss). Zur Wissenschafttheorie Und Metaphysik.* Leipzig: Verlag von Wilhelm Engelmann, 1887.
Riehl, A. A. *Teoriia nauki i metafizika s tochki zreniia filosofskogo krititsizma.* Translated by E. Korsh. Moscow: Tipografiia V. V. Islen'eva, 1887.
Scott, J. C. *Weapons of the Weak: Everyday forms of peasant resistance.* New Haven, CT: Yale University Press, 1985.
Shalamov, V. T. *Sobranie sochinenii.* Vol 1. 6 vols. Moscow: Terra, 2004.
Shalev, S. *A Sourcebook on Solitary Confinement.* London: Mannheim Centre for Criminology, London School of Economics, 2008. www.solitaryconfinement.org/sourcebook.
Shalev, S. *Supermax: Controlling risk through solitary confinement.* Abingdon: Routledge, 2009.
Shumovskii, T. A. *Svet s vostoka.* St Petersburg: Izdatel'stvo S-Peterburgskogo universiteta, 2006.
Sorokin, P. A. *A Long Journey.* New Haven, CT: College and University Press, 1963.
Tolokonnikova, N. *Read and Riot: A Pussy Riot guide to activism.* London: Coronet, 2019.
Venturi, F. *Roots of Revolution: A history of the Populist and Socialist movements in nineteenth-century Russia.* Translated by F. Haskell. London: Weidenfeld & Nicolson, 1960.
Voronina, T. 'Fasting in the life of Russians: 19th–20th centuries'. *Acta Ethnographica Hungarica* 51, no. 3–4 (2006): 235–55. https://doi.org/10.1556/AEthn.51.2006.3-4.1.
Wood, A. 'Administrative exile and the criminals' communes in Siberia'. In *Land Commune and Peasant Community in Russia: Communal forms in Imperial and early Soviet society.* Edited by R. Bartlett, 395–414. Basingstoke: Macmillan, 1990.
Young, S. J. 'Knowing Russia's convicts: The Other in narratives of imprisonment and exile of the late Imperial era'. *Europe-Asia Studies* 65, no. 9 (2013): 1700–15. https://doi.org/10.1080/09668136.2013.844509.
Young, S. J. 'Framing Gulag memoirs: A distant reading'. In *Rethinking the Gulag: sources, identities, legacies.* Edited by Alan Barenberg and Emily D. Johnson. Bloomington: Indiana University Press, forthcoming.
Zim, R. *The Consolations of Writing: Literary strategies of resistance from Boethius to Primo Levi.* Princeton, NJ: Princeton University Press, 2014. https://www.jstor.org/stable/10.2307/j.ctt6wq0m7.

Index

acoustics, new prison's 21, 47, 92, 144, 146–9
activities, communal 26, 30
   celebrations 67, 70, 116, 180, 206
   lectures and study 12, 14, 22, 66–7, 70–1, 104–5, 115–17, 119, 125, 202–3
   singing 67, 180–1, 205–6
administration, Shlissel'burg prison 7, 55–6, 71–2, 93, 94, 98–9, 108, 123–4, 144–5, 182
   changes to 55, 63–4, 71, 167–8
   conditions for 56, 96–7, 140–1, 186, 200
   transferred from the Peter and Paul Fortress 42, 56, 136, 141
Alexander II, Tsar
   attempted assassination of 77, 78
   assassination of 6, 81
Alexander III, Tsar 67, 86
allotments 12, 17–18, 58, 61–2, 89, 106–7, 122, 164–5
   congregation of inmates on 70–1, 99–100, 116, 125, 155, 181–2, 202, 206
   construction of 42, 88, 154
   horticulture on 90, 106–8, 118, 154–5, 172, 175–6, 181–3
   removal of barriers between 18, 20, 66, 99, 100, 112, 116
   self-governance of 62, 94
amnesty
   reduction in sentences due to 37, 40, 72, 75, 119, 129, 133, 203–4
   rumours regarding 186, 207
Andreiushkin, Pakhomii Ivanovich 67, 77, 213, 215
animals, raised by inmates 105–6, 120, 183–4
Antonov, Petr Leont'evich 133, 215
   activities in Shlissel'burg of 108, 123, 135, 180
Antonovich, Ioann (Emperor Ivan VI) 3, 42, 110, 123
Aronchik, Aizik Borisovich 35, 212, 215–16
   illness and death of 42, 50, 52, 61, 80, 142
arrival at Shlissel'burg Prison, inmates' 25, 43–4, 68–9, 79, 81, 95, 120–3, 147, 164, 213
Ashenbrenner, Mikhail Iul'evich 35, 37, 81, 82–4, 135, 212, 216
   memoirs of 2, 13–24, 27, 29–30

Balmashev, Stefan Valer'ianovich 81, 123, 128, 216
bathing 145, 151–2
Bezrodnov, Nikolai Sergeevich, Dr 91, 99, 114, 117, 118, 125
Bogdanovich, Iurii Nikolaevich 35, 142, 151, 216
   activities in Shlissel'burg of 102, 162
   illness and death of 58–9, 61, 79, 129, 163, 212
books 12, 60, 69, 99, 103–5, 113, 119, 125, 189
   absence of 47, 85, 148–9, 153
   access to inmates' own 87–8, 160
   accessed via bookbinding workshop 65, 113
   as reward for good behaviour 9, 16, 139
   deprivation of as punishment 92, 139, 146, 158
   funds for 111–12, 114–15, 177, 208
   mismanagement of provision of 64, 87, 187
   new 57, 59, 63–4, 87, 162, 167, 187
   poor quality of existing 47, 53, 85, 151
   promised by inspectors 62, 178
   protests to improve provision of 48, 59, 86, 89
   translations of by inmates 12, 103
   withdrawn by inspectors 59, 71, 88, 123, 125, 165, 190
burial, inmates' 67, 75, 80
Burtsev, Vladimir L'vovich 34, 38, 39, 77
Butsevich, Aleksandr Vikent'evich 83, 212, 217
   illness and death of 50–1, 142, 151
Butsinskii, Dmitrii Timofeevich 35, 102, 217
   illness and death of 61, 72, 142, 170
   transfer to Shlissel'burg of 25, 136–7, 212

cells 5, 7, 11, 46, 89, 138–9, 146, 160
   corners blocked off 52, 109, 163
   damp and cold in 9, 33, 111
   darkness of 7, 21, 93, 181
   lights in 111, 130, 189
   glass in windows of 42, 46, 93, 98, 138, 154, 181–2
   plumbing in 7, 46
   use of plumbing to communicate 58–60, 163, 166
   ventilation of 95, 137, 160

Chepegin, Nikita Koz'mich 217
Chernyshevskii, Nikolai Gavrilovich 82, 127
Chertkov, Vladimir Grigor'evich 38, 40
collective 10, 13–16, 26–7, 29, 54, 161
   decision-making 14, 59, 71, 162, 191, 197, 208
   protest 52, 57, 156, 161
   voice in memoirs 24–5, 28, 103
commune 31, 33, 73, 88, 90, 97, 104
communication 17–19, 53–4, 92, 99, 111, 144
   absence of, with outside world 6, 7, 9–10, 14, 71
   as resistance 10–11, 22–3, 92
   attempts to prevent 9, 11, 46–7, 92
   by tapping. *See* wall alphabet
   difficulty of 85, 97, 141, 162
   no longer punished 11–12, 52, 159
   removal of obstacles to 18, 20, 99–100
confinement, solitary 2, 5, 7, 12, 31, 66, 70, 136
   psychological effects of 20, 46, 50–1, 53–4, 126, 160
conflict
   between inmates 30, 167, 173–5, 201, 208
   with administration 72, 85–6, 156, 158, 176, 192–4, 197–8
correspondence with families 141, 150, 207–8
   censorship of 65–6, 112, 122–5, 177–8
   demands for 76, 86, 98, 112, 142–3, 178, 200
crazes, inmates' 29, 100–8, 120, 155, 158, 160–1, 172, 175, 181–3, 202

death 24–5, 27–8, 45, 49–54, 57, 59, 61–2, 64, 72, 74–5, 86, 128–9, 147–8, 155–6, 170, 203
   psychological effects of 9, 51, 151, 155, 163–4, 167, 170
death sentences
   carried out at Shlissel'burg Fortress 1, 37, 41–2, 67–8, 77, 123, 146, 160, 212
   commuted to hard labour 1, 37, 81, 84, 128, 133
   for infractions of prison regulations 48–50, 54, 142–3
debates, inmates' 22, 115–17, 202
Decembrists 4, 10, 12, 32
departure from Shlissel'burg Prison, inmates' 45, 52, 74–5, 78–9, 119–20, 126, 129, 164, 188–9, 198–201, 204–6, 209–10
Dolgushin, Aleksandr Vasil'evich 35, 212, 217
   illness and death of 51, 142
Dostoevskii, Fedor Mikhailovich 23–4, 32, 33, 80, 120, 212
Durnovo, Petr Nikolaevich 60, 87, 98, 165, 178

exercise 42, 58, 73, 145, 160
   individual 9, 121, 141, 145
   deprivation of, as punishment 60, 125, 159, 185
   inmates organizing own schedule for 65, 76, 88
   pairs assigned for 12, 50–1, 58, 70, 88, 99, 150–1, 176
   salutary effects of 86, 89, 168
exile-settlement
   transfer to 37–8, 45, 75, 84, 119–20, 126, 133–4, 188, 205–6
   psychological effects of 207, 210

faith 27, 52
   devotional books provided 5, 9, 65, 85
   inmates rejecting 27, 67, 74, 99
feast days
   religious 56, 90, 111, 148–9, 153
Figner, Vera Nikolaevna 83, 126, 217–18
   activities in Shlissel'burg of 114, 122, 183–4, 202, 207
   communal activities of 19, 111, 155, 174–5, 180, 204–6
   intellectual work in Shlissel'burg of 102–4, 161, 175
   moral leadership of 29, 38, 119, 126–7, 156
   physical work in Shlissel'burg of 110, 169
   protests by 124–5, 156, 160, 167, 180, 187, 193, 210
   trial of 37, 84, 125–6, 146, 211–12
   writings of 5, 18, 22–3, 26, 27–8, 30, 33, 35, 102, 104, 174
food 5, 9, 42, 90, 141, 152–3, 212
   absence of invalid rations 49, 61, 143–4
   alcohol and tobacco production 73, 117–19, 178–9, 200
   improvements to 12, 58, 64–5, 91–2, 162, 177
   increase in allowance for 64, 91–2
   inmates controlling budget and menus for 65, 91, 177
   inmates cooking their own 17, 61–2, 67, 70, 107–8, 117, 180, 206
   inmates growing their own 12, 65, 90, 106–7, 120
   on religious feast days 149, 152
   religious fasts 90–1, 109
freedom
   desire for 46, 69, 74, 108, 138
   psychological effects of 76, 126–7, 207, 210
Frolenko, Mikhail Fedorovich 35, 43, 78, 83, 116, 102, 142, 218–19
   activities in Shlissel'burg of 88, 90, 102, 106–7, 151, 180
   writings of 14, 19, 24, 26, 34, 102

Gellis, Meier Iankelevich 212, 219
   illness and death of 51, 142, 147
Generalov, Vasilii Denisovich 67, 77, 213, 219
Gershkovich, Girsh A. 81, 219
Gershuni, Grigorii Andreevich 34, 128, 220
   memoirs of 14, 25, 26, 33
Ginsburg, Sof'ia Mikhailovna 81, 220
   transfer and suicide of 68, 95, 120
Ginzburg, Evgeniia Semenovna 24, 78
Goremykin, Ivan Logginovich 81, 74, 98, 112, 199–200
Gor'kii, Maksim 119, 126

Grachevskii, Mikhail Fedorovich 35, 77, 142, 151, 212, 220
   suicide of 21–2, 55, 57, 86, 95–6, 107 128, 130, 159, 161–2
Gulag 31
   narratives of 10, 23–4, 27, 34

hard labour 1, 4, 24, 32, 43, 50, 77–8, 136, 201
   attempted escapes from 75, 104
   inmates sentenced to 37, 84, 98, 112, 133
   Shlissel'burg as hard labour prison 8, 80
Hegel, Georg Wilhelm Friedrich 82, 117, 131
Herod. *See* Sokolov, Matvei

Ianovich, Liudvig. *See* Janavičius, Liudvikas
illness
   mental 9, 17, 28, 42–3, 49–50, 52, 62–3, 69, 73–4, 76, 86, 142, 147, 153–4, 162, 167–9, 183–6, 194–5
   psychological effect on other inmates of 73, 101, 120, 187, 199
   recovery from 63, 76, 128, 142, 176
   removal of inmates to psychiatric hospital 45, 73–4, 112, 198–200, 213
illness
   physical 9, 42, 49, 53–4, 61–2, 72, 141, 147–8, 203
   care for sick inmates 61–4, 74–5, 99
   deterioration of vision 21, 93–4, 98, 126, 157–8
   malnutrition 5, 9, 42, 49–50, 61, 107
   pulmonary disease 9, 49–51, 54, 58, 60–1, 72, 101, 139, 141, 147, 151, 164
   recovery from 12, 72, 115–16, 169
   removal of sick inmates to old prison 41, 54, 163–4, 194
incarceration, psychological effects of 53, 60, 69–70, 85–6, 94–5, 116, 126–7, 138, 146–8, 150–1, 153, 155, 158–9, 170–1
inspections 52, 71, 98–9, 108, 143, 199–200, 210
   complaints made during 48, 87, 150, 164
   privileges hidden during 18, 66, 101, 118, 178, 189–90
   regime becoming harsher after 59, 88, 165
   regime improving after 57–8, 87, 200
   requests made during 74, 98, 112, 164, 187, 199
instructions, prison 5, 7, 48, 93, 95–6, 124, 139, 146, 177–8
   See also regime, prison.
introspection 41, 59, 76, 85–6, 126–7, 143, 146, 151
Isaev, Grigorii Prokof'evich 35, 78, 212, 221
   illness and death of 54, 142, 147, 151
isolation 7, 9–13, 18–21, 39, 46–7, 49, 54, 85, 139
   from outside world 29, 85, 108, 122
   of women inmates 60, 62
Iurkovskii, Fedor Nikolaevich 142, 221
   activities in Shlissel'burg of 88, 99, 103–4
   illness and death of 70, 74, 203
Iuvachev, Ivan Pavlovich 77, 212, 222
   memoirs of 8, 19–20, 34
   mental illness of 52, 128, 154
   transfer to exile-settlement of 52, 79, 214
Ivanov, Ignatii Kirillovich 212, 222
   mental illness and death of 50, 54, 128, 142, 152
Ivanov, Sergei Andreevich 77, 126, 129, 205, 213, 223
   activities in Shlissel'burg of 22, 97, 106–8, 161
   confrontations in Shlissel'burg involving 124, 165, 169, 196–7, 208
   health of 19, 61, 115
   writings of 104, 115–16, 173
Ivanov, Vasilii Grigorovich 77, 212, 223
   activities in Shlissel'burg of 114, 150, 178–9

Janavičius, Liudvikas (Liudvig Ianovich) 126, 213, 223–4
   amnesty and exile-settlement of 75, 119, 204
   memoirs of 21, 26
journals 63–4, 103, 112–15, 122, 125, 174–5, 201–2, 208
   binding volumes of 64–5, 102, 113–14
   inmates producing their own 23, 105, 172–5

Kachura, Foma Korneevich 123, 224
Kaliaev, Ivan Platonovich 34, 81, 224
Karaulov, Vasilii Andreevich 133, 164, 212, 224–5
Karpovich, Petr Vladimirovich 78, 120–2, 225
Klimenko, Mikhail Filimonovich 142, 212, 225
   suicide of 48, 57, 153, 150
Kobylianskii, Liudvig Aleksandrovich 51–2, 142, 212, 213, 226
Konashevich, Vasilii Petrovich (Konoshevich) 213, 226
   mental illness of 62–3, 73, 167, 185, 194–6, 199–200
   transfer to psychiatric hospital of 74, 200–1
Konopliannikova, Zinaida Vasil'evna 81, 226

Lagovskii, Mikhail Fedorovich (Logovskii, Logovskoi) 226–7
   activities in Shlissel'burg of 105, 187–8
   administrative sentence of 61, 98, 170–2, 213
lectures, inmates' 12, 14, 22, 73, 115, 125, 168, 202
   by Lukaszewicz 104–5, 116–17, 119
Lenin, Vladimir Il'ych (Ul'ianov) 35, 135
library, inmates' 80, 85, 115, 160, 165, 190
Lopatin, German Aleksandrovich 1, 35, 77, 129, 213, 227
   intellectual work in Shlissel'burg of 102–3, 105, 174
   life in Shlissel'burg of 88, 126, 180
Lukaszewicz, Jyzef (Iosif Dement'evich Lukashevich) 77, 213, 227
   activities in Shlissel'burg of 104–5, 106, 114, 116–19

Malavskii, Vladimir Evgenievich 34, 212, 227–8
  illness and death of 50, 139, 142, 147, 151
Manucharov, Ivan L'vovich (Ovanes Ashotovich Manuchariants) 119, 188–9, 213, 228
Martynov, Kalinnik Fedulovich 93, 119, 133, 126, 213, 228
  activities in Shlissel'burg of 102, 180, 192–3
Marx, Karl 88, 120
  Marxism 104, 127–8, 131
medical care 53, 61, 74, 148, 164
  absence of 9, 47, 49, 51, 53, 59, 61, 156, 164
  doctors failing to provide 47, 49, 61, 74, 99, 142–3, 144, 164
  doctors clashing with administration over 157–8, 179
  doctors providing 63, 73, 114, 125, 147–8, 176, 181, 183, 194, 198, 203
  inmates providing 64, 70, 72, 74, 170, 194, 203
  meetings, inmates' 50–4, 60, 64, 70, 71, 73, 116–17, 125, 154, 155–6, 164–5, 168, 172
  deprivation of 39, 85, 98, 142
  in exercise pens 66–7, 88, 150
  protests to obtain 48, 50, 86, 121
Mel'nikov, Mikhail Mikhailovich 228
memoirs, inmates' 1–2, 5, 13–30
  as carceral writing 23–4, 26–7, 29, 30
  collective emphasized in 13, 16, 23–5, 26–30, 54
  genre conventions of 25–8
  identity in 14–15, 25–6, 28
  in revolutionary mythology 1–2, 25, 35
  memorialization in 2, 24, 27, 41, 80, 103
  trauma in 15, 27–8, 41, 126–7
memory 25, 74, 85, 155, 182, 209
  of freedom 46, 148–9, 153
  revolutionary 29, 34–5
Mikhailovskii, Nikolai Konstantinovich 100, 119
Minakov, Egor Ivanovich 86–7, 212, 229
  execution of 48, 50, 143
  protest by 48, 86, 142, 189
Morozov, Nikolai Aleksandrovich 34, 35, 77, 212, 229–30
  health of 61, 115–16, 142
  intellectual work in Shlissel'burg by 102, 104–5, 117, 119, 182
  life in Shlissel'burg of 78, 151, 154
  writings of 19, 26, 56, 80, 102, 104, 161
museum, inmates' 108, 114–15, 202
Myshkin, Ippolit Nikitich 35, 77, 212, 230
  execution of 50, 55, 87, 128
  protest of 48–9, 86, 142, 149, 159

Narodnichestvo, Narodniki. *See* Populism, Russian
Nemolovskii, Appolon Irineevich 77, 212–13, 230
  illness and death of 50, 51, 147
Nicholas I, Tsar 5, 6
Nicholas II, Tsar 37, 71, 135

noise 20–1, 47, 126, 149
  as resistance 20, 92, 156, 161–2
  guards creating 21, 49, 92, 157–9, 192
Novorusskii, Mikhail Vasil'evich 34, 114, 130, 230–1
  transfer to Shlissel'burg of 79, 81, 213

Orzhevskii, Petr Vasil'evich 7, 42, 48, 52, 98, 143, 150, 204
Orzhikh, Boris Dmitrievich 78, 79, 164, 186, 231
  application for pardon by 209–10
Osipanov, Vasilii Stepanovich 67, 77, 213, 232

Pankratov, Vasilii Semenovich 35, 103, 133–5, 213, 232
  amnesty and exile-settlement of 78, 119–20, 205
  memoirs of 2, 14–16, 19–21, 23, 25, 30
People's Will, The (*Narodnaia volia*) 1, 6, 37, 40, 77–8, 81, 83, 127–8, 133
Peter and Paul Fortress (St Petersburg) 6, 7, 26, 37, 63, 77–8, 84, 212
  Shlissel'burg Fortress as replacement for 42–4, 46, 48, 56, 106, 136
Peter the Great, Tsar 2–3
petitions, inmates' 48, 63–4, 73–4, 112, 143, 150, 178, 199, 209–10
Petrov, General Nikolai Ivanovich 55–9, 87, 213
Populism, Russian (*Narodnichestvo*) 31, 104, 127
  Russian Populists 1, 9, 33, 129
privileges 12, 25, 60, 62, 70, 86, 98, 117, 168, 180–1
  rejected when not applied to all inmates 54, 63–4, 155–6
  reversed 9, 12, 70–1, 87–8, 122, 124–5, 181, 190
  sacrifices made to gain 86, 166–7, 169
Plehve, Viacheslav Konstantinovich von 7, 87, 96, 125
Pokhitonov, Nikolai Danilovich 77, 103, 128, 212, 232
  mental illness of 73, 95, 186–7, 192–4
  transfer to hospital of 194, 198–9
  transfer to Shlissel'burg of 25, 136–7
Polivanov, Petr Sergeevich 142, 119–20, 212, 232–3
  activities in Shlissel'burg of 105–7, 161
  suicide of 126, 129
  writings of 34, 102–4, 161
Popov, Mikhail Rodionovich 106, 129, 142, 207, 212, 233
  activities in Shlissel'burg of 22, 97, 106–7, 123–5, 142, 180
  writings of 34, 173
priest
  rejected by inmates 67, 74
  visits from 16, 99, 139, 146
punishment 8, 9, 16, 33, 53, 62, 92, 93, 95–6, 125, 190, 194
  beating 20, 47–8, 93, 124, 150, 192–3
  deprivation of books 47, 156, 158, 190
  deprivation of physical activity 9, 60, 159, 185, 190, 194

execution 48–9, 50, 54, 86
for tapping 11, 92, 124, 139, 147, 156
instructions defining 46, 48, 93, 95–6, 124, 146
old prison, used as isolation block for 7, 41, 47, 49–50, 54–5, 92–3, 150, 153, 156–7, 161–2
straitjacket used as 20, 47, 93, 95, 124, 195
waived for sick inmates 55, 72, 74

reading 12, 69, 89, 93–4, 113–15, 125, 165
group 58, 66–7, 70–1, 111, 113, 115–16, 119, 202
salutary effects of 12, 90, 93–4
regime, Shlissel'burg Prison 5, 7–10, 25, 46–7, 52–4, 70–1, 94–5, 141, 190
improvements to 12, 27, 57, 63–7, 109, 162, 164–5, 177
unsustainability of 9, 21–2, 62, 72, 76, 86, 95–6, 101, 168
See also instructions, prison.
resistance 2, 13, 14, 17–18, 20, 22, 47, 158–9, 161, 163, 189
collective 10, 23, 34–5, 49, 54, 57, 59–60, 156–7, 165–7
complicity of administration in 18, 62, 71–2, 98, 101, 165
conflict between inmates about 167, 171, 197
conflict with administration over 60–2, 71–2, 85–6, 97, 189–92, 196–8
hunger strikes as 14, 48, 50, 59–60, 88, 121, 142, 165–7
individual acts of 48, 50, 121, 124, 141–2, 149–50
writing as 25–7, 30
Rogachev, Nikolai Mikhailovich 68, 77, 146, 212–13, 233

Sazonov. *See* Sozonov, Egor Sergeevich
searches 62
of cells 71, 96, 138, 144–5, 189
personal 15, 52–3, 57, 210
self-governance, inmates' 65, 71, 88, 91, 176–7, 190
clubs organized by inmates 58–60, 66–7, 70, 88–9, 116, 121
control of funds by inmates 65, 89, 90–2, 168, 176, 208
elder 90, 92, 97, 115, 118, 176, 191–2, 196–8
librarian 97, 115, 208
sentences 53–4
administrative 4, 61, 98, 170–1, 213
Shchedrin, Nikolai Pavlovich 50, 212, 234
mental illness of 17, 50, 73, 76, 142, 147, 152, 184–5
transfer to psychiatric hospital of 74, 200–1
Shebalin, Mikhail Petrovich 75, 78, 119, 128, 133, 213, 234
activities in Shlissel'burg of 88, 102, 103, 180
protests in prison by 50, 156
Shebeko, Nikolai Ignat'evich 22, 58–60, 79, 98, 160, 161–3

Shevyrev, Petr Iakovlevich 67, 77, 213, 234
Shlissel'burg Fortress, institution of,
comparison with other prisons 7, 13–14, 207
earlier inmates in 3–5, 10, 42, 110, 123
history of 2–6, 41
place of in Russia's criminal justice system 6–7, 48, 75–6, 112
Shlissel'burg Fortress, physical spaces of,
allotments 99, 116, 154
topography 8, 11, 19, 41–2, 55, 68, 88, 123, 138, 182
workshops 70, 89, 110–11, 190
Shlissel'burg old prison 3–5, 7, 41–2
removal of sick to 17, 50–1, 63, 74, 167
used as accommodation for prisoners before execution 67–8, 123
used as punishment block 7, 41, 47, 49–50, 54–5, 92–3, 150, 153, 156–7, 161–2
workshops in 41, 68, 89, 110–11, 122
Shtromberg, Aleksandr Pavlovich 68, 77, 146, 212–13, 234–5
Sikorskii, Shimel'-Leiba Vul'fovich 235
silence 5, 6, 11–12, 20, 23, 48, 55, 86, 137, 146–7, 149, 161, 164
of guards 23, 138–9, 140–1
Sipiagin, Dmitrii Sergeevich 87, 96, 123
Socialist Revolutionary Party 32, 58, 84, 127–8, 131, 133–5, 212
Sokolov, Matvei, Superintendent ('Herod') 7, 16–17, 55–7, 96, 139–40, 142, 151–62
strictness of regime under 56, 87, 139, 144–5, 151–2, 156
treatment of gendarmes by 56, 140–1, 145
treatment of inmates by 52–3, 93, 143, 148
Sozonov, Egor Sergeevich (Sazonov) 32, 34, 123, 235
Starodvorskii, Nikolai Petrovich 79, 119, 205 213, 235–6
activities in Shlissel'burg of 104, 173
study, by inmates 12, 29, 63, 70–1, 87, 103–5, 151, 153, 203
Sudeikin, Georgii Porfir'evich 127, 140
suicide 9, 48, 55, 64, 68, 77, 95, 120, 128, 150, 162, 213
after release 35, 126, 129
attempts 68, 73, 95, 143, 150, 167
changes following 57, 79, 86, 96, 107, 150, 162
execution as a form of 9, 48, 143
thoughts of 86, 88, 101, 147
Surovtsev, Dmitrii Iakovlevich 75, 77, 119, 212, 236
surveillance 7–9, 22, 71, 109–10, 138, 145, 146
on allotments 62, 67, 94
during exercise 100, 109, 141, 154
psychological effects of 50, 52, 94–5
survival 70, 76, 158–9

Tikhanovich, Aleksandr Pakhomovich 49, 77, 128, 150, 212–13, 236
translation 30, 131
work by inmates on 12, 128, 103
'Trial of the 50' (1877) 77
'Trial of the 193' (1877–8) 36, 77, 78

'Trial of the 20' (1882) 42–3, 78
'Trial of the 14' (1884) 15, 37, 43, 68, 77, 84, 128, 146, 212
Trial of 1 March (1887) 67, 213
'Trial of the 21' (Lopatin case) (1887) 213
Trigoni, Mikhail Nikolaevich 35, 78, 120, 126, 142, 236
    activities in Shlissel'burg of 22, 114, 180

Ul'ianov, Aleksandr Il'ich 35, 67, 77, 213, 237
uniform, guards' 106, 145, 149, 186, 199, 203
uniform, inmates' 61, 79, 98, 107, 111, 212
    allocation of new underwear 56, 138, 145
    change of, for transfer 205–6, 208
    unsuitability for the climate 49, 160

Vasil'ev, Aleksandr 81, 237
Vasil'ev-Finkel'shtein, Iakov Borisovich 81, 237
violence
    of guards against inmates 20, 47, 93, 96, 123–4, 150
    of inmates against administration 48, 73, 93, 142, 149, 161, 194
Volkenshtein, Liudmila Aleksandrovich 29, 36–8, 119, 205–6, 212, 237
    activities in Shlissel'burg of 95, 106–7, 111, 115, 155, 163, 180
    memoirs of 2, 13–15, 17, 19–22, 24, 27, 28–9, 30, 39–40

wall alphabet
    attempts to prevent use of 46–7, 49, 53–4, 61, 92, 95, 139–41, 157, 159, 168
    communication via 19–21, 47, 49–54, 56, 61, 86, 144, 147, 149, 153–7, 168, 175, 204, 207
    difficulty of using 85, 92, 120, 141

leniency regarding use of 12, 52, 54, 159–60
punishment for using 11, 124, 156, 161
resistance via 10–11, 22–3, 59, 61, 149
Waryński, Ludwik Tadeusz 79, 213, 237–8
    illness and death of 58, 61–2, 164
women, activities of 61–2, 110, 155, 169, 182–3, 203
    conditions for 49, 53
    treatment of 52–3, 58, 60–2, 81, 180, 212
    relations with male inmates 74, 111, 116, 180, 204, 206
work 88–90, 121, 168–9, 176
    absence of 5, 8, 46, 53, 146
    allotments used for 58, 62, 65, 106–7, 116, 164–5, 183
    as reward for good behaviour 9, 16, 139
    liberties increased as a result of 111, 181, 190–1
    salutary effects of 12, 21, 85, 90, 115–17, 169
workshops 12, 41, 64, 70–1, 110–11, 122, 164, 168–9, 176
    commissions for fortress administration undertaken in 65, 114–15, 177, 182
    conflict over 168, 190–1, 196–7
    congregation of inmates around 72, 111, 180–2, 190, 204–6
    closed to accommodate new inmates 41, 68, 122
writing, inmates' 23–4, 53, 58, 102–5, 119, 160–1, 172–5
    notebooks provided for 58, 87, 167, 199–200

Zlatopol'skii, Savelii Solomonovich 51, 142, 212, 238
Zvolianskii, Sergei Erastovich 98, 187–8, 199

Lightning Source UK Ltd.
Milton Keynes UK
UKHW021127170621
385676UK00003B/88